UNDERSTANDING

DEATH AND THE
RESURRECTION

UNDERSTANDING
DEATH AND THE
RESURRECTION

JAY A. PARRY • DONALD W. PARRY

DESERET
BOOK

SALT LAKE CITY, UTAH

Also in this series:

Understanding Isaiah
Understanding the Book of Revelation
Understanding the Signs of the Times

Library of Congress Cataloging-in-Publication Data

Parry, Jay A.
    Understanding death and the Resurrection / Jay A. Parry, Donald W. Parry.
      p.   cm.
    Includes bibliographical references and index.
    ISBN 1-57008-826-8 (alk. paper)
    1. Death—Religious aspects—Church of Jesus Christ of Latter-day Saints.   2. Jesus Christ—Resurrection.   3. Church of Jesus Christ of Latter-day Saints—Doctrines.
I. Parry, Donald W.   II. Title.

BX8643.D4P37   2003
236'.1—dc21   2003009153

Printed in the United States of America   72076-6953
Publishers Printing, Salt Lake City, UT

10   9   8   7   6   5   4   3   2   1

Dedicated to our dear loved ones
who have moved ahead of us to the next world:

John Atwell Parry (1900–1972)
Nina Virginia McEntire Parry (1904–1998)
Donald Wayne Hughes (1905–1983)
Almeda Tolman Hughes (1905–1981)
Donald Louis Hughes (1938–1993)
Karen Louise Parry (1958–1959)
Jennifer Hughes LaSane (1970–2002)
Jennifer Lee McIntyre (1972–1972)

And to our fathers and mothers of
many generations before, whom we never met here
but whose faith continues to bless us.

"What is the object of our coming into existence, then dying and falling away, to be here no more? It is but reasonable to suppose that God would reveal something in reference to the matter, and it is a subject we ought to study more than any other. We ought to study it day and night. . . . If we have any claim on our Heavenly Father for anything, it is for knowledge on this important subject."

—JOSEPH SMITH

CONTENTS

Introduction 1

PART 1 UNDERSTANDING DEATH 5

1. Death Is Part of God's Plan 10
2. Mortality and Death 33
3. Conditions and Circumstances of the Dead 58
4. Christ Has Power Over Death 137

PART 2 UNDERSTANDING THE RESURRECTION . . 155

5. The Resurrection: Foreshadowed with Types 160
6. Jesus Christ and the Resurrection 183
7. The Form and Nature of Resurrected Beings 213
8. Times and Order of the Resurrection 261
9. Blessings Associated with the Resurrection 298

Notes 353
Bibliography 363
Scripture Index 369
Subject Index 377

INTRODUCTION

Death has aroused faith and fear, anticipation and anxiety in
mankind almost from the beginning of time. The first recorded
commandment given to Adam included spiritual and physical death
as a consequence of its violation: "I, the Lord God, commanded the
man, saying: Of every tree of the garden thou mayest freely eat, but
of the tree of the knowledge of good and evil, thou shalt not eat of it,
nevertheless, thou mayest choose for thyself, for it is given unto thee;
but, remember that I forbid it, for in the day thou eatest thereof thou
shalt surely die" (Moses 3:16–17). The seeming finality of death has
preoccupied poets and philosophers and led to the creation of religions. Some religions and philosophies have gone far afield from the
truth, creating a cosmos that scarcely resembles the reality revealed
by God. Others have been impressively close to the mark.

Throughout the ages, many wonderful men and women have
understood that the soul is immortal and continues to progress beyond
the grave, even though they did not have the fulness of the gospel. For
instance, the ancient Roman politician and orator Cicero (who lived
in the century before Christ) said, "When I consider the wonderful
activity of the mind, so great a memory of what is past, and such
capacity for penetrating the future; when I behold such a number of
arts and sciences, and such a multitude of discoveries . . . I believe and
am firmly persuaded that a nature which contains so many things
within itself cannot but be immortal."[1]

Not long before he died, Victor Hugo gave us this impressive
insight: "The nearer I approach the end the plainer I hear around me
the immortal symphonies of the world which invites me. It is

marvelous yet simple. For half a century I have been writing my thoughts in prose and in verse; history, philosophy, drama, romance, tradition, satire, ode and song; I have tried all. But I feel I have not said the thousandth part of what is in me. When I go down to the grave I can say like many others,—'I have finished my day's work.' But I cannot say, 'I have finished my life's work.' My day's work will begin again the next morning. The tomb is not a blind alley; it is an open thoroughfare. It closes on the twilight, it opens on the dawn. My work is only beginning; my work is hardly above the foundation. I could gladly see it mounting forever. The thirst for the infinite proves infinity."[2]

And when Benjamin Franklin wrote his own epitaph, he said, "Like the cover of an old book, its contents torn out and stripped of its lettering and gilding, lies here food for worms. But the work shall not be lost, for it will, as he believes, appear once more in a new and more elegant edition, revised and corrected by the Author."

Poets likewise have expressed deep truths and testimonies about man's ultimate victory over death. John Donne, a contemporary of William Shakespeare, wrote these famous lines:

> Death, be not proud, though some have callèd thee
> > Mighty and dreadful, for thou art not so:
> For those whom thou think'st thou dost overthrow
> > Die not, poor Death; nor yet canst thou kill me. . . .
> One short sleep past, we wake eternally,
> > And Death shall be no more: Death, thou shalt die!

And Alfred, Lord Tennyson, gave this stirring witness of our immortality, comparing death to a sailor putting out to sea:

> Sunset and evening star,
> > And one clear call for me!
> And may there be no moaning of the bar,
> > When I put out to sea. . . .
>
> Twilight and evening bell,
> > And after that the dark!
> And may there be no sadness of farewell,
> > When I embark;

> For tho' from out our bourne of Time and Place
> The flood may bear me far,
> I hope to see my Pilot face to face
> When I have crossed the bar.

The world is full of information (and speculation) about death and our experience after death. Best-selling books have told of brief entry into a spiritual existence through what is commonly known as a "near-death experience." Those called spiritualists or mediums claim special communication with the dead. Where can the truth be found?

The Lord gave us the answer through Isaiah: "When they shall say unto you: Seek unto them that have familiar spirits, and unto wizards that peep and mutter—should not a people seek unto their God for the living to hear from the dead?" (2 Nephi 18:19). If we want to "hear from the dead," or if we want to learn about the spirit world or the resurrection, we should not go to wizards or mediums. Instead, we must turn to God, learn from him, and listen to his prophets. They will teach us what we should know, and they will give us the truth, pure and undefiled by the philosophies of men or the deceptions of devils.

That is what we have sought to do in this work. We have gone to the scriptures to identify what the Lord's recorded word tells us about these things. We have also looked for further light from our latter-day prophets. As Joseph Smith taught, life, death, and the resurrection are subjects about which God is pleased to inform us: "All men know that they must die. And it is important that we should understand the reasons and causes of our exposure to the vicissitudes of life and of death, and the designs and purposes of God in our coming into the world, our sufferings here, and our departure hence. What is the object of our coming into existence, then dying and falling away, to be here no more? It is but reasonable to suppose that God would reveal something in reference to the matter, and it is a subject we ought to study more than any other. We ought to study it day and night, for the world is ignorant in reference to their true condition and relation. If we have any claim on our Heavenly Father for anything, it is for knowledge on this important subject."[3]

Christ's victory over death has inspired the words of true prophets as they have given wonderful reassurance and hope. Death is part of

God's plan, the prophets have taught. Yes, it is a time of separation, loss, and appropriate grief. But it is not the end. We continue to live in spirit form as we undergo new experiences in a spirit world. In time, our spirits and bodies will be reunited through the miracle of resurrection. We will come forth with glorified bodies, our physical and spiritual elements permanently and perfectly united.

What a glorious message this is! Death, then, is a gift of God provided through the agency and sacrifice of Adam and Eve, our first parents. Resurrection with glorified, immortal bodies is a gift of God provided through the agency and sacrifice of Jesus Christ, father of our spiritual life.

We would like to thank all those who helped make this book a reality, including our friends at Deseret Book Company, Cory Maxwell, Jack Lyon, Richard Erickson, and Kent Minson; Ron Stucki for the wonderful cover design; and Nila Hughes, Lindsay McAllister, Christine Neilson, and Vicki Parry for proofreading and research assistance.

PART 1

UNDERSTANDING DEATH

*C*an we have hope in the face of one of the greatest enemies of mankind, that cruel and unfeeling reality we call death? The gospel answers in a resounding affirmative.

Yet some families have suffered so terribly it seems that hope would be an absolute impossibility. Elder James E. Faust told the story of Stillman Pond, a member of the Church who was driven out of Nauvoo in September 1846: "The early winter that year brought extreme hardships, including malaria, cholera, and consumption. The family was visited by all three of these diseases.

"Maria contracted consumption, and all of the children were stricken with malaria. Three of the children died while moving through the early snows. Stillman buried them on the plains. Maria's condition worsened because of the grief, pain, and the fever of malaria. She could no longer walk. Weakened and sickly, she gave birth to twins. They were named Joseph and Hyrum, and both died within a few days.

"The Stillman Pond family arrived at Winter Quarters and, like many other families, they suffered bitterly while living in a tent. The death of the five children coming across the plains to Winter Quarters was but a beginning.

"The journal of Horace K. and Helen Mar Whitney verifies the following regarding four more of the children of Stillman Pond who perished:

"'On Wednesday, the 2nd of December 1846, Laura Jane Pond, age 14 years, . . . died of chills and fever.' Two days later on 'Friday, the 4th of December 1846, Harriet M. Pond, age 11 years, . . . died with chills.' Three days later, 'Monday, the 7th of December, 1846, Abigail A. Pond, age 18 years, . . . died with chills.' Just five weeks later, 'Friday, the 15th of January, 1847, Lyman Pond, age 6 years, . . . died with chills and fever.' Four months later, on the 17th of May,

1847, his wife Maria Davis Pond also died. Crossing the plains, Stillman Pond lost nine children and a wife. He became an outstanding colonizer in Utah, and became the senior president of the thirty-fifth Quorum of Seventy."

Then Elder Faust gives us this essential lesson:

"Having lost these nine children and his wife in crossing the plains, Stillman Pond did not lose his faith. He did not quit. He went forward. He paid a price, as have many others before and since, to become acquainted with God."[1]

It was a hope in Christ that enabled Stillman Pond to remain faithful, despite his terrible losses. It is a hope in Christ that enables us also to stand firm.

"All of us have to deal with death at one time or another," said President Gordon B. Hinckley, *"but to have in one's heart a solid conviction concerning the reality of eternal life is to bring a sense of peace in an hour of tragedy that can come from no other source under the heavens."*[2]

Understanding the words of the prophets will help us increase our *"conviction concerning the reality of eternal life."* When we die we do not cease to exist. Instead we simply move to another room in our Father's house. We continue to associate with loved ones. If we have been faithful in this life, we will experience circumstances of peace and enjoyment beyond our present anticipations. If we have been faithful in this life, we will go forth into an existence of blessing and delight.

In a masterful discourse on this subject, Elder Russell M. Nelson wrote, *"Life does not begin with birth, nor does it end with death. Prior to our birth, we dwelled as spirit children with our Father in Heaven. There we eagerly anticipated the possibility of coming to earth and obtaining a physical body. Knowingly we wanted the risks of mortality, which would allow the exercise of agency and accountability. . . . But we regarded the returning home as the best part of that long-awaited trip, just as we do now. Before embarking on any journey, we like to have some assurance of a round-trip ticket. Returning from earth to life in our heavenly home requires passage through— and not around—the doors of death. We were born to die, and we die to live. (See 2 Corinthians 6:9.) As seedlings of God, we barely blossom on earth; we fully flower in heaven."*[3]

This section of Understanding Death and the Resurrection *will explore the doctrine of "the doors of death." It will discuss*

- *the ways in which death is essential to the plan of our Father in Heaven,*
- *the relation of death and the fall of Adam and Eve,*
- *what happens to little children who die,*
- *the experience of death in the Millennium,*
- *the purposes of mortality,*
- *what it means to "die in the Lord,"*
- *the place of mourning and grief,*
- *our spiritual condition when we die,*
- *the location and conditions in the spirit world,*
- *the conditions in hell,*
- *missionary work in the spirit world,*
- *communication between the spirit and mortal worlds,*
- *Christ's power over death,*
- *Christ's visit to the spirit world, and*
- *how hope in Christ can help us overcome fear of death.*

"Death can be comforting and sweet and precious or it can thrust upon us all the agonies and sulphurous burnings of an endless hell," wrote Elder Bruce R. McConkie. "And we—each of us individually—make the choice as to which it shall be."[4]

CHAPTER 1

DEATH IS PART
OF GOD'S PLAN

W hat peace, what joy can come to our souls when we know that
we are in the hands of a loving God, a God of power, who in
his infinite wisdom has decreed that death be part of our passage from
life to life. What a blessing to understand that death is not the end of
our being, that it is only a temporary condition, that "no bodily
change, no earthly vicissitude affects the integrity and the permanence
of the self. The spirit does not age with the body nor does it perish
with the body. It is a divine effluence of reality, and as such must
always persist. The self, by its very nature, transcends mortality."[1]

Such knowledge is available to those who embrace the truths of
the gospel of Jesus Christ. When we come to know as the prophets
know, we can rejoice in an understanding that death was part of the
plan of salvation from the beginning, that the fall of Adam and Eve
and our resulting mortal state were part of a divine design, that the
dead are alive to God, and that the dead will have all the opportunities for salvation that the living have.

Alma spoke in some detail to his son Corianton about the "great
plan of happiness" and the role death has in that plan:

"Behold, after the Lord God sent our first parents forth from the
garden of Eden, . . . we see, that there was a time granted unto man to
repent, yea, a probationary time, a time to repent and serve God.

"For behold, if Adam had put forth his hand immediately, and partaken of the tree of life, he would have lived forever, according to the
word of God, having no space for repentance; yea, . . . and the great
plan of salvation would have been frustrated. But behold, it was

appointed unto man to die . . . and man became lost forever, yea, they became fallen man. . . .

"Now behold, it was not expedient that man should be *reclaimed from this temporal death,* for that would *destroy the great plan of happiness.* Therefore, as the soul could never die, and the fall had brought upon all mankind a spiritual death as well as a temporal, that is, they were cut off from the presence of the Lord, it was expedient that mankind should be reclaimed from this spiritual death. . . .

"And now remember, my son, *if it were not for the plan of redemption,* (laying it aside) *as soon as they were dead their souls were miserable,* being cut off from the presence of the Lord. . . .

"And now, the plan of mercy could not be brought about except an atonement should be made; therefore God himself atoneth for the sins of the world, to bring about the plan of mercy, to appease the demands of justice, that God might be a perfect, just God, and a merciful God also" (Alma 42:2, 4–6, 8–9, 11, 15; emphasis added).

According to the eternal plan, then, "every man that is born into the world will die. It matters not who he is, nor where he is, whether his birth be among the rich and the noble, or among the lowly and poor in the world, his days are numbered with the Lord, and in due time he will reach the end." Yet this need not be a cause of fear or dismay. "I rejoice that I am born to live, to die, and to live again. I thank God for this intelligence. It gives me joy and peace that the world cannot give, neither can the world take it away. . . . Therefore I have nothing to be sad over, nothing to make me sorrowful. All that I have to do within the world is calculated to buoy me up to give me joy and peace, hope and consolation, in this present life, and a glorious hope of salvation and exaltation in the presence of my God in the world to come."[2]

We knew these things even before coming to earth: "We knew before we were born that we were coming to the earth for bodies and experience and that we would have joys and sorrows, ease and pain, comforts and hardships, health and sickness, successes and disappointments. We knew also that after a period of life we would die. We accepted all these eventualities with a glad heart, eager to accept both the favorable and the unfavorable. We eagerly accepted the chance to come earthward even though it might be for only a day or a year.

Perhaps we were not so much concerned whether we should die of disease, of accident, or of senility. We were willing to take life as it came and as we might organize and control it, and this without murmur, complaint, or unreasonable demands.

"In the face of apparent tragedy we must put our trust in God, knowing that despite our limited view, his purposes will not fail. With all its troubles, life offers us the tremendous privilege to grow in knowledge and wisdom, faith and works, preparing to return and share God's glory."[3]

WHAT IS DEATH?

Ecclesiastes 12:7

> 7 Then shall the dust return to the earth as it was: and the spirit shall return unto God who gave it.

This passage sums up the two essential elements of the experience of death: the body decays in the earth, and the spirit moves on to another sphere of existence. The Lord said through Joseph Smith that "the spirit and the body are the soul of man" (D&C 88:15). It is when the spirit and the body are separated that death occurs. James put it succinctly: "The body without the spirit is dead" (James 2:26).

And yet we know from the witnesses of many prophets that the spirit lives on. When we know the gospel plan, we understand that death is merely a transition from one state to another.

In an attempt to help us understand what happens when we die, a number of the prophets and apostles have compared death to birth. A few examples:

"Mortal death is no more an ending than birth was a beginning."[4]

"We shall suffer no more in putting off this flesh and leaving the spirit houseless than the child, in its capacity, does in its first efforts to breathe the breath of this mortal life."[5]

"While mortals mourn 'a man is dead,' angels proclaim 'a child is born.'"[6]

"In every death there is a birth; the spirit leaves the body dead to us and passes to the other side of the veil alive to that great and noble company that are also working for the accomplishment of the purposes of God."[7]

To understand death as the prophets do is to see that it can be a very positive thing.

"Death . . . releases a spirit for growth and development," President Spencer W. Kimball said, "and places a body in the repair shop of Mother Earth, there to be recast, remolded into a perfect body, an immortal glorious temple, clean, whole, perfected, and ready for its occupant for eternity."[8]

When we pass into death, Brigham Young said, we will say "why this is the greatest advantage of my whole existence, for I have passed from a state of sorrow, grief, mourning, woe, misery, pain, anguish and disappointment into a state of existence where I can enjoy life to the fullest extent as far as that can be done without a body. My spirit is set free, I thirst no more, I want to sleep no more, I hunger no more, I tire no more, I run, I walk, I labor, I go, I come, I do this, do that, whatever is required of me, nothing like pain or weariness, I am full of life, full of vigor, and I enjoy the blessings of my Heavenly Father, by the power of His Spirit."[9]

NOTES AND COMMENTARY

Ecclesiastes 12:7 *the dust return to the earth.* The Genesis account of the creation of Adam and Eve says, "The Lord God formed man of the dust of the ground, and breathed into his nostrils the breath of life; and man became a living soul" (Genesis 2:7; see also Moses 3:7). The description of death as found in Ecclesiastes reverses the process of creation: the dust returns to earth, and the spirit goes back to "God who gave it."

the spirit shall return unto God who gave it. This has reference to the spirit world. For a discussion on the idea of returning to God, see "At Death We Are Taken Home to God," below.

THE COMMON LOT OF MAN

Job 34:15, 20

15 All flesh shall perish together, and man shall turn again unto dust. . . .

20 In a moment shall they die, and the people shall be

troubled at midnight, and pass away: and the mighty shall be taken away without hand.

Death is one of the few great universals in this mortal existence. No one who comes to this earth will leave it without passing through the separation of spirit and body called death. There are no exceptions— even those who are translated must experience the change, though it will come "in the twinkling of an eye" (D&C 43:32). We know from our own observation and experience that all will die. Who among our neighbors or associates is older than 90 or 100 or, in the rarest of cases, 105 or 110? All eventually die and their bodies return to dust.

Even though we can see this from our own observation, it is significant that the Lord also tells us clearly through the scriptures that death is one of the constants of life. Perhaps he states what we all know to be obvious because he must make clear to us that it is indeed part of his plan.

As President Spencer W. Kimball said, "Death is a part of life. People must die. There can never be total victory over disease and death until the end of time. . . . Die we must; otherwise there could be no resurrection, and without that there could be no immortality and further development."[10]

NOTES AND COMMENTARY

Job 34:15 *All flesh shall perish.* Death comes to all—rich and poor, strong and weak, wise and foolish. We read elsewhere in Job, "One dieth in his full strength, being wholly at ease and quiet. . . . And another dieth in the bitterness of his soul, and never eateth with pleasure. They shall lie down alike in the dust, and the worms shall cover them" (Job 21:23–26; see also Ecclesiastes 2:16; 8:8; 2 Nephi 9:6).

man shall turn again unto dust. This refers back to the day when Adam was created. The Lord said, "I, the Lord God, formed man from the dust of the ground, and breathed into his nostrils the breath of life; and man became a living soul, the first flesh upon the earth, the first man also" (Moses 3:7). Just as the bodies of men and women have been formed from dust, or the elements of the earth, so shall they return to the elemental state after death. The Lord said to Adam, "By the sweat of thy face shalt thou eat bread, until thou shalt return unto the ground—for thou shalt surely die—for out of it wast thou taken: for dust thou wast, and unto dust shalt thou return" (Moses 4:25).

Job 34:20 *In a moment shall they die.* Death may come slowly, as when a person is suffering from a terminal disease. But the actual experience of death does indeed take but a moment for all; in one instant a person is alive, and in the next the spirit has left the body and the person is dead.

the mighty shall be taken away without hand. Certainly some people are taken in death by the hand of others—millions are killed in the battlefield or on the highways, for example. But many millions more die from disease or the dangers incident to life, without the involvement of another human being. Yes, man has power to take another's life, but all will certainly die, whether that death is immediately caused by the hand of another or not.

DEATH RESULTS FROM THE FALL

Moses 6:48

48 And [Enoch] said unto them: Because that Adam fell, we are; and by his fall came death; and we are made partakers of misery and woe.

Before Adam and Eve partook of the fruit, there was no death on the earth. But the Lord told them that death would result from their eating of the tree of the knowledge of good and evil (Moses 3:16–17), which was what actually happened (Moses 4:8–25). Eve and then Adam partook of the fruit; their transgression constituted the Fall, and the promised consequence of that fall was both spiritual and physical death. Had Adam and Eve not transgressed, they would have remained in the Garden of Eden forever, without offspring (2 Nephi 2:22–23). But after the Fall they were cast out of the Garden, were able to have children, and with their children were subject to death.

Without the Fall there would still be no death on the earth, even now, thousands of years later. But, at the same time, we would not be here. The Father's plan was such that we would come to earth as mortals, beings designed to die.

NOTES AND COMMENTARY

Moses 6:48 *Because that Adam fell, we are.* This teaching of Enoch was echoed millennia later by Lehi: "Adam fell that men might be; and men are, that they might have joy" (2 Nephi 2:25).

by his fall came death. "In Adam all die," Paul taught (1 Corinthians 15:22). "As by one man sin entered into the world, and death by sin; . . . so death passed upon all men, for that all have sinned" (Romans 5:12; see also Moses 6:59).

we are made partakers of misery and woe. Lehi taught that joy could be the result of Adam's fall, while Enoch noted that misery and woe flow from that fall. Both, of course, are correct. Mortal life, concluding always in death, does indeed bring trial and affliction; none escape difficulties in health, hunger and thirst, emotional pain, worries about loved ones, or concerns about temporal matters. But life can also bring joy when one turns to Christ—and it can bring eternal joy to all who accept the ordinances and covenants of the gospel with all their hearts.

THE ROLE OF DEATH IN GOD'S ETERNAL PLAN

2 Nephi 9:6

> 6 Death hath passed upon all men, to fulfil the merciful plan of the great Creator. . . .

Why has death passed upon all men, and in what way is this plan of God merciful? The scriptures and latter-day prophets give us some clues as to why death is an essential part of our experience in the eternal plan.

First, as Lehi taught, we must have "opposition in all things." Without opposition, which includes both death and life, everything would "remain as dead, having no life neither death, nor corruption nor incorruption, happiness nor misery, neither sense nor insensibility." In such a state, "righteousness could not be brought to pass, neither wickedness, neither holiness nor misery, neither good nor bad" (2 Nephi 2:11; see also Ecclesiastes 3:1–8).

Second, death is a necessary part of the trial we must go through as we seek to grow (through grace) unto godhood: "Be not afraid of your enemies, for I have decreed in my heart, saith the Lord, that I will prove you in all things, whether you will abide in my covenant, even unto death, that you may be found worthy" (D&C 98:14). Loss, pain, and grief can serve as tests of our faith and help us grow in eternally important ways.

Third, death is a necessary step toward resurrection. As we read in the Doctrine and Covenants, "Thus did I, the Lord God, appoint unto man the days of his probation—that by his natural death he might be raised in immortality unto eternal life, even as many as would believe" (D&C 29:43). Without death we can never come to the blessing of immortal, glorified, resurrected bodies. As we sing in our sacrament services,

> Upon the cross he meekly died
> For all mankind to see
> That death unlocks the passageway
> Into eternity.

Elder Bruce R. McConkie wrote, "We shouted for joy at the privilege of becoming mortal because without the tests of mortality there could be no eternal life. We now sing praises to the great Redeemer for the privilege of passing from this life because without death and the resurrection we could not be raised in immortal glory and gain eternal life."[11]

Death is indeed a merciful part of the plan of our great Creator.

NOTES AND COMMENTARY

2 Nephi 9:6 *Death hath passed upon all men.* See the discussion under "The Common Lot of Man," above.

the merciful plan of the great Creator. Alma explained how the different elements of God's plan fit together, including the element of death. Here are the essential points of his message:

• When God sent Adam and Eve out of the Garden of Eden, He set up a barrier ("cherubim, and a flaming sword") to prevent our first parents from partaking of the tree of life. Should they have done so, they would have lived forever in a sinful state and would thereby have frustrated "the great plan of salvation" (Alma 42:5).

- As part of the plan, "it was appointed unto man to die" (v. 6). But through the Fall, mankind "were cut off both temporally and spiritually from the presence of the Lord" (v. 7). Should they die in that state, having no redemption, they would be "lost forever" (v. 6).

- If God were to cause that man should not suffer temporal death, it "would destroy the great plan of happiness" (v. 8). As Elder Boyd K. Packer observed regarding this verse, "Alma did not say that setting mortal death aside would merely delay or disturb the plan of happiness; he said it would destroy it. The words death and happiness are not close companions in mortality, but in the eternal sense they are essential to one another. Death is a mechanism of rescue. Our first parents left Eden lest they partake of the tree of life and live forever in their sins. The mortal death they brought upon themselves, and upon us, is our journey home."[12]

- Since "the soul could never die," and since all mankind had suffered both spiritual and temporal death, some means had to be provided to reclaim man from the spiritual death (v. 9).

- If there were no plan of redemption, men would be miserable when they died, since they would be "cut off from the presence of the Lord" (v. 11) and would remain that way forever (v. 14).

- Since mankind "had become carnal, sensual, and devilish, by nature," earth life was provided as a time to prepare for eternal life (v. 10). It was a time in which man could repent of his sins and learn to serve God (v. 4). Repentance was the only way men could receive the blessings of "the plan of redemption." Through repentance they would receive mercy (vv. 12–13). Without repentance they would be punished (v. 16).

- "The plan of mercy" required the performance of an atonement, which would be performed by "God himself . . . that God might be a perfect, just God, and a merciful God also" (v. 15).

- The "plan of happiness," which includes all the elements described above, is "as eternal . . . as the life of the soul" (v. 16).

It is comforting to know that death, universal and unavoidable death, is part of the perfect plan of a loving Father.

THE DEAD ARE ALIVE TO GOD

Luke 20:38

38 For he is not a God of the dead, but of the living: for all live unto him.

Since all living things have a spirit that gives them life, death is not a cessation of existence to God. When we die and the spirit leaves the body, God regards the spirit and sees that it has gone from one state of existence to another. He continues to be concerned about the body; he knows that a fulness of joy requires a perfected spirit in a glorified body (D&C 93:33–34). But the spirit is that which gives life to the body; the spirit comes before and continues after our mortal life. All beings are alive unto God, whether they live in the premortal world, the mortal earth, the postmortal spirit world, or the resurrected state (see also Matthew 22:31–32; Mark 12:26).

THE DEAD WILL BE JUDGED BY GOD, JUST AS THE LIVING ARE

Acts 10:42

42 And he [Jesus] commanded us to preach unto the people, and to testify that it is he which was ordained of God to be the Judge of quick and dead.

Peter teaches here that Jesus Christ is the Judge of the entire human race, whether they are alive or dead. Peter repeated this truth in his first epistle, saying that Christ was "ready to judge the quick and the dead," adding, "For this cause was the gospel preached also to them that are dead, that they might be judged according to men in the flesh, but live according to God in the spirit" (1 Peter 4:5–6). Christ's power reaches even unto the dead.

NOTES AND COMMENTARY

Acts 10:42 *quick and dead.* The *quick* are those who are alive, whose bodies are *quickened,* or made alive, by their spirits.

THE DEATH OF LITTLE CHILDREN

D&C 137:10

10 And I also beheld that all children who die before they arrive at the years of accountability are saved in the celestial kingdom of heaven.

One of the greatest heartaches parents can have is to lose a child in death. Only those who have experienced this tragedy know fully the depth of their pain and loneliness. The despair can increase when the bereaved parents are taught (as sometimes happens) that little children are damned if they haven't received baptism before death. This, of course, is a false doctrine, as we learn clearly from the Book of Mormon (Moroni 8:5–22). Mormon taught that the practice of baptizing little children (those before the age of accountability) was a "gross error" (v. 6) and "solemn mockery before God" (v. 9). "Little children are whole, for they are not capable of committing sin" (v. 8); they are "alive in Christ" (v. 12) and therefore "need no repentance, neither baptism" (v. 11).

How grateful we are for the glorious truth, as revealed to Joseph Smith, that "all little children who die before they arrive at the years of accountability are saved in the celestial kingdom of heaven."

Joseph Smith gave this further comforting truth: "The Lord takes many away, even in infancy, that they may escape the envy of man, and the sorrows and evils of this present world; they were too pure, too lovely, to live on earth; therefore, if rightly considered, instead of mourning we have reason to rejoice as they are delivered from evil, and we shall soon have them again."[13]

When parents are faithful to their covenants, they have the assurance that "they will not only meet their children in the spirit world, but will also recognize them and know them as they knew them in this life."[14]

The gospel gives us at least one additional glorious doctrine concerning the death of little children. Our latter-day prophets have taught that when a righteous mother is "deprived of the pleasure and joy" of rearing her child to adulthood because of premature death, that mother will have that privilege "renewed to her" in the resurrection. But the circumstances will be much more favorable—parents will then be able to rear their children without sickness, sin, teenage rebellion, negative societal influences, and so forth.[15]

NOTES AND COMMENTARY

D&C 137:10 *I also beheld.* This is part of a vision Joseph Smith saw in the Kirtland Temple in January 1836.

the years of accountability. With a few exceptions (such as those who are mentally impaired), this has been defined by the Lord as age eight (D&C 68:25–27).

saved in the celestial kingdom of heaven. The scriptures give many evidences of this truth. Abinadi taught, "Little children also have eternal life" (Mosiah 15:25). And the Lord said to Joseph Smith in 1830, "Little children are redeemed from the foundation of the world through mine Only Begotten" (D&C 29:46).

SALVATION FOR THE DEAD

Doctrine and Covenants 128:5, 15–19, 22

5 You may think this order of things to be very particular; but let me tell you that it is only to answer the will of God, by conforming to the ordinance and preparation that the Lord ordained and prepared before the foundation of the world, for the salvation of the dead who should die without a knowledge of the gospel. . . .

15 And now, my dearly beloved brethren and sisters, let me assure you that these are principles in relation to the dead and the living that cannot be lightly passed over, as pertaining to our salvation. For their salvation is necessary and essential to our salvation, as Paul says concerning the fathers— that they without us cannot be made perfect—neither can we without our dead be made perfect.

16 And now, in relation to the baptism for the dead, I will give you another quotation of Paul, 1 Corinthians 15:29: Else what shall they do which are baptized for the dead, if the dead rise not at all? Why are they then baptized for the dead?

17 And again, in connection with this quotation I will give you a quotation from one of the prophets, who had his eye fixed on the restoration of the priesthood, the glories to be revealed in the last days, and in an especial manner this most glorious of all subjects belonging to the everlasting gospel, namely, the baptism for the dead; for Malachi says, last chapter, verses 5th and 6th: Behold, I will send you Elijah the prophet before the coming of the great and dreadful day of the Lord: And he shall turn the heart of the fathers to the children, and the heart of the children to their fathers, lest I come and smite the earth with a curse.

18 I might have rendered a plainer translation to this, but it is sufficiently plain to suit my purpose as it stands. It is sufficient to know, in this case, that the earth will be smitten with a curse unless there is a welding link of some kind or other between the fathers and the children, upon some subject or other—and behold what is that subject? It is the baptism for the dead. For we without them cannot be made perfect; neither can they without us be made perfect. Neither can they nor we be made perfect without those who have died in the gospel also; for it is necessary in the ushering in of the dispensation of the fulness of times, which dispensation is now beginning to usher in, that a whole and complete and perfect union, and welding together of dispensations, and keys, and powers, and glories should take place, and be revealed from the days of Adam even to the present time. And not only this, but those things which never have been revealed from the foundation of the world, but have been kept hid from the wise and prudent, shall be revealed unto babes and sucklings in this, the dispensation of the fulness of times.

19 Now, what do we hear in the gospel which we have received? A voice of gladness! A voice of mercy from heaven; and a voice of truth out of the earth; glad tidings for the dead; a voice of gladness for the living and the dead; glad tidings of great joy. How beautiful upon the mountains are the feet of those that bring glad tidings of good things, and that say unto Zion: Behold, thy God reigneth! As the dews of Carmel, so shall the knowledge of God descend upon them! . . .

22 Brethren, shall we not go on in so great a cause? Go forward and not backward. Courage, brethren; and on, on to the victory! Let your hearts rejoice, and be exceedingly glad. Let the earth break forth into singing. Let the dead speak forth anthems of eternal praise to the King Immanuel, who hath ordained, before the world was, that which would enable us to redeem them out of their prison; for the prisoners shall go free.

It is a law that all our Father's children must be saved under the same conditions—hearing the word of truth and accepting it, making gospel covenants and receiving the ordinances, obeying God's commandments and the voice of the Spirit, enduring in faith, hope, and charity to the end.

If God has equal requirements of all his children, he must provide equal opportunity to them all. Then what of salvation for those who die without gospel knowledge, ordinances, and covenants? The Church of Jesus Christ of Latter-day Saints stands alone in understanding that the dead (who are not dead to God) will receive an opportunity to hear and accept the gospel in the spirit world if they did not have such an opportunity in mortality.

And what constitutes an "opportunity in mortality"? Only the Lord can say. We lack sufficient knowledge of the intricacies of the plan, as well as the true motivations of the human heart, to be able to judge. But we know as an article of our faith that God will judge all things perfectly.

In the spirit world, righteous spirits with authority from God go forth as missionaries to teach the gospel. Those who receive the message are able to receive the blessing of repentance; when the ordinance of baptism is performed for them in mortal temples, they can receive that ordinance (followed by the other ordinances of salvation). Through their faith and obedience, and through the atonement of Christ, they may become heirs of salvation and receive all the blessings they would have received had they been able to fully come unto Christ and his Church and gospel in mortality.

The teachings of our latter-day prophets and apostles have greatly amplified our understanding of the marvelous truths about salvation for the dead. In summary, we learn:

- "All who have died without a knowledge of this gospel, who would have received it if they had been permitted to tarry, shall be heirs of the celestial kingdom of God" (D&C 137:7).

- "All children who die before they arrive at the years of account-ability are saved in the Celestial Kingdom of heaven (D&C 137:10).

- "In our Father's mercy every soul has opportunity to accept or reject the gospel message, either in this life or in the spirit world."[16]

- "There is no such thing as a second chance to gain salvation. . . . For those who do not have an opportunity in this life, the first chance to gain salvation will come in the spirit world. If those who hear the word for the first time in the realms ahead are the kind of people who would have accepted the gospel here, had the oppor-tunity been afforded them, they will accept it there. Salvation for the dead is for those whose first chance to gain salvation is in the spirit world."[17] (Again we must note that only the Lord knows when a person has received a true chance to understand and accept or reject the gospel.)

- Ordinances for the salvation of the dead could not be performed until after Jesus Christ had performed his atonement and con-quered death.[18]

- Ordinances for the salvation of the dead are for those "who did not have the opportunity to receive the gospel [or all its ordi-nances] in this life."[19]

- Baptism and the other ordinances belong to this mortal, temporal, physical world. Apparently, in the plan of God, it is not enough for a spirit to be baptized with "spiritual water"; our physical bod-ies must be baptized with physical water. Those who die without

baptism can receive that ordinance through the actions of authorized administrators on the mortal earth; these baptize worthy men
and women (and boys and girls) as proxy for those who cannot
participate personally in the ordinance because they are in the
spirit world.[20]

• "These ordinances become efficacious for those who have died
when those individuals demonstrate faith in Christ, repent of their
sins, and accept vicarious baptism for the remission of their
sins."[21]

• "It takes just as much to save a dead man as a living man."[22]
Therefore, "it is not only necessary that you should be *baptized*
for your dead, but you will have to go through *all* the ordinances
for them, the same as you have gone through to save yourselves."[23]

• Ordinances for the dead are performed in temples dedicated for
the work of the Lord. Since the number of dead are so many, we
begin by "doing the work for all of *our kindred,* with hope, of
course, on our part that all of them will receive the truth."[24]

• "If the dead could, they would speak in language loud as ten thousand thunders, calling upon the servants of God to rise up and
build temples, magnify their calling and redeem their dead."[25]

As he contemplated these truths, Wilford Woodruff exclaimed,
"Oh, I wish many times that the veil were lifted off the face of the
Latter-day Saints. I wish we could see and know the things of God as
they do who are laboring for the salvation of the human family who
are in the spirit world; for if this were so, this whole people, with very
few, if any, exceptions, would lose all interest in the riches of the
world, and instead thereof their whole desires and labors would be
directed to redeem their dead, to perform faithfully the work and mission given us on earth; so that when we ourselves should pass behind
the veil and meet with Joseph and the ancient apostles, and others who
are watching over us and who are deeply interested in our labors, we
might feel satisfied in having done our duty."[26]

NOTES AND COMMENTARY

D&C 128:5 *this order of things.* This phrase has reference to the requirement that all baptisms for the dead be performed before witnesses and be recorded in the official records of the Church. These instructions were given in a letter from Joseph Smith to the Church in September 1842.

ordained and prepared before the foundation of the world. Even before the creation of this earth, our Father in Heaven established it as part of his plan that those "who should die without a knowledge of the gospel" would be given full opportunities and blessings in the spirit world.

D&C 128:15 *cannot be lightly passed over.* We cannot take lightly our responsibility to seek out the names of our dead and perform sacred, saving ordinances for them in God's holy temples.

their salvation is necessary and essential to our salvation. Our Heavenly Father covenanted with his children before they came to earth that each one would be given an opportunity to receive the gospel before the final judgment.[27] Some will be privileged to receive the good news in mortality. In exchange for that great blessing, they have the obligation to do all they can to take the gospel to others, both through missionary labors and through family history and temple work. Our ancestors thus cannot be made perfect without our efforts. But we also cannot be made perfect without doing our part to fulfill God's premortal promise to his children.

Joseph Fielding Smith said that "some members of the Church have wondered . . . Will not a man who keeps the commandments of the Lord, who is faithful and true so far as he himself is concerned, receive perfection? Yes, provided his worthy dead also receive the same privileges, because there must be a family organization, a family unit, and each generation must be linked to the chain that goes before in order to bring perfection in family organization."[28]

D&C 128:16 *baptized for the dead, if the dead rise not at all?* In asking this question, Paul bore witness of the reality of the resurrection, using baptism for the dead as an evidence of the doctrine that we shall indeed rise from the dead.

D&C 128:17 *this most glorious of all subjects.* The most glorious of all subjects in the gospel Joseph Smith names here as "the baptism for the dead." These truths were revealed by the Lord well before Joseph received an understanding of the sealing ordinance for the living and the dead, which ordinance is another facet of the transcendent truth of salvation for the dead.

Joseph Smith wrote, "This doctrine appears glorious, inasmuch as it exhibits the greatness of divine compassion and benevolence in the extent of the plan of human salvation. This glorious truth is well calculated to enlarge the understanding, and to sustain the soul under troubles, difficulties and distress."[29]

he shall turn the heart of the fathers to the children, and the heart of the children to their fathers. Joseph Smith said, "Now, the word *turn* here should be translated bind, or seal."[30] Through restoring the sealing power to the earth, Elijah would open the door to the performance of essential and eternal ordinances in the temples of God. With temples constructed and functioning, the dead fathers would look to their living children with new hope, and the living children would look to their dead fathers with renewed interest and commitment. As these hearts turn to each other, the work of God would move forward, and the Lord's purposes on earth would begin to be more completely fulfilled.

Regarding the turning of the hearts of the fathers, George Q. Cannon declared, "They pray for you today in the spirit world, as they have been no doubt from the beginning praying for their descendants that they may be faithful to the truth. . . . Their hearts yearn after us, their constant desire being that we may be faithful and maintain our integrity and be prepared to bring salvation to them and redeem them by going forth and obeying every ordinance which God has established in the Church for the salvation of the living and the dead."[31]

As the spirits of our dead ancestors turn their hearts to us, so must we turn our hearts to them, seeking the binding or sealing that Joseph Smith spoke of. This is done, of course, through genealogical research and the vicarious performance of the temple ordinances for the dead. As we do this work, we must remember that those who inhabit the spirit world are real people with real hopes, wishes, and dreams. Without the temple ordinances, said Joseph Fielding Smith, "none of these families can thus be sealed for eternity in an eternal family union. Delay to them must be disappointing in the extreme."[32]

lest I come and smite the earth with a curse. If the righteous descendants of Adam and Eve are not sealed as one great family, the eternal union designed for that family will not become a reality, and one of the supreme purposes for the earth will be thwarted. If we as the Lord's church don't make an earnest effort to fulfill this charge, doing as much as we can before the Lord comes, he will smite the earth with a curse at his second coming. (Baptism for the dead, mentioned here by Joseph Smith as the necessary "welding link" (D&C 128:18) between the generations, is the first step toward the priesthood sealing of couples and families.)

D&C 128:18 *I might have rendered a plainer translation to this.* On 6 April 1830, the Lord said to Joseph Smith, "Thou shalt be called a seer, a translator, a prophet, an apostle of Jesus Christ, an elder of the church" (D&C 21:1). Joseph Smith had the divine gift of translation, and with that gift he could translate ancient records according to the will of the Lord.

necessary in the ushering in of the dispensation of the fulness of times. The dispensation of the fulness of times, which is the dispensation in which we now live, involves a restoration and uniting of all previous "dispensations, and keys, and powers, and glories." As part of that uniting, or "welding together," the fathers of old and their descendants will be bound or sealed into one great family.

things which never have been revealed from the foundation of the world. In the last days, the Lord will reveal great things even to "babes and sucklings." Here the prophet is contrasting those viewed by the world as "wise and prudent" with those viewed by the world as "babes and sucklings"—the weak and simple things of the earth. It is to the weak and simple, the humble and innocent, that the Lord most often reveals his secrets.

D&C 128:19 *glad tidings for the dead.* These are glad tidings indeed: the dead who die without Christ shall not continue in bondage to Satan. If they repent and receive the proffered temple ordinances, they can, through the grace of Christ, come unto exaltation.

How beautiful upon the mountains are the feet of those that bring glad tidings. We know this as symbolic language referring to the work of missionaries and others as they take the gospel to those who do not have it. But those beautiful feet will also be found in the spirit world, taking the same glad tidings to those bound in prison there.

As the dews of Carmel, so shall the knowledge of God descend upon them! In the northern area of Israel is a mountain range called Carmel where the morning dew is unusually heavy. This dew is very welcome to the inhabitants of the area and at times is the only source of life-giving moisture. Joseph Smith here testifies that the knowledge of God will descend like a blanket of dew upon those who will receive it.

D&C 128:22 *Let the dead speak forth anthems of eternal praise.* This is poetic language, but it is also literal. The dead will sing out praise "to the King Immanuel, who hath ordained, before the world was, that which would enable us to redeem them out of their prison; for the prisoners shall go free."

SAVIORS ON MOUNT ZION

Obadiah 1:21

21 And saviours shall come up on mount Zion to judge the mount of Esau; and the kingdom shall be the Lord's.

Joseph Smith spoke of this doctrine by asking, "How are [the saints] to become saviors on Mount Zion?" He then answered the question, saying, "By building their temples, erecting their baptismal fonts, and going forth and receiving all the ordinances, baptisms, confirmations, washings, anointings, ordinations and sealing powers upon their heads, in behalf of all their progenitors who are dead, and redeem them that they may come forth in the first resurrection and be exalted to thrones of glory with them." In this work, he said, "is the chain that binds the hearts of the fathers to the children, and the children to the fathers, which fulfills the mission of Elijah."[33]

It is a glorious work to participate in the plan of salvation as saviors of our fellowmen, working in harmony with the Savior of all, and acting through his power. This plan was in place from the beginning. John A. Widtsoe taught that we made a "certain agreement with the Almighty" at the grand council in premortality. "Since the plan is intended for all men, we became parties to the salvation of every person under that plan. We agreed, right then and there, to be not only saviors for ourselves but measurably, saviors for the whole human family. We went into a partnership with the Lord. The working out of the plan became then not merely the Father's work, and the Savior's work, but also our work."[34]

NOTES AND COMMENTARY

Obadiah 1:21 *mount Zion.* Anciently Mount Zion was another name for Mount Moriah, the mountain in Jerusalem where the temple stood. Thus the name represented the city of Jerusalem as well as the Lord's temple. In the latter days, Mount Zion also refers both to the city of New Jerusalem and to its temple. Also, by extension, Mount Zion is a symbolic expression referring to all of the Lord's temples in the last dispensation (see D&C 76:66; 84:2, 32; 133:56).

to judge the mount of Esau. The mount of Esau stands in contrast to Mount Zion. In this context, Esau symbolizes the wicked world.[35] As the Saints participate in the work of salvation in the Lord's temples (Mount Zion), those for whom they do the work (including those who have been part of the wicked world, or Mount Esau) will have opportunity for greater blessings as well as for greater judgments.

DEATH IN THE MILLENNIUM

D&C 63:50–51

50 And he that liveth when the Lord shall come, and hath kept the faith, blessed is he; nevertheless, it is appointed to him to die at the age of man.

51 Wherefore, children shall grow up until they become old; old men shall die; but they shall not sleep in the dust, but they shall be changed in the twinkling of an eye.

Death in the Millennium will have three major differences from how we know it now. First, there will be no premature death, either among children or adults. All will live to "the age of man." Second, when people die, their bodies will not be laid in the ground to decay and await the resurrection. Instead, they will be changed from a mortal to a resurrected state in an instant, "in the twinkling of an eye." As a result of these circumstances, those on earth will no longer experience any sorrow at the "death" of loved ones (D&C 101:29).

The third difference is a logical consequence of the second: no longer will people go to the spirit world when they die, but as the Lord said in this dispensation, "when he dies he shall not sleep, that is to say in the earth, but shall be changed in the twinkling of an eye, and shall be caught up, and his rest shall be glorious" (D&C 101:31–32).

NOTES AND COMMENTARY

D&C 63:50 *die at the age of man.* Isaiah gave us a helpful alternate reading to this phrase when he said, "There shall be no more thence an infant of days, nor an old man that hath not filled his days: for the child shall die an hundred years old" (Isaiah 65:20). Elsewhere in the Doctrine and Covenants we read, "In that day an infant shall not die until he is old; and his life shall be as the age of a tree" (D&C 101:30). The common thread running between all these expressions is that there is an ideal length of a person's life, a lifespan that truly enables people to fulfill the measure of their creation. That is the length of life all those on earth during the years of the Millennium will enjoy.

D&C 63:51 *changed in the twinkling of an eye.* Throughout the long ages of the earth's existence, death has involved a separation of the spirit and the body, with the body going into the grave and the spirit going forth into the spirit world. During the Millennium, however, death as we know it will be no longer. Instead, when we have enjoyed a full allotment of years of mortal life, we will be "changed in the twinkling of an eye"—meaning, in an instant—from mortality to a glorified immortality.

WORK FOR THE DEAD IN THE MILLENNIUM

Brigham Young

> Do you know what the Millennium is for, and what work will have to be done during that period? . . . I think there is a work to be done then which the whole world seems determined we shall not do. What is it? To build temples . . . and work for the salvation of our forefathers.[36]

Salvation for the dead is the "great work of the millennium."[37] But because communication in the Millennium will flow freely between the spheres, that work will proceed much more efficiently than it does at the present time. We currently perform ordinances for thousands and millions of the dead based simply on our ability to establish their key vital statistics. We do not know which of the dead desire the temple ordinances. Further complicating our effort, we are unaware even of the identity of countless numbers of those who have died.

In the Millennium, the Lord will allow those in the spirit world to openly contact us "so that we may not work by chance, or by faith alone, without knowledge, but with the actual knowledge revealed unto us."[38] As Charles W. Penrose said, "The veil will be taken away which separates us from our brethren who have gone before, and we will work with them, and they with us. We will be in perfect harmony; and the Priesthood behind the veil will reveal to the Priesthood in the flesh in the holy Temples of God where these conversations will take place, the names of those for whom we must officiate which we cannot obtain by the means now at our command."[39]

Of this thrilling time, Brigham Young said, "Some of those who are not in mortality will come along and say, 'Here are a thousand names I wish you to attend to in this temple, and when you have got through with them I will give you another thousand;' and the Elders of Israel and their wives will go forth to officiate for their forefathers, the men for the men, and the women for the women."[40]

CHAPTER 2

MORTALITY AND DEATH

Mortality and death are inextricably intertwined. In fact, the very word *mortal* contains the root of the word for death. The Latin *mort-* and *mors* both mean death; *mortuary, mortician,* and *murder* all share the same root.[1] A *mortality table* is used by insurance companies to determine patterns in the deaths of populations. Thus, when we speak of being mortal, by definition we say that the most singular fact of our existence is that we are moving, whether quickly or slowly, toward an appointment with death.

"This is only our place of temporary existence. We cannot live here always with our bodies full of pain and subject to decay. Deprive us of food and we die; deprive us of water, and after a short time we die; deprive us of air, and we live but a few moments. We all know that this is not the state for us to live in and endure to eternity."[2]

Though mortality leads invariably toward death, the two are not the same. When we speak of mortal man and woman, we speak of individuals who are still alive on the earth. They are in this school of probation, being tested and tried by the difficulties of life—and by the death of loved ones and the certain prospect of death for themselves. With death as such a certainty, and with the veil generally so impenetrable, our faith faces a stiff and painful trial. Will we believe and follow the directives of Christ, even though we cannot see him, even though we do see loved ones leaving in death and not returning, even though we know we ourselves will likewise lay down the flesh and go away, our existence vanishing to the eyes of all those who remain?

Despite the sure prospect of death, mortal life is a gift from our Father in Heaven. It is given as a space in time to allow us to prepare to die, to ready ourselves for the next stage of existence, to prepare for the eventual blessing of becoming immortal. To those who walk by faith, believing the prophets (who also are usually unseen to us—they have long since died or, if they still live, they usually live, walk, and minister in areas where we are not), their immortal lives will be like that which God enjoys. Such are said to have died "in the Lord." Those who reject the prophets, either in word or in deed, will receive much lesser blessings in immortality.

Elder Russell M. Nelson captured the connection between mortality and death when he wrote, "Viewed from an eternal perspective, we live to die; and we die to live again. . . . Birth is the gateway to mortal life; death is the gateway to immortality and eternal life."[3]

And President J. Reuben Clark Jr. gave us a valuable perspective in his clear statement: "Death is, in the eternal plan, co-equal with birth."[4]

Gospel understanding teaches us that there is purpose in death, that in fact our bodies are designed to wind down toward death, and that sometimes little holds us here besides our ties to loved ones on the mortal earth.

"Our spirits are entangled in these bodies—held captive as it were for a season," Heber C. Kimball wrote of the mortal problem; on the one hand, our spirits long to be free; on the other hand, freedom from our bodies also separates us from loved ones who remain in mortality. "[Our spirits] are like the poor Saints, who are for a time obliged to dwell in miserable mud shanties that are mouldering away, and require much patching and care to keep them from mingling with mother earth before the time. They feel miserable in these old decaying tabernacles, and long for the day when they can leave them to fall and take possession of a good new house.

"It seems natural for me to desire to be clothed upon with immortality and eternal life, and leave this mortal flesh; but I desire to stick to it as long as I can be a comfort to my sisters, brethren, wives, and children. Independent of this consideration I would not turn my hand over to live twenty-five minutes. What else could give birth to a single desire to live in this tabernacle, which is more or less shattered by the merciless storms which have beat upon it, to say nothing of the ravages made upon it by the tooth of time? While I cling to it I must of necessity suffer many pains, rheumatism, head ache, jaw ache, and heart ache; sometimes in one part of my body and sometimes in another. It is all right; it is so ordained that we may not cling with too great a tenacity to mortal flesh; but be willing to pass through the vail and meet with Joseph and Hyrum and Willard and Bishop Whitney, and thousands of others in the world of spirits."[5]

MORTALITY—LAND OF THE SHADOW OF DEATH

Isaiah 9:2

2 The people that walked in darkness have seen a great light: they that dwell in the land of the shadow of death, upon them hath the light shined.

This is a prophecy of the coming of Christ to the earth, and of the effect of his atonement on both sin and death. The people were in spiritual darkness, a result of sin, and Jesus, the light of the world, came among them, so that "upon them hath the light shined." Further, all the people of the earth dwelled "in the land of the shadow of death." In time, all those who live in that shadow (whether in mortality or in the spirit world) will hear of Christ and receive the blessings of his light.

When John was brought to the temple in Jerusalem as an eight-day-old baby to be circumcised, his father, Zacharias, lifted his voice in prophecy and said, "Thou, child, shalt be called the prophet of the Highest: for thou shalt go before the face of the Lord to prepare his ways; to give knowledge of salvation unto his people by the remission of their sins, through the tender mercy of our God; whereby the dayspring from on high hath visited us, to give light to them that sit in darkness and in the shadow of death, to guide our feet into the way of peace" (Luke 1:76–79). Jesus Christ is the dayspring from on high, the dawning of the light of mercy in our lives, and even though we may be "in darkness and in the shadow of death," he will give us light and "guide our feet into the way of peace."

NOTES AND COMMENTARY

Isaiah 9:2 *walked in darkness . . . seen a great light.* The people of the earth were in spiritual darkness, in apostasy from the truth. But

Christ came, specifically to the inhabitants of Zebulun and Naphtali (mentioned in Isaiah 9:1) during his mortal mission. Upon those people the great light shined.

the land of the shadow of death. All of earth's inhabitants dwell in the land of the shadow of death. Death comes to all; it casts its shadow over everyone who lives on the earth. The land of the shadow of death is different from the land of the dead, the spirit world. We live under death's shadow until death takes us; then we live in the land of the dead—the spirit world. Those who live on the mortal earth, under death's shadow, will see the light of Christ and be blessed by a knowledge of the power and universality of his resurrection.

David also spoke of this land. In his most famous Psalm (the twenty-third), he spoke of how the Lord will bless us as we walk through life's experience, with the fear of both physical and spiritual death: "The Lord is my shepherd; I shall not want. . . . He leadeth me in the paths of righteousness for his name's sake. Yea, though I walk through the valley of the shadow of death, I will fear no evil: for thou art with me; thy rod and thy staff they comfort me" (Psalm 23:1, 3–4). Even though we are subject to both physical and spiritual death, David says, even though they are so much with us that they cast a shadow over our lives, yet we need not fear, for if we walk in righteousness the Lord is with us.

MORTALITY GIVES A TIME TO PREPARE FOR DEATH AND ETERNITY

Alma 12:22, 24, 26–27

22 Now Alma said unto him: . . . Now we see that Adam did fall by the partaking of the forbidden fruit, according to the word of God; and thus we see, that by his fall, all mankind became a lost and fallen people. . . .

24 And we see that death comes upon mankind, yea, the death which has been spoken of by Amulek, which is the temporal death; nevertheless there was a space granted unto man in which he might repent; therefore this life became a probationary state; a time to prepare to meet God; a time to prepare for that endless state which has been spoken of by us, which is after the resurrection of the dead. . . .

26 And now behold, if it were possible that our first parents could have gone forth and partaken of the tree of life they would have been forever miserable, having no preparatory state; and thus the plan of redemption would have been frustrated, and the word of God would have been void, taking none effect.

27 But behold, it was not so; but it was appointed unto men that they must die; and after death, they must come to judgment, even that same judgment of which we have spoken, which is the end.

The fall of Adam and Eve affected all those who followed them. The entire family of man was "lost and fallen" from their previous position of innocence and glory. Another result of the transgression of Adam and Eve was death, both spiritual and temporal. Without the foresight of the plan of the Father, that death would have been eternal, never ending. But in his mercy and perfect compassion, God provided "a space" wherein we could repent and "prepare to meet God." After this "probationary state," we die, which death is eventually followed by the last judgment.

Years after teaching these things to the people of Ammonihah, Alma taught many of the same truths to his son Corianton. After God cast Adam and Eve out of the Garden of Eden, he granted "a time . . . unto man to repent, yea, a probationary time, a time to repent and serve God. . . . Therefore, according to justice, the plan of redemption could not be brought about, only on conditions of repentance of men in this probationary state, yea, this preparatory state; for except it were for these conditions, mercy could not take effect except it should destroy the work of justice. Now the work of justice could not be destroyed; if so, God would cease to be God" (Alma 42:4, 13).

NOTES AND COMMENTARY

Alma 12:22 *by his fall, all mankind became a lost and fallen people.* Because of the fall of Adam and Eve, all their descendants also are fallen. All mankind lives in a fallen world, and all have, to one degree or another (until they are changed by the power of the Atonement) a fallen nature. All are also lost to the opportunity to dwell with God (until they partake of the blessings of the Atonement). As Alma taught in another setting, "Our first parents were cut off both temporally and spiritually from the presence of the Lord; and thus we see they became subjects to follow after their own will. . . . They had become carnal, sensual, and devilish, by nature" (Alma 42:7, 10).

Alma 12:24 *there was a space granted.* The immediate result of the Fall was that "all mankind became a lost and fallen people" (v. 22). But, because of the love of God, He provided a period of time wherein his children could come unto Christ in faith, repent of their sins, receive of his power to change their hearts, and, as a result, qualify to be lifted from the Fall to a glorified state.

this life became a probationary state. This probationary state is "a time to prepare to meet God; a time to prepare for that endless state which has been spoken of by us, which is after the resurrection of the dead."

In latter-day revelation, the Lord tells us more about the purpose of this probationary state. During the days of our probation, the Lord said, he would "send forth angels to declare unto [us] repentance and redemption," through faith on the name of his Only Begotten Son. "And thus did I, the Lord God, appoint unto man the days of his probation—that by his natural death he might be raised in immortality unto eternal life, even as many as would believe" (D&C 29:42–43). Why did the Lord give us a space to prepare? So we would be given an opportunity to develop faith in Christ and repent—to the end that after death we could be "raised . . . unto eternal life" rather than be lost to such blessings and cast into hell.

Alma's missionary companion, Amulek, spoke in some detail about this life as a probationary state. In words that are familiar to many Latter-day Saints, he said, "Behold, now is the time and the day of your salvation. . . . For behold, this life is the time for men to prepare to meet God; yea, behold the day of this life is the day for men to perform their labors. . . . Therefore, I beseech of you that ye do not procrastinate the day of your repentance until the end; for after this day of life, which is given us to prepare for eternity, behold, if we do not improve our time while in this life, then cometh the night of darkness wherein there can be no labor performed. . . . For behold, if ye have procrastinated the day of your repentance even until death, behold, ye have become subjected to the spirit of the devil, and he doth seal you his" (Alma 34:31–33, 35).

Clearly, for those who have a full opportunity to receive and apply the gospel during mortality, this life is the "time and the day of your salvation"; it is "the time for men to prepare to meet God; . . . the day for men to perform their labors."

But this probationary test continues into the spirit world in at least three ways. First, those who have not heard the gospel word in mortality will receive that opportunity in the spirit world, where they will be allowed to exercise faith, repentance, and obedience. Second, those who heard and rejected the gospel here can experience some advancement (though limited) in the world to come if they decide to repent at that point. Third, those who receive the gospel here and seek to live it with all their hearts will be able to continue to progress and grow in the spirit world. (For further discussion of these doctrines, see chapter 3, Conditions and Circumstances of the Dead.)

Even those who do not hear the gospel in this life have the blessing of the light of Christ (D&C 84:45–46). It is the responsibility of all God's children to hearken to the light they are given and conform their lives to that light. To a degree, then, this life is a probationary state for all who dwell here, regardless of their gospel opportunities.

Joseph Smith emphasized the importance of making the most of the opportunities God gives us in this life. "A man can do as much in this life in one year as he can do in ten years in the spirit world without the body," the Prophet said.[6]

Elder Melvin J. Ballard repeated the statement of Joseph Smith and then further explained,

"It is much easier to overcome and serve the Lord when both flesh and spirit are combined as one. This is the time when men are more pliable and susceptible. When clay is pliable, it is much easier to change than when it gets hard and sets.

"This life is the time to repent. That is why I presume it will take a thousand years after the first resurrection until the last group will be prepared to come forth. It will take them a thousand years to do what it would have taken, but three score years and ten to accomplish in this life."[7]

Alma 12:26 *they would have been forever miserable.* If Adam and Eve had partaken of the fruit of the tree of life without the experience of mortality—with its trials, mistakes, and opportunities for repentance—they would have short-circuited the process of progress our Father in Heaven established. Instead of preparing themselves for eternity through the mortal and spirit-world experiences, they would have been transformed immediately into an immortal state—but an immortal state where they had not been cleansed from sin. The result would have been an eternity of misery. As Alma taught his son Corianton, "As the soul could never die, and the fall had brought upon all mankind a spiritual death as well as a temporal, . . . if it were not for the plan of redemption, (laying it aside) as soon as they were dead their souls were miserable, being cut off from the presence of the Lord" (Alma 42:9, 11).

the plan of redemption would have been frustrated. The plan of redemption called for a Savior to perform an atonement, which would allow for a cleansing and glorification of the Father's children upon the conditions of faith, repentance, and obedience. If Adam and Eve had partaken of the fruit of the tree of life without receiving the blessings of a savior, they would have lived forever in their sin. Thus "the plan of redemption would have been frustrated."

Alma 12:27 *it was appointed unto men that they must die.* Death is part of the plan of salvation the Lord has given us. See the discussion on this doctrine under the heading "Appointed unto Death."

after death, they must come to judgment. After death and before the resurrection, each of us will be judged according to our works and our hearts. The resurrection we receive will be based on the judgment we receive.

APPOINTED UNTO DEATH

Doctrine and Covenants 42:43–48

43 And whosoever among you are sick, and have not faith to be healed, but believe, shall be nourished with all

tenderness, with herbs and mild food, and that not by the hand of an enemy.

44 And the elders of the church, two or more, shall be called, and shall pray for and lay their hands upon them in my name; and if they die they shall die unto me, and if they live they shall live unto me.

45 Thou shalt live together in love, insomuch that thou shalt weep for the loss of them that die, and more especially for those that have not hope of a glorious resurrection.

46 And it shall come to pass that those that die in me shall not taste of death, for it shall be sweet unto them;

47 And they that die not in me, wo unto them, for their death is bitter.

48 And again, it shall come to pass that he that hath faith in me to be healed, and is not appointed unto death, shall be healed.

All are appointed to die eventually; as Alma said, "It was appointed unto men that they must die; and after death, they must come to judgment" (Alma 12:27). In other words, death is a natural and universal consequence of mortal life.

And yet the Lord sometimes has purposes wherein, at specific times, he "appoints" to a given person the blessing of continuing to live for a time. Elder Spencer W. Kimball gave a helpful commentary on this scripture:

"If not 'appointed unto death' and sufficient faith is developed, life can be spared. But if there is not enough faith, many die before their time. It is evident that even the righteous will not always be healed and even those of great faith will die when it is according to the purpose of God. Joseph Smith died in his thirties as did the Savior. Solemn prayers were answered negatively.

"'If he is not appointed unto death!' That is a challenging statement. I am confident that there is a time to die. I am not a fatalist. I believe that many people die before 'their time' because they are careless, abuse their bodies, take unnecessary chances, or expose themselves to hazards, accidents, and sickness. . . .

"And God will sometimes use his power over death to protect us. . . .

"God can control our lives. He guides and blesses us, but gives us our agency. We may live our lives in accordance with His plan for us or we may foolishly shorten or terminate them.

"I am positive in my mind that the Lord has planned our destiny. We can shorten our lives but I think we cannot lengthen them very much. Sometime we'll understand fully, and when we see back from the vantage point of the future we shall be satisfied with many of the happenings of this life which seemed too difficult for us to comprehend."[8]

Often an appointment to die is based on the Lord's need for a person's talents and service in the spirit world. "A mortal life may need to be 'shortened' by twenty years as we might view it," Elder Neal A. Maxwell wrote, "but if so, it may be done in order for special services to be rendered by that individual in the spirit world, services that will benefit thousands of new neighbors with whom that individual will live in all of eternity. . . . Our omniloving and omniscient Father will release us when it is best for us to be released. But each such release of a righteous person is also a call to new labors!"[9]

Wilford Woodruff told of a remarkable experience with his wife, where she died but apparently was not appointed unto death. Through his administrations, and through the exercise of agency by his wife, she was restored to life. As he recorded in his journal, on December 4, 1838, "she seemed to be gradually sinking and in the evening her spirit apparently left her body, and she was dead.

"The sisters gathered around her body, weeping, while I stood looking at her in sorrow. The spirit and power of God began to rest upon me until, for the first time during her sickness, faith filled my soul, although she lay before me as one dead.

"I had some oil that was consecrated for my anointing while in Kirtland. I took it and consecrated it again before the Lord for anointing the sick. I then bowed down before the Lord and prayed for the life of my companion, and I anointed her body with the oil in the name of the Lord. I laid my hands upon her, and in the name of Jesus Christ

I rebuked the power of death and the destroyer, and commanded the same to depart from her, and the spirit of life to enter her body.

"Her spirit returned to her body, and from that hour she was made whole; and we all felt to praise the name of God, and to trust in Him and to keep His commandments.

"While this operation was going on with me (as my wife related afterwards) her spirit left her body, and she saw it lying upon the bed, and the sisters weeping. She looked at them and at me, and upon her babe, and, while gazing upon this scene, two personages came into the room carrying a coffin and told her they had come for her body. One of these messengers informed her that she could have her choice: she might go to rest in the spirit world, or, on one condition she could have the privilege of returning to her tabernacle and continuing her labors upon the earth. The condition was, if she felt that she could stand by her husband, and with him pass through all the cares, trials, tribulation and afflictions of life which he would be called to pass through for the gospel's sake unto the end. When she looked at the situation of her husband and child she said: 'Yes, I will do it!'

"At the moment that decision was made the power of faith rested upon me, and when I administered unto her, her spirit entered her tabernacle, and she saw the messengers carry the coffin out at the door."[10]

NOTES AND COMMENTARY

D&C 42:43 *have not faith to be healed, but believe.* There are different levels of faith. Some believe in Christ and in the true gospel, but they do not have a strong enough faith to receive a miracle of healing. These should be treated and helped with tenderness. And, the Lord adds, "they who have not faith to do these things [that is, to be healed], but believe in me, have power to become my sons" (D&C 42:52), suggesting that they may still have sufficient faith to receive the saving blessings of the gospel.

not by the hand of an enemy. An enemy likely will not fully have the sick person's interests at heart. Further, the sick are to be "nourished with all tenderness, with herbs and mild food." If the herbs and mild food are given "by the hand of an enemy," the tenderness will be missing. Apparently the emotional support we offer those who are sick is an important element of the healing process.

D&C 42:44 *if they die they shall die unto me.* We may submit ourselves to a priesthood blessing in faith and righteousness, hoping to be healed, and yet may nevertheless die. In such a case, we die unto the Lord, meaning we die according to his will, we die into his kingdom in the spirit world, we die in order to do his work and continue labors of righteousness in paradise. On the other hand, if we are healed through that blessing, we live unto the Lord, meaning that we continue our works for him, with his blessing, in his kingdom here in mortality.

D&C 42:45 *weep for the loss of them that die.* When we "live together in love" we cherish our associations with family and friends. When they die, even though we have a firm testimony of continuing life in the spirit world and a lively hope of the resurrection, we miss those associations and have cause to weep for lost closeness, lost relationships, lost opportunities. The Lord acknowledges the depth of our feelings when he allows (or instructs) us to "weep for the loss of them that die." He further knows our fear and distress for those who may have rejected repentance and an earnest striving for obedience, saying that we should "more especially" weep for the dead who "have not hope of a glorious resurrection."

D&C 42:46 *those that die in me shall not taste of death.* The next phrase qualifies and clarifies. Those who die in the Lord shall taste of death, meaning they shall indeed die, but the taste shall not be bitter but sweet. Elder Spencer W. Kimball explained this phrase by saying, "I think that means they are not going into the other world feeling resentment and reticence. After they get past a certain point they go with happiness, peace and contentment."[11]

Those with this view of death will understand the truths Joseph F. Smith taught at a funeral in 1878: "There is no death where we . . . have hope of a glorious resurrection. . . . We live, then; we do not die; we do not anticipate death but we anticipate life, immortality, glory, exaltation, and to be quickened by the glory of the celestial kingdom."[12]

D&C 42:47 *And they that die not in me, wo unto them, for their death is bitter.* In contrast to those who die in the Lord, those who die in sin shall taste all the bitterness of death.

"Fear, and tremble before God," Abinadi said, "for ye ought to tremble; for the Lord redeemeth none such that rebel against him and die in their sins; yea, even all those that have perished in their sins ever since the world began, that have wilfully rebelled against God, that have known the commandments of God, and would not keep them; these are they that have no part in the first resurrection" (Mosiah 15:26; see also Moroni 10:26).

D&C 42:48 *not appointed unto death.* Certain people at certain times may be near death, but it may not be the Lord's will that they die at that point. If they exercise faith in Christ, such people may be blessed with a continuation of life in mortality. Of course, others may also be preserved without specific exercise of faith if it is the Lord's will.

DYING IN THE LORD

Doctrine and Covenants 124:85–86

85 Let no man go from this place who has come here essaying to keep my commandments.

86 If they live here let them live unto me; and if they die let them die unto me; for they shall rest from all their labors here, and shall continue their works.

This passage teaches a key principle—that whether we live or die, we should let God be the center and focus of our being. Alma described this way of life: "Cry unto God for all thy support; yea, let all thy doings be unto the Lord, and whithersoever thou goest let it be in the Lord; yea, let all thy thoughts be directed unto the Lord; yea, let the affections of thy heart be placed upon the Lord forever. Counsel with the Lord in all thy doings, and he will direct thee for good; yea, when thou liest down at night lie down unto the Lord, that he may watch over you in your sleep; and when thou risest in the morning let thy heart be full of thanks unto God; and if ye do these things, ye shall be lifted up at the last day" (Alma 37:36–37).

Paul explained the same idea in a different way: "He that regardeth the day, regardeth it unto the Lord; and he that regardeth not the day, to the Lord he doth not regard it. He that eateth, eateth to the Lord, for he giveth God thanks; and he that eateth not, to the Lord he eateth not, and giveth God thanks. For none of us liveth to himself, and no man dieth to himself. For whether we live, we live unto the Lord; and whether we die, we die unto the Lord: whether we live therefore, or die, we are the Lord's. For to this end Christ both died, and rose, and revived, that he might be Lord both of the dead and living" (Romans 14:6–9).

The Lord should be our guide and support and all our desire in mortality, and as we go into the spirit world, we can take that same heart and mind with us.

In a classic address, Elder Bruce R. McConkie explained the meaning and significance of dying in the Lord: "Those who have been true and faithful in this life will not fall by the wayside in the life to come. If they keep their covenants here and now and depart this life firm and true in the testimony of our blessed Lord, they shall come forth with an inheritance of eternal life.

"We do not mean to say that those who die in the Lord, and who are true and faithful in this life, must be perfect in all things when they go into the next sphere of existence. . . . There are many things they will do and must do, even beyond the grave, to merit the fulness of the Father's kingdom in that final glorious day. . . .

"But what we are saying is that when the saints of God chart a course of righteousness, when they gain sure testimonies of the truth and divinity of the Lord's work, when they keep the commandments, when they overcome the world, when they put first in their lives the things of God's kingdom: when they do all these things, and then depart this life—though they have not yet become perfect—they shall nonetheless gain eternal life in our Father's kingdom; and eventually they shall be perfect as God their Father and Christ His Son are perfect."[13]

Of such as these, George Q. Cannon said, "How delightful it is to contemplate the departure of those who have been faithful, as far as their knowledge permitted, to the truth which God has revealed! There is no sting nor gloom nor inconsolable sorrow about the departure of such persons. Holy angels are around their bedside to administer unto them. The Spirit of God rests down upon them, and His messengers are near them to introduce them to those who are on the other side of the veil."[14]

Others have spoken of such messengers. Joseph Smith said of his brother, Alvin, for example, "He was one of the soberest of men, and when he died the angel of the Lord visited him in his last moments."[15]

NOTES AND COMMENTARY

D&C 124:85 *Let no man go from this place.* This revelation was given in Nauvoo, Illinois, in January 1841. The Saints had been driven from Missouri and had gathered in Nauvoo. The Lord was encouraging them to remain in Nauvoo, where they could serve him and build up the Church.

D&C 124:86 *if they die let them die unto me.* The very experience of death is different for those who live and die unto the Lord. As we read earlier, "Those that die in me shall not taste of death, for it shall be sweet unto them; and they that die not in me, wo unto them, for their death is bitter" (D&C 42:46–47; see also discussion on these verses above). Those who die in the Lord shall eventually "come forth . . . to receive a crown of righteousness, and to be clothed upon, even as I am, to be with me, that we may be one" (D&C 29:13). In their resurrection they shall "receive an inheritance before the Lord, in the holy city" (D&C 63:49).

they shall rest from all their labors here, and shall continue their works. Those who die in righteousness go to a place of rest. But they do not rest from all their labors—only from their mortal labors. In paradise, they "continue their works" for the kingdom, continuing to contribute their all to the cause of God (see also Revelation 14:13). As the Psalmist said, "Precious in the sight of the Lord is the death of his saints" (Psalm 116:15). The Lord rejoices with them in their release from the trials and pains of mortality, while at the same time he is grateful for their continuing service in blessing their fellowmen.

FEAR OF DEATH

Psalm 55:4–5

4 My heart is sore pained within me: and the terrors of death are fallen upon me.

5 Fearfulness and trembling are come upon me, and horror hath overwhelmed me.

Death is a source of great fear for the wicked and those who lack faith in God and his plan, as well as those without knowledge, but for the righteous, death can be sweet (see D&C 42:46–47). Those without faith are fearful of annihilation, of ceasing to exist. Those in sin fear the punishments they will receive from God after they die.

Paul wrote, "O death, where is thy sting? O grave, where is thy victory?" He answered his own question by saying, "The sting of death is sin." But, he concluded, "thanks be to God, which giveth us the victory through our Lord Jesus Christ" (1 Corinthians 15:55–57; see also Alma 22:14). Paul understood that death for the righteous is marked by the victory of the atonement of Jesus Christ. But the wicked feel the "sting of death."

Other prophets have written of this fear of death. Enos wrote of the wicked in his day that only by "continually reminding them of death, and the duration of eternity, and the judgments and the power of God" were the preachers of righteousness able to "keep them from going down speedily to destruction" (Enos 1:23). Fear of death can sometimes provide a motivation to repent.

Abinadi warned the people of Noah that "the Lord redeemeth none such that rebel against him and die in their sins." The people should therefore "fear, and tremble before God" (Mosiah 15:26).

Elder Russell M. Nelson tells of an experience he had that brought him face to face with death—and the complete lack of fear he was able to enjoy:

"I remember vividly an experience I had as a passenger in a small two-propeller airplane. One of the engines suddenly burst open and caught on fire. The propeller of the flaming engine was starkly stilled. As we plummeted in a steep spiral dive toward the earth, I expected to die. Some of the passengers screamed in hysterical panic. Miraculously, the precipitous dive extinguished the flames. Then, by starting up the other engine, the pilot was able to stabilize the plane and bring us down safely.

"Throughout that ordeal, though I felt that sudden death was coming, my paramount feeling was that I was not afraid to die. I remember a sense of returning home to meet ancestors for whom I had done temple work. I remember my deep sense of gratitude that my sweetheart and I had been sealed eternally to each other and to our children born and reared in the covenant. I realized that our marriage in the temple was our most important accomplishment. Honors bestowed upon me by men could not begin to approach the inner peace provided by sealings performed in the House of the Lord."[16]

If we are in sin or lack faith, we will experience "that awful fear of death which fills the breasts of all the wicked" (Mormon 6:7). But if we have entered into sacred covenants with the Lord, and have been true to those covenants, we can have peace in the face of imminent death.

NOTES AND COMMENTARY

Psalm 55:4 *My heart is sore pained within me.* David spoke of the "oppression of the wicked," who hated him "in wrath" (v. 3). These things caused him anguish of heart.

terrors of death. Elder George Q. Cannon described the terrors of death: "How is it with the wicked and the apostate? . . . With what horror and dread do they look forward to the time of their death! In their sight death is a grim and terrible monster. They have no cheering promises of God to lean upon. The road before them, which leads to the spirit land, is dark and dismal; they have a foretaste of that which awaits them, and they shrink back with affright."[17]

In Psalm 88, the Psalmist gave voice to the trouble of spirit felt by a man facing death with fear:

"My soul is full of troubles: and my life draweth nigh unto the grave.

"I am counted with them that go down into the pit: I am as a man that hath no strength. . . .

"Thou hast laid me in the lowest pit, in darkness, in the deeps.

"Thy wrath lieth hard upon me, and thou hast afflicted me with all thy waves. . . .

"Thou hast put away mine acquaintance far from me; thou hast made me an abomination unto them: I am shut up, and I cannot come forth. . . .

"Lord, why castest thou off my soul? why hidest thou thy face from me?

"I am afflicted and ready to die from my youth up: while I suffer thy terrors I am distracted.

"Thy fierce wrath goeth over me; thy terrors have cut me off.

"They came round about me daily like water; they compassed me about together.

"Lover and friend hast thou put far from me, and mine acquaintance into darkness" (Psalm 88:3–4, 6–8, 14–18).

MOURNING FOR THE DEAD

Doctrine and Covenants 42:45

45 Thou shalt live together in love, insomuch that thou shalt weep for the loss of them that die, and more especially for those that have not hope of a glorious resurrection.

When we love another person, we feel deeply the loss that comes with the separation from him or her at death. We anticipate the lost companionship, the lost opportunities of love and association, possibly the hours of loneliness yet to come. Those emotions often come readily to the surface and are manifest in the tears of mourning. The Lord approves such outward expressions of our grief; he knows that such feelings are a natural part of being mortal.

Even Joseph Smith, with his intimate and personal knowledge of the plan of salvation, suffered deep grief when his older brother died at a young age: "I remember well the pangs of sorrow that swelled my youthful bosom and almost burst my tender heart when he died."[18]

Our feelings of loss are heightened when we fear that our deceased loved one will not have "hope of a glorious resurrection." When our loved ones die in sin, we fear that they may lose the blessings and promises given to the faithful in God's kingdom. As a consequence, we know that our ties with them of kinship or friendship may well not survive death and resurrection; our parting with them in mortality may be our last. Further, we fear that they have failed of the eternal blessings that they might have gained through faithfulness. Small wonder that we are instructed to "more especially" weep on such occasions.

Being open to the pain of those who suffer bereavement is part of being a saint. Alma said to his converts at the waters of Mormon that they must be "willing to mourn with those that mourn; yea, and comfort those that stand in need of comfort" (Mosiah 18:9).

Elder Russell M. Nelson wrote sympathetically of the reality of grief when he said, "The separation imposed by the departure of a loved one evokes pangs of sorrow and shock among those left behind. The hurt is real. . . . Even though we understand the doctrine—even though we dearly love God and his eternal plan—mourning remains. It is not only normal; it is a healthy reaction. Mourning is one of the purest expressions of deep love. . . . The only way to take sorrow out of death is to take love out of life. . . .

"Where can we turn for peace? We can come unto the Lord Jesus Christ. With consummate love, he said: 'Peace I leave with you, my peace I give unto you: not as the world giveth, give I unto you. Let not your heart be troubled, neither let it be afraid.' (John 14:27.)"[19]

Even though mourning is a natural reaction to the death of those we love, it need not be a lasting condition. Jesus said, "Blessed are they that mourn: for they shall be comforted" (Matthew 5:4).

President Heber J. Grant, seventh president of the Church, told of a poignant experience in his family where he and his children received the great blessing of comfort from the Lord. President Grant's wife was deathly ill, and his daughter asked him to heal her mother by the power of the priesthood.

"I told my little girl that we all had to die sometime, and that I felt assured in my heart that her mother's time had arrived. She and the rest of the children left the room.

"I then knelt down by the bed of my wife (who by this time had lost consciousness) and I told the Lord I acknowledged His hand in life, in death, in joy, in sorrow, in prosperity, or adversity. I thanked Him for the knowledge I had that my wife belonged to me for all eternity, that the gospel of Jesus Christ had been restored, that I knew that by the power and authority of the Priesthood here on the earth that I could and would have my wife forever if I were only faithful as she had been. But I told the Lord that I lacked the strength to have my wife die and to have it affect the faith of my little children in the ordinances of the gospel of Jesus Christ; and I supplicated the Lord with all the strength that I possessed, that He would give to that little girl of mine a knowledge that it was His mind and His will that her mamma should die.

"Within an hour my wife passed away, and I called the children back into the room. My little boy about five and a half or six years of age was weeping bitterly, and the little girl twelve years of age took him in her arms and said: 'Do not weep, do not cry, Heber; since we went out of this room the voice of the Lord from heaven has said to me, "In the death of your mamma the will of the Lord shall be done."'

"Tell me, my friends, that I do not know that God hears and answers prayers! Tell me that I do not know that in the hour of adversity the Latter-day Saints are comforted and blessed and consoled as no other people are!"[20]

The comfort that Latter-day Saints can receive in the hour of bereavement is real and substantial. "The promise 'Those that die in me shall not taste [the bitterness of] death, for it shall be sweet unto them' extends often to those bereaved," wrote Truman Madsen. "When death comes at a ripe climax of a life well lived, there is a noticeable absence of agony, a fervent sense of culmination, and even, at times, rejoicing. . . . The closest analogy to a Mormon funeral at graveside is a missionary farewell. Here is a group of loved ones, not hard-faced and stoical, not blank and numb, but sensitized. There is apparent grief, but not despair. There is warmth and promise."[21]

"I have no reason to mourn, not even at death," Joseph F. Smith said. "It is true . . . I may shed tears when I see the grief of others. I have sympathy in my soul for the children of men. I can weep with them when they weep; I can rejoice with them when they rejoice; but I have no cause to mourn, nor to be sad because death comes into the world. I am speaking now of the temporal death, the death of the body. All fear of this death has been removed from the Latter-day Saints. They . . . know that as death came upon them by the transgression of Adam, so by the righteousness of Jesus Christ shall life come unto them, and though they die they shall live again. Possessing this knowledge, they have joy even in death, for they know that they shall rise again and shall meet again beyond the grave. They know that the Spirit dies not at all; that it passes through no change, except the change from imprisonment in this mortal clay to freedom and to the sphere in which it acted before it came to this death."[22]

FUNERALS

2 Samuel 3:31–33, 35

31 And David said to Joab, and to all the people that were with him, Rend your clothes, and gird you with sackcloth, and mourn before Abner. And king David himself followed the bier.

32 And they buried Abner in Hebron: and the king lifted up his voice, and wept at the grave of Abner; and all the people wept.

33 And the king lamented over Abner. . . .

35 And when all the people came to cause David to eat meat while it was yet day, David sware, saying, So do God to me, and more also, if I taste bread, or ought else, till the sun be down.

Not all cultures hold funerals as people in America do, with speeches and flowers. The ancient Israelites, for example, followed a pattern like that shown in 2 Samuel—rending their clothes, putting on sackcloth, weeping, lamenting, and fasting.

The scriptures say little about funerals. But, thankfully, our latter-day leaders have given helpful instructions about the form and spirit of our funerals.

Latter-day Saint funerals are considered worship services and are typically conducted under the direction of a bishop. The bishop is the presiding authority and should follow the directions given in the *Church Handbook of Instructions.* The spirit of funerals should be similar to the spirit found in sacrament meetings, and talks, music, and prayers that would be inappropriate in sacrament meeting should be considered inappropriate for a funeral. Speakers should take the opportunity to teach the comforting doctrines of the gospel and to bear testimony of Jesus Christ and the reality of his atonement.

In an important conference address, Elder Boyd K. Packer emphasized the spirit that should prevail at Latter-day Saint funerals: "One of the most solemn and sacred meetings of the Church is the funeral for a departed member. It is a time of caring and support when families gather in a spirit of tender regard for one another. It is a time to soberly contemplate doctrines of the gospel and the purposes for the ministry of the Lord Jesus Christ. . . .

"A comforting, spiritual funeral is of great importance. It helps console the bereaved and establishes a transition from mourning to the reality that we must move forward with life. Whether death is expected or a sudden shock, an inspirational funeral where the doctrines of resurrection, the mediation of Christ, and certainty of life after death are taught strengthens those who must now move on with life.

"Many attend funerals who do not come to church regularly. They come subdued in spirit and are teachable. How sad when an opportunity for conversion is lost because a funeral is less than it might have been. . . .

"We are close, very close, to the spirit world at the time of death. There are tender feelings, spiritual communications really, which may easily be lost if there is not a spirit of reverence. . . .

"The Comforter works, as far as I have experienced, in moments of reverence and quiet and solemnity. How sad if our own conduct is irreverent at a time when others are seeking so desperately for spiritual strength."[23]

President Wilford Woodruff recorded some guidelines for his own funeral, which he desired to be a simple affair. "I wish my body washed clean and clothed in clean white linen, according to the order of the Holy Priesthood," he wrote, "and put into a plain, decent coffin, made of native wood, with plenty of room. *I do not wish any black made use of about my coffin, or about the vehicle that conveys my body to the grave.* I do not wish my family or friends *to wear any badge of mourning for me* at my funeral or afterwards, for, if I am true and faithful unto death, there will be no necessity for anyone to mourn for me. . . . Their speech will be to the living. *If the laws and customs of the spirit world will permit, I should wish to attend my funeral but I shall be governed by the counsel I receive in the spirit world.*"[24]

Finally, President Spencer W. Kimball gave a thoughtful caution to those who offer eulogies at funerals: "The practice of speakers wiping out every fault and magnifying every seeming virtue of faithless persons as soon as they are dead, leaves the false impression that the acceptance of the gospel and complete obedience to its standards while in this life are not important. Extravagant statements, promises, or assurances, unless clearly dictated by the Spirit, should not be made at funerals."[25]

NOTES AND COMMENTARY

2 Samuel 3:31 *Rend your clothes, and gird you with sackcloth.* It was a common practice in ancient Israel for people to mourn a death by tearing their clothes and putting on sackcloth (see, for example, Genesis 37:34; Isaiah 15:3).

the bier. The bier was probably like a litter on which the body of the deceased was carried. The bier was borne by the nearest relatives, and it was followed by the group of mourners to the place of burial.

2 Samuel 3:35 *So do God to me, and more also.* This is a figure of speech called a "curse formula," often found in the Old Testament (see, for example, Ruth 1:17; 1 Samuel 3:17; 14:44; 2 Samuel 3:9). In this instance, David is inviting a curse upon himself if he does not adequately mourn the death of Abner.

if I taste bread, or ought else, till the sun be down. David is pledging to observe a strict fast until after sunset, which is when the Hebrew day ended. Fasting was an expression of grief, sorrow, or deep regret.

BURIAL

Genesis 47:29–30

29 And the time drew nigh that Israel must die: and he called his son Joseph, and said unto him, If now I have found grace in thy sight, put, I pray thee, thy hand under my thigh, and deal kindly and truly with me; bury me not, I pray thee, in Egypt:

30 But I will lie with my fathers, and thou shalt carry me out of Egypt, and bury me in their buryingplace. And he said, I will do as thou hast said.

The place of burial was of vital importance to the ancient people of Israel—so much so that Israel (Jacob) asked his son to promise that he would make the long and difficult journey from Egypt to Canaan to bury him "with [his] fathers" (see also Genesis 49:29–32; 50:4–13). A generation later, Joseph made the same request of "his brethren": "I die: and God will surely visit you, and bring you out of this land unto the land which he sware to Abraham, to Isaac, and to Jacob . . . and ye shall carry up my bones from hence" (Genesis 50:24–25). Joseph's request was remembered and honored by Moses hundreds of years later (Exodus 13:19).

Joseph Smith taught that the desire of Jacob and Joseph was based on a true principle. When Lorenzo Dow Barnes died in December 1842, while serving a mission in England, he was buried in Leeds. Joseph Smith subsequently said in a sermon preached at the Nauvoo Temple:

"I would esteem it one of the greatest blessings . . . to have the privilege of having our dead buried on the land where God has appointed to gather His Saints together, and where there will be none but Saints, . . . that in the morn of the resurrection they may . . . come up out of their graves and strike hands immediately in eternal glory and felicity, rather than be scattered thousands of miles apart. There is something good and sacred to me in this thing. The place where a man is buried is sacred to me. . . .

"When I heard of the death of our beloved Brother Barnes, it would not have affected me so much, if I had the opportunity of burying him in the land of Zion.

"I believe those who have buried their friends here, their condition is enviable. Look at Jacob and Joseph in Egypt, how they required their friends to bury them in the tomb of their fathers. See the expense which attended the embalming and the going up of the great company to the burial.

"It has always been considered a great calamity not to obtain an honorable burial: and one of the greatest curses the ancient prophets could put on any man, was that he should go without a burial.

"I have said, Father, I desire to die here among the Saints. But if this is not Thy will, and I go hence and die, wilt thou find some kind friend to bring my body back, and gather my friends who have fallen in foreign lands, and bring them up hither, that we may all lie together.

"I will tell you what I want. If tomorrow I shall be called to lie in yonder tomb, in the morning of the resurrection let me strike hands with my father, and cry, 'My father,' and he will say, 'My son, my son,' as soon as the rock rends and before we come out of our graves."[26]

Certainly Joseph Smith was not preaching that all the Saints should be buried in one place, nor will a righteous soul suffer if he or she is buried in a foreign land, in the depths of the ocean, on the plains, or in some other less favorable spot. There will be no loss of blessings to the righteous whose bodies are destroyed by burning, who are lost at war, or who live in a place where burial is not possible. But as much as possible, we should seek to give our dead honorable burials, and we should bury family members together, as the Prophet suggested.[27]

NOTES AND COMMENTARY

Genesis 47:29 *If now I have found grace in thy sight.* The NIV translates "grace" as "favor." In essence, Jacob is saying to Joseph, "If you are willing to do me a favor."

put, I pray thee, thy hand under my thigh. This is a particularly solemn form of oath. "It is from the thighs that one's descendants come, so that to take an oath with one hand under the thigh would be equivalent to calling upon these descendants to maintain an oath which has been fulfilled, and to avenge one which has been broken."[28] Our modern equivalent would be to put our hand on a Bible when swearing an oath. Jacob was asking Joseph to swear a solemn oath that he would take Jacob's body to the family burial place.

≈≈≈

CHAPTER 3

CONDITIONS AND
CIRCUMSTANCES OF THE DEAD

Though the body is mortal and must die, the spirit is immortal. "The part of you that looks out through your eyes and allows you to think and smile and act and know and be, that is your spirit and that is eternal," Elder Boyd K. Packer has taught. "It cannot die."[1] Elder Russell M. Nelson added that it is the spirit that "provides the body with animation and personality."[2] The "animation and personality" of the spirit continues even after the body is dead. That spirit goes into another state or dimension called the spirit world, there to dwell until the time of the resurrection.

In this, as in all things, Jesus is our example: "As Jesus' spirit left his body hanging on the cross and later lying in the tomb, so shall our spirits eventually leave our bodies lying lifeless. As Jesus preached to spirits in the spirit world in his spiritual state, so shall our spirits continue active and expand and develop."[3]

There are many questions one might ask about the spirit's mode of existence in the next sphere:

- When we die, what becomes of the agreements we've made with others?

- In what ways do we change—or not change—when we die?

- What do the scriptures mean in saying that at death we are "taken home to God"?

- What is the gulf between the righteous and wicked in the world to come?

- What is paradise like?

- What is the spirit prison like?
- Is there really such a place as hell?
- What are the "gates of hell"?
- How is the gospel taken to the wicked in the spirit world?
- What kind of communication can occur between the two worlds?

The prophets have taught us much about these things, and Latter-day Saints know more about the spirit world than any other people on earth. Our interest in the spirit world is not a simple curiosity. For one thing, we know that we ourselves will soon enough go into that world. For another, "every one who departs from this mortal state of existence only adds another link to the chain of connection. . . . Those of us who have lost children, brothers and sisters and parents, feel an increased interest in the spirit world; the ties between such and the spirit world, have become binding, and we can contemplate, if not with delight, at least with no great sorrow, our removal from this state of existence to the next."[4]

WHAT IS THE SPIRIT?

Ether 3:16

16 Behold, this body, which ye now behold, is the body of my spirit; and man have I created after the body of my spirit; and even as I appear unto thee to be in the spirit will I appear unto my people in the flesh.

Death has been defined as the separation of the body and the spirit. The body goes into the grave, lifeless, while the spirit continues. But what is the spirit?

Spirits are the living, highly intelligent offspring of God. As Paul wrote, we have "fathers of our flesh" whom we seek to obey—but far better it is to be "in subjection to the Father of Spirits" (Hebrews 12:9).

In the remarkable account in the book of Ether, Jehovah, the premortal Jesus Christ, appeared to the brother of Jared in the spirit. The brother of Jared was astounded to see the form in which the Lord appeared. "The Lord stretched forth his hand and . . . the veil was taken from off the eyes of the brother of Jared, and he saw the finger of the Lord; and it was as the finger of a man, like unto flesh and blood."

In the ensuing dialogue, the Lord said to the brother of Jared, "Seest thou that ye are created after mine own image? Yea, even all men were created in the beginning after mine own image."

Moroni concluded, "Jesus showed himself unto this man in the spirit, even after the manner and in the likeness of the same body even as he showed himself unto the Nephites" (Ether 3:6, 15, 17).

We can understand our spirits by observing our physical bodies. The "body" of the spirit looks essentially like the physical body we are given here on earth. Our spirits are composed of "matter," but they are "more fine or pure" than our physical bodies and "can only be discerned by purer eyes" (D&C 131:7).

The spirit is the basic and essential element of our being. "Man *is* spirit," the Lord has revealed (D&C 93:33; emphasis added). The spirit is also eternal. "The spirit of man is not a created being," said Joseph Smith, referring to that part of the spirit which we sometimes call "intelligence." "It existed from eternity and will exist to eternity. Anything created cannot be eternal; and earth, water, etc., had their existence in an elementary state, from eternity."[5] On another occasion, the Prophet said, "I am dwelling on the immortality of the spirit of man. The intelligence of spirits had no beginning, neither will it have an end. That is good logic. That which has a beginning may have an end. There never was a time when there were not spirits; for they are co-equal [co-eternal] with our Father in heaven."[6]

Not only will the spirit continue forever, but it will also retain its individual identity. President Joseph F. Smith taught that we are "just as truly individuals" as Jesus Christ is.[7]

"The spirits of our children are immortal before they come to us, and their spirits, after bodily death, are like they were before they came. They are as they would have appeared if they had lived in the flesh, to grow to maturity, or to develop their physical bodies to the full stature of their spirits. . . .

" . . . the Spirit of Jesus Christ was full-grown before he was born into the world; and so our children were full-grown and possessed their full stature in the spirit, before they entered mortality, the same stature that they will possess after they have passed away from mortality, and as they will also [eventually] appear after the resurrection."[8]

When a husband and wife are reunited in the resurrection, President Smith said, "neither would be changed, except from mortality to immortality; neither would be other than himself or herself, but they will have their identity in the world to come precisely as they exercise their individuality and enjoy their identity here."[9]

With his usual eloquence, Parley P. Pratt described the characteristics of our spirits:

"Jesus . . . conveyed the idea in the clearest terms, that an individual intelligence or identity could never die.

"The . . . thinking being, the individual, active agent or identity that inhabited that tabernacle, never ceased [at death] to exist, to think, act, live, move, or have a being; never ceased to exercise those sympathies, affections, hopes, and aspirations, which are founded in the very nature of intelligences, being the inherent and invaluable principles of their eternal existence.

"No, they never cease. They live, move, think, act, converse, feel, love, hate, believe, doubt, hope, and desire.

"But what are they, if they are not flesh and bones? What are they, if they are not tangible to our gross organs of sense? Of what are they composed, that we can neither see, hear, nor handle them, except we are quickened, or our organs touched by the principles of vision . . . or spiritual sight? . . . They are made of the element which we call spirit, which is as much an element of material existence, as earth, air, electricity, or any other tangible substance recognized by man; but so subtle, so refined is its nature, that it is not tangible to our gross organs. . . .

"We would call it a spiritual body, an individual intelligence, an agent endowed with life, with a degree of independence, or inherent will, with the powers of motion, of thought, and with the attributes of moral, intellectual, and sympathetic affections and emotions.

"We would conceive of it as possessing eyes to see, ears to hear, hands to handle; as in possession of the organ of taste, of smelling, and of speech.

"Such beings are we, when we have laid off this outward tabernacle of flesh. We are in every way interested, in our relationships, kindred ties, sympathies, affections, and hopes, as if we had continued to live, but had stepped aside, and were experiencing the loneliness of absence for a season. Our ancestors, our posterity, to the remotest ages of antiquity, or of future time, are all brought within the circle of our sphere of joys, sorrows, interests, or expectations; each forms a link in the great chain of life, and in the science of mutual salvation, improvement, and exaltation through the blood of the Lamb."[10]

NOTES AND COMMENTARY

Ether 3:16 *the body of my spirit.* This has reference to the form of the spirit. It is not "immaterial matter," for no such thing exists (D&C 131:7). It has form and substance, just as the mortal body does, although of a different kind. "Spirit is a substance," the Prophet Joseph Smith said. "It is material, but . . . it is more pure, elastic and refined matter than the body; . . . it existed before the body, can exist in the body; and will exist separate from the body, when the body will be mouldering in the dust; and will in the resurrection, be again united with it."[11]

man have I created after the body of my spirit. The physical appearance of mankind is patterned after the spiritual appearance of the premortal Jehovah. As the body has eyes, ears, mouth, nose, hands, arms, feet, and so forth, so also does the spirit.

even as I appear unto thee to be in the spirit will I appear unto my people in the flesh. The spirit looks like the body. Jehovah here tells the brother of Jared that when he comes to earth in the body, his appearance will be like that of his spirit. We read in the Doctrine and Covenants that "that which is spiritual [is] in the likeness of that which is temporal; and that which is temporal [is] in the likeness of that which is spiritual; the spirit of man in the likeness of his person, as also the spirit of the beast, and every other creature which God has created" (D&C 77:2).

WE LEAVE ALL BEHIND AT DEATH

Job 1:21

21 Naked came I out of my mother's womb, and naked shall I return thither: the Lord gave, and the Lord hath taken away; blessed be the name of the Lord.

Paul expressed the same idea to Timothy in different words: "We brought nothing into this world, and it is certain we can carry nothing out" (1 Timothy 6:7). And the Preacher in Ecclesiastes said, "As he came forth of his mother's womb, naked shall he return to go as he came, and shall take nothing of his labour, which he may carry away in his hand. . . . [I]n all points as he came, so shall he go: and what profit hath he that hath laboured for the wind?" (Ecclesiastes 5:15–16; see also Psalm 49:12–20).

There is a saying that "you can't take it with you," and this is absolutely true. When we die, we leave all temporal things behind: houses, lands, cars, boats, bank accounts, toys, appliances, computers, clothing, books, academic degrees and professional titles, earthly professions, and the honors of men. We even leave behind our bodies and the very casket in which we are laid.

Elder Spencer W. Kimball once told of a friend who took him to his ranch. The friend showed off his fine new car and then drove Elder Kimball to a "beautiful new landscaped home, and he said with no little pride, 'This is my home.'

"He drove to a grassy knoll. . . . With a wide sweeping gesture, he boasted, 'From the clump of trees, to the lake, to the bluff, and to the ranch buildings and all between—all this is mine. And the dark specks in the meadow—those cattle also are mine.' . . .

"That was long years ago. I saw him lying in his death among luxurious furnishings in a palatial home. His had been a vast estate. And I folded his arms upon his breast, and drew down the little curtains over his eyes. I spoke at his funeral, and I followed the cortege from the good piece of earth he had claimed to his grave, a tiny, oblong area the length of a tall man, the width of a heavy one.

"Yesterday I saw that same estate, yellow in grain, green in lucerne, white in cotton, seemingly unmindful of him who had claimed it. Oh, puny man, see the busy ant moving the sands of the sea."[12]

Elder ElRay Christiansen, an Assistant to the Twelve for many years, "told of a wealthy man in Denmark who was converted to the gospel and had migrated to Utah. His commitment caused the loss of much of his fortune, but, after settling here, he again had the ability to amass riches and, in the process, lost his faith and testimony. As his brethren tried to counsel him about his eternal purpose, he would not listen. Finally one of them said to him, 'Lars, it is not good to think only of money. You cannot take it with you, you know.'

"Lars answered, 'Vat is that you say?' and he was told again, 'I say you cannot take it with you.'

"Lars responded, 'Vell, den, I vill not go.'

"Elder Christiansen's report was that he had gone anyway."[13]

If we cannot take our worldly goods with us, what *can* we take with us when we die?

We can take our—

- testimony
- character
- relationships (when we are bound by and true to covenant)
- memory of experiences
- priesthood
- covenant promises
- knowledge
- spiritual gifts

Simply put, death will strip us of every earthly thing. Only those things that are spiritual and eternal will continue with us into the next sphere of existence.

ALL COVENANTS AND AGREEMENTS HAVE AN END AT DEATH, EXCEPT THOSE SEALED BY PRIESTHOOD

Doctrine and Covenants 132:13–14

13 And everything that is in the world, whether it be

ordained of men, by thrones, or principalities, or powers, or
things of name, whatsoever they may be, that are not by me
or by my word, saith the Lord, shall be thrown down, and
shall not remain after men are dead, neither in nor after the
resurrection, saith the Lord your God.
14 For whatsoever things remain are by me; and whatso-
ever things are not by me shall be shaken and destroyed.

Just as we lose all our temporal possessions at death, so also do we lose all agreements and covenants we have made on earth, unless those covenants have been authorized, blessed, and sealed by the Lord. Even agreements or covenants or contracts that are made under authority of kings and rulers shall have an end at death. This includes the marriage agreement. The Lord outlined this truth as follows:

"All covenants, contracts, bonds, obligations, oaths, vows, per-formances, connections, associations, or expectations, that are not made and entered into and sealed by the Holy Spirit of promise, of him who is anointed, both as well for time and for all eternity, and that too most holy, by revelation and commandment through the medium of mine anointed, whom I have appointed on the earth to hold this power (and I have appointed unto my servant Joseph to hold this power in the last days, and there is never but one on the earth at a time on whom this power and the keys of this priesthood are conferred), are of no efficacy, virtue, or force in and after the resurrection from the dead; for all contracts that are not made unto this end have an end when men are dead. . . .

"Therefore, if a man marry him a wife in the world, and he marry her not by me nor by my word, and he covenant with her so long as he is in the world and she with him, their covenant and marriage are not of force when they are dead, and when they are out of the world; therefore, they are not bound by any law when they are out of the world" (D&C 132:7, 15).

The Lord's law is very clear. No matter what our intentions or desires, if we join with another person in any covenant, contract, or agreement here on earth, and if that agreement has not been bound by the keys of the priesthood and sealed by the Holy Spirit of promise, then the agreement is over at the time of death. Interestingly, many marriages performed in our culture are pronounced valid "until death shall you part" or "as long as you both shall live." The very words of such ceremonies reinforce the truth that earthly covenants and vows are valid only for our days on the mortal earth.

The Holy Spirit of promise mentioned here is the Holy Ghost, acting in his office as one who gives final ratification and approval to all the ordinances and covenants we enter into in righteousness. The appointed keys of power and authority mentioned are the sealing power, held in its fulness only by the president of The Church of Jesus Christ of Latter-day Saints but delegated to those authorized by him to seal in the holy temples.

NOTES AND COMMENTARY

D&C 132:13 *And everything that is in the world.* The Lord gives a list of what this includes: any agreement or law set up and ordained of men, even men of authority and power. If the agreement is of the Lord, both by authority and Spirit, it shall remain and continue in the resurrection. If it is of men only, it will end at death.

things of name. The meaning of this expression is not clear; however, it may have reference to things that are well known and famous, things that have a name. Perhaps the Lord is saying that even those things that have earthly fame, "whatsoever they may be," do not have power to establish anything that lasts beyond death.

D&C 132:14 *whatsoever things remain are by me.* In the resurrection, only one category of things will remain: those that are set up, sponsored, initiated, or authorized by the Lord.

WE CONTINUE IN THE SAME SPIRITUAL CONDITION WHEN WE DIE

Alma 34:34–35

34 Ye cannot say, when ye are brought to that awful crisis, that I will repent, that I will return to my God. Nay, ye cannot say this; for that same spirit which doth possess your bodies at the time that ye go out of this life, that same spirit will have power to possess your body in that eternal world.

35 For behold, if ye have procrastinated the day of your

repentance even until death, behold, ye have become sub-
jected to the spirit of the devil, and he doth seal you his;
therefore, the Spirit of the Lord hath withdrawn from you, and
hath no place in you, and the devil hath all power over you;
and this is the final state of the wicked.

Nephi taught regarding the resurrection that at that time "they who are righteous shall be righteous still, and they who are filthy shall be filthy still" (2 Nephi 9:16). As we see from the teachings of Amulek above, the same principle clearly holds true when we pass from mortal life into the spirit world—the state of our soul and our character here continue to be the same there.

"Have you ever realized that there is no magic in death," President Spencer W. Kimball asked, "that ceasing to breathe does not make angels of careless people, does not make believers of disbelievers, does not bring faith where there was skepticism?"[14]

Brigham Young taught the same principle: "Suppose . . . that a man is evil in his heart—wholly given up to wickedness, and in that condition dies, his spirit will enter into the spirit world intent upon evil. On the other hand, if we are striving with all the powers and faculties God has given us to improve upon our talents, to prepare ourselves to dwell in eternal life, and the grave receives our bodies while we are thus engaged, with what disposition will our spirits enter their next state? They will be still striving to do the things of God, only in a much greater degree—learning, increasing, growing in grace and in the knowledge of the truth."[15]

It must be noted, however, that some people have difficulties in the mortal sphere that will be removed in the spirit world. The person who is in a physically or sexually abusive relationship, with its resulting dampening effects on the spirit, will enjoy a much changed experience in the spirit world. The same could perhaps be said of those who suffer from clinical depression or chronic, severe physical illness.

In the same way that the nature of the spirit continues to be the same after death, so does our level of knowledge. In his well-known address on the three degrees of glory, Elder Melvin J. Ballard said, "Do not let any of us imagine that we can go down to the grave not having overcome the corruptions of the flesh and then lose in the grave all our sins and evil tendencies. They will be with us. They will be with the spirit when separated from the body. . . .

"Some folk get the notion that the problems of life will at once clear up, and they will know that this is the gospel of Christ when they die. I have heard people say they believe when they die, they will see Peter and that he will clear it all up. I said, 'You never will see Peter until you accept the gospel of the Lord Jesus Christ, at the hands of the elders of the Church, living or dead. They will meet these men to whom this right and authority has been given, for this generation shall receive it at the hands of those who have been honored with the priesthood of this dispensation. Living or dead, they shall not hear it from anyone else.'

"So, men won't know any more when they are dead than when they are living, only they will have passed through the change called death. They will not understand the truths of the gospel only by the same process as they understand and comprehend them here. . . . When you die and go to the spirit world, you will labor for years, trying to convert individuals who will be taking their own course. Some of them will repent; some of them will listen. Another group will be rebellious, following their own will and notion, and that group will get smaller and smaller until every knee shall humbly bow and every tongue confess."[16]

NOTES AND COMMENTARY

Alma 34:34 *that awful crisis.* The "awful crisis" men face is dying without being prepared by faith and repentance to conclude this mortal probation.

that same spirit. The spirit that possesses our bodies in this life will also possess our bodies in the world to come. The expression "same spirit" can be applied in several ways. First, Amulek seemed to be explicitly referring to the spirit of the devil and the Spirit of the Lord. Whichever spirit we allow to guide and direct us in mortality will continue to influence us in the spirit world and beyond.

Second, Amulek's words can be applied to our "disposition, attitude, proclivity, spiritual direction. Men and women will not have an immediate reversal of attitude at the time of death. If they have desired evil things; if they have sold their souls for attention and applause and acclaim; if they have craved carnal pleasures alone—if their lives have followed this course, they need not expect to inherit spirituality in the world to come."[17]

As Elder Bruce R. McConkie put it, "Men have the same talents and intelligence there which they had in this life. They possess the same attitudes, inclinations, and feelings there which they had in this life. They believe the same things, as far as eternal truths are concerned; they continue, in effect, to walk in the same path they were following in this life. . . . Thus if a man has the spirit of charity and love of the truth in his heart in this life, that same spirit will possess him in the spirit world. If he has the spirit of unbelief and hate in his heart here, so will it be with him when he passes through the door into the spirit world."[18]

Third, George Q. Cannon spoke of our spirits being "animated" here by the spirit of the kingdom we would eventually receive: "We shall enter into the other sphere of existence with the same spirit that we have here. If we were animated by the spirit of the Telestial Kingdom we shall have that, if by the spirit of the Terrestrial Kingdom we shall have that, if by the spirit of the Celestial Kingdom we shall have that. We shall go from this condition of existence into the other sphere with the same feelings, to some extent at least, as we have here. If we have had knowledge, we shall have it there."[19]

Alma 34:35 *subjected to the spirit of the devil.* If we make choices to follow Satan and his will, and if we fail to repent when we're given the opportunity (whether in the mortal or the spiritual world), we become his subjects. Amulek said to those who continue in that spirit that in time the devil will "seal you his," and he will have "all power over you."

hath no place in you. If we "give place" for the Spirit of the Lord in our lives, allowing him to be our companion and guide, he will continue with us. But if we choose to follow the spirit of the devil and refuse to repent, the Spirit of the Lord will leave us, while the devil will continue with us.

AT DEATH WE ARE "TAKEN HOME TO GOD"

Alma 40:11

11 Now, concerning the state of the soul between death and the resurrection—Behold, it has been made known unto me by

*an angel, that the spirits of all men, as soon as they are
departed from this mortal body, yea, the spirits of all men,
whether they be good or evil, are taken home to that God who
gave them life.*

In these verses, Alma teaches us two fundamental truths about life
after death. First, we are not resurrected immediately after we die.
Second, when we die our spirits are "taken home to . . . God." But
what does it mean to be taken home to God? If even the wicked come
into the presence of God at death, what does that do to their agency as
certain elements of their test continue in the spirit world? After all,
those who have not received the opportunity to hear the gospel in mortality will have that chance in the spirit world—and it must be an
opportunity that will truly test their hearts. An essential element of
such a test is a willingness to exercise faith even when we are outside
the presence of God.

One explanation of this passage is that God's presence really is
everywhere. As the Psalmist said,

"Whither shall I go from thy spirit? or whither shall I flee from
thy presence?

"If I ascend up into heaven, thou art there: if I make my bed in
hell, behold, thou art there.

"If I take the wings of the morning, and dwell in the uttermost
parts of the sea; even there shall thy hand lead me, and thy right hand
shall hold me.

"If I say, Surely the darkness shall cover me; even the night shall
be light about me.

"Yea, the darkness hideth not from thee; but the night shineth as
the day: the darkness and the light are both alike to thee" (Psalm
139:7–12).

This idea accords with the teaching of George Q. Cannon:

"Alma, when he says that 'the spirits of all men, as soon as they
are departed from this mortal body . . . are taken home to that God
who gave them life,' has the idea doubtless, in his mind that our God
is omnipresent—not in His own personality but through His minister,
the Holy Spirit.

"He does not intend to convey the idea that they are immediately ushered into the personal presence of God. He evidently uses that phrase in a qualified sense. . . . Alma says plainly that the spirits of the righteous go into a state of happiness, etc. He says the spirits of the wicked are cast into outer darkness, etc. Now, then, how can those spirits who are cast into outer darkness be in the personal presence of God? God does not dwell where they are, and they certainly do not go where He is. And yet He is there by His Spirit and by His power."[20]

Another interpretation is that God lives in a spiritual realm, and that when we die we "go home" to that realm. As Joseph Fielding Smith said, "These words of Alma as I understand them, do not intend to convey the thought that all spirits go back into the presence of God for an assignment to a place of peace or a place of punishment and before him receive their individual sentence. 'Taken home to God,' simply means that their mortal existence has come to an end, and they have returned to the world of spirits, where they are assigned to a place according to their works with the just or with the unjust, there to await the resurrection. 'Back to God' is a phrase which finds an equivalent in many other well known conditions. For instance: a man spends a stated time in some foreign mission field. When he is released and returns to the United States, he may say, 'It is wonderful to be back home'; yet his home may be somewhere in Utah or Idaho or some other part of the West."[21]

President Harold B. Lee concurred:

"In discussing this matter I have found the quotation from President Brigham Young contained in his *Discourses,* which says: '[The scripture] reads that the spirit goes to God who gave it. Let me render this scripture a little plainer; when the spirits leave their bodies they are in the presence of our Father and God, they are prepared then to see, hear and understand spiritual things. . . .

"'If the wicked wish to escape from his presence, they must go where he is not, where he does not live, where his influence does not preside. To find such a place is impossible, except they go beyond the bounds of time and space.'[22]

". . . When we go home to God, it is just like going back to our home country. We may not go into the presence of the governor of the state where we live, but we will go to the home country, and there we shall find our level among the people with whom we are most accustomed to associate."[23]

NOTES AND COMMENTARY

Alma 40:11 *the spirits of all men, as soon as they are departed from this mortal body, . . . are taken home to that God who gave them life.* As noted above, Latter-day Saint authorities agree that Alma's teaching here is to be taken figuratively rather than literally. Some of the righteous may well have the privilege of standing in the presence of God as they make the transition from mortal to spirit life, just as some of the righteous have the privilege of heavenly visitations while they are still on this earth. But most men and women do not have that privilege, either here or in the spirit world. There *is* a time when "all men" will literally stand before God, however; this will occur in conjunction with the judgment that takes place at the resurrection (2 Nephi 9:15; Alma 33:22).

SEPARATION OF BODY AND SPIRIT IS BONDAGE

Doctrine and Covenants 138:50

50 For the dead had looked upon the long absence of their spirits from their bodies as a bondage.

In Joseph F. Smith's vision of the redemption of the dead, he saw a great gathering of "an innumerable company of the spirits of the just." These were righteous spirits "who had been faithful in the testimony of Jesus while they lived in mortality." They were not suffering the torments of the damned, nor were they in suspense as to their eventual destiny. Their faith in Christ was firm and true, and they had confidence both in his plan and in their place in that plan.

Nevertheless, they "were rejoicing together because the day of their deliverance was at hand." Deliverance from what? As President Smith saw, they knew the Lord was coming "to declare their redemption from the bands of death.

"Their sleeping dust was to be restored unto its perfect frame, bone to his bone, and the sinews and the flesh upon them, the spirit and the body to be united never again to be divided, that they might receive a fulness of joy" (D&C 138:12–17).

This passage is filled with remarkable truth. The spirits President Smith saw were blessed with the joys of righteousness. They were in a state where there is no sickness, hunger, or fatigue, no bodily ills of any kind, no concern about money or debt or temporal matters of any kind. They had passed the tests of mortality and no longer had the fear of spiritual failure. And yet they had learned firsthand what the Lord revealed to Joseph Smith: "The elements are eternal, and spirit and element, inseparably connected, receive a fulness of joy; and when separated, man cannot receive a fulness of joy" (D&C 93:33).

Only those who are most like God are fashioned to enjoy the greatest joy. God is a resurrected, glorified man, whose being is composed of "spirit and element, inseparably connected." Thus, despite the seeming advantages of a life in spirit form, the dead look "upon the long absence of their spirits from their bodies as a bondage" (D&C 138:50; see also D&C 45:17).

"Just as we need this physical body to experience things that never would have been ours while we were in the spirit world awaiting this opportunity," said Elder Melvin J. Ballard, "so the spirit after death will want the body, because it will live in a world that is real. God designed and intended that his whole realm, which is both spiritual and material, shall be the abode and habitation of man, and without the physical body it would be impossible for us to contact with physical objects as we do here and now."[24]

On another occasion Elder Ballard added, "I grant you that the righteous dead will be at peace, but I tell you that when we go out of this life, leave this body, we will desire to do many things that we cannot do at all without the body. . . .

"The point I have in mind is that we are sentencing ourselves to long periods of bondage, separating our spirits from our bodies, or we are shortening that period, according to the way in which we overcome and master ourselves."[25]

THE WORLD OF SPIRITS

Alma 40:6–7

6 Now there must needs be a space betwixt the time of death and the time of the resurrection.

7 And now I would inquire what becometh of the souls of men from this time of death to the time appointed for the resurrection?

In this passage, Alma asks the question of the ages. What happens to us when we die? Where do we go? It's obvious that the body goes into the grave and decays into nothingness—but what becomes of the soul, the spirit?

Thankfully, our latter-day prophets have given us much light and knowledge on this subject. Through their inspired teachings, they have removed much of the mystery and fear from death.

When we die, the spirit goes into a spiritual world. "The earth itself and the living things on the earth have spirit counterparts that existed before the physical creation, and a living soul consists of a spirit body united with a physical body. This spirit existence, where living things are composed of organized, refined spirit matter, extends beyond the human family and includes animals and plants. Little is revealed about plant spirits beyond the fact that all living things, including plants, were created as spirits before they were created with physical bodies (Moses 3:5, 9). However, latter-day revelation indicates that human and animal spirits are living, active, intelligent beings and that spirits do not need physical bodies for existence. Since spirits exist before mortality as well as afterward, there is both a premortal and a postmortal spirit world.

"The premortal spirit existence, for mankind at least, was 'in heaven,' in the kingdom where God lives. Explaining this phase of the Creation, the Lord said, 'I, the Lord God, created all things . . . spiritually, before they were naturally upon the face of the earth, . . . for in heaven created I them' (Moses 3:5)."[26]

Our entry into the spirit world through death is much like our entry into the mortal world through birth. In both cases, our spirit leaves a familiar environment and goes to one that is new and unfamiliar. We leave loved ones behind. But other loved ones await us, people who knew us before and who are anxious to greet us, to love us and to bless us. When we are born, we take a mortal body. When we die, we leave that body behind.[27]

When we die, we are subjected to what President Joseph F. Smith

called a "partial judgment" of our works on the earth. This judgment
determines whether we will be sent to paradise or to spirit prison, the
two divisions of the spirit world. He wrote,

"The spirits of all men, as soon as they depart from this mortal
body, whether they are good or evil, we are told in the Book of
Mormon, are taken home to that God who gave them life, where *there*
is a separation, a partial judgment, and the spirits of those who are
righteous are received into a state of happiness which is called paradise. . . . The wicked, on the contrary, have no part nor portion in the
Spirit of the Lord, and they are cast into [spirit prison], being led captive, because of their own iniquity, by the evil one."[28] For further information on paradise and spirit prison, see the discussions below. See
the discussion beginning on the next page for additional prophetic
insights into the spirit world.

NOTES AND COMMENTARY

Alma 40:6 *a space betwixt the time of death and the time of the*
resurrection. Death started at the time of the Fall and will continue as
we know it until the Millennium. In the Millennium, as discussed elsewhere in this book, people will be changed from mortal life to a
resurrected state "in the twinkling of an eye" (D&C 43:32). But during
the nonmillennial years of the earth's temporal existence, there is a
space of time between death and the resurrection. During that space,
the spirits of all those who die go to the spirit world.

Alma 40:7 *the time appointed for the resurrection.* The Lord has
revealed three specific times of resurrection for the people of the
earth: (1) When Jesus Christ was resurrected as the first fruits, many
of the righteous dead were also resurrected. Other righteous souls
since that time have also been resurrected, including such men as
Peter, James, and Moroni. (2) When Christ comes again, the righteous
dead will be resurrected to meet him; the remaining righteous will
continue to be resurrected (changed in the twinkling of an eye)
throughout the Millennium. (3) After the Millennium, the unrighteous
and unrepentant dead will finally be resurrected. For more details on
the times appointed for the resurrection, see chapter 8, Times and
Order of the Resurrection.

Here are some additional truths from our leaders about the spirit world.

THE SPIRIT WORLD IS HERE ON EARTH

"Where is the spirit world?" asked Elder Harold B. Lee. "Is it away up in the heavens? That isn't what the scriptures and our brethren explain. They have told us the spirit world is right here round about us, and the only spirits who can live here are those who are assigned to fill their missions here on earth. This is the spirit world. And if our eyes could be opened we could see those who have departed from us—a father, mother, brother, a sister, a child."[29]

THE SPIRIT WORLD IS A PLACE OF CONTINUING PROBATION

This earth life is a time of probation. As Lehi taught, after Adam and Eve were cast out of the Garden of Eden, "the days of the children of men were prolonged, according to the will of God, that they might repent while in the flesh; wherefore, their state became a state of probation, and their time was lengthened, according to the commandments which the Lord God gave unto the children of men" (2 Nephi 2:21). During our time on earth, we are tested to see if we will "do all things whatsoever the Lord [our] God shall command" us (Abraham 3:25). We are given our agency and the light of Christ to guide us, and the Lord desires to see whether we will "choose liberty and eternal life, through the great Mediator of all men, or to choose captivity and death, according to the captivity and power of the devil" (2 Nephi 2:27). Those who pass the test here—meaning those who fully accept the gospel of Jesus Christ, receive all the ordinances, and walk in true faith and reliance on Christ—will go into the spirit world with their exaltation assured.

But those who fail in any of those particulars will continue in a probationary state in the spirit world. As Parley P. Pratt taught, "The spirit world is . . . an intermediate state, a probation, a place of preparation, improvement, instruction, or education, where spirits are chastened and improved, and where, if found worthy, they may be taught a knowledge of the Gospel."[30]

Elder George Q. Cannon added, "We will have to work there to grow and to make progress just as we have here. . . . But we shall find that knowledge and power will not come to us there as the rain that falls upon us, without any effort of ours to acquire them. We shall have to exercise ourselves and exert our powers there just as we have to here. We shall be rewarded according to our diligence and faithfulness in the exercise of our agency."[31]

Victor L. Ludlow has written similarly: "The postmortal spirit world is a natural continuation of earth life. It comprises the other vital portion of our second estate. The second estate began with our birth as our spirit and physical body were joined together, and it continues until they are reunited again in a resurrected state. . . . Both phases of the second estate are probationary periods where we learn, develop, and test our spiritual commitments. Our priorities must be developed and refined before we can exit from the postmortal spirit world."[32]

Elder Neal A. Maxwell has made it clear that we continue to walk by faith in the postmortal spirit world. "We do not now know precisely how God handles things in the spirit world so that life there is an extension of walking by faith," he wrote. "Death does not suddenly bestow upon the disbeliever full awareness of all reality, thereby obviating the need for any faith. Instead, what follows death is a continuum of the basic structure in mortality—until the Judgment Day, when every knee shall bow and every tongue confess that Jesus is the Christ (see Romans 14:11; Philippians 2:10; D&C 76:110). Until then, we 'walk by faith, not by sight' (2 Corinthians 5:7).

"How will God ensure this condition in the spirit world? We do not know. Yet He has certainly so handled the second estate in relation to the first estate, hasn't He? The memories of the first estate are not accessible in the second estate. The spirit world will be so arranged that there will be no legitimate complaints later over the justice and mercy of God (see Mosiah 27:31; Alma 12:15)."[33]

IN THE SPIRIT WORLD, WE CONTINUE IN
BONDAGE TO THE CRAVINGS OF THE FLESH

"When we go out of this life, leave this body," wrote Elder Melvin J. Ballard, "we will desire to do many things that we cannot do at all without the body. We will be seriously handicapped, and we will long for the body; we will pray for that early reunion with our bodies. . . . Then, every man and woman who is putting off until the next life the task of correcting and overcoming the weakness of the flesh are sentencing themselves to years of bondage, for no man or woman will come forth in the resurrection until they have completed their work, until they have overcome, until they have done as much as they can do."[34]

CHILDREN WHO DIE HAVE ADULT SPIRITS IN THE SPIRIT WORLD

The Church teaches that we are all spirit children of our Father in Heaven, and that we were reared in the premortal world until our spirits had reached maturity. Then, in due time, those adult spirits were given the opportunity to gain bodies on earth, which they did by entering their assigned infant bodies. When that body dies, whether as an infant, a child, a teenager, or a mature adult, the spirit will again appear in its natural form, as an adult. Thus, all those who dwell in the postmortal spirit world are adult spirits.

Elder Melvin J. Ballard wrote of a manifestation he received that supports this teaching. He said, "I lost a son six years of age and I saw him a man in the spirit world after his death, and I saw how he had exercised his own freedom of choice and would obtain of his own will and volition a companionship, and in due time to him and all those who are worthy of it, shall come all of the blessings and sealing privileges of the House of the Lord."[35]

Sometimes, however, the Lord may allow the spirit of one who is dead to appear to loved ones in the form in which they would recognize them. Thus, one who died as a child may appear in a child's form to those who loved him or her in mortality.[36]

THERE ARE MANY VARIETIES AND GRADES OF SPIRITS IN THE SPIRIT WORLD

Some people suppose that there are only two kinds of spirits in the spirit world—the righteous in paradise and the wicked in the spirit prison. It is true that there is a basic division between the righteous and the wicked in the spirit world. But there are also as many kinds and grades of spirits there as we have here on earth. George Q. Cannon taught, "There will be just as much distinction between spirits there as you find between spirits here. Those who have made good use of their opportunities here will have the benefit of their diligence and faithfulness there. Those who have been careless and indifferent and have not acquired knowledge and power through the exercise of faith will find themselves lacking there."[37] And Elder Alvin R. Dyer added, "The spirit world will contain the same cross-section of diversity of race and creed that exist upon the earth. The spirit will awaken there with the same religious concept, or the lack of it. There will be Catholics and Protestants of every sect, Jews, Mohammedans, Hindus, Buddhists and others as well as the infidels. All must be taught; must come to a knowledge of the plan of salvation and of the mission of Jesus Christ."[38]

Joseph Smith emphasized that the spirit paradise and spirit prison are both part of the same world: "I will say something about the spirits in prison. There has been much said by modern divines about the words of Jesus (when on the cross) to the thief, saying, 'This day shalt thou be with me in paradise.' King James' translators make it out to say paradise. But what is paradise? It is a modern word: it does not answer at all to the original word that Jesus made use of. . . . There is nothing in the original word in Greek from which this was taken that signifies paradise; but it was—This day thou shalt be with me in the world of spirits: then I will teach you all about it and answer your inquiries. . . .

" . . . There has been much said about the word hell, and the sectarian world have preached much about it, describing it to be a burning lake of fire and brimstone. But what is hell? It is another modern term, and is taken from hades. . . .

"Hades, the Greek, or Sheol, the Hebrew: these two significations mean a world of spirits. Hades, Sheol, paradise, spirits in prison, are all one: it is a world of spirits.

"The righteous and the wicked all go to the same world of spirits until the resurrection."[39]

LIFE IN THE SPIRIT WORLD IS MUCH LIKE LIFE HERE ON EARTH

As mentioned above, the spirit world is an extension of our second estate. In that world, "Life there is the spiritual equivalent of life here. The spirit world, itself, is but the spiritual equivalent of earth."[40] The people there "converse together the same as we do on the earth."[41] Elder Bruce R. McConkie explained, "Life and work and activity all continue in the spirit world. Men have the same talents and intelligence there which they had in this life. They possess the same attitudes, inclinations, and feelings there which they had in this life."[42]

Because life in the spirit world may be said to mirror life here, the wicked there continue to fight against the truth just as they did here. "The wicked spirits that leave here and go into the spirit world, are they wicked there? Yes," said Brigham Young. " . . . They are in the spirit world, and are just as busy as they possibly can be to do everything they can against the prophet and the apostles, against Jesus and his kingdom. They are just as wicked and malicious in their actions against the cause of truth as they were while on the earth."[43]

While the wicked continue their works of wickedness in the spirit world, the righteous continue their works of righteousness. Wilford Woodruff taught, "All men who go into the spirit world, and who bear the Holy Priesthood, will continue their labors. Their work will follow them. Their work will not cease when they lay their tabernacles down here in the tomb."[44]

In his testimony of a remarkable experience he had, President Wilford Woodruff explained that righteous spirits may be even busier in the spirit world than they were here on earth:

"Joseph Smith continued visiting myself and others up to a certain time and then stopped. The last time I saw him was in heaven. In the night vision I saw him at the door of the Temple in heaven. He came and spoke to me. He said he could not stop to talk to me because he was in a hurry. The next man I met was Father Smith; he couldn't talk to me because he was in a hurry. I met a half a dozen brethren who held high positions on earth, and none of them could stop to talk with me because they were in a hurry. I was much astonished.

"By and by I saw the Prophet again, and I got the privilege to ask him a question. 'Now,' said I, 'I want to know why you are in a hurry? I have been in a hurry all my life, but I expected my hurry would be over when I got into the Kingdom of Heaven, if I ever did.'

"Joseph said, 'I will tell you, Brother Woodruff, every dispensation that has had the priesthood on earth and has gone into the celestial kingdom, has had a certain amount of work to do to prepare to go to the earth with the Savior when he goes to reign on earth. Each dispensation has had ample time to do this work. We have not. We are the last dispensation, and so much work has to be done and we need to be in a hurry in order to accomplish it.'

"Of course, that was satisfactory with me, but it was new doctrine to me."[45]

The righteous in the spirit world function under the direction of the priesthood, just as they do here. Priesthood authority oversees the labors of the righteous there and blesses those who will heed the Lord's messengers, and priesthood power protects the righteous from the evil spirits who dwell there.[46]

Relationships in the Spirit World

What are relationships like in the spirit world? The prophets have taught that we shall know each other there just as we do here. "I have a father, brothers, children, and friends who have gone to a world of spirits," Joseph Smith said. "They are only absent for a moment. They are in the spirit, and we shall soon meet again. . . . When we depart, we shall hail our mothers, fathers, friends, and all whom we love, who have fallen asleep in Jesus."[47]

"Spirits are just as familiar with spirits as bodies are with bodies," Brigham Young taught. "They walk, converse, and have their meetings."[48] "We have more friends behind the veil than on this side," President Young taught on another occasion, "and they will hail us more joyfully than you were ever welcomed by your parents and friends in this world; and you will rejoice more when you meet them than you ever rejoiced to see a friend in this life."[49]

For commentary on how relationships in the spirit world are largely determined by righteous or unrighteous choices on earth (or subsequent acceptance or rejection of the gospel in the spirit world), see this chapter's discussions on paradise and the spirit prison.

The Second Coming and the Spirit World

Since Christ is the God of the dead as well as the living, those in the spirit world have as great an interest in his second coming as do those on the earth. When Christ comes again, conditions in the spirit world will greatly change, for the righteous will be lifted up in the resurrection and only the wicked will remain. Latter-day revelation explains this doctrine: "The saints that are upon the earth, who are alive, shall be quickened and be caught up to meet him.

"And they who have slept in their graves shall come forth, for their graves shall be opened; and they also shall be caught up to meet him in the midst of the pillar of heaven—they are Christ's, the first fruits, they who shall descend with him first, and they who are on the earth and in their graves, who are first caught up to meet him; and all this by the voice of the sounding of the trump of the angel of God.

"And after this another angel shall sound, which is the second trump; and then cometh the redemption of those who are Christ's at his coming; who have received their part in that prison which is prepared for them, that they might receive the gospel, and be judged according to men in the flesh.

"And again, another trump shall sound, which is the third trump; and then come the spirits of men who are to be judged, and are found under condemnation; and these are the rest of the dead; and they live not again until the thousand years are ended, neither again, until the end of the earth" (D&C 88:96–101).

At the second coming of Christ, then, all the righteous, living and dead, will be lifted up to meet him as he descends from the heavens. At that time the righteous dead will be resurrected. Paul made it plain that the righteous dead would be lifted up first: "This we say unto you by the word of the Lord, that they who are alive at the coming of the Lord, shall not prevent [precede] them who . . . are asleep. For the Lord himself shall descend from heaven with a shout, with the voice of the archangel, and with the trump of God: and the dead in Christ shall rise first; then they who are alive, shall be caught up together into the clouds with them who remain, to meet the Lord in the air; and so shall we ever be with the Lord" (JST 1 Thessalonians 4:15–17). Then those who received the gospel in the spirit world will be lifted up, also in resurrected form. Finally, it appears that the spirits of the wicked will temporarily come forth to see the Lord's return, but they will remain in the spirit until after the Millennium is over (D&C 88:96–101).

Those who die during the Millennium will not go into the spirit world but will be changed to a resurrected state in the twinkling of an eye. Of course, missionary work must continue in the spirit world during the Millennium—and will likely move forward at an increased pace as temple work in the mortal world is hastened during that same period. Perhaps the missionaries at that time will not be spirits but resurrected beings. As Joseph Smith said of the spirit world, "Flesh and blood cannot go there; but flesh and bones, quickened by the Spirit of God, can."[50]

THE GULF BETWEEN RIGHTEOUS AND WICKED

Luke 16:19–31

19 There was a certain rich man, which was clothed in purple and fine linen, and fared sumptuously every day:

20 And there was a certain beggar named Lazarus, which was laid at his gate, full of sores,

21 And desiring to be fed with the crumbs which fell from the rich man's table: moreover the dogs came and licked his sores.

22 And it came to pass, that the beggar died, and was carried by the angels into Abraham's bosom: the rich man also died, and was buried;

23 And in hell he lift up his eyes, being in torments, and seeth Abraham afar off, and Lazarus in his bosom.

24 And he cried and said, Father Abraham, have mercy on me, and send Lazarus, that he may dip the tip of his finger in water, and cool my tongue; for I am tormented in this flame.

25 But Abraham said, Son, remember that thou in thy lifetime receivedst thy good things, and likewise Lazarus evil things: but now he is comforted, and thou art tormented.

26 And beside all this, between us and you there is a great gulf fixed: so that they which would pass from hence to you cannot; neither can they pass to us, that would come from thence.

27 Then he said, I pray thee therefore, father, that thou wouldest send him to my father's house:

28 For I have five brethren; that he may testify unto them, lest they also come into this place of torment.

29 Abraham saith unto him, They have Moses and the prophets; let them hear them.

30 And he said, Nay, father Abraham: but if one went unto them from the dead, they will repent.

31 And he said unto him, If they hear not Moses and the prophets, neither will they be persuaded, though one rose from the dead.

This parable, which was told by Jesus during his mortal ministry, illustrates the fact that we should help the poor according to our means. But it also contains an important point of doctrine: there was "a great gulf fixed" between the righteous and the wicked in the spirit world (see 2 Nephi 9:12–13). The wicked could not go where the righteous were and the righteous could not go where the wicked were, even though they both dwelled in the same world.

Latter-day prophets have made it clear that this gulf was bridged by Christ when he visited the spirit world. "Christ came and through his death bridged that gulf, proclaimed liberty to the captives, and the opening of this prison door to those who sat in darkness and captivity," wrote Joseph Fielding Smith. "From that time forth this gulf is bridged so that the captives, after they have paid the full penalty of their misdeeds, satisfied justice, and have accepted the gospel of Christ, having the ordinances attended to in their behalf by their living relatives or friends, receive the passport that entitles them to cross the gulf."[51]

NOTES AND COMMENTARY

Luke 16:22 *Abraham's bosom.* This is symbolic language for paradise, where Abraham dwelled between his death and his resurrection.

Luke 16:24 *water.* In the parable, this refers to water that would quench the rich man's thirst. But symbolically it may have reference to the living waters of the gospel, which were not available to those in the spirit prison until Jesus opened the door for that blessing during his brief ministry in the spirit world.

I am tormented in this flame. These are the flames of hell, which will torment all those who choose wickedness in any form while they are here on earth. These are not literal flames, however. See the discusson on "The State Called Hell," below.

Luke 16:26 *between us and you there is a great gulf fixed.* The gulf represented some kind of barrier that prevented those who wanted to go back and forth between paradise and the spirit prison from doing so. Jesus' visit to the spirit world made it possible for those in paradise to visit those in prison to teach them the gospel, and it enabled the repentant in the spirit prison, who received the gospel ordinances, to leave the prison.

Luke 16:31 *neither will they be persuaded, though one rose from the dead.* People are converted through the testimony of the Holy Ghost, not by visits from spirits from the spirit world.

THE STATE CALLED PARADISE

Alma 40:11–12

> 11 Now, concerning the state of the soul between death and the resurrection . . .
>
> 12 the spirits of those who are righteous are received into a state of happiness, which is called paradise, a state of rest, a state of peace, where they shall rest from all their troubles and from all care, and sorrow.

Paradise seems to have several meanings in scripture. The tenth Article of Faith says that "the earth will be renewed and receive its paradisiacal glory," meaning that the earth will return to the state it enjoyed when Adam and Eve were in the Garden of Eden. Eden, then, was a form of paradise, and it would fit well with the description of the spirit world paradise given above.

The word *paradise* comes from the Persian by way of the Greek, meaning a park or a garden.[52] The original word may have had symbolic rather than literal meaning; thus, paradise in the spirit world may not be a literal park or garden as the Garden of Eden was, but instead it may be a particularly pleasing place, a place of rest and enjoyment as a quiet earthly park or garden can be. The park that is paradise stands in impressive contrast to the prison that is the portion of the spirit world called hell.

Some uses of *paradise* in the New Testament (the word does not appear in the Old Testament) seem to refer to the celestial kingdom. For example, Paul spoke of a man (likely Paul himself) who was "caught up into paradise, and heard unspeakable words, which it is not lawful for a man to utter." This same man was "caught up to the third heaven," which may have been the same experience, taking him to the same place (2 Corinthians 12:2, 4). John wrote in his Revelation, "He that hath an ear, let him hear what the Spirit saith unto the churches; To him that overcometh will I give to eat of the tree of life, which is in the midst of the paradise of God" (Revelation 2:7). The tree of life, of course, is a symbol for Christ and eternal life, both of which are found in the celestial world.

Usually, however, *paradise* refers to the blessed state where the righteous live and perform their labors for God's kingdom in the period between death and the resurrection. They will "rest from all their labors" of the mortal world (D&C 59:2), but they will remain anxiously engaged in the work of the Lord. Joseph Smith said of this work, "The spirits of the just are exalted to a greater and more glorious work; hence they are blessed in their departure to the world of spirits. Enveloped in flaming fire, they are not far from us, and know and understand our thoughts, feelings, and motions, and are often pained therewith."[53] Paradise is the abode of faithful saints who endured to the end and of innocent children who died before the age of eight, as well as all those who were innocent and not accountable in mortality because of mental deficiency.

In the last days of his life, a very ill Jedediah M. Grant, then a member of the First Presidency, visited the spirit world (particularly paradise) "two nights in succession." He recovered briefly, long enough to tell his fellow counselor Heber C. Kimball about his experience, and then passed away. Here is a record of Elder Grant's experience, as related at his funeral by Elder Kimball:

"He said to me, 'Brother Heber, I have been into the spirit world two nights in succession, and, of all the dreads that ever came across me, the worst was to have to again return to my body, though I had to do it. But O,' says he, 'the order and government that were there! When in the spirit world, I saw the order of righteous men and women; beheld them organized in their several grades, and there appeared to be no obstruction to my vision; I could see every man and woman in their grade and order. I looked to see whether there was any disorder there, but there was none; neither could I see any death nor any darkness, disorder or confusion.' He said that the people he there saw were organized in family capacities; and when he looked at them he saw grade after grade and all were organized and in perfect harmony. . . .

"He saw the righteous gathered together in the spirit world, and there were no wicked spirits among them. He saw his wife; she was the first person that came to him. He saw many that he knew, but did not have conversation with any except his wife, Caroline. She came to him, and he said that she looked beautiful and had their little child, that died on the Plains, in her arms, and said, 'Mr. Grant, here is little Margaret; you know that the wolves ate her up, but it did not hurt her; here she is all right.'

"'To my astonishment,' he said, 'when I looked at families there was a deficiency in some, there was a lack, for I saw families that would not be permitted to come and dwell together, because they had not honored their calling here.'

"He asked his wife, Caroline, where Joseph and Hyrum and Father Smith and others were; she replied, 'they have gone away ahead, to perform and transact business for us.' The same as when Brother Brigham and his brethren left Winter Quarters and came here to search out a home; they came to find a location for their brethren.

"He also spoke of the buildings he saw there, remarking that the Lord gave Solomon wisdom and poured gold and silver into his hands that he might display his skill and ability, and said that the temple erected by Solomon was much inferior to the most ordinary buildings he saw in the spirit world.

"In regard to gardens, says Brother Grant, 'I have seen good gardens on this earth, but I never saw any to compare with those that were there. I saw flowers of numerous kinds, and some with from fifty to a hundred different colored flowers growing upon one stalk.' We have many kinds of flowers on the earth, and I suppose those very articles came from heaven, or they would not be here.

"After mentioning the things that he had seen, he spoke of how much he disliked to return and resume his body, after having seen the beauty and glory of the spirit world, where the righteous spirits are gathered together."[54]

President Joseph F. Smith, who also had much understanding of the spirit world, gave us this insight into those who die having qualified for exaltation (or who so qualify after death): "The disembodied spirit during the interval of the death of the body and its resurrection from the grave is not perfect, hence it is not prepared to enter into the exaltation of the celestial kingdom; but it has the privilege of soaring in the midst of immortal beings, and of enjoying, to a certain extent, the presence of God, not the fulness of his glory, not the fulness of the reward which we are seeking and which we are destined to receive, if found faithful to the law of the celestial kingdom, but only in part."[55]

In some ways these promises are similar to those given to the faithful and spiritually advanced here in mortality. To an extent they are able to enjoy the presence of God, though not to a fulness, and they may also enjoy, according to God's will, the ministry of "immortal beings," or angels.

President Smith continued, speaking of those "who lived true and faithful to [their] covenants": "The righteous spirit that departs from this earth is assigned its place in the Paradise of God; it has its privileges and honors which are in point of excellency, far above and beyond human comprehension; and in this sphere of action, enjoying this partial reward for its righteous conduct on the earth, it continues its labors. . . . For while the body sleeps and decays, the spirit receives a new birth; to it the portals of life are opened. It is born again into the presence of God. . . . Returning there from the mission it has been performing in this state of probation, having been absent a few years from father, mother, kindred, friends, neighbors, and from all that was dear; it has returned nearer to the home-circle, to old associations and scenes, much in the same way as a man who comes home from a foreign mission, to join again his family and friends and enjoy the pleasures and comforts of home. . . . Instead of continuing here among the things of time, surrounded as we are with the weaknesses of a fallen world, and subject to earthly cares and sorrows, they are freed from them to enter a state of joy, glory and exaltation; not a fulness of any one of them but to await the morning of the resurrection of the just."[56]

Finally, we have this witness from Brigham Young: "The brightness and glory of the next apartment is inexpressible. . . . When we pass into the spirit world [meaning, into paradise] we shall possess a measure of [God's] power. Here, we are continually troubled with ills and ailments of various kinds. In the spirit world we are free from all this and enjoy life, glory, and intelligence; and we have the Father to speak to us, Jesus to speak to us, and angels to speak to us, and we shall enjoy the society of the just and the pure who are in the spirit world until the resurrection."[57]

NOTES AND COMMENTARY

Alma 40:12 *the spirits of those who are righteous.* Those who live in the part of the spirit world called paradise are the righteous: those who have received and honored sacred covenants, loved God and their fellow man, and lived up to their privileges as Saints of God.

a state of happiness, which is called paradise. In the spirit world, the righteous will dwell in peace; "they shall rest from all their troubles and from all care, and sorrow." They will live and mingle with others who were righteous in mortality and will no longer be troubled by the wicked. In such a place, knowing they have passed the mortal test and are assured of eternal life, no wonder they live in "a state of happiness."

SPIRIT PRISON

Alma 40:11, 13–14

11 Now, concerning the state of the soul between death and the resurrection . . .

13 . . . the spirits of the wicked, yea, who are evil—for behold, they have no part nor portion of the Spirit of the Lord; for behold, they chose evil works rather than good; therefore the spirit of the devil did enter into them, and take possession of their house—and these shall be cast out into outer darkness; there shall be weeping, and wailing, and gnashing of teeth, and this because of their own iniquity, being led captive by the will of the devil.

14 Now this is the state of the souls of the wicked, yea, in darkness, and a state of awful, fearful looking for the fiery indignation of the wrath of God upon them; thus they remain in this state, as well as the righteous in paradise, until the time of their resurrection.

In the first part of this passage, cited in the previous section, Alma spoke of the state of the righteous after death. Here he gives a picture of the state of the wicked. Of course, this explanation gives us the two extreme ends of the spectrum. Alma speaks of the wicked who were "led captive by the will of the devil," who shall be in "a state of awful, fearful looking for the fiery indignation of the wrath of God." Of course, many among God's children are not fully righteous and yet are not fully given over to the works of Satan. This great middle group, which would include many of the honorable people of the earth, will also be sent to the spirit prison at the time of their death. They will remain there in a degree of darkness that corresponds to the light and darkness they accepted and lived by in mortality.

This separation of the righteous and wicked at the time of death has been referred to as a "partial judgment." At the time of death, President Joseph F. Smith wrote, "there is a separation, a partial judgment, and the spirits of those who are righteous are received into a state of happiness which is called paradise. . . . The wicked, on the contrary, have no part nor portion in the Spirit of the Lord, and they are cast into outer darkness, being led captive, because of their own iniquity, by the evil one."[58]

Our spirit world has been the abode of the dead since the first people died on this earth. And there has been a form of separation between the righteous and wicked dead since the beginning. Before the time of Christ, this separation between paradise and spirit prison was a great gulf over which spirits could not cross. But once Jesus Christ visited the spirit world, that gulf was bridged and there could be communication and interaction between paradise and prison; righteous spirits could then take the gospel message to those in prison, and those who repented and accepted the fulness of the gospel, with all its requirements, could leave the prison and enter paradise.[59] Joseph Smith taught, "Every man that has been baptized and belongs to the kingdom has a right to be baptized for those who have gone before; and as soon as the law of the Gospel is obeyed here [the gospel ordinance] by their friends who act as proxy for them, the Lord has administrators there to set them free."[60]

Even though the spirit prison is a separate designation in the spirit world, in some ways the entire world is a prison. To an extent, even the righteous are in a prison, since they no longer have physical bodies, a limitation that they view as a form of bondage (see D&C 45:17; 138:50). "The whole spirit world, and not only that portion designated as hell, is considered to be a spirit prison. When Jesus came to them he declared 'liberty to the captives who had been faithful,' for they 'had looked upon the long absence of their spirits from their bodies as a bondage.'"[61] Perhaps it was in this sense that Jesus went to the spirits in prison when he went to the spirit world, as taught by Peter (see 1 Peter 3:18–20; 4:6; see also D&C 138:20–22, 29–32).

Brigham Young suggested that there is no physical separation of the righteous and the wicked in the spirit world. "If we go back to our mother country, the States, we find there the righteous, and we there find the wicked," he wrote. "If we go to California, we there find the righteous and the wicked; all dwelling together; and when we go beyond this veil, and leave our bodies which were taken from mother earth, and which must return, our spirits will pass beyond the veil; we go where both Saints and sinners go; they all go to one place."[62]

Even if the spirit prison and paradise share the same geography, there is still a separation between the righteous and the wicked. Here in mortality, people tend to find and associate with those who have similar values and beliefs. We may do business with those who have different life-styles and worldviews from our own, but as a rule those we spend time with when we have a choice are those who feel and believe and live as we do. So it will be in the spirit world. Righteous souls will mingle and live with those of a like spirit, and the same is true of the wicked.

"Can those persons who pursue a course of carelessness, neglect of duty and disobedience, when they depart from this life, expect that their spirits will associate with the spirits of the righteous in the spirit world?" Heber C. Kimball asked. Then he answered: "I do not expect

it, and when you depart from this state of existence, you will find it
out for yourselves."[63] It may be that this separation is not enforced by
God but instead is put in place by the natural desires and inclinations
of those who live in that world. Moroni wrote, "Ye would be more
miserable to dwell with a holy and just God, under a consciousness of
your filthiness before him, than ye would to dwell with the damned
souls in hell" (Mormon 9:4).

For further discussion on the spirit prison, see "The State Called
Hell," below.

NOTES AND COMMENTARY

Alma 40:13 *the spirits of the wicked.* The wicked of whom Alma
speaks here appear to be the worst of the worst. They are "evil, . . .
they have no part nor portion of the Spirit of the Lord; . . . they chose
evil works rather than good; . . . the spirit of the devil did enter into
them, and take possession of their house . . . [they were] led captive
by the will of the devil." Others also will be sent to the spirit prison,
including all those who reject the gospel on the earth, even though
they might otherwise be good people, or those who accept the gospel
but do not honor their covenants, or those who do not receive the
opportunity to hear the gospel while in mortality; all these will be in a
state of darkness until they receive the gospel light.

cast out into outer darkness. This does not appear to be the outer
darkness that is the final state of the sons of perdition, for this condition of outer darkness will end at "the time of their resurrection" (Alma
40:14). Thus, *outer darkness* here seems to be another name for the
darkness of the spirit prison (see D&C 38:5; Moses 7:57).

Alma 40:14 *this is the state of the souls of the wicked.* The state
of the souls of the wicked is one of fear and trouble, "looking for the
fiery indignation of the wrath of God upon them." Verse 21 adds that
the wicked will be "in misery." Joseph Smith defined the nature of that
misery: "The great misery of departed spirits in the world of spirits,
where they go after death, is to know that they have come short of the
glory that others enjoy and that they might have enjoyed themselves,
and they are their own accusers."[64]

Another source of misery for those in spirit prison is a lack of
hope. For those billions who have never heard of the gospel plan, the

conditions in spirit prison appear to be their final state. They no longer suffer the physical troubles of mortality—sickness, hunger, fatigue, and death—but spiritual and emotional travails continue and perhaps are heightened because the physical distractions are no longer there. This can be an exquisite form of hell indeed.[65]

THE STATE CALLED HELL

Doctrine and Covenants 76:84–85, 106

> 84 These are they who are thrust down to hell.
>
> 85 These are they who shall not be redeemed from the devil until the last resurrection, until the Lord, even Christ the Lamb, shall have finished his work. . . .
>
> 106 These are they who are cast down to hell and suffer the wrath of Almighty God, until the fulness of times, when Christ shall have subdued all enemies under his feet, and shall have perfected his work.

The word *hell* has at least two meanings. In one sense it refers to the final state of those called sons of perdition who will be cast into outer darkness with Satan and his angels. But hell also commonly refers to the spirit prison portion of the spirit world. When we read the scriptures, we must take care not to confuse one usage for the other. In this book we will use those references to hell that refer to the spirit prison.

In Joseph Smith's great vision of the three degrees of glory (D&C 76), he saw those who would inherit the least of the glories bestowed by God, the telestial. Such people are those who had been "thrust down to hell" (v. 84), meaning they were locked up in the spirit prison between their death and resurrection. Their time of resurrection would come after all others of God's children had been resurrected. While awaiting that resurrection, they would "suffer the wrath of God" (v. 104). The degree of wrath they suffer would vary depending on the degree of sinfulness they had yielded themselves to while in mortality.

Hell is a condition of spiritual death, one of the manifestations of the wrath of God. As we read in 2 Nephi, "O how great the goodness of our God, who prepareth a way for our escape from the grasp of this awful monster; yea, that monster, death and hell, which I call the death of the body, and also the death of the spirit. . . . And this death of which I have spoken, which is the spiritual death, shall deliver up its dead; which *spiritual death is hell;* wherefore, death and hell must deliver up their dead, and hell must deliver up its captive spirits, and the grave must deliver up its captive bodies, and the bodies and the spirits of men will be restored one to the other; and it is by the power of the resurrection of the Holy One of Israel" (2 Nephi 9:10, 12).

Spiritual death is a separation from the Spirit of the Lord. Such is the state of those in hell as long as they dwell there. Then, when they finally ascend from the torments of hell to receive the glory of the telestial world, their time of spiritual death is ended, for they receive the blessings "of the Holy Spirit through the ministration of the terrestrial" (D&C 76:86).

Those who suffer the torments of hell are those who choose wickedness in their mortal life and refuse to repent when the opportunity is offered. In contrast, those who sin in mortality but then repent with all their hearts will either escape the torments of hell entirely (if they repent in mortality) or will be redeemed from hell before "the fulness of times" (if they repent in the spirit world when they finally have an opportunity to receive the true gospel). As Alma said, "May the Lord grant unto you repentance, that ye may not bring down his wrath upon you, that ye may not be bound down by the chains of hell, that ye may not suffer the second death" (Alma 13:30). One's escape and redemption from hell, of course, are available through the atonement of Christ, a genuine change of heart leading to a spiritual rebirth, and a reception of all the laws and ordinances of the gospel.

Lehi's plea for his children is extended to all: "O that ye would awake; awake from a deep sleep, yea, even from the sleep of hell, and shake off the awful chains by which ye are bound, which are the chains which bind the children of men, that they are carried away captive down to the eternal gulf of misery and woe. . . . But behold, the Lord hath redeemed my soul from hell; I have beheld his glory, and I am encircled about eternally in the arms of his love" (2 Nephi 1:13, 15).

Hell is not designed for punishment only. One great purpose of hell (and the punishment there) is to help souls eventually come unto repentance and turn to Christ as their Redeemer. Heber C. Kimball said, "The spirits of . . . those who are not just, will be left where they will be scourged, tormented and afflicted, until they can bring their spirits unto subjection and be like clay in the hands of the potter, that the potter may have power to mould and fashion them into any kind of vessel, as he is directed by the Master Potter."[66] Thus hell is designed to be a learning experience, and people can escape their imprisonment in hell as quickly as they learn the things required of them—and apply those lessons, with all their hearts, to the improvement of their souls. There are some who are sunk so deeply in sin, however, that they will require an additional thousand years after all others are resurrected before they finally qualify for the blessings of grace and resurrection for themselves.

For discussion and commentary on the missionary effort to hell and the opportunities for repentance there, see "Missionary Work in the Spirit World" and "Repentance in the Spirit World" below.

NOTES AND COMMENTARY

D&C 76:84 *these are they*. This part of the great vision of the three degrees of glory is about those who eventually receive a telestial inheritance. They first are thrust down to hell, where they suffer, learn, and eventually qualify to emerge to a kingdom of glory. It appears from this statement that all who go to hell will, in time, be assigned to the telestial kingdom if they refuse to repent (although a few will continue in hell forever, as sons of perdition). Since the spirit prison also includes terrestrial souls (D&C 76:71–74), it may be that the spirt prison includes more than one level, the lower (or lowest) of which is hell. The scriptures refer in two places to the "lowest hell" (see Deuteronomy 32:22; Psalm 86:13). These may be references to the final state of Satan, his angels, and the sons of perdition, or they may refer to the gradations or levels of the spirit prison.

The scriptures teach plainly that the eternal world has three degrees of glory (D&C 76:70–71, 81), that the celestial world has three levels (D&C 131:1–4), and that the telestial glory has many levels (D&C 76:98). Hell likewise has many levels, and the spirit prison also appears to have such levels. Our Father's children are all different from one another, and it is only just that there be many levels of punishment and blessing in the world to come. "Salvation is graded ever upward until it culminates in the glorious condition of exaltation," taught Elder James E. Talmage. "So [also] damnation is graded; else what did the Lord mean as recorded in the twelfth chapter of Mark. . . . 'These shall receive greater damnation'? Well, if there be a greater damnation there are lesser degrees of damnation and the term is used in the sense of deprivation and forfeiture. That man enters into a degree of damnation who has forfeited his opportunities and therefore has rendered himself incapable of the advancement that would otherwise be possible."[67]

thrust down to hell. Who is thrust down to hell? Who goes into this state of bondage, there to remain until their redemption is won through the Atonement, through their repentance (which may require personal sufferings), and through their obedience to the laws and ordinances (including proxy ordinances) of the gospel? The scriptures tell in careful detail who it is that will be thrust down to hell, if they continue in their sin without repentance. (The following list is not exhaustive; items are listed in random order.)

- Those who are filled with pride (2 Nephi 26:10; 28:15).

- Those who "yield unto the devil and choose works of darkness rather than light" (2 Nephi 26:10).

- Those who follow "the will of the flesh and the evil which is therein" (2 Nephi 2:29).

- Those who "harden their hearts . . . until . . . they are taken captive by the devil" (Alma 12:11).

- Those who allow the devil to stir up their hearts "to anger against that which is good," and who lie to seek to destroy the Lord's work (2 Nephi 28:20; D&C 10:24–26).

- Those who succumb to the temptations of harlots (Proverbs 5:3–5; 7:10, 27; 9:13–18).

- Those who "preach false doctrines . . . and pervert the right way of the Lord" (2 Nephi 28:15).

- "All those who commit whoredoms" (2 Nephi 28:15).

- Those who allow the devil to "lull them away into carnal security" (2 Nephi 28:21).

- Those who believe there is no hell and no devil (2 Nephi 28:22).

- Those who commit adultery (3 Nephi 12:27–30).

- Those who deny "the mercies of Christ" and suppose "that little children need baptism" (Moroni 8:12–21).

- Those who receive not "the gospel, neither the testimony of Jesus, neither the prophets, neither the everlasting covenant" (D&C 76:101).

- Those who "are liars, and sorcerers, and adulterers, and whore-mongers, and whosoever loves and makes a lie" (D&C 76:103).

- Those who "take of the abundance which [the Lord has] made, and impart not [their] portion, according to the law of [the] gospel, unto the poor and the needy" (D&C 104:18).

- "All those that discomfort [the Lord's] people, and drive, and murder, and testify against them" (D&C 121:23).

- "Whosoever is angry with his brother without a cause" (Matthew 5:22).

- Those who condemn the Book of Mormon (Mormon 8:16–17).

- All those who have "gone astray, and have denied [the Lord], and have sought their own counsels in the dark; and in their own abominations have they devised murder, and have not kept the commandments" (Moses 6:28).

- Those who have "all the commandments of God, . . . and that transgresseth them, and that wasteth the days of [their] probation" (2 Nephi 9:27).

- Those who "think they are wise" because "they are learned" and therefore "hearken not unto the counsel of God, for they set it aside" (2 Nephi 9:28).

- The rich who "despise the poor, and . . . persecute the meek, and [whose] hearts are upon their treasures; wherefore, their treasure is their god" (2 Nephi 9:30).

- Those who refuse to hear the word of God (2 Nephi 9:31).

- Those who are liars (2 Nephi 9:34).

- "The murderer who deliberately killeth" (2 Nephi 9:35).

- "Those that worship idols" (2 Nephi 9:37).

- "All those who die in their sins" (2 Nephi 9:38).

- Those who yield "to the enticings of that cunning one" (2 Nephi 9:39).

- Those who are "carnally-minded" (2 Nephi 9:39).

Unfortunately, as additional souls are "thrust down to hell," "hell hath enlarged herself, and opened her mouth without measure." Those who die and go to hell are thoroughly diminished; "their glory, and their multitude, and their pomp, and he that rejoiceth, shall descend into it. And the mean man shall be brought down, and the mighty man shall be humbled, and the eyes of the lofty shall be humbled" (Isaiah 5:14–15).

D&C 76:85 *shall not be redeemed from the devil until the last resurrection.* Those souls who willingly give themselves over to Satan and his works shall suffer bondage to the devil (see Alma 12:11) until all the righteous have been resurrected. Then, at the end of this earth's temporal existence, hell will be emptied as all are resurrected. Jesus Christ holds the "keys of hell and of death" (Revelation 1:18). With those keys he exercises the power of redemption.

D&C 76:106 *suffer the wrath of Almighty God.* Hell is a place of torment. In his famous discourse, King Benjamin taught, "If [a] man repenteth not, and remaineth and dieth an enemy to God, the demands of divine justice do awaken his immortal soul to a lively sense of his own guilt, which doth cause him to shrink from the presence of the Lord, and doth fill his breast with guilt, and pain, and anguish, which is like an unquenchable fire, whose flame ascendeth up forever and ever" (Mosiah 2:38).

The scriptures give us several examples of what the torments of hell might be like. The first is from the book of Alma, where we read the story of Zeezrom. Through lies and deceit, Zeezrom caused Alma and Amulek to be imprisoned and, he supposed, slain. But in time "his soul began to be harrowed up under a consciousness of his own guilt; yea, he began to be encircled about by the pains of hell" (Alma 14:6). As his condition worsened, he grew sick "with a burning fever, which was caused by the great tribulations of his mind on account of his wickedness." His many sins "did harrow up his mind until it did become exceedingly sore, having no deliverance; therefore he began to be scorched with a burning heat" (Alma 15:3). Because of Zeezrom's godly sorrow, he was healed by priesthood power, released from the pains of hell he was suffering, and went forth to become a powerful disciple of God.

Later in that same book we read the story of Alma the younger, who sought "to destroy the church of God" (Alma 36:11). His actions resulted in the spiritual death of many people, a sin so great he called it murder (Alma 36:14). After an angel appeared and rebuked him, he later reported, "I was struck with such great fear and amazement lest perhaps I should be destroyed. . . . I was racked with eternal torment, for my soul was harrowed up to the greatest degree and racked with all my sins. Yea, I did remember all my sins and iniquities, for which I was tormented with the pains of hell; yea, I saw that I had rebelled against my God, and that I had not kept his holy commandments. . . . So great had been my iniquities, that the very thought of coming into the presence of my God did rack my soul with inexpressible horror. Oh, thought I, that I could be banished and become extinct both soul and body, that I might not be brought to stand in the presence of my God, to be judged of my deeds. And now, for three days and for three nights was I racked, even with the pains of a damned soul."

He described himself as being "in the gall of bitterness, and . . . encircled about by the everlasting chains of death," noting, "There could be nothing so exquisite and so bitter as were my pains."

While he was "thus racked with torment," Alma's father and other faithful Saints were fasting and praying for him. Their prayers were answered, and Alma the younger was able to cry out in his heart, in faith, to the Lord, pleading for mercy.

"And now, behold, when I thought this, I could remember my pains no more; yea, I was harrowed up by the memory of my sins no more. And oh, what joy, and what marvelous light I did behold; yea, my soul was filled with joy as exceeding as was my pain!" (Alma 36:11–20).

A third scriptural example of the torments of hell is found in Doctrine and Covenants 19. There the Lord speaks with great plainness to Martin Harris, commanding him to repent, "lest I smite you by the rod of my mouth, and by my wrath, and by my anger, and your sufferings be sore—how sore you know not, how exquisite you know not, yea, how hard to bear you know not. For behold, I, God, have suffered these things for all, that they might not suffer if they would repent; But if they would not repent they must suffer even as I; which suffering caused myself, even God, the greatest of all, to tremble because of pain, and to bleed at every pore, and to suffer both body and spirit—and would that I might not drink the bitter cup, and shrink—nevertheless, glory be to the Father, and I partook and finished my preparations unto the children of men.

"Wherefore, I command you again to repent, . . . lest you suffer these punishments of which I have spoken, of which in the smallest, yea, even in the least degree you have tasted at the time I withdrew my Spirit" (D&C 19:15–20).

Joseph Smith said, in speaking of the torments of hell known symbolically as "the lake that burns with fire and brimstone": "A man is his own tormenter and his own condemner. . . . The torment of disappointment in the mind of man is as exquisite as a lake burning with fire and brimstone. I say, so is the torment of man."[68]

until the fulness of times. This expression means that they will suffer just punishments from God, while they are still in the spirit state, until all the purposes of the earth have been fulfilled. When every soul assigned to our earth has been born, lived, and died (or been changed "in the twinkling of an eye" [D&C 43:32]); when every righteous soul has been resurrected; when every wicked soul has paid the price of rebellion and finally bowed the knee in submission to Christ; then the fulness of times (for this purpose) can be said to have come. Then the wicked who have continued in the spirit world can finally be granted the blessing of resurrection.

THE GATES OF HELL

Doctrine and Covenants 98:22

*22 And again I say unto you, if ye observe to do whatso-
ever I command you, I, the Lord, will turn away all wrath and
indignation from you, and the gates of hell shall not prevail
against you.*

The term "gates of hell" is confusing to many. We first find that
expression in the scriptures in the book of Matthew:

"When Jesus came into the coasts of Caesarea Philippi, he asked
his disciples, saying, Whom do men say that I the Son of man am?

"And they said, Some say that thou art John the Baptist: some,
Elias; and others, Jeremias, or one of the prophets.

"He saith unto them, But whom say ye that I am?

"And Simon Peter answered and said, Thou art the Christ, the Son
of the living God.

"And Jesus answered and said unto him, Blessed art thou, Simon
Bar-jona: for flesh and blood hath not revealed it unto thee, but my
Father which is in heaven. And I say also unto thee, That thou art
Peter, and upon this rock I will build my church; and the gates of hell
shall not prevail against it" (Matthew 16:13–18). Some have inter-
preted this to mean that Satan would not prevail against the early
church, that it would never fall into apostasy. But the brethren of the
early church were unanimous in their understanding that there would
indeed be an apostasy, that the church and priesthood and divine ordinances would all be taken from the earth until the "times of restitution
of all things" (Acts 3:21).[69]

If the expression *gates of hell* does not refer to the power of Satan,
what does the expression mean? Hugh Nibley gives one helpful
interpretation:

"To the Jews 'the gates of hell' meant something very specific. Both
Jews and Christians thought of the world of the dead as a prison—
carcer, phylake, phroura—in which the dead were detained but not necessarily made to suffer any other discomfort. In the Jewish tradition the
righteous dead are described as sitting impatiently in their place of
detention awaiting their final release and reunion with their resurrected

bodies and asking, 'How much longer must we stay here?' The Christians talked of 'the prison of death' to which baptism held the key of release. . . .

"It is the proper function of a gate to shut creatures in or out of a place; when a gate 'prevails,' it succeeds in this purpose; when it does not 'prevail,' someone succeeds in getting past it. But *prevail* is a rather free English rendering of the far more specific Greek *katischyo,* meaning to overpower in the sense of holding back, holding down, detaining, suppressing, etc. . . . Since all have fallen, all are confined in death which it is the Savior's mission to overcome; their release is to be accomplished through the work of the church. . . . In one of the very earliest Christian poems Christ is described as going to the under-world to preach to the dead, 'And the dead say to him, . . . "Open the gate to us!"' whereupon the Lord, 'heeding their faith,' gives them the seal of baptism. Baptism for the dead, then, was the key to the gates of hell. . . .

"'The gates of hell,' then, does not refer to the devil at all. . . . The gates of hell are the gates of hell—the 'holding back' of those who are in the spirit world from attaining the object of their desire."[70]

One way, then, in which the gates of hell do not prevail is through baptism. Those who are baptized and keep their covenants are not bound by hell but enter paradise. Baptism for the dead frees those who did not have opportunity to receive the gospel in mortality but who received it with all their hearts in the spirit world. In such cases, the gates of hell swing wide and the new convert escapes.

The scriptures give a variety of instances when the gates of hell shall not prevail, meaning that souls will not be bound in hell if they do what is required. We read that hell's gates will not prevail against—

- those who repent and are baptized (3 Nephi 11:38; D&C 33:11–13)

- those who join the Lord's true church and endure to the end (D&C 10:69)

- those who keep the commandments of God (D&C 17:8; 98:22)

- those who "give heed" to all the "words and commandments" of the president of the Church, "in all patience and faith" (D&C 21:4–5)

- those whose hearts are broken and whose spirits are contrite (2 Nephi 4:32)
- those who partake of the sacrament worthily (3 Nephi 18:1–13)
- those who help to build up the true Church "upon the foundation of my gospel and my rock" (D&C 18:5).

NOTES AND COMMENTARY

D&C 98:22 *turn away all wrath and indignation from you.* Those who are obedient to the Lord escape the wrath of his judgments. Should they suffer because of judgments that are poured out on the wicked, they nevertheless will be spared God's wrath; when they die, they will go to paradise and eventually a blessing of highest glory. The combination of this promise with the next one ("the gates of hell shall not prevail against you") suggests that if we are obedient, we will be protected from wrath in mortality and hell in the next sphere.

the gates of hell. The gates of hell are not literal but metaphorical, a figure of speech used to represent that which keeps a person in hell. Those gates essentially represent the failure to make and keep gospel covenants, particularly baptism. The "chains of hell" and "chains of darkness" are similar metaphors found in the scriptures, but their meaning is different. These expressions refer to the binding power of the devil, by which he drags souls down in sin and darkness. As we read in Alma, "They that will harden their hearts, to them is given the lesser portion of the word until they know nothing concerning his mysteries; and then they are taken captive by the devil, and led by his will down to destruction. Now this is what is meant by the chains of hell" (Alma 12:11; see also Alma 5:7–10; 13:30; 26:14).

MISSIONARY WORK IN THE SPIRIT WORLD

Doctrine and Covenants 138:29–30

29 . . . *the Lord went not in person among the wicked and the disobedient who had rejected the truth, to teach them;*
30 But behold, from among the righteous, he organized his

forces and appointed messengers, clothed with power and authority, and commissioned them to go forth and carry the light of the gospel to them that were in darkness, even to all the spirits of men; and thus was the gospel preached to the dead.

This is one of the great messages of hope in the gospel: after Christ's crucifixion, while his body lay in the tomb, his spirit went to the spirit world to proclaim the gospel to those who were held captive there. And who were the captives? All who dwelled in that world, for they had no power to leave the spirit world, having no power of resurrection. Death held them bound, and without Christ's victory over death, there was no escape.

When Jesus visited their world, he bore a message of eternal joy: he had conquered death and would soon be resurrected, and because he had won the battle with death and sin, all mankind would likewise be resurrected. He then organized a missionary force among the righteous to carry that same message to all who would listen, in all parts of their world. President Joseph F. Smith gave us this glorious account of Christ's visit to the spirit world:

"On the third of October, in the year nineteen hundred and eighteen, I sat in my room pondering over the scriptures. . . . I opened the Bible and read the third and fourth chapters of the first epistle of Peter, and as I read I was greatly impressed, more than I had ever been before, with the following passages: 'For Christ also hath once suffered for sins, the just for the unjust, that he might bring us to God, being put to death in the flesh, but quickened by the Spirit: By which also he went and preached unto the spirits in prison; Which sometime were disobedient, when once the long-suffering of God waited in the days of Noah, while the ark was a preparing, wherein few, that is, eight souls were saved by water.' (1 Peter 3:18–20.) 'For for this cause was the gospel preached also to them that are dead, that they might be judged according to men in the flesh, but live according to God in the spirit.' (1 Peter 4:6.)

"As I pondered over these things which are written, the eyes of my understanding were opened, and the Spirit of the Lord rested upon me, and I saw the hosts of the dead, both small and great.

CONDITIONS AND CIRCUMSTANCES OF THE DEAD   •   [105]

"And there were gathered together in one place an innumerable company of the spirits of the just, who had been faithful in the testimony of Jesus while they lived in mortality. . . . They were assembled awaiting the advent of the Son of God into the spirit world, to declare their redemption from the bands of death. . . . While this vast multitude waited and conversed, rejoicing in the hour of their deliverance from the chains of death, the Son of God appeared, declaring liberty to the captives who had been faithful; and there he preached to them the everlasting gospel, the doctrine of the resurrection and the redemption of mankind from the fall, and from individual sins on conditions of repentance.

"But unto the wicked he did not go, and among the ungodly and the unrepentant who had defiled themselves while in the flesh, his voice was not raised. . . .

"I marveled, for I understood that the Savior spent about three years in his ministry among the Jews and those of the house of Israel, endeavoring to teach them the everlasting gospel and call them unto repentance; and yet, notwithstanding his mighty works, and miracles, and proclamation of the truth, in great power and authority, there were but few who hearkened to his voice, and rejoiced in his presence, and received salvation at his hands. But his ministry among those who were dead was limited to the brief time intervening between the crucifixion and his resurrection; and I wondered at the words of Peter—wherein he said that the Son of God preached unto the spirits in prison, who sometime were disobedient, when once the long-suffering of God waited in the days of Noah—and how it was possible for him to preach to those spirits and perform the necessary labor among them in so short a time.

"And as I wondered, my eyes were opened, and my understanding quickened, and I perceived that the Lord went not in person among the wicked and the disobedient who had rejected the truth, to teach them; but behold, from among the righteous, he organized his forces and appointed messengers, clothed with power and authority, and commissioned them to go forth and carry the light of the gospel to them that were in darkness, even to all the spirits of men; and thus was the gospel preached to the dead. And the chosen messengers went forth to declare the acceptable day of the Lord and proclaim liberty to the captives who were bound, even unto all who would repent of their sins and receive the gospel.

"Thus was the gospel preached to those who had died in their sins, without a knowledge of the truth, or in transgression, having rejected the prophets. These were taught faith in God, repentance from sin, vicarious baptism for the remission of sins, the gift of the Holy Ghost by the laying on of hands, and all other principles of the gospel that were necessary for them to know in order to qualify themselves that they might be judged according to men in the flesh, but live according to God in the spirit. And so it was made known among the dead, both small and great, the unrighteous as well as the faithful, that redemption had been wrought through the sacrifice of the Son of God upon the cross.

"Thus was it made known that our Redeemer spent his time during his sojourn in the world of spirits, instructing and preparing the faithful spirits of the prophets who had testified of him in the flesh; that they might carry the message of redemption unto all the dead, unto whom he could not go personally, because of their rebellion and transgression, that they through the ministration of his servants might also hear his words. . . .

"I beheld that the faithful elders of this dispensation, when they depart from mortal life, continue their labors in the preaching of the gospel of repentance and redemption, through the sacrifice of the Only Begotten Son of God, among those who are in darkness and under the bondage of sin in the great world of the spirits of the dead. The dead who repent will be redeemed, through obedience to the ordinances of the house of God, and after they have paid the penalty of their transgressions, and are washed clean, shall receive a reward according to their works, for they are heirs of salvation" (D&C 138:1, 6–12, 16, 18–20, 25–37, 57–59).

NOTES AND COMMENTARY

D&C 138:29 *the Lord went not in person among the wicked.* This is consistent with the Lord's pattern in general (with the exception of his mortal ministry, when the glory of his spirit was veiled by his flesh). The scriptures teach that "no man hath seen God at any time, except them who believe" (JST 1 John 4:12). Further, we read that those who inherit the telestial kingdom will not enjoy the presence of either the Son or the Father but will receive blessings of the Holy Spirit (D&C 76:86). Just as it is on earth, and just as it shall be in eternity, so in the spirit world the wicked do not have the privilege of seeing Christ the Lord.

D&C 138:30 *from among the righteous, he organized his forces and appointed messengers.* This is the same pattern the Lord followed in his ministry among the Nephites. He appeared to the righteous who were gathered at the temple, taught them the basic principles of his gospel, and ordained and sent forth messengers to the other inhabitants of the land.

clothed with power and authority. This, of course, has reference to the priesthood. The metaphor of being clothed suggests that the power and authority are fully a part of who these messengers are— they are fully covered by it. In a conference talk some years earlier, President Joseph F. Smith used this same image to refer to the messengers of the Lord in mortality: "Following the raising of this ensign [the establishment of the Church], the Lord sent forth His elders clothed with the priesthood and with power and authority, among the nations of the earth, bearing witness unto all peoples of the restoration of His Church, and calling upon the children of men to repent and receive the gospel."[71]

carry the light of the gospel to them that were in darkness. This may be a fulfillment of the prophecy of Isaiah: "The people that walked in darkness have seen a great light: they that dwell in the land of the shadow of death, upon them hath the light shined" (Isaiah 9:2). Of course, there are likely other applications of this prophecy as well.

to all the spirits of men. See the discussion below.

The vision of Joseph F. Smith teaches the following additional lessons about missionary work in the spirit world:

ALL THE DEAD WILL HEAR THE GOSPEL

Jesus sent his "messengers" to "carry the light of the gospel to them that were in darkness, even to all the spirits of men." Later, the account of the vision reiterates that they were to "carry the message of redemption unto all the dead" (D&C 138:30, 37). Joseph Fielding Smith wrote, "The Lord has so arranged his plan of redemption that all who have died without this opportunity shall be given it in the spirit world. There the elders of the Church who have died are proclaiming the gospel to the dead. All those who did not have an opportunity here to receive it, who there repent and receive the gospel, shall be heirs of the celestial kingdom of God."[72]

The work to take the word of the gospel to the many billions who never heard it on earth is immense. "Compare those inhabitants on the earth who have heard the Gospel in our day, with the millions who have never heard it, or had the keys of salvation presented to them, and you will conclude at once as I do, that there is an almighty work to perform in the spirit world," wrote Brigham Young. " . . . Reflect upon the millions and millions and millions of people that have lived and died without hearing the Gospel on the earth, without the keys of the Kingdom. They were not prepared for celestial glory, and there was no power that could prepare them without the keys of this Priesthood."[73]

With so much work to do, the Lord's messengers are literally in a hurry. Wilford Woodruff had a fascinating experience that underscored this truth. In a vision, President Woodruff saw the spirit of Joseph Smith. But "he said he could not stop to talk with me because he was in a hurry. . . . I met half a dozen brethren who had held high positions on earth, and none of them could stop to talk with me because they were in a hurry." Later, Joseph Smith explained to him, "Every dispensation that has had the priesthood on the earth and has gone into the celestial kingdom has had a certain amount of work to do to prepare to go to the earth with the Savior when he goes to reign on the earth. Each dispensation has had ample time to do this work. We have not. We are the last dispensation, and so much work has to be done, and we need to be in a hurry in order to accomplish it."[74]

Brigham Young made a similar statement about the hurry of the work in the spirit world: "Father Smith and Carlos [Smith] and Brother Partridge, yes, and every other good Saint, are just as busy in the spirit world as you and I are here. They can see us, but we cannot see them unless our eyes were opened. What are they doing there? They are preaching, preaching all the time, and preparing the way for us to hasten our work in building temples here and elsewhere. . . . They are hurrying to get ready by the time we are ready, and we are all hurrying to get ready by the time our Elder Brother is ready."[75]

THE FAITHFUL IN MORTALITY CONTINUE AS MISSIONARIES IN THE SPIRIT WORLD

President Smith taught, "The faithful elders of this dispensation, when they depart from mortal life, continue their labors in the preaching of the gospel of repentance and redemption . . . among those who are in darkness and under the bondage of sin in the great world of the spirits of the dead" (D&C 138:57).

He added on another occasion, "This gospel [is] . . . being preached to the spirits in prison, to those who have passed away from this stage of action into the spirit world without the knowledge of the gospel. Joseph Smith is preaching the gospel to them, so is Hyrum Smith, so is Brigham Young, and so are all the faithful apostles who lived in this dispensation, under the administration of the Prophet Joseph. They are there, having carried with them from here the holy Priesthood which they received under the hands and by the authority of the Prophet Joseph Smith. With that authority, conferred upon them in the flesh, they are preaching the gospel to the spirits in prison, as Christ directed when his body lay in the tomb, and he went to proclaim liberty to the captives, and to open the prison doors to them that were bound. Not only are these engaged in that work, but hundreds and thousands of others. The elders who have died in the mission field have not finished their missions, but they are continuing them in the spirit world."[76]

This is consistent with the teaching of Joseph Smith: "All those [who] die in the faith go to the prison of spirits to preach to the dead in body, but they are alive in the spirit; and those spirits preach to the spirits that they may live according to God in the spirit, and men do minister for them in the flesh; and angels bear the glad tidings to the spirits, and they are made happy by these means."[77]

A corollary truth is that sometimes people are called from mortality for the express purpose of serving as missionaries in the spirit world. Elder Spencer W. Kimball once remarked at the funeral service of a young man that he had been called to the spirit world to preach the gospel to the countless thousands who had been killed in World War II. Elder Harold B. Lee gave a similar testimony and further said on a later occasion, "Who knows but that many of our choicest young men bearing the Holy Priesthood, whose lives have been taken in these terrible world conflicts, might not have been called to go to the spirit world while their bodies lie in the grave, as did the Savior's, to preach repentance to the millions of those who have died without a knowledge of the gospel."[78]

The missionary force in the spirit world is augmented not only by those who die; new converts there can also join the effort. Thus the work continues on without interruption, growing, spreading, and ever increasing in power.

THE SUCCESS ATTENDING MISSIONARY WORK IN THE SPIRIT WORLD

President Smith does not seem to address the issue of how successful the missionaries in the spirit world will be, although other prophets have done so. Interestingly, different authorities seem to take different positions on the issue. But on reflection, these differing views seem to be two sides of one coin, and thus one can readily be reconciled with the other.

Some of the early Brethren taught that most of the souls in the spirit world would accept the gospel. For instance, Lorenzo Snow taught, "I believe . . . that when the gospel is preached to the spirits in prison, the success attending that preaching will be far greater than that attending the preaching of our elders in this life. I believe there will be very few indeed of those spirits who will not gladly receive the gospel when it is carried to them. The circumstances there will be a thousand times more favorable."[79]

In a similar vein, President Wilford Woodruff, in an April 1894 conference address, quoted what is now part of Doctrine and Covenants 137: "All who have died without a knowledge of this gospel, who would have received it if they had been permitted to tarry, shall be heirs of the celestial kingdom of God; also all that shall die henceforth without a knowledge of it, who would have received it with all their hearts, shall be heirs of that kingdom; for I, the Lord, will judge all

men according to their works, according to the desire of their hearts"
(vv. 7–9).

Then President Woodruff added, "So it will be with your fathers.
There will be very few, if any, who will not accept the Gospel. Jesus,
while his body lay in the tomb, went and preached to the spirits in
prison, who were destroyed in the days of Noah. After so long an
imprisonment, in torment, they doubtless gladly embraced the Gospel,
and if so they will be saved in the kingdom of God. The fathers of this
people will embrace the Gospel. . . . I tell you when the prophets and
apostles go to preach to those who are shut up in prison, and who have
not received the Gospel, thousands of them will there embrace the
Gospel. They know more in that world than they do here."[80]

We should also note that President Woodruff was speaking
specifically of "the fathers" of those who became faithful Latter-day
Saints. The Lord uses and honors certain lineages to accomplish his
work and sends spirits to certain bloodlines to accomplish his purposes. Perhaps the fathers of the Saints will be more open to the
gospel message because their children received that message, or
because the children are praying and working for them, or because the
Lord has sent "believing spirits" to those lines.

Brigham Young seemed to take a different point of view in regard
to the openness of spirits to the gospel message. "Every departed spirit
is subject to the laws that govern the spirit world. There are wicked
men in the spirit world. Millions of them will have the privilege of
receiving the Gospel in the spirit, that they may be judged according
to men in the flesh, and no doubt but many will reject the Gospel
there."[81]

And Elder Neal A. Maxwell wrote, "The gospel, when preached in
the spirit world, will bring the same responses as here: 'some believed
the things which were spoken, and some believed not' (Acts 28:24)."[82]

Will people in the spirit world accept the gospel more readily than
they do here? The answer appears to be yes—and no. On the one
hand, those in the spirit world may seem to have some advantages.
They no longer need to work to provide food and shelter for themselves and others, and they have no need for sleep. Brigham Young
described these conditions of the spirit world: "I [will] have passed

from a state of sorrow, grief, mourning, woe, misery, pain, anguish and disappointment into a state of existence, where I can enjoy life to the fullest extent as far as that can be done without a body. My spirit is set free, I thirst no more, I want to sleep no more, I hunger no more, I tire no more, I run, I walk, I labor, I go, I come, I do this, I do that, whatever is required of me, nothing like pain or weariness, I am full of life, full of vigor, and I enjoy the presence of my heavenly Father, by the power of his Spirit."[83]

In such conditions, spirits have more time to study and learn. In addition, they have the long years where they are bound in the prison, and during those years, century upon century, they have continuing opportunity to think, to feel, and to seek understanding of truth. During those same seemingly endless years, they may be able to observe the joy and peace of those who have embraced the gospel. In those ways, as President Snow put it, "the circumstances there will be a thousand times more favorable."[84]

On the other hand, we do not change our natures just by going into the spirit world.[85] That seems to be the truth behind the teaching of Elder Maxwell that some will believe and others will not, just the same as we see here. People will have their agency to accept or reject the gospel, and as Brigham Young said, many will reject it. People will have their agency to use their increased time in the spirit world to learn and grow or to waste it in other pursuits—and many will certainly waste it.

Nor is it true that there is no opposition in the spirit world. As the Lord's missionaries go forth to serve among those in the spirit prison, others at the same time are preaching against the truth. Brigham Young said, "Those who have died without the Gospel are continually afflicted by those evil spirits, who say to them—'Do not go to hear that man Joseph Smith preach, or David Patten, or any of their associates, for they are deceivers.'"[86]

When it comes to opportunities to hear and accept the gospel, people on earth will not have an advantage over those in the spirit world—nor will the reverse be true. Somehow, in the justice of God, those on both sides of the veil will have a level playing field when the totality of their experiences and opportunities are compared.

Accepting the gospel, of course, does not equate with entering the celestial kingdom, even when the needed ordinances are made available. Doctrine and Covenants 76 tells us that those in the terrestrial world include those "who are the spirits of men kept in prison, whom the Son visited, and preached the gospel unto them, that they might be judged according to men in the flesh; who received not the testimony of Jesus in the flesh [after being given the opportunity], but afterwards received it" (vv. 73–74).

Thus, every soul in the celestial and terrestrial kingdoms will have accepted the gospel of Jesus Christ, either here on earth or in the spirit world.

Those who go to the telestial kingdom never do accept the fulness of the gospel—or if they accept it, they subsequently violate their covenants. "These are they who received not the gospel of Christ, neither the testimony of Jesus. . . . For these are they who are of Paul, and of Apollos, and of Cephas. These are they who say they are some of one and some of another—some of Christ and some of John, and some of Moses, and some of Elias, and some of Esaias, and some of Isaiah, and some of Enoch; but received not the gospel, neither the testimony of Jesus, neither the prophets, neither the everlasting covenant" (D&C 76:82, 99–101).

Even though those assigned to the telestial glory do not accept the gospel or testimony of Christ, eventually even they will acknowledge the Kingship of the Lord and will serve him:

"Behold, and lo, we saw the glory and the inhabitants of the telestial world, that they were as innumerable as the stars in the firmament of heaven, or as the sand upon the seashore; and heard the voice of the Lord saying: These all shall bow the knee, and every tongue shall confess to him who sits upon the throne forever and ever; for they shall be judged according to their works, and every man shall receive according to his own works, his own dominion, in the mansions which are prepared; and they shall be servants of the Most High; but where God and Christ dwell they cannot come, worlds without end" (D&C 76:109–12).

Are these telestial souls many or few? Joseph Smith's vision gives

us the answer: "They were as innumerable as the stars in the firmament of heaven, or as the sand upon the seashore."

On one occasion, Lorenzo Snow added, "Very, very few of those
who die without the Gospel will reject it on the other side of the
veil."[87] Perhaps Elder Snow was referring to the fact that very few of
the Father's children would become sons of perdition. All others will
"bow the knee" and "confess" with their tongue and "be servants of
the Most High."

A related question has to do with how much those in the spirit
world actually know. Elder Melvin J. Ballard taught, "When a man
and woman are dead, they will not know the truth any more than we
do. They will not be given a flood of light that will make them see
everything. You will see in the spirit world every phase of religion.
They will be free to do as they please, each following his will o' the
wisp. . . . Men in the spirit world will be tested in exactly the same
conditions as if here upon the earth. They will have to manifest the
same courage and the same faith. And there are thousands of them,
hundreds of thousands and millions of them in the spirit world who
long to receive this gospel and have been waiting hundreds of years
for their deliverance."[88]

Parley P. Pratt taught similarly when he said, "I will suppose, in
the spirit world, a grade of spirits of the lowest order, composed of
murderers, robbers, thieves, adulterers, drunkards, and persons ignorant, uncultivated, &c., who are in prison, or in hell, without hope,
without God, and unworthy as yet of Gospel instruction. Such spirits,
if they could communicate, would not tell you of the resurrection or
of any of the Gospel truths, for they know nothing about them. They
would not tell you about heaven, or Priesthood, for in all their mean-
derings in the world of spirits, they have never been privileged with
the ministry of a holy Priest. If they should tell all the truth they possess, they could not tell much.

"Take another class of spirits—pious, well-disposed men; for
instance, the honest [follower of religion] who, although honest, and
well disposed, had not, while in the flesh, the privilege of the
Priesthood and Gospel. They believed in Jesus Christ, but died in
ignorance of his ordinances, and had not clear conceptions of his

doctrine, and of the resurrection. They expected to go to that place called heaven, as soon as they were dead, and that their doom would then and there be fixed, without any further alteration or preparation. Suppose they should come back, with liberty to tell all they know? How much light could we get from them? They could only tell you about the nature of things in the world in which they live. . . .

"What, then, could you get from them? Why, common chit chat, in which there would be a mixture of truth, and of error and mistakes, in mingled confusion: all their communications would betray the same want of clear and logical conceptions, and sound sense and philosophy, as would characterize the same class of spirits in the flesh."[89]

These teachings seem to be supported by Joseph F. Smith's vision of the redemption of the dead. While in the spirit world, Jesus appointed and organized his messengers, and sent them forth to "carry the light of the gospel to them that were in darkness, even to all the spirits of men. . . . Thus was the gospel preached to those who had died in their sins, without a knowledge of the truth, or in transgression, having rejected the prophets. These were taught faith in God, repentance from sin, vicarious baptism for the remission of sins, the gift of the Holy Ghost by the laying on of hands, and all other principles of the gospel that were necessary for them to know in order to qualify themselves that they might be judged according to men in the flesh, but live according to God in the spirit. And so it was made known among the dead, both small and great, the unrighteous as well as the faithful, that redemption had been wrought through the sacrifice of the Son of God upon the cross" (D&C 138:30, 32–35).

The dead needed the truths of the gospel and they did not have them. They needed to be taught. Just like people here on earth, they were ignorant of essential, saving truths until the missionaries came.

In his epistle to the Romans, Paul taught an eternal truth by asking questions: "Whosoever shall call upon the name of the Lord shall be saved. How then shall they call on him in whom they have not believed? and how shall they believe in him of whom they have not heard? and how shall they hear without a preacher? And how shall they preach, except they be sent?" (Romans 10:13–15).

If the spirits in prison do not know the gospel truth until they receive the missionaries, what might Wilford Woodruff have had in mind when he said, "They know more in that world than they do here"?[90] Perhaps he was considering the long years during which those spirits suffered in prison, unable to move forward in progression and unable to understand why. Perhaps he had reference to their knowledge of suffering, or of their long experience with bondage and their overwhelming desire to be released. Or he may have been referring to their now-certain knowledge that there is life after death. They would also know more than we do about the nature of spirits and what life is like after death. Nevertheless, until they were taught, they would still lack knowledge of God's plan and of the ultimate destiny of souls.

Learning in any sphere is based on agency. Those who exercise agency to learn in the spirit world are able to do so more quickly there. As mentioned, it appears there are fewer distractions and obstacles to learning there. On the other hand, many avenues of learning are closed to those in the spirit world. Living in a sphere with no hunger, sickness, or death, no pain or disease, places some limitations on what one can learn through experience. Yet for the wicked, the suffering and torment of the spirit are very real. In the spirit world, spirits can advance quickly in learning that involves the Spirit, intellect, and suffering for sin and wrong choices, if they will.

One final note on the success of the missions in the spirit world and the subsequent growth of the church in that sphere. There are two ways we build the Church here on earth—through conversion (coupled with ordinances) and through the birth of children into member families. In the same way, there are two ways we build the Church in the spirit world—through conversion (coupled with proxy ordinances) and through the death (and "birth" into the spirit world) of people who are faithful members here.

REPENTANCE IN THE SPIRIT WORLD

President Joseph F. Smith's vision of the redemption of the dead emphasized the reality of repentance in the spirit world. He recorded, "The chosen messengers went forth to declare the acceptable day of the Lord and proclaim liberty to the captives who were bound, even unto all who would repent of their sins and receive the gospel. . . . These were taught faith in God, repentance from sin, vicarious baptism for the remission of sins, the gift of the Holy Ghost by the laying on of hands, and all other principles of the gospel that were necessary for them to know. . . .

"I beheld that the faithful elders of this dispensation, when they depart from mortal life, continue their labors in the preaching of the gospel of repentance and redemption. . . . The dead who repent will be redeemed, through obedience to the ordinances of the house of God, and after they have paid the penalty of their transgressions, and are washed clean, shall receive a reward according to their works, for they are heirs of salvation" (D&C 138:31, 33–34, 57, 58–59).

But in some ways repentance is more challenging in the spirit world. "Clearly it is difficult to repent in the spirit world of sins involving physical habits and actions. There one has spirit and mind but not the physical power to overcome a physical habit. He can desire to change his life, but how can he overcome the lusts of the flesh unless he has flesh to control and transform? How can he overcome the tobacco or the drink habit in the spirit world where there is no liquor nor tobacco and no flesh to crave it? Similarly with other sins involving lack of control over the body."[91]

Preaching to the spirits in prison can bring one of four outcomes.

1. The spirit can reject the message and continue in hell.

2. The spirit can accept the message and move into paradise. If that spirit had first received the opportunity to receive the testimony of Jesus on earth but rejected that opportunity, he or she will eventually inherit the terrestrial kingdom. (Thankfully, the Lord, with his divine combination of perfect knowledge, justice, and love will judge when and where we have had sufficient opportunity to hear and embrace the gospel message.)

3. If the spirit received the gospel in mortality but then failed to honor covenants, he or she may hear the preaching in the spirit world and repent. Such a spirit will eventually inherit the terrestrial kingdom.[92]

4. If the spirit who accepts the message never had an opportunity to do so in mortality, he or she may eventually inherit the celestial kingdom.

Those who receive the gospel message can thus receive great blessings. Repentance combined with ordinances opens the doors to the spirit prison and allows the spirit to move into the company of the righteous in paradise.

The Book of Mormon gives us two interesting accounts of the deliverance of souls from hell. Each of these experiences is about the deliverance of people who were still in mortality, but the descriptions are also remarkably effective in understanding the feelings of rejoicing that would accompany the deliverance of souls from the spirit prison. The first account contains the words of Alma, speaking to the people of Zarahemla and remembering with them the way in which the Lord had "delivered their [fathers'] souls from hell":

"Behold, he changed their hearts; yea, he *awakened them out of a deep sleep,* and they awoke unto God. Behold, they were *in the midst of darkness;* nevertheless, their souls were illuminated by the light of the everlasting word; yea, they were *encircled about by the bands of death,* and the *chains of hell,* and an *everlasting destruction did await them.*

"And now I ask of you, my brethren, . . . were the *bands of death* broken, and the *chains of hell* which encircled them about, were they loosed? I say unto you, Yea, they were loosed, and their souls did expand, and they did *sing redeeming love.* And I say unto you that they are saved.

"And now I ask of you on what conditions are they saved? Yea, what grounds had they to hope for salvation? What is the cause of their being loosed from the *bands of death,* yea, and also the *chains of hell?* Behold, I can tell you— . . . they humbled themselves and put their trust in the true and living God" (Alma 5:6–11, 13; emphasis added).

The second account, by Ammon, relates his feelings about his mission to the Lamanites, who also were redeemed from hell:

"Behold, how many thousands of our brethren has he loosed from the *pains of hell;* and they are brought to *sing redeeming love,* and this because of the power of his word which is in us, therefore have we not great reason to rejoice? Yea, we have reason to praise him forever, for he is the Most High God, and has loosed our brethren from the *chains of hell.* Yea, they were encircled about with *everlasting darkness and destruction;* but behold, he has brought them into his everlasting light, yea, into everlasting salvation; and they are encircled about with the matchless bounty of his love; yea, and we have been instruments in his hands of doing this great and marvelous work.

"Therefore, let us glory, yea, we will glory in the Lord; yea, *we will rejoice, for our joy is full;* yea, we will praise our God forever. Behold, who can glory too much in the Lord? Yea, who can say too much of his great power, and of his mercy, and of his long-suffering towards the children of men? Behold, I say unto you, I cannot say the smallest part which I feel" (Alma 26:13–16; emphasis added).

THE CONNECTION BETWEEN MISSIONARY WORK IN THE SPIRIT WORLD AND TEMPLES ON EARTH

President Joseph F. Smith learned in his vision that some of the dead who "are in darkness and under the bondage of sin" could still become "heirs of salvation." The requirements: that they repent, pay "the penalty of their transgressions," and receive "the ordinances of the house of God" (D&C 138:57–59). Since the ordinances of the temple are directly accessible only to those on earth, mortals must perform temple work by proxy for the dead. When the spirits of the dead embrace the gospel message as well as the saving ordinances, they can then be freed from the bonds that hold them in prison.

The building of temples for the blessing of the dead is as important as missionary work for the living. President Spencer W. Kimball noted, "Most members of the Church are aware of our intense interest in the missionary work in the church and the appeals we have made in many lands for the rededication to preaching the gospel and preparing missionaries to carry the good news of the restoration to the people everywhere. I feel the same sense of urgency about temple work for the dead as I do about missionary work for the living, since they are basically one and the same."[93]

Elder Neal A. Maxwell taught an important truth about the connection between the two worlds: "[The Lord] will hasten His work in its time. (See D&C 88:73.) When He hastens His work, He hastens it on both sides of the veil. This is why, of course, the holy temples are so crucial especially at this time in human history. The constituency in the spirit world, by the way, is many times larger, numerically, than here. Whenever we open new nations on this side of the veil, as is now happening, we have simultaneously opened the door to thousands beyond the veil. The temple provides the precious spiritual linkage."[94]

Not only do the repentant dead receive the gospel message, but they also know of the temple-building efforts of the Saints on earth: "Oh, what rejoicing there must now be in the world of spirits among our Father's faithful children as they see our modern temples being built," exclaimed Elder Marion G. Romney.[95] When we do work for the dead in the temples, the missionaries in the spirit world will say to their investigators, as Brigham Young put it, "Do you not see somebody at work for you? The Lord remembers you and has revealed to his servants on the earth, what to do for you."[96]

COMMUNICATION BETWEEN THE SPIRIT AND MORTAL WORLDS

Moroni 10:14

14 And again, to another, the beholding of angels and ministering spirits.

These blessings are among the gifts of the Spirit listed by Moroni. It is part of the Lord's plan that there be communication from the spirit and eternal worlds back to certain of his children in mortality. Parley P. Pratt described some of the reasons for such visits:

"Who . . . is prepared, among the spirits in the spirit world, to communicate the truth on the subject of salvation, to guide the people, to give advice, to confer consolation, to heal the sick, to administer joy, and gladness, and hope of immortality and eternal life, founded on manifest truth? . . . Peter, James, Joseph, Hyrum, Father Smith, any, or all of those ancient or modern Saints, who have departed this life, who are clothed upon with the powers of the eternal Apostleship, or Priesthood, who have gone to the world of spirits, not to sorrow, but as joyful messengers, bearing glad tidings of eternal truth to the spirits in prison—could not [they] teach us good things? Yes, if they were permitted so to do. . . .

" . . . what then do we wish, in communicating with the eternal

world, by visions, angels, or ministering spirits? Why, if a
sick they would like to be visited, comforted, or healed by an angel or
spirit! If a man is in prison, he would like an angel or spirit to visit
him, and comfort or deliver him. A man shipwrecked would like to be
instructed in the way of escape for himself and fellows from a watery
grave. In case of extreme hunger a loaf of bread brought by an angel
would not be unacceptable.

"If a man were journeying, and murderers were lying in wait for
him in a certain road, an angel would be useful to him in telling him of
the circumstance, and to take another road.

"If a man were journeying to preach the Gospel, an angel would
be useful to tell the neighbors of his high and holy calling, as in case
of Peter and Cornelius. Or would you not like to have angels all
around you, to guard, guide, and advise you in every emergency?"[97]

Such angelic and spirit visitations are often unseen, though they
are nonetheless real. President Woodruff said, "The living cannot see
the departed spirits, but the latter can see and administer to those in
the flesh, even though the latter know it not."[98]

And Elder Dallin H. Oaks has taught, "The ministering of angels
can also be unseen. Angelic messages can be delivered by a voice or
merely by thoughts or feelings communicated to the mind. President
John Taylor described 'the action of the angels, or messengers of God,
upon our minds, so that the heart can conceive . . . revelations from
the eternal world.'[99]

"Nephi described three manifestations of the ministering of angels
when he reminded his rebellious brothers that (1) they had 'seen an
angel,' (2) they had 'heard his voice from time to time,' and (3) also
that an angel had 'spoken unto [them] in a still small voice' though
they were 'past feeling' and 'could not feel his words' (1 Nephi
17:45). The scriptures contain many other statements that angels are
sent to teach the gospel and bring men to Christ (see Hebrews 1:14;
Alma 39:19; Moroni 7:25, 29, 31–32; D&C 20:35). Most angelic
communications are felt or heard rather than seen."[100]

NOTES AND COMMENTARY

Moroni 10:14 *the beholding of angels.* An angel can be one of
several different kinds of beings—either resurrected and glorified

beings, translated beings, premortal spirits, or spirits of just men made perfect through Christ. In a technical sense, all angels are resurrected beings (D&C 129:1). But Joseph Smith taught that translated beings are "held in reserve to be ministering angels."[101] And "ministering spirits" are also often referred to as angels. Because Christ was the first person ever resurrected on this sphere, and since "there are no angels who minister to this earth but those who do belong or have belonged to it" (D&C 130:5), we know that all angelic visitations before the resurrection of Christ were either translated beings or spirits. This would include the angel who visited Adam and Eve and taught them the gospel (Moses 5:6), the angels who appeared to Jacob (Genesis 32:1), and the visitations of Gabriel to Daniel (see Daniel 8:16; 9:21), Mary (Luke 1:26–27), and Zacharias (see Luke 1:5–19).

The Book of Mormon is filled with examples of ministering angels, including those that visited Nephi (1 Nephi 11:14), King Benjamin (Mosiah 3:2), Alma the younger (Mosiah 27:10–11; Alma 8:14), Amulek (Alma 10:7), Samuel the Lamanite (Helaman 13:7), Nephi the disciple of the Lord (3 Nephi 7:17–18), and others.

Some angels, of course, are resurrected beings. Well-known examples include the appearance of Moroni and John the Baptist to Joseph Smith (Joseph Smith–History 1:30–33, 68–72, D&C 128:20).

ministering spirits. Ministering spirits, or righteous spirits who go from the spirit world to visit man for God's purposes, are often referred to as angels. "The spirits of just men are made ministering servants to those who are sealed unto life eternal," Joseph Smith taught. " . . . The spirits of the just are exalted to a greater and more glorious work; hence they are blessed in their departure to the world of spirits."[102]

The teachings of the latter-day prophets give us a number of other insights into the rich blessing of communication between the spirit and mortal worlds. Here are a few principles and experiences they have shared with the Saints.

THE SPIRITS OF THE DEAD WATCH US AND DESIRE TO HELP

In April 1896, President Joseph F. Smith wrote a letter to his missionary son, Hyrum M., answering his questions about the spirit world. One of Hyrum's questions was "To what extent do our relatives and friends who have died have cognizance of us and our actions?" President Smith answered, "That will depend on the condition of our departed kindred and friends. All spirits are subject to the laws of the spirit world. For instance, the Prophet Joseph Smith, on October 9, 1843, said: 'Spirits can only be revealed in flaming fire or glory. (That is, disembodied spirits.) Angels have advanced further, their light and glory being tabernacled, and hence, they appear in bodily shape. (Angels here referred to are resurrected beings.) The spirits of just men are made ministering servants to those who are sealed unto life eternal. . . . ' But Joseph continues: 'The spirits of the just are exalted to a greater and more glorious work; hence they are blessed in their departure to the World of Spirits. Enveloped in flaming fire *they are not far from us* and know and understand our thoughts and feelings and notions and are *often pained therewith.'* . . .

"Now, if our departed kindred and friends are just (righteous) spirits, exalted to this greater and more glorious work, they may be very near us, enveloped in flaming glory, taking notes, or observing actions of our thought, feelings, and actions, rejoicing because of our virtues and integrity to the truth, or sorrowing and weeping over our sins and transgressions. And not only so, but able to render assistance, when our spirits are susceptible to the power they wield. . . . I believe that our departed kindred and loved ones are far more mindful of us and solicitous for our salvation day by day than they ever were in the flesh, because they know more."[103]

Twenty years later, near the end of his life, President Smith said, "I believe we move and have our being in the presence of heavenly messengers and of heavenly beings. We are not separated from them. . . . I claim that we live in their presence, they see us, they are solicitous for our welfare, they love us now more than ever. For now they see the dangers that beset us; they can comprehend better than ever before, the weaknesses that are liable to mislead us into dark and forbidden paths. They see the temptations and the evils that beset us in life, and the proneness of mortal beings to yield to temptation and to wrong doing; hence their solicitude for us and their love for us and their desire for our well being must be greater than that which we feel for ourselves."[104]

Prophets from our generation have added their witness to this truth. Harold B. Lee, for example, said, "Sometimes we think the whole job is up to us, forgetful that there are loved ones beyond our sight who are thinking about us and our children."[105] And Ezra Taft Benson taught, "Visitors, seen and unseen, from the world beyond, are often close to us. This is part of eternity which we are living today—part of God's plan. There is no veil to the Lord."[106]

It is a blessing to know that those who have passed on may be praying for us, and that their prayers are answered just as ours are. Elder Melvin J. Ballard asked, "Why is it that sometimes only one of a city or household receives the Gospel?" His answer reveals a great truth. He said, "It was made known to me that it is because the righteous dead who have received the Gospel in the spirit world are exercising themselves, and in answers to their prayers elders of the Church are sent to the homes of their posterity . . . , and that descendant in the flesh is then privileged to do the work for his dead kindred. I want to say to you that it is with greater intensity that the hearts of the fathers and mothers in the spirit world are turned to their children now in the flesh than that our hearts are turned to them."[107]

THE LEADERS OF OUR PAST ALSO WATCH US AND DESIRE TO HELP

Not only are loved ones near, keeping watch over us and seeking to help us, but Church leaders from the past are doing the same. Wilford Woodruff spoke of this often. In April conference, 1880, he said, "The eyes of the heavenly hosts are over us; the eyes of God himself and his Son Jesus Christ; the eyes of all the prophets and Apostles who have dwelt in the flesh; they are watching our works. . . . We are not shut out from God, we are not shut out from our brethren, though the vail is between us. They understand our works, our conditions, our position."[108]

At the following conference President Woodruff continued this theme. "I believe the eyes of the heavenly hosts are over this people," he said; "I believe they are watching the elders of Israel, the prophets and apostles and men who are called to bear off this kingdom. I believe they watch over us all with great interest.

" . . . After the death of Joseph Smith I saw and conversed with him many times in my dreams in the night season. On one occasion he and his brother Hyrum met me when on the sea going on a mission to England. I had Dan Jones with me. He received his mission from Joseph Smith before his death; and the prophet talked freely to me about the mission I was then going to perform. And he also talked to me with regard to the mission of the Twelve Apostles in the flesh, and he laid before me the work they had to perform; and he also spoke of the reward they would receive after death. And there were many other things he laid before me in his interview on that occasion. . . .

"I have had many interviews with Brother Joseph until the last 15 or 20 years of my life; I have not seen him for that length of time. But during my travels in the southern country last winter I had many interviews with President Young, and with Heber C. Kimball, and Geo. A. Smith, and Jedediah M. Grant, and many others who are dead. They attended our conference, they attended our meetings. And on one occasion, I saw Brother Brigham and Brother Heber ride in a carriage ahead of the carriage in which I rode when I was on my way to attend conference; and they were dressed in the most priestly robes. When we arrived at our destination I asked Prest. Young if he would preach to us. He said, 'No, I have finished my testimony in the flesh I shall not talk to this people any more. But (said he) I have come to see you; I have come to watch over you, and to see what the people are doing. Then (said he) I want you to teach the people—and I want you to fol-low this counsel yourself—that they must labor and so live as to obtain the Holy Spirit, for without this you cannot build up the king-dom; without the spirit of God you are in danger of walking in the dark, and in danger of failing to accomplish your calling as apostles and as elders in the church and kingdom of God. And, said he, Brother Joseph taught me this principle.' . . . Do you not think they are inter-ested about us? I tell you they are."[109]

At the dedication of the Tokyo Temple, President Spencer W. Kimball remarked, "I expect that every one of the presidents of the Church, all twelve of us, have been dreaming glorious dreams about a temple in Tokyo. This world is not so far from the world of those who have passed on. We feel certain that they are permitted to visit the earth at times, and I think that Joseph Smith, Brigham Young, and all of the presidents, including Heber J. Grant, are surely not far from us this day."¹¹⁰

Church leaders from the past also seem to have some influence on the Church in the present. After he was called to be an apostle, Elder Heber J. Grant struggled mightily with feelings of inadequacy. In his wrestlings, he sought the Lord for solace and reassurance. At one point he was riding alone on horseback. "As I was riding along . . . I seemed to see, and I seemed to hear, what to me is one of the most real things in all my life. I seemed to hear the words that were spoken. I listened to the discussion with a great deal of interest. The First Presidency and the Quorum of the Twelve Apostles had not been able to agree on two men to fill the vacancies in the Quorum of the Twelve. There had been a vacancy of one for two years, and a vacancy of two for one year, and the conferences had adjourned without the vacancies' being filled. In this council the Savior was present, my father was there, and the Prophet Joseph Smith was there. They discussed the question that a mistake had been made in not filling those two vacancies and that in all probability it would be another six months before the Quorum would be completed. And they discussed as to whom they wanted to occupy those positions, and decided that the way to remedy the mistake that had been made in not filling these vacancies was to send a revelation. It was given to me that the Prophet Joseph Smith and my father [Jedediah M. Grant] mentioned me and requested that I be called to that position. I sat there and wept for joy. It was given to me that I had done nothing to entitle me to that exalted position, except that I had lived a clean, sweet life. It was given to me that because of my father's having practically sacrificed his life in what was known as the great reformation, so to speak, of the people in early days, having been practically a martyr, that the Prophet Joseph and my father desired me to have that position, and it was because of their faithful labors that I was called, and not because of anything I had done of myself or any great thing that I had accomplished. It was also given to me that that was all these men, the Prophet and my father, could do for me. From that day it depended upon me and upon me alone as to whether I made a success of my life or a failure."¹¹¹

From this experience, Elder Grant was convinced that the

prophets and apostles in the spirit world still have some influence on the workings of the Church in mortality.

Wilford Woodruff related an understanding of a council held for a different purpose: "I have felt of late as if our brethren on the other side of the veil had held a council, and that they had said to this one, and that one, 'Cease thy work on earth, come hence, we need help,' and they have called this man and that man. It has appeared so to me in seeing the many men who have been called from our midst lately.

"Perhaps I may be permitted to relate a circumstance with which I am acquainted in relation to Bishop Roskelley, of Smithfield, Cache Valley. On one occasion he was suddenly taken very sick—near to death's door. While he lay in this condition, President Peter Maughan, who was dead, came to him and said: 'Brother Roskelley, we held a council on the other side of the veil. I have had a great deal to do, and I have the privilege of coming here to appoint one man to come and help. I have had three names given to me in council, and you are one of them. I want to inquire into your circumstances.'

"The Bishop told him what he had to do, and they conversed together as one man would converse with another. President Maughan then said to him: 'I think I will not call you. I think you are wanted here more than perhaps one of the others.' Bishop Roskelley got well from that hour.

"Very soon after, the second man was taken sick, but not being able to exercise sufficient faith, Brother Roskelley did not go to him. By and by this man recovered, and on meeting Brother Roskelley he said: 'Brother Maughan came to me the other night and told me he was sent to call one man from the ward,' and he named two men as had been done to Brother Roskelley. A few days afterwards the third man was taken sick and died.

"Now, I name this to show a principle. They have work on the other side of the veil; and they want men, and they call them. And that was my view in regard to Brother George A. Smith. When he was almost at death's door, Brother Cannon administered to him, and in thirty minutes he was up and ate breakfast with his family. We labored with him in this way, but ultimately, as you know, he died. But it taught me a lesson. I felt that man was wanted behind the veil. We labored also with Brother Pratt; he, too, was wanted behind the veil."[112]

SPIRITS OF LOVED ONES CAN BRING A VARIETY OF BLESSINGS

Ministering spirits can bring a variety of wonderful blessings when they come. Joseph F. Smith said, "Our fathers and mothers, brothers, sisters and friends who have passed away from this earth, having been faithful, and worthy to enjoy these rights and privileges, may have a mission given them to visit their relatives and friends upon the earth again, bringing from the divine Presence messages of love, of warning, or reproof and instruction, to those whom they had learned to love in the flesh."[113]

Spirits can come bringing comfort. President Harold B. Lee once related an experience in the life of John Wells, who at one time was a member of the Presiding Bishopric. "A son of Bishop Wells was killed in Emigration Canyon on a railroad track. Brother John Wells was a great detail man and prepared many of the reports we are following up now. His boy was run over by a freight train. Sister Wells was inconsolable. She mourned during the three days prior to the funeral, received no comfort at the funeral, and was in a rather serious state of mind.

"One day soon after the funeral services while she was lying on her bed relaxed, still mourning, she says that her son appeared to her and said, 'Mother do not mourn, do not cry. I am all right.' He told her that she did not understand how the accident happened and explained that he had given the signal to the engineer to move on, and then made the usual effort to catch the railing on the freight train; but as he attempted to do so his foot caught on a root and he failed to catch the hand rail, and his body fell under the train. It was clearly an accident.

"Now, listen. He said that as soon as he realized that he was in another environment he tried to see his father, but *he couldn't reach him. His father was so busy with the duties in his office he could not respond to his call.* Therefore he had come to his mother. He said to her, 'You tell father that all is well with me, and I want you not to mourn any more.'"[114]

Spirits can help us in our trials. At one point Parley P. Pratt lay for months in a Missouri dungeon, utterly discouraged to have been imprisoned for so long. One thought ruled his mind: "Shall I ever, at any time, however distant it may be, or whatever I may suffer first; shall I ever be free again in this life?" As he pondered the question, an answer came. Here is what he recorded:

"After some days of prayer and fasting, and seeking the Lord on the subject, I retired to my bed in my lonely chamber at an early hour, and while the other prisoners and the guard were chatting and beguiling the lonesome hours in the upper apartment of the prison, I lay in silence, seeking and expecting an answer to my prayer, when suddenly I seemed carried away in the spirit, and no longer sensible to outward objects with which I was surrounded. A heaven of peace and calmness pervaded my bosom; a personage from the world of spirits stood before me with a smile of compassion in every look, and pity mingled with the tenderest love and sympathy in every expression of the countenance. A soft hand seemed placed within my own, and a glowing cheek was laid in tenderness and warmth upon mine. A well-known voice saluted me, which I readily recognized as that of the wife of my youth, who had for one or two years been sweetly sleeping where the wicked cease from troubling and the weary are at rest. I was made to realize that she was sent to commune with me, and answer my question.

"Knowing this, I said to her in a most eager and inquiring tone: Shall I ever be at liberty again in this life and enjoy the society of my family and the Saints, and preach the gospel as I have done? She answered definitely and unhesitatingly: 'YES!' I then recollected that I had agreed to be satisfied with the knowledge of that one fact, but now I wanted more.

"Said I: Can you tell how, or by what means, or where I shall escape? She replied: 'THAT THING IS NOT MADE KNOWN TO ME YET.' I instantly felt that I had gone beyond my agreement and my faith in asking this last question, and that I must be contented at present with the answer to the first.

"Her gentle spirit then saluted me and withdrew. I came to myself. The doleful noise of the guards, and the wrangling and angry words of the old apostate again grated on my ears, but heaven and hope were in my soul.

"Next morning I related the whole circumstance of my vision to my two fellow prisoners, who rejoiced exceedingly. This may seem to some like an idle dream, or a romance of the imagination; but to me it was, and always will be, a reality, both as it regards what I then experienced and the fulfillment afterwards."[115]

Spirits may visit to take other loved ones in death. Heber J. Grant related a visit of his deceased wife for that purpose: "I have been blessed with only two sons. One of them died at five years of age and the other at seven.

"My last son died of a hip disease. I had built great hopes that he would live to spread the gospel at home and abroad and be an honor to me. About an hour before he died I had a dream that his mother, who was dead, came for him, and that she brought with her a messenger, and she told this messenger to take the boy while I was asleep. In the dream I thought I awoke and I seized my son and fought for him and finally succeeded in getting him away from the messenger who had come to take him, and in so doing I dreamed that I stumbled and fell upon him.

"I dreamed that I fell upon his sore hip, and the terrible cries and anguish of the child drove me nearly wild. I could not stand it, and I jumped up and ran out of the house so as not to hear his distress. I dreamed that after running out of the house I met Brother Joseph E. Taylor and told him of these things.

"He said: 'Well, Heber, do you know what I would do if my wife came for one of her children—I would not struggle for that child; I would not oppose her taking that child away. If a mother who had been faithful had passed beyond the veil, she would know of the suffering and the anguish her child may have to suffer. She would know whether that child might go through life as a cripple and whether it would be better or wiser for that child to be relieved from the torture of life. And when you stop to think, Brother Grant, that the mother of that boy went down into the shadow of death to give him life, she is the one who ought to have the right to take him or leave him.'

"I said, 'I believe you are right, Brother Taylor, and if she comes again, she shall have the boy without any protest on my part.'

"After coming to that conclusion, I was waked by my brother, B. F. Grant, who was staying that night with us.

"He called me into the room and told me that my chi

"I went in the front room and sat down. There was a between me and my wife who is now living, and I felt the presence of that boy's deceased mother, sitting in that chair. I did not tell anybody what I felt, but I turned to my living wife and said: 'Do you feel anything strange?' She said: 'Yes, I feel assured that Heber's mother is sitting between us, waiting to take him away.'

"Now, I am naturally, I believe, a sympathetic man. I was raised as an only child with all the affection that a mother could lavish upon a boy. I believe that I am naturally affectionate and sympathetic and that I shed tears for my friends—tears of joy for their success and tears of sorrow for their misfortunes. But I sat by the deathbed of my little boy and saw him die, without shedding a tear. My living wife, my brother, and I, upon that occasion experienced a sweet, peaceful, and heavenly influence in my home, as great as I have ever experienced in my life. And no person can tell me that every other Latter-day Saint that has a knowledge of the gospel in his heart and soul, can really mourn for his loved ones; only in the loss of their society here in this life."[116]

The Lord can use spirits to reveal truth to us. In 1896 Elder Abraham H. Cannon, a member of the Quorum of the Twelve, was suddenly and unexpectedly taken in death. He was only thirty-seven years old and had served in the quorum for nearly seven years. Wilford Woodruff was troubled by the early death of this brother, as were other leaders and members of the Church. And yet President Woodruff trusted in the Lord, saying, "There is a meaning to this. Many times things take place with us that we do not comprehend, unless it is given to us by revelation. But there is a meaning in the loss of that young apostle. I had a manifestation of that while in San Francisco recently.

"One evening, as I fell asleep, I was very much troubled with evil spirits that tried to afflict me; and while laboring to throw off these spirits and their influence, there was another spirit visited me that seemed to have power over the evil spirits, and they departed from me. Before he left me he told me not to grieve because of the departure of Abraham Hoagland Cannon; for the Lord had called him to fill another important mission in the spirit world, as a pure and holy apostle from

Zion in the Rocky Mountains—a labor which would not only prove a great benefit to his father's household, but to the Church and kingdom of God on the earth. I feel to name this, because it is true."[117]

Brigham Young said, "About the time the temples are ready, the strangers will be along and will converse with you, and will inquire of you, probably, if you understand the resurrection of the dead. You might say you have heard and read a great deal about it, but you do not properly understand it; and they will then open your minds and tell you the principles of the resurrection of the dead and how to save your friends; they will point out Scriptures in the Old and New Testament, in the Book of Mormon, and other revelations of God, saying, 'Don't you recollect reading so and so, that saviors should come up on Mount Zion?' etc., and they will expound the Scriptures to you."[118]

THE LORD WILL ALLOW SPIRITS TO COMMUNICATE TO FACILITATE WORK FOR THE DEAD

The spirits of the dead are often very interested in temple work, both for themselves and for others they love. In one famous example, the signers of the Declaration of Independence, led by George Washington, appeared to Wilford Woodruff and demanded that he do their temple work for them. "They waited on me for two days and two nights. I thought it very singular, that notwithstanding so much work had been done, and yet nothing had been done for them. . . . I straightway went into the baptismal font and called upon Brother McAllister to baptize me for the signers of the Declaration of Independence, and fifty other eminent men, making one hundred in all, including John Wesley, Columbus, and others. I then baptized him for every President of the United States, except three; and when their cause is just, somebody will do the work for them."[119] They also ordained the men to the priesthood and had an endowment performed, by proxy, for each one.

Elder Melvin J. Ballard related an experience of Edward J. Wood, who was first president of the Cardston Alberta Temple. "While sealing a group of children to their parents, in the midst of the ceremony he felt an impression to ask the mother who was present, 'Sister, does this list contain the names of all your children?' She said, 'Yes.' He began again but once more he stopped and asked if the list named all her children. She told him there were no more children. He attempted to proceed, but a third time was impelled to ask: 'My Sister, have you not lost a child whose name is not on this list?' Then she said, 'Yes, I do remember now. We did lose a little baby. It was born alive and then died soon after. I had forgotten to put its name down.' The name was given, and then it, being the first born, was named first and all were sealed to the parents.

"Then President Wood said: 'Every time I started to seal the children I heard a voice say: "Mother, don't forget me," and I could not go any farther.' The appeal was made each time until the omission was discovered."[120]

These spirits can help as we do family history research. Elder Ballard taught, "They know where their records are, and . . . the spirit and influence of your dead will guide those who are interested in finding those records. . . . If there is anywhere on the earth anything concerning them, you will find it. . . . If we have done our best and have searched and have discovered all that is available, then the day will come when God will open and part the veil, and the records . . . will be revealed."[121] Elder David B. Haight added his witness to this truth: "I believe that when you diligently seek after your ancestors—in faith— needed information will come to you even when no mortal records of their lives are available."[122] And Brigham Young said that "the time will come [when] . . . some of those who are not in mortality will come along and say, 'Here are a thousand names I wish you to attend to in this temple, and when you have got through with them I will give you another thousand;' and the Elders of Israel and their wives will go forth to officiate for their forefathers, the men for the men, and the women for the women."[123]

He also said, "[Those in the temple] will often have occasion to say, 'Somebody came to the temple last night; we did not know who he was, but he was no doubt a brother, and told us a great many things we did not before understand. He gave us the names of a great many of our forefathers that are not on record, and he gave me my true lineage and the names of my forefathers for hundreds of years back. He said to me, you and I are connected in one family; there are the names of your ancestors; take them and write them down, and be baptized and confirmed, and save such and such ones, and receive of the blessings of the eternal Priesthood for such and such an individual, as you do for yourselves.'"[124]

Those who are diligent in seeking out their dead will receive help in other ways as well. As Elder John A. Widtsoe said, "Those who give themselves with all their might and main to this work [family history work] receive help from the other side. Whoever seeks to help those on the other side receives help in return in all the affairs of life."[125]

Spirit Communication Is Directed by the Priesthood

Visits and communication through the veil must be authorized and directed by the priesthood, specifically by those authorities who direct the work in the spirit world. President Joseph F. Smith said, "Our fathers and mothers, brothers, sisters and friends who have passed away from this earth, having been faithful, and worthy to enjoy these rights and privileges, may have a mission given them to visit their relatives and friends upon the earth again, bringing from the divine Presence messages of love, of warning, of reproof and instruction, to those whom they had learned to love in the flesh. . . . There are laws to which they who are in the paradise of God must be subject, as well as laws to which we are subject."[126] Thus, according to law and by assignment ("may have a mission given them"), the spirits of the dead may visit the living.

In an article called "Do the Dead Return?" Elder Orson F. Whitney spoke of the idea of mortals making compacts, or agreements, with each other to return from the dead with a message. Then he said, "That the inhabitants of the spirit world, or some of them, return at times and communicate with mortals, I am perfectly well assured. But I am not convinced that any and every spirit is at liberty to return, whatever the 'compacts' that may have been entered into beforehand. Some spirits are 'in prison.' Of what avail would a compact be in their case, unless their jailor or some higher power were a party to it? Evidently the spirits that communicate with mortals are not of that class, unless it be in exceptional cases, where leave of absence has been granted for some special reason.

"God's house is a house of order, and the spirit world is a room in that house. This being the case, it is only reasonable to conclude that

before anything important or unusual can take place there, th
of the Mansion must first give consent. Otherwise confusic ̲ ̲ ̲u̲r̲u
prevail, and the divine purpose for which the veil was dropped
between the two worlds might be thwarted. . . . Permission from the
Great Father would have to be obtained before one of his children,
[who is] . . . a disembodied spirit, could make itself manifest to
mortals.

"Moreover, . . . not every mortal is qualified to receive a message
from 'the other side.' One must be fittingly endowed, must have the
proper gift, in order to get a communication of that kind. Earthly ties
would not necessarily govern. Other and higher relationships are
involved. There must be capacity as well as a desire to receive.
Because men like Moses and Joseph Smith saw God, is no sign that
any man can see him. 'Choice seers' were they, very different from
ordinary men. All human beings can obtain blessings from heaven, but
not always in the same way. There are diversities of gifts and varying
degrees of receptivity. Wireless telegraphy furnishes a hint in this connection. Unless there be a receiving station with an apparatus properly
attuned, a message launched upon the ether would find, like Noah's
dove, 'no rest for the sole of her foot.'"[127]

Unfortunately, not all spirits are righteous, and not all contact
between the worlds is positive. "There are influences in the atmos-
phere that are invisible to us," Elder George Q. Cannon noted. ". . . I
have no doubt that many of my brethren and sisters have sensibly felt
in various places and at various times evil influences around them."
He then noted, "Brother Joseph Smith gave an explanation of this.
There are places in the Mississippi Valley where the influence or the
presence of invisible spirits are very perceptibly felt. He said that
numbers had been slain there in war and that there were evil influences or spirits which affect the spirits of those who have tabernacles
on the earth. I myself have felt those influences in other places besides
the continent of America; I have felt them on the old battle grounds
on the Sandwich Islands.

"I have come to the conclusion that if our eyes were open to see the
spirit world around us, we should feel differently on this subject than
we do; we would not be so unguarded and careless and so indifferent

whether we had the spirit and power of God with us or not; but we would be continually watchful and prayerful to our Heavenly Father for His Holy Spirit and His holy angels to be around about us to strengthen us to overcome every evil influence."[128]

Brigham Young taught a similar principle: "There are myriads of disembodied evil spirits—those who have long ago laid down their bodies here and in the regions round about among and around us; and they are trying to make us and our children sick, and are trying to destroy us and tempt us to evil."[129]

If we have a visitation through the veil, how can we discern the difference between a righteous spirit and an evil or unrighteous one? Joseph Smith gave us an important key: "Some will say that they have seen a spirit; that he offered them his hand, but they did not touch it. This is a lie. First, it is contrary to the plan of God: a spirit cannot come but in glory; an angel has flesh and bones; we see not their glory."[130] He gave further instructions at Nauvoo, Illinois, in February 1843; these instructions were later published as part of section 129 in the Doctrine and Covenants:

"When a messenger comes saying he has a message from God, offer him your hand and request him to shake hands with you. If he be an angel he will do so, and you will feel his hand. If he be the spirit of a just man made perfect he will come in his glory; for that is the only way he can appear—ask him to shake hands with you, but he will not move, because it is contrary to the order of heaven for a just man to deceive; but he will still deliver his message. If it be the devil as an angel of light, when you ask him to shake hands he will offer you his hand, and you will not feel anything; you may therefore detect him.

"These are three grand keys whereby you may know whether any administration is from God" (vv. 4–9).

CHAPTER 4

CHRIST HAS POWER
OVER DEATH

O death, where is thy sting?" Paul asked. "O grave, where is thy victory?" He then gave the answer: "The sting of death is sin; and the strength of sin is the law." But that solemn truth is tempered by the infinite blessing of the atonement of Jesus Christ: "But thanks be to God, which giveth us the victory through our Lord Jesus Christ" (1 Corinthians 15:55–57).

Harold B. Lee echoed Paul's words when he said, "The heavy hand of death becomes lighter, the pall of gloom is pierced and throbbing wounds are soothed as faith lifts us beyond the sordid trials and sorrows of mortal life and gives a vision of brighter days and more joyous prospect, as has been revealed, when 'God shall wipe away all tears from their eyes; and there shall be no more death, neither sorrow, nor crying, neither shall there be any more pain: for the former things are passed away' (Revelation 21:4) through the atonement of the Lord Jesus Christ. With such faith and understanding you who may be called upon to mourn can sing as it has been written, 'Death is swallowed up in victory. O death, where is thy sting? O grave, where is thy victory?' (1 Corinthians 15:54–55.)"[1]

Without Christ death is nothing less than a "monster" (2 Nephi 9:10), something to be feared above all else. But Christ has conquered death for us, removing for the believer both the fear of death and much of its emotional pain.

It is Christ and his atonement that enables those of faith to understand such statements as this stirring testimony of Orson F. Whitney: "We are not going to die. We are deathless beings. We lived before we came into this world, and we shall live after we go out of it. What we call death is not worthy the name. There is no death for the righteous. Christ died to destroy death. The change called death is but a temporary separation of the spirit from the body; and while the body goes back to mother earth, the spirit returns to God who gave it—it enters paradise, the place of departed spirits, there to await the resurrection. Yes; the day will come when spirit and body will reunite, to be no more subject to these mortal conditions, and the soul shall inherit eternal life, a fulness of joy. Such are the hopes and promises held out by the gospel.

"None of our dear departed ones are dead. They have but gone before. This so-called death, when properly understood, is simply a going back home. There is a universal law requiring all things to return to whence they came and to where they belong. It is the law of restitution, spoken of by the holy prophets since the world began. This sublime lesson is taught not only in the scriptures, but in the Book of Nature. The rain-drops, the moment they strike the ground, begin to trickle back to the ocean, or evaporate to the clouds from which they fell. Up from the bosom of the mighty deep and over the broad land are carried the waters that are showered upon the earth to make it green and flowery and fruitful; and when those waters have fulfilled their mission they are gathered back to their ocean reservoir. Not a drop of dew is lost.

"Matter is eternal, spirit is eternal, intelligence or the light of truth is eternal; and our spirits that come from God, the moment they are born into this world begin traveling back to eternity—begin moving toward the great sea out of which they were taken! . . . No soul that believes in Jesus Christ and keeps his commandments need fear to die. It is nothing but a return home."[2]

Those with a gospel perspective and faith in the power of Christ can rejoice with President Heber J. Grant, who said, "I never think of my wives and my dear mother and my two boys, my daughter, and my departed friends, and beloved associates being in the graveyard. I think only of the joy and the happiness and the peace and satisfaction . . . they have in meeting with father and mother and loved ones who have been true and faithful to the gospel of the Lord Jesus Christ. My mind reaches out to the wonderful joy and satisfaction and happiness that they are having, and it robs the grave of its sting."[3]

GOD HAS POWER OVER DEATH AND HELL

Doctrine and Covenants 63:2–4

2 Yea, verily, I say, hear the word of him whose anger is kindled against the wicked and rebellious;

3 Who willeth to take even them whom he will take, and preserveth in life them whom he will preserve;

4 Who buildeth up at his own will and pleasure; and destroyeth when he pleases, and is able to cast the soul down to hell.

God has power over all things, including both death and hell. As we read in Joseph Smith's vision of the three degrees of glory, of those who become gods it is said, "All things are theirs, whether life or death, or things present, or things to come, all are theirs and they are Christ's, and Christ is God's" (D&C 76:59). Thus the gods have controlling power over all things, including life and death; Christ has dominion over the other gods; and the Father has dominion over all.

The Lord has given us many scriptural examples of his power over death. One such example is found in a prophecy given to Ezekiel. In Ezekiel 32 the Lord compared the king of Egypt to a great whale that moved freely in the seas and the rivers. But, the Lord said, "I will . . . spread out my net over thee," capturing the whale.

"Then will I leave thee upon the land, I will cast thee forth upon the open field, and will cause all the fowls of the heaven to remain upon thee, and I will fill the beasts of the whole earth with thee. And I will lay thy flesh upon the mountains, and fill the valleys with thy height. I will also water with thy blood the land wherein thou swimmest, even to the mountains; and the rivers shall be full of thee. . . .

"For thus saith the Lord God; The sword of the king of Babylon shall come upon thee. By the swords of the mighty will I cause thy multitude to fall, the terrible of the nations, all of them: and they shall spoil the pomp of Egypt, and all the multitude thereof shall be destroyed" (vv. 3–6, 11–12).

Egypt was mighty as a whale—but the Lord was mightier still, and the Lord would freely exercise his power to lay waste to Egypt, destroying "the multitude thereof," casting them from mortal life to death.

Just as the Lord can take life according to his will, so can he preserve it. Once Hezekiah, king of Judah, was "sick unto death." But the king desired to continue to live, and he "turned his face toward the wall, and prayed unto the Lord, and said, Remember now, O Lord, I beseech thee, how I have walked before thee in truth and with a perfect heart, and have done that which is good in thy sight. And Hezekiah wept sore.

"Then came the word of the Lord to Isaiah, saying, Go, and say to Hezekiah, Thus saith the Lord, the God of David thy father, I have heard thy prayer, I have seen thy tears: behold, I will add unto thy days fifteen years" (Isaiah 38:1–5).

The prophecy came to pass just as Isaiah said, because of God's power over death.

NOTES AND COMMENTARY

D&C 63:3 *willeth to take even them whom he will take, and preserveth in life them whom he will preserve.* The Lord has power to take or preserve life according to his will. The Psalmist spoke of the Lord's power to preserve, even in the midst of destruction: "Behold, the eye of the Lord is upon them that fear him, upon them that hope in his mercy; to deliver their soul from death, and to keep them alive in famine. Our soul waiteth for the Lord: he is our help and our shield" (Psalm 33:18–20).

D&C 63:4 *is able to cast the soul down to hell.* Satan entices us to sin, but it is Christ who holds the keys to death and hell. Keys are the governing, controlling power, the power to bind and loose, the power to send one to hell or to set one free. Such is the power of the Lord.

THE PRIESTHOOD CAN RAISE THE DEAD

Doctrine and Covenants 124:100

100 And what if I will that he should raise the dead, let him not withhold his voice.

One of the most famous miracles of Jesus was the raising of Lazarus from the dead. On that occasion, he stood at the entrance to Lazarus' tomb and called in a loud voice, "Lazarus, come forth!" Then Lazarus, even though he had been dead four days, emerged from the tomb wrapped in the bandages of burial. This miracle was a marvelous manifestation of the power of God over death (see John 11:11–45).

The scriptures give many other evidences of this power. Here are a few examples:

- Elisha raised from death the son of the Shunammite woman (2 Kings 4:32–37).
- Jesus sent his apostles forth with the command to raise the dead (Matthew 10:8).
- Jesus told John's disciples that they should view Jesus' raising the dead as a sign that he was sent from God (Matthew 11:4–5).
- Jesus raised the widow's son from the dead (Luke 7:12–15).
- Paul included raising the dead on his list of the works of faith (Hebrews 11:35).
- When Benjamin spoke of the works of the coming Lord, he included raising the dead (Mosiah 3:5).
- A disciple of Christ named Nephi raised his brother from the dead (3 Nephi 7:19).
- Jesus raised a man from the dead when he ministered among the Nephites (3 Nephi 26:15).
- The disciples of Jesus among the Nephites raised the dead (4 Nephi 1:5).

This power has also been made manifest among the Latter-day Saints. One powerful example is seen in the life of Lorenzo Snow. Ella Jensen, a young girl who belonged to a family that was closely acquainted with President Snow, died from scarlet fever. Her father, Jacob Jensen, drove into town, which was more than a mile away, to ask President Snow to arrange for Ella's funeral. Instead President

Snow decided to visit the home, accompanied by Rudger Clawson. Elder Clawson recorded their experience:

"As we entered the home we met Sister Jensen, who was very much agitated and alarmed. We came to Ella's bedside and were impressed by the thought that her spirit had passed out of the body and gone beyond.

"Turning to me President Snow said: 'Brother Clawson, will you anoint her,' which I did. We then laid our hands upon her head and the anointing was confirmed by President Snow, who blessed her and among other things, used this very extraordinary expression, in a commanding tone of voice, 'Come back, Ella, come back. Your work upon the earth is not yet completed, come back.'"

Jacob Jensen, Ella's father, continues the account:

"After President Snow had finished the blessing, he turned to my wife and me and said, 'Now do not mourn or grieve any more. It will be all right. . . . '

"Ella remained in this condition for more than an hour after President Snow administered to her, or more than three hours in all after she died. We were sitting there watching by the bedside, her mother and myself, when all at once she opened her eyes. She looked about the room, saw us sitting there, but still looked for someone else. And the first thing she said was: 'Where is he? Where is he?'

"We asked, 'Who? Where is who?'

"'Why, Brother Snow,' she replied. 'He called me back.'"[4]

NOTES AND COMMENTARY

D&C 124:100 *if I will that he should raise the dead, let him not withhold his voice.* The Lord can inspire those who hold the priesthood to exercise power to command the dead to return to life. When God directs a man to use priesthood power in this way, even if the direction comes quietly, through the whisperings of the Spirit, the man must act as he is prompted to act and "not withhold his voice."

CHRIST REDEEMS US FROM DEATH AND HELL

2 Nephi 9:10–13, 19

10 O how great the goodness of our God, who prepareth a way for our escape from the grasp of this awful monster; yea, that monster, death and hell, which I call the death of the body, and also the death of the spirit.

11 And because of the way of deliverance of our God, the Holy One of Israel, this death, of which I have spoken, which is the temporal, shall deliver up its dead; which death is the grave.

12 And this death of which I have spoken, which is the spiritual death, shall deliver up its dead; which spiritual death is hell; wherefore, death and hell must deliver up their dead, and hell must deliver up its captive spirits, and the grave must deliver up its captive bodies, and the bodies and the spirits of men will be restored one to the other; and it is by the power of the resurrection of the Holy One of Israel.

13 O how great the plan of our God! For on the other hand, the paradise of God must deliver up the spirits of the righteous, and the grave deliver up the body of the righteous; and the spirit and the body is restored to itself again, and all men become incorruptible, and immortal, and they are living souls, having a perfect knowledge like unto us in the flesh, save it be that our knowledge shall be perfect. . . .

19 O the greatness of the mercy of our God, the Holy One of Israel! For he delivereth his saints from that awful monster the devil, and death, and hell, and that lake of fire and brimstone, which is endless torment.

Death and hell are "death of the body, and also the death of the spirit," or spiritual death. Jesus Christ redeems us from both conditions, the first as a free gift, the second as we have faith, repent, and come unto him, meeting all the requirements he places upon us.

The scriptures give frequent and clear testimony that Christ redeems us from death. Through Hosea, for example, Jehovah says, "I will ransom them from the power of the grave; I will redeem them from death: O death, I will be thy plagues; O grave, I will be thy destruction" (Hosea 13:14).

In the Book of Mormon we read, "If Christ had not come into the world, . . . there could have been no redemption. And if Christ had not risen from the dead, or have broken the bands of death that the grave should have no victory, and that death should have no sting, there could have been no resurrection. But there is a resurrection, therefore the grave hath no victory, and the sting of death is swallowed up in Christ. He is the light and the life of the world; yea, a light that is endless, that can never be darkened; yea, and also a life which is endless, that there can be no more death" (Mosiah 16:6–9).

And again: "He will take upon him death, that he may loose the bands of death which bind his people" (Alma 7:12).

These blessings are for all mankind: "Behold, the resurrection of Christ redeemeth mankind, yea, even all mankind, and bringeth them back into the presence of the Lord" (Helaman 14:17).

Christ also redeems the repentant from hell. This occurs in two ways. First, because of his atonement, many people are able to repent of their sins while they are still in their mortal probation, and thus they are able to avoid hell entirely, going straight to paradise when they die. Without the atonement, there would be no paradise in the spirit world, but only hell. Second, those who repent in the spirit prison can then escape hell and begin at that point to enjoy the blessings of paradise. Eventually, at the time of the final resurrection, all will emerge from that hell located in the spirit world, and that hell will be no more (see commentary on hell above); the only remaining hell will be that suffered by the devil, his angels, and the sons of perdition.

The scriptures also give many witnesses of this blessing of redemption from hell. After his transgression, David wrote of his faith that the powers of the atonement would eventually redeem his soul from hell. "Therefore my heart is glad," he wrote, "and my glory rejoiceth: my flesh also shall rest in hope. For thou wilt not leave my soul in hell" (Psalm 16:9–10). "Behold, the Lord hath redeemed my soul from hell," Lehi said to his children shortly before he died. "I have beheld his glory, and I am encircled about eternally in the arms of his love" (2 Nephi 1:15). Nephi added his testimony near the end of his own life: "I glory in my Jesus, for he hath redeemed my soul from hell" (2 Nephi 33:6).

NOTES AND COMMENTARY

2 Nephi 9:10 *O how great the goodness of our God.* God rescues us from the "awful monster" of death and hell (see below) not so much because of our goodness or righteousness, but because of his. "Since man had fallen he could not merit anything of himself; but the sufferings and death of Christ atone for their sins, through faith and repentance, and so forth; and that he breaketh the bands of death, that the grave shall have no victory, and that the sting of death should be swallowed up in the hopes of glory" (Alma 22:14). King David wrote of this goodness of God: "I will call upon the Lord, who is worthy to be praised: so shall I be saved from mine enemies. The sorrows of death compassed me, and the floods of ungodly men made me afraid. The sorrows of hell compassed me about: the snares of death prevented me. In my distress I called upon the Lord, and cried unto my God: he heard my voice out of his temple, and my cry came before him, even into his ears" (Psalm 18:3–6; see also 2 Samuel 22:4–7). On another occasion he prayed, "I will praise thee, O Lord my God, with all my heart: and I will glorify thy name for evermore. For great is thy mercy toward me: and thou hast delivered my soul from the lowest hell" (Psalm 86:12–13).

prepareth a way. The way that "our God" has prepared for our rescue is the atonement of Jesus Christ, his sufferings in the Garden of Gethsemane and on the cross, and his triumph at the garden tomb.

the grasp of this awful monster; yea, that monster, death and hell. This expression is repeated in verse 19. Earlier in the chapter Nephi describes in a graphic way why death and hell are considered to be such awful monsters. Without the atonement of Christ, we would stay permanently in the state of death and hell, "to an endless duration." Our bodies would have been "laid down to rot and to crumble to . . . mother earth, to rise no more." Under those circumstances, our spirits would "become subject" to Satan, and "must have become like unto him, and we become devils, . . . to remain with the father of lies, in misery, like unto himself" (2 Nephi 9:7–9). No wonder he felt to exclaim, "How great the goodness of our God!"

2 Nephi 9:11 *the way of deliverance.* The Lord Jehovah, even Jesus Christ, is our Deliverer (see Psalm 18:2; 40:17; 70:5; 144:2). The way of deliverance is his atonement. "And so all Israel shall be saved: as it is written, There shall come out of Sion the Deliverer, and shall turn away ungodliness from Jacob: For this is my covenant unto them, when I shall take away their sins" (Romans 11:26–27). When Joseph F. Smith saw his vision of the spirit world, he witnessed the Saints rejoicing in their redemption, and they "bowed the knee and acknowledged the Son of God as their Redeemer and Deliverer from death and the chains of hell" (D&C 138:23).

2 Nephi 9:12 *death and hell must deliver up their dead.* Through the power of Christ, both death and hell have been conquered, and eventually the spirit world, including that portion called hell, will be completely emptied. "Hell must deliver up its captive spirits, and the grave must deliver up its captive bodies, and the bodies and the spirits of men will be restored one to the other; and it is by the power of the resurrection of the Holy One of Israel," Jacob wrote in this same verse. At the same time, "the paradise of God must deliver up the spirits of the righteous, and the grave deliver up the body of the righteous" (v. 13) in the glorious resurrection.

2 Nephi 9:13 *all men become incorruptible, and immortal, and they are living souls.* These are descriptions of resurrected bodies. For further discussion on the resurrection, see part 2 of this book.

CHRIST'S VISIT TO THE SPIRIT WORLD

1 Peter 3:18–19 (JST)

18 For Christ also hath once suffered for sins, the just for the unjust, being put to death in the flesh, but quickened by the Spirit, that he might bring us to God.

19 For which cause also, he went and preached unto the spirits in prison.

This event was prophesied by Jesus himself: "The hour is coming, and now is, when the dead shall hear the voice of the Son of God: and they that hear shall live" (John 5:25). Christ's visit marked a historic first, a triumphal occasion in a world that lives in much darkness; it was the time not only for Christ to enter that world, but also for him to let his voice be heard in preaching, and to turn the key for others to preach the gospel as well. "The Son of God . . . was the first who declared the gospel unto the dead. No one else preached unto the dead until Christ went to them and opened the doors, and from that time forth the elders of Israel, who have passed away, have had the privilege of going to the spirit world and declaring the message of salvation"[5]

The Lord said through Zechariah, "By the blood of thy covenant I have sent forth thy prisoners out of the pit wherein is no water" (Zechariah 9:11). This may well have reference to the spirit prison. Until Christ's atonement and visit to the spirit world, there was no living water among the prisoners. Jesus brought that water by proclaiming the sweet and good news that the Atonement had been accomplished and that the prisoners—as they met the requirements of faith, repentance, and receiving the ordinances—could be set free.

President Joseph F. Smith gives us the most complete view of this marvelous occasion when Christ, after his crucifixion, went into the world of the dead to preach.[6] Here is part of what President Smith saw:

"As I pondered over these things which are written, the eyes of my understanding were opened, and the Spirit of the Lord rested upon me, and I saw the hosts of the dead, both small and great. And there were gathered together in one place an innumerable company of the spirits of the just, who had been faithful in the testimony of Jesus while they lived in mortality; and who had offered sacrifice in the similitude of the great sacrifice of the Son of God, and had suffered tribulation in their Redeemer's name. All these had departed the mortal life, firm in the hope of a glorious resurrection, through the grace of God the Father and his Only Begotten Son, Jesus Christ.

"I beheld that they were filled with joy and gladness, and were rejoicing together because the day of their deliverance was at hand. They were assembled awaiting the advent of the Son of God into the spirit world, to declare their redemption from the bands of death. . . .

"While this vast multitude waited and conversed, rejoicing in the hour of their deliverance from the chains of death, the Son of God appeared, declaring liberty to the captives who had been faithful; and there he preached to them the everlasting gospel, the doctrine of the resurrection and the redemption of mankind from the fall, and from individual sins on conditions of repentance.

"But unto the wicked he did not go, and among the ungodly and the unrepentant who had defiled themselves while in the flesh, his voice was not raised; . . .

"And the saints rejoiced in their redemption, and bowed the knee and acknowledged the Son of God as their Redeemer and Deliverer from death and the chains of hell. Their countenances shone, and the radiance from the presence of the Lord rested upon them, and they sang praises unto his holy name. . . .

"Thus was it made known that our Redeemer spent his time during his sojourn in the world of spirits, instructing and preparing the faithful spirits of the prophets who had testified of him in the flesh; that they might carry the message of redemption unto all the dead, unto whom he could not go personally, because of their rebellion and transgression, that they through the ministration of his servants might also hear his words.

"Among the great and mighty ones who were assembled in this vast congregation of the righteous were Father Adam, the Ancient of Days and father of all, and our glorious Mother Eve, with many of her faithful daughters who had lived through the ages and worshiped the true and living God. Abel, the first martyr, was there, and his brother Seth, one of the mighty ones, who was in the express image of his father, Adam. Noah, who gave warning of the flood; Shem, the great high priest; Abraham, the father of the faithful; Isaac, Jacob, and Moses, the great law-giver of Israel; and Isaiah, who declared by prophecy that the Redeemer was anointed to bind up the broken-hearted, to proclaim liberty to the captives, and the opening of the prison to them that were bound, were also there. Moreover, Ezekiel, who was shown in vision the great valley of dry bones, which were to be clothed upon with flesh, to come forth again in the resurrection of the dead, living souls; Daniel, who foresaw and foretold the establishment of the kingdom of God in the latter days, never again to be destroyed nor given to other people; Elias, who was with Moses on the Mount of Transfiguration; and Malachi, the prophet who testified of the coming of Elijah—of whom also Moroni spake to the Prophet Joseph Smith, declaring that he should come before the ushering in of the great and dreadful day of the Lord—were also there. . . . All these and many more, even the prophets who dwelt among the Nephites and testified of the coming of the Son of God, mingled in the vast assembly and waited for their deliverance, for the dead had looked upon the long absence of their spirits from their bodies as a bondage.

"These the Lord taught, and gave them power to come forth, after his resurrection from the dead, to enter his Father's kingdom, there to be crowned with immortality and eternal life" (D&C 138:11–16, 18–20, 23–24, 36–46, 49–51).[7]

Christ's visit to the spirit world is a wonderful testimony of his power over death. The spirits of the dead were gathered because of their faith in Christ and his power. "They were filled with joy and gladness, and were rejoicing together because the day of their deliverance was at hand." They were waiting expectantly for Christ "to declare their redemption from the bands of death," knowing they would soon be resurrected. When Christ appeared, he did indeed declare "liberty to the captives who had been faithful," and he preached "the doctrine of the resurrection and the redemption of mankind from the fall." The Saints responded by rejoicing "in their redemption," and they bowed before Christ "and acknowledged [him] as their Redeemer and Deliverer from death and the chains of hell." After teaching them, Jesus "gave them power to come forth, after his resurrection," in a resurrection of their own. Thus did he give them his greatest two gifts—"immortality and eternal life"—the first a gift that comes to all, the second a gift we receive "on conditions of repentance."

When Jesus announced himself as Messiah at the little synagogue in Nazareth, he quoted much of what we now have as Isaiah 61:1–2 (see Luke 4:16–19). Those words are a prophecy essentially outlining the mission of Jesus Christ to the people of the earth. But Isaiah's prophecy may have a dual application, also applying to Christ's mission to the spirit world: "The Spirit of the Lord God is upon me; because the Lord hath anointed me to preach good tidings unto the meek; he hath sent me to bind up the brokenhearted, to proclaim liberty to the captives, and the opening of the prison to them that are bound; to proclaim the acceptable year of the Lord, and the day of vengeance of our God; to comfort all that mourn; to appoint unto them that mourn in Zion, to give unto them beauty for ashes, the oil of joy for mourning, the garment of praise for the spirit of heaviness" (Isaiah 61:1–3).[8]

Elder Bruce R. McConkie described the scene when Jesus preached in paradise: "In his mortal ministry, Jesus the King, as a mortal, had spoken such words as never before man spake; yet they were addressed to weak and faltering and oftentimes rebellious mortals, none of whose hearts had yet begun to burn with the fires of the Spirit. Now in the paradise of God, among the righteous, who already knew the doctrines of salvation; who already had a hope of eternal life; and, above all, whose souls were already afire with the Holy Spirit of God—what wonders of divine truth he must have spoken as he prepared them for their not-distant resurrection! We assume he ministered and spoke almost continuously from the hour of his death to the hour of his resurrection, for, among them, there was no need to rest; none would grow weary or become inattentive. The weaknesses of the flesh were no longer theirs. Perhaps, also, he opened their minds and quickened their understandings so that they saw in vision the wonders of eternity. That we have not yet learned by revelation what was said and done there simply means that our weak and fragile spiritual stature does not as yet qualify us to know and understand what others more worthy and more qualified have received."[9]

NOTES AND COMMENTARY

1 Peter 3:18 *Christ also hath once suffered for sins.* No one has ever suffered as our Savior suffered. As he said in latter-day revelation, "Behold, I, God, have suffered these things for all, that they might not suffer if they would repent; but if they would not repent they must suffer even as I; which suffering caused myself, even God, the greatest of all, to tremble because of pain, and to bleed at every pore, and to suffer both body and spirit—and would that I might not drink the bitter cup, and shrink" (D&C 19:16–18). As this passage makes plain, we also suffer for sins if we do not repent—but the sins we suffer for are our own, while Christ suffered entirely because of and in behalf of others.

the just for the unjust. Jesus was "just," meaning justified or right or perfect in all he did. We are unjust, or unjustified. Another way to put this would be "the righteous for the unrighteous." It is a measure of Christ's infinite love for us that he suffered for us while we were yet in our sins.

quickened by the Spirit. Through his resurrection, Christ would be able to "bring us to God" if we took advantage of the other blessings of the Atonement. In the resurrection, he was "quickened by the Spirit," as Lehi taught: "The Holy Messiah . . . layeth down his life according to the flesh, and taketh it again by the power of the Spirit, that he may bring to pass the resurrection of the dead, being the first that should rise" (2 Nephi 2:8).

1 Peter 3:19 *by which also he went and preached.* For the cause of helping us return to our Father, Jesus went into the spirit world to preach the good news of his gospel of redemption.

Hugh Nibley has shared with us some valuable insights into the Lord's brief ministry to the spirit world, as seen through the eyes of some of the earliest Christian sources: "Following 1 Peter 4:6, it was believed in the early church that Christ preached 'to them that are dead.' 'For this reason,' says the Lord in the 'Discourse to the Apostles,' 'have I gone below and spoken to Abraham, Isaac, and Jacob, to your fathers, the prophets, and preached to them, that they might enjoy their rest in heaven.' To quote more fully a passage already cited from the Epistle of Barnabas, 'He opens to us, who were enslaved by death, the doors of the temple, that is the mouth; and by giving us repentance introduced us into the . . . spiritual temple builded for the Lord.' Christ is the king 'of those beneath the earth,' says Hippolytus, 'since he also was reckoned among the dead, while he was preaching the gospel to the spirits of the saints [or holy or righteous ones].' The same writer says Jesus 'became the evangelist of the dead, the liberator of spirits and the resurrection of those who had died.' The idea is thus expressed by the author of the Sibylline Discourses: 'He will come to Hades with tidings of hope to all the saints, and [tidings] of the end of time and the last day.' Clement of Alexandria is thus following the accepted doctrine when he says: 'Christ went down to Hades for no other purpose than to preach the gospel.' . . .

"'Descending into the other world,' says the old hymn, Christ 'prepared a road, and led in his footsteps all those whom he shall ransom, leading them into his flock, there to become indistinguishably

mingled with the rest of his sheep.' 'I made a congregation of the living in the realm of the dead,' says the Lord in the Odes of Solomon, 'I
spake to them with living lips . . . and sealed my name upon their
heads, because they are free and belong to me.' Another Ode says: 'I
went to all my imprisoned ones to free them . . . and they gathered
themselves together to me and were rescued; because they were members of me and I was their head.' 'He went down alone,' writes
Eusebius, citing a popular formula, 'but mounted up again with a great
host towards the Father.' Tertullian is more specific: 'Christ . . . did
not ascend to the higher heavens until he had descended to the lower
regions [lit. lower parts of the worlds], there to make the patriarchs
and prophets his compotes.' The word compos [singular form] in
Tertullian always denotes 'one who shares secret knowledge;' he made
them his disciples in the other world."[10]

the spirits in prison. As we learn in Joseph F. Smith's great vision
of the redemption of the dead, Jesus did not personally go to the
wicked in the spirit world but organized a missionary force to accomplish that task. Yet, in one sense, He did indeed preach to the spirits in
prison, since even paradise is a form of prison, as spirits labor in a
form of bondage until they can be reunited with their bodies. See the
discussion on the spirit prison above.

CHRIST OVERCOMES FEAR OF DEATH

Alma 27:28

> 28 . . . *they never did look upon death with any degree of
> terror, for their hope and views of Christ and the resurrection;
> therefore, death was swallowed up to them by the victory of
> Christ over it.*

Fear of death is commonplace among mankind. Much of the fear
stems from the fact that, without faith, we have no understanding of
what happens to our identity after we die.

This attitude is evident in portions of the book of Job. There Job
asks, "Are not my days few? cease then, and let me alone, that I may
take comfort a little, before I go whence I shall not return, even to
the land of darkness and the shadow of death; a land of darkness, as

darkness itself; and of the shadow of death, without any order, and where the light is as darkness" (Job 10:20–22).

In this passage Job expresses a feeling that is held by many in the world, particularly those who do not know Christ or his gospel: the world of the dead is a place of darkness, shadow, lack of order. In fact, the words darkness and shadow are repeated six times in two verses.

A few chapters later Job repeats a similar feeling of despair: "Man that is born of a woman is of few days, and full of trouble. He cometh forth like a flower, and is cut down: he fleeth also as a shadow, and continueth not. . . .

"For there is hope of a tree, if it be cut down, that it will sprout again, and that the tender branch thereof will not cease. Though the root thereof wax old in the earth, and the stock thereof die in the ground; yet through the scent of water it will bud, and bring forth boughs like a plant.

"But man dieth, and wasteth away: yea, man giveth up the ghost, and where is he? As the waters fail from the sea, and the flood decayeth and drieth up: so man lieth down, and riseth not: till the heavens be no more, they shall not awake, nor be raised out of their sleep" (Job 14:1–2, 7–12).[11]

Others in scripture have also given voice to these feelings of lack of hope in the face of death. The Psalmist wrote, "O Lord, deliver my soul: oh save me for thy mercies' sake. For in death there is no remembrance of thee: in the grave who shall give thee thanks?" (Psalm 6:4–5). The Preacher in Ecclesiastes said, "Whatsoever thy hand findeth to do, do it with thy might; for there is no work, nor device, nor knowledge, nor wisdom, in the grave, whither thou goest" (Ecclesiastes 9:10).

We learn from the Book of Mormon that the source of such doctrine is the devil. Korihor, who was led by the devil, taught that "when a man was dead, that was the end thereof" (Alma 30:18).

It is true that without Christ there is great cause to fear death. Jacob taught that without the Atonement "this corruption could not put on incorruption. . . . And if so, this flesh must have laid down to rot and to crumble to its mother earth, to rise no more. . . . [And] behold, if the flesh should rise no more our spirits must become subject to that angel who fell from before the presence of the Eternal God, and became the devil, to rise no more. And our spirits must have become like unto him, and we become devils, angels to a devil, to be shut out from the presence of our God, and to remain with the father of lies, in misery, like unto himself" (2 Nephi 9:7–9).

Without Christ, death is an "awful monster" (2 Nephi 9:10). But Satan's lie is that there is no Atonement, that the promises of Christ are not real or valid. As Paul wrote, "If in this life only we have hope in Christ, we are of all men most miserable" (1 Corinthians 15:19). But we do have hope in Christ, both in this life and in the life to come. We need not fear, because we have a Savior who has conquered death for us all: "Now is Christ risen from the dead, and become the first-fruits of them that slept. . . . For as in Adam all die, even so in Christ shall all be made alive" (1 Corinthians 15:20, 22).

It is because of Christ that we can feel as the people of Anti-Nephi-Lehi did: "They never did look upon death with any degree of terror, for their hope and views of Christ and the resurrection; therefore, death was swallowed up to them by the victory of Christ over it" (Alma 27:28).

"Wherefore," the Lord said to the people of this dispensation, "fear not even unto death; for in this world your joy is not full, but in me your joy is full. Therefore, care not for the body, neither the life of the body; but care for the soul, and for the life of the soul" (D&C 101:36–37).

When we have hope in Christ, we can have the attitude toward death that Brigham Young spoke of at the funeral of his sister, Fanny Young. He said, "I do not mourn for Sister Fanny: I rejoice. She has lived upwards of three score years and ten, and exhibited the retention of sound sense to her last days with us here. She said to her sister, Nancy, a short time ago, 'If you hear of my being dead before you come to see me again, let the first thing you say be "Hallelujah!"' That remark, to me, evidences the retention of sound judgment."[12]

PART 2

UNDERSTANDING THE RESURRECTION

*O*ur prophets have spoken of the atoning sacrifice and resurrection of Jesus Christ as the greatest event in human history.[1] Such a statement is self-evident to all who give it any consideration—what could be greater than the act that provided our rescue from sin and death?

Sin and death are the two greatest enemies of the human race, both introduced into the world by the fall of Adam and Eve. The atonement of Jesus Christ conquered both those enemies, overcoming death for all mankind and overcoming sin for all who will repent and follow their Redeemer.

"The atonement," wrote President Gordon B. Hinckley, "is the greatest miracle" of all time.[2] What could be a greater miracle than cleansing a soul spotted with sin, or raising a long-dead, totally disintegrated body from the grave? Other miracles—walking on water, calming the seas, healing the blind, multiplying the bread and the fishes—are of great importance. But the miracles that flow from the Atonement, the miracles that vanquish death, the miracles that help us overcome sin—these are what open wide the door to our eternal exaltation.

The atonement for sin and the atonement for death work in tandem with each other. Both are essential for us to come to true godliness. If we were redeemed from death but not cleansed from sin, we would rise from the grave as corrupted souls. If we were sanctified from sin but never resurrected, we would not be corporeal as God is, and we would never attain to a fulness of joy (see D&C 93:33–34). No wonder prophets and saints alike have raised their voices in praise of our Father and his Beloved Son, who provided an escape from the clutches of these great enemies. But their love is so perfect and their plan so divine that they did much more than enable us to be raised from death to sinless, immortal bodies. They intend to raise us to glory!

*The resurrection was the culminating act of the marvelous atone-
ment of Christ. It is "the visible, outward manifestation of the more
invisible and inward spiritual triumph of the Atonement." As such,
"it remains the grand, central fact at the heart of the Christian message. It is the sublime reality that sets Christianity apart from all
other religions."³ Thus the resurrection, supremely important in its
own right, also stands as a symbol of the many other blessings of the
Atonement. If the resurrection is real and true, then Christ's other
powers to bless and lift us unto the Father are likewise real.*

*Speaking of the resurrection as the culmination of the Atonement,
President Hinckley said, "Of all the victories in human history, none is
so great, none so universal in its effect, none so everlasting in its consequences as the victory of the crucified Lord who came forth in the
Resurrection that first Easter morning.*

*"We laud the captains and the kings, we praise the nations that
are victorious against oppressors. We appropriately build monuments
to remember their sacrifices and their triumphs over the forces of
oppression. But great and important as are these achievements, none
can compare with the victory of the lonely, pain-racked figure on
Calvary's cross who triumphed over death and brought the gift of eternal life to all mankind."⁴*

*The scope of the resurrection is infinite. It affects every member
of the human family in every age of the world. It blesses every person
from every world created by Christ. It reaches back to the beginning of
time and forward to the end of the world. It blesses animals, plants,
and the earth itself. No dead body will ever be forgotten—all will be
resurrected. No body will be lost in the utmost parts of the earth—the
Lord knows all, and all will rise from the dead. God will indeed resurrect every member of the human family, with no exceptions. With
reference to the resurrection, John Taylor assured us, "Its scope
embraced all peoples, nations and tongues."⁵*

*As we seek a deeper understanding of the glorious doctrine of the
resurrection, this section of the book will discuss*

- *the many types and shadows pointing to the resurrection,*
- *the keys Jesus Christ holds that make the resurrection possible,*

- *how Jesus Christ destroyed death and has mankind,*
- *the resurrection as part of Christ's infinite atonement.*
- *the many witnesses and descriptions of the resurrected Lord,*
- *the many wonderful capabilities possessed by resurrected beings,*
- *celestial, terrestrial, and telestial beings in the resurrection,*
- *the times and the order of the resurrection,*
- *the continuation of family relationships among the righteous after the resurrection,*
- *how we would be without hope, without comfort, and without ultimate redemption if there were no resurrection,*
- *the existence and advantage after the resurrection of intelligence gained in mortality,*
- *how understanding the resurrection guides us to righteousness, and*
- *the universal nature of the resurrection.*

Few gospel topics bring as much comfort and peace as the resurrection. In fact, Paul instructed us to give comfort to one another by teaching the resurrection. After speaking of Jesus' resurrection and our subsequent resurrection, Paul charged, "Comfort one another with these words . . ." (see 1 Thessalonians 4:14–18). In association with this, Elder Neal A. Maxwell taught, "Our 'brightness of hope' [see 1 Nephi 31:20] . . . means that at funerals our tears are genuine, but not because of termination—rather because of interruption. Though just as wet, our tears are not of despair but are of appreciation and anticipation. Yes, for disciples, the closing of a grave is but the closing of a door which later will be flung open with rejoicing. We say humbly but firmly that it is the garden tomb—not life—that is empty."[6]

CHAPTER 5

THE RESURRECTION: FORESHADOWED WITH TYPES

The prophets, both ancient and modern, have provided us with a host of clear statements that help us understand the resurrection. In addition to these statements, they have also taught us much about the resurrection by using types and shadows. In the language of the Book of Mormon, a type is an event or image of something that encourages one to *look forward* to the future. The Law of Moses, for instance, encouraged the Israelites to "*look forward* to the coming of Christ, considering that the law of Moses was a type of his coming" (Alma 25:15; emphasis added). Also, "these ordinances were given after this manner, that thereby the people might *look forward* on the Son of God, it being a type of his order, or it being his order, and this that they might *look forward* to him for a remission of their sins" (Alma 13:16; emphasis added). King Benjamin declared that God had given to ancient Israel "many signs, and wonders, and types, and shadows" (Mosiah 3:15).

Most types and shadows point to Jesus Christ. According to Nephi, "all things which have been given of God from the beginning of the world, unto man, are the typifying of him" (2 Nephi 11:4). And the Lord revealed through Moses, "All things have their likeness, and all things are created and made to bear record of me, both things which are temporal, and things which are spiritual; things which are in the heavens above, and things which are on the earth, and things which are in the earth, and things which are under the earth, both above and beneath: all things bear record of me" (Moses 6:63). What *things* bear record of Jesus? Temporal things, spiritual things, things in heaven and on earth, and in the earth, and under the earth, and so on.

As stated above, most types refer to Jesus Christ, his atonement, mission, and ministry. In this chapter we will examine a number of scriptural types that pertain to his resurrection and the resurrection of all humanity. As with all types, those presented here are designed to encourage the reader to *look forward,* in this case to the resurrection. These types are a great blessing to us as they add to our understanding and prepare us for what is to come.

Sleep. Our nightly sleep is a type and a shadow for death, and awakening in the morning symbolizes the resurrection. (See also the parallels listed under "Morning," below.) Daniel used the word *sleep* to refer to death and *awake* to refer to the resurrection. "And many of them that sleep in the dust of the earth shall awake, some to everlasting life, and some to shame and everlasting contempt" (Daniel 12:2). Other prophets have used similar language. (See commentary on "Those Who Sleep in the Dust Shall No Longer Slumber.")

Jonah and the Great Fish. Jonah's experience with the great fish typified Jesus' death and resurrection. Both were buried deep in their respective tombs, Jonah in the belly of the fish and Jesus in the belly of the earth. Both spent approximately three days and three nights there; and both were brought forth on the third day. As Bruce R. McConkie wrote, "Jonas's burial in and coming forth from the 'great fish' (Jonah 1:15–17; 2) symbolizes the death, burial, and resurrection of Christ."[1] (See commentary on "The Sign of the Prophet Jonah.")

Baptism. Our baptism into The Church of Jesus Christ of Latter-day Saints represents death and resurrection. On the one hand, it represents the "death" of our disobedient, sinful selves, and our spiritual "resurrection" into a newness of life. But it also represents our physical death and resurrection. Immersion prefigures death and burial, and coming forth from the water anticipates resurrection, or coming forth from the grave. In Romans 6:3–11, a discourse on baptism, Paul used many terms that pertain to death—*dead, buried, death,* and *died.* He also used terms that speak of the resurrection—*raised up, newness of life, resurrection, live, raised from the dead, liveth,* and *alive.* (See commentary on "Baptism—Symbol of Death and Resurrection.")

Raising of Lazarus. The raising of Lazarus from the dead typifies the resurrection from the dead. Language used in the Lazarus account pertains to both death and the resurrection—*died, rise again,* and *life* (see John 11:21–26). Just as Lazarus died and was brought back to life through the power of Jesus Christ, so too will all the dead be brought back to life in the resurrection through the power of Jesus' atonement. It is likely that every person who has ever been raised from the dead by the power of the priesthood is a type and a shadow of the resurrection. (See commentary on "The Raising of Lazarus: A Type of the Resurrection.")

Translated Beings. Souls who have been translated by the power of God typify resurrected beings. Those who have been translated are changed in their bodies so that they cannot suffer physical pain, sickness, hunger, thirst, or fatigue. They cannot die until God so ordains, but they will yet die. Both translated and resurrected beings have remarkable bodies that are not akin to mortal bodies. Like translated beings, resurrected souls will never taste of death or experience physical pain, and Satan has no power over them. Both resurrected personages and translated beings have the power to hide their true identity from mortals, and both have power over the elements of the earth. (For further discussion on the nature of translated beings, see commentary on "'A Greater Change': Translated and Resurrected Beings," in this chapter.)

Morning. Our prophets have frequently referred to the "morning of the first resurrection," which is the resurrection that will take place at Christ's second coming. Brigham Young, for example, declared, "The very particles that compose our bodies will be brought forth in the morning of the resurrection, and our spirits will then have tabernacles to be clothed with, as they have now, only they will be immortal tabernacles—spiritual tabernacles."[2] It may be that the *morning* of the day is a type that looks forward to the resurrection. The first obvious parallel is that Christ was resurrected in the morning (Mark 16:1–6), Sunday morning, now known as Easter morning.

There are other parallels. Morning comes at daybreak or sunrise, which corresponds with the increased light that people will gain at the resurrection. During the night, we sleep, a similitude to those who are sleeping in their graves. Then in the morning, we rise out of bed, in likeness of our rising out of the grave. During our sleep, we have no consciousness, but when we awake we have full consciousness. Similarly, during our sleep of death our bodies have no consciousness, but at the resurrection our bodies, united with our spirits, will have full consciousness. Morning brings physical refreshment to those who have slept just as the resurrection will give eternal vigor to our souls. "As we rise in the morning from our night's rest, so it will be with us in the resurrection," said Charles W. Penrose.[3]

Birth. Our birth into mortality occurred after our spirits entered our bodies and subsequent to our mothers' delivery. Similarly, our resurrection will occur after our spirits enter our bodies and subsequent to our delivery from the grave. Hence, our birth into mortality is a type of our resurrection into immortality. Brigham Young once stated, "The resurrection from the dead may also, with propriety, be called a birth."[4] Elder Charles W. Penrose, too, likened birth to the resurrection. "I want to impress . . . the fact that the resurrection will prove to be just as natural as birth."[5]

The items listed above—sleep, Jonah and the fish, baptism, the raising of Lazarus, translated beings, morning, and birth—embrace only a few of the types that look forward to death or resurrection. Other items may be considered. For instance, the Mosaic laws that pertain to leprosy (Leviticus 13–14) and to corpses (Numbers 19) have symbolic elements that point to or anticipate death and resurrection.

THOSE WHO SLEEP IN THE DUST SHALL NO LONGER SLUMBER

Daniel 12:2–3

2 And many of them that sleep in the dust of the earth shall awake, some to everlasting life, and some to shame and everlasting contempt.

3 And they that be wise shall shine as the brightness of the firmament; and they that turn many to righteousness as the stars for ever and ever.

Many of Daniel's prophecies pertain to the last days and the end of times. He prophesied of the restoration of the latter-day kingdom

of God upon the earth, of the great meeting that will be held at Adam-
ondi-Ahman, and of various things that pertain to the latter days. In
the beginning verses of chapter 12, the prophet foretold of the resurrection. He referred to death as sleeping in the earth's dust and to resurrection as awakening from that sleep. His use of the symbol of *sleep*
for *death* has subsequently been used by many other prophets and
scriptural writers (see examples in Notes and Commentary, below).
President John Taylor, for example, used *slumber* in the following
assertion: "Man is an eternal being; his body is eternal. It may die and
slumber, but it will burst the barriers of the tomb and come forth in
the resurrection of the just."[6] Joseph F. Smith used slumber similarly
in a discussion of death and resurrection: "That which we call death
is merely the slumber and rest of this mortal clay, and that only for a
little season."[7]

NOTES AND COMMENTARY

Daniel 12:2 *them that sleep in the dust of the earth.* This refers
to those who have died, whose bodies are in the earth and whose spirits are in the spirit world awaiting the resurrection. The power of
Jesus Christ and his atonement enables humanity to awake from their
sleep, for without the Atonement their sleep would be an "endless
sleep"—they would never receive a resurrection. Mormon 9:13 reads,
"Because of the redemption of man, which came by Jesus Christ,
they are brought back into the presence of the Lord; yea, this is
wherein all men are redeemed, because the death of Christ bringeth to
pass the resurrection, which bringeth to pass a redemption from an
endless sleep."

shall awake. At the resurrection, the bodies of the dead will
become animate and awaken when their spirits reunite with them. The
righteous will be blessed to awaken and receive the resurrection some
time before the wicked. The Lord revealed to Joseph Smith, "The
trump of God shall sound both long and loud, and shall say to the
sleeping nations: Ye Saints arise and live; ye sinners stay and sleep
until I shall call again" (D&C 43:18).

*some to everlasting life . . . some to shame and everlasting con-
tempt.* Depending on their works and choices during mortality, people
will receive one of two resurrections. The righteous will awaken to

everlasting or eternal life, but the wicked will awaken to "shame and everlasting contempt." Jesus' words correspond with Daniel's: "The hour is coming, in the which all that are in the graves shall hear his voice, and shall come forth; they that have done good, unto the resurrection of life; and they that have done evil, unto the resurrection of damnation" (John 5:28–29).

Daniel 12:3 *they that be wise shall shine as the brightness of the firmament.* Those who made wise choices during mortality, who kept the commandments and worshiped the true and living God, will be blessed with light and glory forever. Daniel compared these to the bright lights of the skies, including the sun and the stars. Doctrine and Covenants 76 provides a more detailed description of the brightness spoken of by Daniel: "These are they who shall have part in the first resurrection. These are they who shall come forth in the resurrection of the just. . . . These are they whose bodies are celestial, whose glory is that of the sun, even the glory of God, the highest of all, whose glory the sun of the firmament is written of as being typical" (D&C 76:64–65, 70; see also Alma 40:25).

they that turn many to righteousness as the stars for ever and ever. Daniel employed two similes in verse 3 to describe the nature of the righteous at the resurrection. The first compares the righteous to the "brightness of the firmament" (discussed above); the second compares the righteous to the stars. Those who direct others to righteousness, taught Daniel, will be like the stars, which produce light, provide direction, and exist eternally in the heavens.

THE SIGN OF THE PROPHET JONAH

Matthew 12:39–41

> *39 But he answered and said unto them, An evil and adulterous generation seeketh after a sign; and there shall no sign be given to it, but the sign of the prophet Jonas:*
>
> *40 For as Jonas was three days and three nights in the whale's belly; so shall the Son of man be three days and three nights in the heart of the earth.*
>
> *41 The men of Nineveh shall rise in judgment with this generation, and shall condemn it: because they repented at*

*the preaching of Jonas; and, behold, a greater than Jonas is
here.*

The experience of Jonah (in Greek, Jonas) and the great fish typified and anticipated the burial and resurrection of Jesus Christ. Long
before Jesus' birth in Bethlehem, the Lord with his divine foreknowl-
edge brought about certain events in Jonah's life that would typify circumstances related to Jesus Christ. For example, the Lord called Jonah
to preach repentance to the people of Nineveh (see Jonah 1:2); then,
after his prophet attempted to flee from him (which, of course, was
very unlike Christ), he worked with the natural world to accomplish
his purposes: he "*sent* out a great wind into the sea . . . so that the ship
was like to be broken" (Jonah 1:4; emphasis added); he "*prepared* a
great fish to swallow up Jonah" (Jonah 1:17; emphasis added); and he
"*spake* unto the fish, and it vomited out Jonah upon the dry land"
(Jonah 2:10; emphasis added). All of these workings with the natural
world served God's purpose several centuries later when Jesus stood
before a group of Pharisees and scribes and told them of the sign of
Jonah, a sign that he, the Lord, would be resurrected after spending
three days and three nights in the tomb.

NOTES AND COMMENTARY

Matthew 12:39 *he answered and said unto them.* Jesus was
speaking to a group of scribes and Pharisees who had asked for a sign.

An evil and adulterous generation seeketh after a sign. One
explanation of this is that the group of sign seekers to whom Jesus was
speaking included evil men and adulterers.

Joseph Smith shared the following experience: "When I was
preaching in Philadelphia, a Quaker called out for a sign. I told him to
be still. After the sermon, he again asked for a sign. I told the congregation the man was an adulterer; that a wicked and adulterous
generation seeketh after a sign; and that the Lord had said to me in a
revelation, that any man who wanted a sign was an adulterous person. 'It is true,' cried one, 'for I caught him in the very act,' which
the man afterwards confessed when he was baptized."[8]

Of course, Jesus could also have been referring to *spiritual* adultery—that is, to idolatry, or having gods other than the Lord. This

symbol was used throughout the Old Testament. Those who ask for a sign are not really seeking the true God but are asking out of their own pride or arrogance, as the Pharisees did, which is a sign of spiritual adultery.

the sign of the prophet Jonas. The sign of Jonah refers to Christ's resurrection. In a number of ways, Jonah served as a type and a shadow of Christ's burial and resurrection: (1) Both Jonah and Jesus were buried in the deep. While inside the fish, Jonah cried out that he was buried in the "belly of hell [*sheol*]" (or the world of spirits);[9] he was "cast . . . into the deep" and "went down to the bottoms of the mountains" (Jonah 2:2, 3, 6). Jesus was buried in a sepulchre in the earth. (2) Both spent "three days and three nights" in their respective tombs—Jonah in the "whale's belly," Jesus "in the heart of the earth" (Matthew 12:40). (3) Both Jesus and Jonah were brought forth from their places of burial. Jonah prayed from the fish's belly: "I went down to the bottoms of the mountains; the earth with her bars was about me for ever: yet hast thou brought up my life from corruption, O Lord my God" (Jonah 2:6). "Brought up" (or "raised up") and "corruption" are both phrases used in connection with the resurrection (for "raised up," see Acts 13:33; Romans 6:4; for "corruption," see 1 Corinthians 15:50; Alma 40:2). Jonah was brought forth from the fish's belly and its corruptible influences; Jesus was raised up from the tomb and his corruptible (mortal) body became incorruptible (immortal).

Matthew 12:40 *For as Jonas was three days and three nights in the whale's belly.* Jesus referred to Jonah and his occupation of the fish's belly for three days and three nights. Then he said, "So shall the Son of man be three days and three nights in the heart of the earth," referring to the time that he would spend in the tomb.

Some students of the scriptures sense a problem with the time period that Christ spent in the tomb: If Jesus died on Friday evening and arose on Sunday morning, how can this be reckoned to be "three days and three nights"? Biblical scholar D. A. Carson explains, "According to Jewish tradition, 'three days and three nights' need mean no more than 'three days' or the combination of any part of three separate days."[10] Thus part of Friday, all day Saturday, and part of Sunday fulfills the requirement of "any part of three separate days."

Matthew 12:41 *The men of Nineveh shall rise in judgment with this generation.* Jonah prophesied of the downfall of Nineveh, the capital city of Assyria, located on the Tigris River. "Yet forty days," the prophet declared, "and Nineveh shall be overthrown" (Jonah 3:4). Jonah's preaching and prophesying was effective because "the people of Nineveh believed God." Moreover, their king proclaimed a fast for both man and beast and commanded, "Let man and beast be covered with sackcloth, and cry mightily unto God: yea, let them turn every one from his evil way, and from the violence that is in their hands" (Jonah 3:5–8). God witnessed the acts of repentance of the inhabitants of Nineveh and determined not to destroy them.

These repentant inhabitants of Nineveh became a sign to the Jews at the time of Jesus. As Jesus stated, "The men of Nineveh shall rise in judgment with this generation, and shall condemn it: because they repented at the preaching of Jonas; and, behold, a greater than Jonas is here." The one greater than Jonah was Jesus himself. Though the men of Nineveh repented after hearing Jonah, the Jews of Jesus' time would not repent at the preaching of Jesus. Therefore the Jews received condemnation, where the people of Nineveh escaped theirs through heeding and repentance.

BAPTISM—SYMBOL OF DEATH AND RESURRECTION

Romans 6:3–11

> *3 Know ye not, that so many of us as were baptized into Jesus Christ were baptized into his death?*
>
> *4 Therefore we are buried with him by baptism into death: that like as Christ was raised up from the dead by the glory of the Father, even so we also should walk in newness of life.*
>
> *5 For if we have been planted together in the likeness of his death, we shall be also in the likeness of his resurrection:*
>
> *6 Knowing this, that our old man is crucified with him, that the body of sin might be destroyed, that henceforth we should not serve sin.*
>
> *7 For he that is dead is freed from sin.*
>
> *8 Now if we be dead with Christ, we believe that we shall also live with him:*

9 Knowing that Christ being raised from the dead dieth no more; death hath no more dominion over him.

10 For in that he died, he died unto sin once: but in that he liveth, he liveth unto God.

11 Likewise reckon ye also yourselves to be dead indeed unto sin, but alive unto God through Jesus Christ our Lord.

Paul, in his epistle to the Romans, likened the ordinance of baptism to death and resurrection. Immersion prefigures death and burial, and coming forth from the water anticipates resurrection, or the coming forth from the grave: "The ordinance of baptism by water, to be immersed therein in order to answer to the likeness of the dead, that one principle might accord with the other; to be immersed in the water and come forth out of the water is in the likeness of the resurrection of the dead in coming out of their graves" (D&C 128:12). Paul used a number of terms that pertain to death: *dead* (five times), *buried, old man is crucified, body . . . might be destroyed, death* (four times), *dieth, died* (twice). He also referred to the resurrection: *raised up, newness of life, resurrection, live, raised from the dead, liveth* (twice), *alive.* The baptismal font itself signifies the grave: "The baptismal font was instituted as a similitude of the grave, and was commanded to be in a place underneath where the living are wont to assemble, to show forth the living and the dead, and that all things may have their likeness" (D&C 128:13).

The entire baptismal ordinance focuses on Jesus Christ. It is conducted in his name, and the priest performing the baptism cites Christ's authority (3 Nephi 11:23–26; D&C 20:73). The priest himself is a type and shadow of Jesus Christ, who is called "a priest for ever after the order of Melchisedec" (Hebrews 7:17; Psalms 110:4). As a type of Jesus, the priest raises the baptismal candidate out of the water just as Jesus Christ's power will one day raise us at the resurrection out of our graves. Additionally, every baptism recalls Christ's own death and resurrection, as Paul explained so clearly to his Roman audience. (See also Colossians 2:12, "Buried with [Christ] in baptism, wherein also ye are risen with him.") Baptism also focuses on Christ in that it is through his atonement that it is possible for the baptismal candidate to become a new creature, alive in Christ. The reality of a physical resurrection adds even more meaning to the concept of a spiritual resurrection from our former ungodly selves.

NOTES AND COMMENTARY

Romans 6:3 *baptized into Jesus Christ.* Jesus Christ is the focus of the baptismal ordinance and of all gospel ordinances, such as the sacrament and administering to the sick. People who are "baptized into Jesus Christ" are those who are "born again; yea, born of God, changed from their carnal and fallen state, to a state of righteousness, being redeemed of God, becoming his sons and daughters" (Mosiah 27:25).

baptized into his death. Throughout Romans 6 Paul compared burial in the waters of baptism to Jesus' burial in the tomb. In verse 3 he uses the phrase "baptized into his death"; in verse 4 he writes, "buried with him by baptism into death"; in verse 5 he explains, "we have been planted together in the likeness of his death"; and in verse 8 he uses the phrase "if we be dead with Christ." In all of these phrases, Jesus Christ is the focal point.

Scripture revealed through Joseph Smith also places baptism and burial in the same context. "This is the testimony of the gospel of Christ concerning them who shall come forth in the resurrection of the just—They are they who received the testimony of Jesus, and believed on his name and were baptized after the manner of his burial, being buried in the water in his name" (D&C 76:50–51). JST Genesis 17:5 also refers to "the burial, or baptism."

In some of his writings, Paul compared baptized individuals to the *dead*, because the individual's former spiritual life is now gone, buried beneath the baptismal waters: "If ye be dead with Christ from the rudiments of the world, why, as though living in the world, are ye subject to ordinances" (Colossians 2:20), he wrote to the Colossians. Also, "Ye are dead, and your life is hid with Christ in God" (Colossians 3:3). And Paul wrote to Timothy, "It is a faithful saying: For if we be dead with him, we shall also live with him" (2 Timothy 2:11).

Romans 6:4 *like as Christ was raised up . . . even so we also should walk in newness of life.* Paul used terms of comparison, "like as . . . even so," to link Christ's resurrection to the baptism of Christ's followers. With both baptism and resurrection, people are "raised up" from either water or the grave. And with both resurrection and baptism, people "walk in newness of life," one as an immortal and the other as a new spiritual being. Jesus Christ, as Paul witnessed, is the source of power that brings the resurrection as well as newness of life to those who receive baptism.

Romans 6:5 *likeness of his death . . . likeness of his resurrection.* Once more Paul compared Christ's death and resurrection to baptism, twice using *likeness,* a term of comparison. Paul's words become more personal to us because he uses the pronoun *we:* "*we* [are] planted in the likeness of his death, *we* shall be also in the likeness of his resurrection.

Romans 6:6 *our old man is crucified with him.* Unrepentant sinners are like old men who are dying, not physically but spiritually. Our unrepentant, guilty selves need to be "put to death," not physically but spiritually. At baptism, Paul says, those who are truly repentant are figuratively crucified with Jesus Christ. That is to say, they acknowledge Jesus' suffering and death on the cross, and they make his atoning sacrifice effective in their own lives. Their old sinful selves "die," and they become like resurrected beings will be, pure and bright before God. Note Paul's language regarding the destruction of the former sinful self: "our old man is crucified" and "the body of sin" is "destroyed." In another setting Paul invited the Ephesians to "put off . . . the old man, which is corrupt according to the deceitful lusts; and be renewed in the spirit of your mind; and that ye put on the new man, which after God is created in righteousness and true holiness" (Ephesians 4:22–24; see also Colossians 3:9).

henceforth we should not serve sin. Individuals who are truly converted to Jesus Christ and his gospel lose the tendency and desire to serve sin. But this loss of desire to serve sin comes only after we have denied ourselves of all ungodliness (as Paul states, "that the body of sin might be destroyed"), and after we have permitted the grace of God to work in our lives. Moroni wrote this significant and illuminating statement: "Come unto Christ, and be perfected in him, and deny yourselves of all ungodliness; and if ye shall deny yourselves of all ungodliness, and love God with all your might, mind and strength, then is his grace sufficient for you, that by his grace ye may be perfect in Christ; and if by the grace of God ye are perfect in Christ, ye can in nowise deny the power of God. And again, if ye by the grace of God are perfect in Christ, and deny not his power, then are ye sanctified in Christ by the grace of God, through the shedding of the blood of Christ, which is in the covenant of the Father unto the remission of your sins, that ye become holy, without spot" (Moroni 10:32–33).

Romans 6:7 *For he that is dead is freed from sin.* The Joseph Smith Translation clarifies this passage with the addition of the words "to sin": "For he that is dead *to sin* is freed from sin."

Romans 6:9 *Christ being raised from the dead dieth no more.* Paul communicated an important doctrine about the resurrection. Once Jesus Christ, and for that matter any individual, has been resurrected, he or she will never die again. "Death hath no more dominion over him" or her.

Romans 6:10 *he died unto sin once.* For more than a millennium, high priests who served under the Mosaic Law offered up animal sacrifices daily. These sacrifices looked forward to the great and last sacrifice of Jesus Christ, who, of course, was not required to die more than once. As Paul explained to the Hebrews, "So Christ was once offered to bear the sins of many" (Hebrews 9:28); and additionally, Jesus, "who needeth not daily, as those high priests, to offer up sacrifice, first for his own sins, and then for the people's: for this he did once, when he offered up himself" (Hebrews 7:27); and again, "By the which will we are sanctified through the offering of the body of Jesus Christ once for all" (Hebrews 10:10).

Romans 6:11 *but alive unto God through Jesus Christ our Lord.* This phrase sums up Paul's discourse on baptism. Baptized individuals who have come unto Christ and have forsaken their sins are spiritually "alive unto God." This is but a type and a shadow of what souls will be like after their resurrection—souls spiritually alive "unto God through Jesus Christ our Lord."

THE RAISING OF LAZARUS: A TYPE OF THE RESURRECTION

John 11:21–26

21 Then said Martha unto Jesus, Lord, if thou hadst been here, my brother had not died.

22 But I know, that even now, whatsoever thou wilt ask of God, God will give it thee.

23 Jesus saith unto her, Thy brother shall rise again.

24 Martha saith unto him, I know that he shall rise again in the resurrection at the last day.

25 Jesus said unto her, I am the resurrection, and the life: he that believeth in me, though he were dead, yet shall he live:

26 And whosoever liveth and believeth in me shall never die. Believest thou this?

The raising of Lazarus from the dead serves as a type and a shadow of the resurrection from the dead. Just as Lazarus died and was brought back to life through the power of Jesus Christ, so too will the dead be brought back to life in the resurrection through the power of Jesus' atonement. Three expressions used in John 11:21–26—*died, rise again,* and *life*—refer to Lazarus' rising from the dead. These three expressions also apply to the resurrection, for those who have *died* will eventually *rise again* into immortal *life* at the resurrection.

Jesus, then, used the setting of Lazarus' death to teach concerning the resurrection. Previous to Lazarus' renewal to life, Jesus instructed Martha, Lazarus' sister, "I am the resurrection, and the life: he that believeth in me, though he were dead, yet shall he live" (v. 25).

NOTES AND COMMENTARY

John 11:21 *Then said Martha unto Jesus.* The conversation between Martha and Jesus begins with Martha's statement about her brother's death, but it soon turns to the topic of the resurrection.

Lord, if thou hadst been here, my brother had not died. These words do not express rebuke on Martha's part but are a manifestation of her faith. Her meaning was that if the Lord had been there, he could have healed Lazarus from his sickness and blessed him with life. The words may have echoed what Martha and Mary had thought or expressed to one another since their brother's death four days earlier. Mary, too, would utter the same words to the Lord during her meeting with him, "Lord, . . . " (John 11:32).

John 11:22 *But I know.* Twice in the narrative Martha uses the expression "I know," here and again in verse 24. Martha knows, "even now," after Lazarus has been dead for four days, that Jesus has the power to raise him from the dead. Martha also knows about the doctrine of the resurrection: "I know that he shall rise again in the resurrection at the last day" (v. 24).

whatsoever thou wilt ask of God, God will give it thee. These words reveal the extent of Martha's faith. Notwithstanding the fact that Lazarus is now dead, she knows that Jesus simply has to pray to the Father and the Father will grant him whatever he asks.

John 11:23 *Thy brother shall rise again.* Jesus' promise that Martha's brother will rise again has a double meaning—(1) very shortly, Lazarus will rise from the dead when Jesus commands him to come forth from the tomb; and (2) Lazarus will rise again at the resurrection. Martha's response to Jesus' promise indicates that she interprets his words to have the second meaning: "I know that he shall rise again in the resurrection at the last day" (v. 24).

John 11:24 *resurrection at the last day.* The knowledge that the resurrection will take place at the end of the world is a certainty for Martha. She knows that her brother will rise again on a far-off day; but she longs for his companionship now.

John 11:25 *I am the resurrection, and the life.* These especially majestic words distinguish Jesus Christ from all others who have lived upon the earth. These words have also served to comfort millions of Christians through the centuries who have lost loved ones to physical death. *Resurrection* points to the immortality that all mortals will someday experience, and *life* seems to speak of the gift of eternal life that is reserved for those who have lived their lives in harmony with God's commandments.

Note that Jesus does not say, "I will be the resurrection and the life," but "I am the resurrection and the life." *I am* establishes that Jesus at that time possessed the power of the resurrection and the power to give life. Hannah, the mother of the prophet Samuel and the wife of Elkanah, had knowledge of this more than a millennium earlier. In what is now known as the Song of Hannah, this inspired woman wrote concerning the Lord's power to give life and to resurrect: "The Lord killeth, and maketh alive: he bringeth down to the grave, and bringeth up" (1 Samuel 2:6).

John 11:26 *whosoever liveth and believeth in me shall never die.* These words do not indicate that those who believe in Jesus Christ will not die a physical death. Certainly millions of Christian believers have died since Jesus uttered these words. And all except Christ himself have suffered spiritual death through sin. But those who believe in and follow Christ will be reborn to a new life, from which, if they remain faithful, they shall never die.

"A GREATER CHANGE": TRANSLATED BEINGS AND RESURRECTED BEINGS

3 Nephi 28:7–9, 15–23, 27–32, 36–40

7 Therefore, more blessed are ye, for ye shall never taste of death; but ye shall live to behold all the doings of the Father unto the children of men, even until all things shall be fulfilled according to the will of the Father, when I shall come in my glory with the powers of heaven.

8 And ye shall never endure the pains of death; but when I shall come in my glory ye shall be changed in the twinkling of an eye from mortality to immortality; and then shall ye be blessed in the kingdom of my Father.

9 And again, ye shall not have pain while ye shall dwell in the flesh, neither sorrow save it be for the sins of the world; and all this will I do because of the thing which ye have desired of me, for ye have desired that ye might bring the souls of men unto me, while the world shall stand. . . .

15 And whether they were in the body or out of the body, they could not tell; for it did seem unto them like a transfiguration of them, that they were changed from this body of flesh into an immortal state, that they could behold the things of God.

16 But it came to pass that they did again minister upon the face of the earth; nevertheless they did not minister of the things which they had heard and seen, because of the commandment which was given them in heaven.

17 And now, whether they were mortal or immortal, from the day of their transfiguration, I know not;

18 But this much I know, according to the record which

hath been given—they did go forth upon the face of the land, and did minister unto all the people, uniting as many to the church as would believe in their preaching; baptizing them, and as many as were baptized did receive the Holy Ghost.

19 And they were cast into prison by them who did not belong to the church. And the prisons could not hold them, for they were rent in twain.

20 And they were cast down into the earth; but they did smite the earth with the word of God, insomuch that by his power they were delivered out of the depths of the earth; and therefore they could not dig pits sufficient to hold them.

21 And thrice they were cast into a furnace and received no harm.

22 And twice were they cast into a den of wild beasts; and behold they did play with the beasts as a child with a suckling lamb, and received no harm.

23 And it came to pass that thus they did go forth among all the people of Nephi, and did preach the gospel of Christ unto all people upon the face of the land; and they were converted unto the Lord, and were united unto the church of Christ, and thus the people of that generation were blessed, according to the word of Jesus. . . .

27 And behold they will be among the Gentiles, and the Gentiles shall know them not.

28 They will also be among the Jews, and the Jews shall know them not.

29 And it shall come to pass, when the Lord seeth fit in his wisdom that they shall minister unto all the scattered tribes of Israel, and unto all nations, kindreds, tongues and people, and shall bring out of them unto Jesus many souls, that their desire may be fulfilled, and also because of the convincing power of God which is in them.

30 And they are as the angels of God, and if they shall pray unto the Father in the name of Jesus they can show themselves unto whatsoever man it seemeth them good.

31 Therefore, great and marvelous works shall be wrought

by them, before the great and coming day when all people must surely stand before the judgment-seat of Christ;

32 Yea even among the Gentiles shall there be a great and marvelous work wrought by them, before that judgment day....

36 And now behold, as I spake concerning those whom the Lord hath chosen, yea, even three who were caught up into the heavens, that I knew not whether they were cleansed from mortality to immortality—

37 But behold, since I wrote, I have inquired of the Lord, and he hath made it manifest unto me that there must needs be a change wrought upon their bodies, or else it needs be that they must taste of death;

38 Therefore, that they might not taste of death there was a change wrought upon their bodies, that they might not suffer pain nor sorrow save it were for the sins of the world.

39 Now this change was not equal to that which shall take place at the last day; but there was a change wrought upon them, insomuch that Satan could have no power over them, that he could not tempt them; and they were sanctified in the flesh, that they were holy, and that the powers of the earth could not hold them.

40 And in this state they were to remain until the judgment day of Christ; and at that day they were to receive a greater change, and to be received into the kingdom of the Father to go no more out, but to dwell with God eternally in the heavens.

Joseph Smith taught regarding the character of a translated being: "Now the doctrine of translation is a power which belongs to this [the Melchizedek] Priesthood. Many have supposed that the doctrine of translation was a doctrine whereby men were taken immediately into the presence of God, and into an eternal fulness, but this is a mistaken idea. Their place of habitation is that of the terrestrial order, and a place prepared for such characters He held in reserve to be ministering angels unto many planets."[11]

"The three Nephites," wrote Elder Franklin D. Richards, "wanted to tarry until Jesus came, and that they might He took them into the heavens and endowed them with the power of translation."[12] 3 Nephi 28 reveals much about "the power of translation." Translated beings "never taste of death" (3 Nephi 28:7) or "endure the pains of death" (3 Nephi 28:8). They experience no physical pain while dwelling in the flesh, nor do they feel "sorrow save it be for the sins of the world" (3 Nephi 28:9). Satan has "no power over them" and cannot tempt them (3 Nephi 28:39). Translated beings can hide their identity as translated beings from others (3 Nephi 28:27–28), and if they "pray unto the Father in the name of Jesus they can show themselves unto whatsoever man it seemeth them good" (3 Nephi 28:30). Translated beings also possess power over earth's elements. With specific reference to the three Nephites, no prison could hold them, nor could the pits of the earth keep them. When they were cast into fiery furnaces or the dens of wild beasts, they escaped with no harm (3 Nephi 28:19–22). In short, "the powers of the earth could not hold them" (3 Nephi 28:39).

The power of translation possessed by the three Nephites gave them a remarkable spiritual and physical standing that in some respects parallels, and even anticipates, that of resurrected beings. In other words, translated beings serve as types and shadows of celestial resurrected beings. Like translated beings, resurrected souls will never taste of death—they are immortal, their spirits and bodies will never again be divided. And also like translated beings, those who are resurrected do not experience physical pain, and Satan has no power over them. Resurrected personages have the power to hide or "veil" their true identity from others, as do those who have been translated. And resurrected beings possess power over the earth's elements; there is no power on earth that can hold them. The same is also true of translated beings.

Joseph Smith explained that translated beings "have not yet entered into so great a fulness as those who are resurrected from the dead. . . . This distinction is made between the doctrine of actual resurrection and translation: translation obtains deliverance from the tortures and sufferings of the body, but their existence will prolong as to the labors and toils of the ministry, before they can enter into so great a rest and glory."[13] Of course, translated beings do not have celestial bodies, but their mortal bodies have been changed to a terrestrial order for the following reasons: (1) so that they cannot suffer physical pain (3 Nephi 28:9); (2) so that Satan cannot tempt them or have power over them: "there was a change wrought upon them, insomuch that Satan could have no power over them, that he could not tempt them" (3 Nephi 28:39); (3) so that they would have powers over the elements: "they were sanctified in the flesh, that they were holy, and that the powers of the earth could not hold them" (3 Nephi 28:39); and (4) "there must needs be a change wrought upon their bodies, or else it needs be that they must taste of death" (3 Nephi 28:37).

This change from a mortal to translated being was designed to be temporary and to last until Christ's judgment day (3 Nephi 28:7–8, 39–40). At that time, translated beings will receive yet another change, called a "greater change" (3 Nephi 28:40)—a change from the status of translated to resurrected. This change will happen instantaneously; they "shall be changed in the twinkling of an eye from mortality to immortality" (3 Nephi 28:8).

NOTES AND COMMENTARY

3 Nephi 28:7 *ye shall never taste of death.* The idea of this phrase is repeated in verse 8: "ye shall never endure the pains of death." Of course, the three Nephites will yet have to die, but they will not feel the pain that often accompanies death. "Translated beings are still mortal and will have to pass through the experience of death, or the separation of the spirit and the body, although this will be instantaneous."[14]

ye shall live to behold all the doings of the Father unto the children of men. The Father's "doings" seems to refer to his work among the nations subsequent to the translation of the three Nephites. Perhaps they witnessed the Father's work during the Dark Ages, the Reformation, and the Restoration, as well as other periods of the earth.

when I shall come in my glory with the powers of heaven. The three Nephites will remain in their translated state until Christ's second coming, when he comes in his glory. This time period is called "the last day" (v. 39) and "the judgment day of Christ" (v. 40). At that time their bodies will be changed instantaneously from a translated state to a resurrected state.

3 Nephi 28:8 *changed in the twinkling of an eye from mortality to immortality.* See commentary on 1 Corinthians 15:52 and Doctrine and Covenants 43:32.

then shall ye be blessed in the kingdom of my Father. The three Nephites are earlier called "blessed" by Jesus for their desire to minister among earth's inhabitants (see verse 7). They will be "blessed" as well after their resurrection and after they enter the Father's kingdom.

3 Nephi 28:9 *all this will I do.* Jesus Christ has all power to change the physical bodies of mortals from one state to another, according to his divine desires and to fulfil his eternal plans. "All this will I do," he promises the three.

for ye have desired that ye might bring the souls of men unto me. These words describe the principal goal of the three Nephites, which is to brings souls to Christ. This goal is repeated throughout the remainder of 3 Nephi 28 in the following words: the three Nephites did "minister unto all people . . . preaching . . . baptizing" (3 Nephi 28:18); they "did preach the gospel of Christ unto all people upon the face of the land" (3 Nephi 28:23); "they shall minister unto all the scattered tribes of Israel, and unto all nations, kindreds, tongues and people, and shall bring out of them unto Jesus many souls, that their desire may be fulfilled, and also because of the convincing power of God which is in them" (3 Nephi 28:29).

3 Nephi 28:17 *from the day of their transfiguration.* The three Nephites were yet mortal (see commentary on verse 7) after they received the power of translation. Nonetheless, they were transfigured, an experience that resulted in "a change wrought upon their bodies" (v. 37) so that their bodies were similar to those of immortal souls. 3 Nephi 28:15 suggests that this transfiguration was so great that the three Nephites themselves "could not tell . . . whether they were in the body or out of the body" and that "it did seem" that they had an immortal body. The three Nephites, then, were both transfigured and translated. As one Book of Mormon commentary states it: "One who is translated is always transfigured, but a person may be transfigured without being translated."[15] Others besides the three Nephites, too, were transfigured during mortality. Moses (Moses 1:11), Peter, James, and John (Matthew 17:1–9) were transfigured. Transfiguration is a temporary condition, where a person is so filled with the Holy Ghost and the power of God that his or her countenance and overall appearance are changed (see, for example, Exodus 34:29–35).

Why are souls transfigured? So that " they [can] behold the things of God" (3 Nephi 28:15). Moses, for example, "beheld God": "Now mine own eyes have beheld God; but not with my natural, but my spiritual eyes, for my natural eyes could not have beheld; for I should have withered and died in his presence; but his glory was upon me; and I beheld his face, for I was transfigured before him" (Moses 1:11). Peter, James, and John, too, beheld the things of God in a vision while on a high mountain (Matthew 17:1–9).

3 Nephi 28:19–22 Translated beings have power over the elements of the earth. In fact, no earthly power can harm them. Numerous attempts were made to harm, contain, or slay the three Nephites subsequent to their translation, although none of these was successful: "they were cast into prison . . . and the prisons could not hold them. . . . And they were cast down into the earth; . . . they were delivered out of the depths of the earth. . . . And thrice they were cast into a furnace and received no harm. And twice were they cast into a den of wild beasts . . . and received no harm" (3 Nephi 28:19–22).

3 Nephi 28:23–29 *they did go forth among all the people.* The three Nephites were assigned to minister to faithful members of the church (3 Nephi 28:26) as well as those not of the faith. The record specifies that they ministered among "all people" (3 Nephi 28:18, 23) or "all nations, kindreds, tongues and people" (3 Nephi 28:29). This includes the Gentiles, Jews, and the scattered tribes of Israel (3 Nephi 28:27–29).

3 Nephi 28:30 *they are as the angels of God, and if they shall pray unto the Father in the name of Jesus they can show themselves unto whatsoever man it seemeth them good.* Resurrected beings can hide their glory from mortals when they appear to them. Jesus appeared to two of his disciples on the road to Emmaus, for example, and they did not detect that he was a resurrected being until he permitted them to comprehend (see commentary on Luke 24:13–32). In this regard, Paul advised, "Be not forgetful to entertain strangers: for thereby some have entertained angels unawares" (Hebrews 13:2). The three Nephites are like angels in that they, too, can "show themselves" in their true form as translated beings to "whatsoever man it seemeth them good." Before doing so, however, they are required to pray to the Father in Christ's name in order to receive that privilege. On most occasions, however, the three Nephites appear unto the Gentiles and Jews and "they know them not" (3 Nephi 28:27–28).

3 Nephi 28:31 *great and marvelous works shall be wrought by them.* Perhaps the greatest and most marvelous work (compare 2 Nephi 25:17–18) the three Nephites have done and will continue to do is bring people to Jesus Christ. Certainly, however, they have done numerous other great acts in moving God's divine work forward as they have worked among the nations since the day of their translation. Verse 32 states, "Even among the Gentiles shall there be a great and marvelous work wrought by them."

3 Nephi 28:38–40 *there was a change wrought upon their bodies.* God changed the mortal bodies of the three Nephites so their bodies were similar to those of immortal souls. That is to say, "they were sanctified in the flesh, that they were holy, and that the powers of the earth could not hold them" (v. 39). Their bodies became translated bodies, not resurrected souls. According to the text, "this change was not equal to that which shall take place at the last day. . . . And in this state they were to remain until the judgment day of Christ; and at that day they were to receive a greater change" (vv. 39–40). The "greater change" refers to the resurrection. At the judgment day, the three Nephites will receive the greater change to their bodies; they will become glorious, resurrected souls.

CHAPTER 6

JESUS CHRIST AND THE RESURRECTION

Jesus Christ holds the keys of death, hell, and the resurrection. To John he revealed, "I am he that liveth, and was dead; and, behold, I am alive for evermore, Amen; and have the keys of hell and of death" (Revelation 1:18). He also disclosed to John, "As the Father hath life in himself, so hath he given to the Son to have life in himself" (John 5:26); and further, "I am the resurrection and the life" (John 11:25).

At the time of Christ's resurrection, a number of individuals saw the Lord and testified of his resurrection. These include (not in chronological order):

1. *Mary.* She was recorded as the first to see the resurrected Lord. On recognizing Jesus, she said "Rabboni" or Master (John 20:16).

2. *Other women.* Angels testified to Mary Magdalene, Mary (the mother of James), Salome (the mother of James and John), and other women, "Ye seek Jesus of Nazareth, which was crucified: he is risen; he is not here: behold the place where they laid him" (Mark 16:6). As the women were on their way to inform others about this event, Jesus met them. They embraced his feet and worshiped him (Matthew 28:9).

3. *Peter.* The scriptural records do not indicate where Peter saw the postmortal Jesus. Luke records, "The Lord is risen indeed, and hath appeared to Simon" (Luke 24:34); and Paul wrote, "He was seen of Cephas, then of the twelve" (1 Corinthians 15:5).

4. *Two disciples on the road to Emmaus.* The two were probably Cleopas and Luke. (See commentary on "The Capabilities of Resurrected Beings," in chapter 7.)

5. *The apostles, except for Thomas.* Jesus appeared to the apostles and instructed them, "Behold my hands and my feet, that it is I myself:

handle me, and see" (Luke 24:39). Soon after, he told them, "Ye are witnesses of these things" (Luke 24:48). (See commentary on "The Resurrected Savior Has Flesh and Bones and Partakes of Mortal Food," in chapter 7.) "But Thomas, one of the twelve, called Didymus, was not with them when Jesus came" (John 20:24). The apostles who saw Jesus on this occasion later testified to Thomas, "We have seen the Lord" (John 20:25).

6. *Thomas and other apostles.* Jesus appeared to Thomas and others. He instructed Thomas, "Reach hither thy finger, and behold my hands; and reach hither thy hand, and thrust it into my side." Thomas then testified, "My Lord and my God" (John 20:27–28).

7. *Seven of Jesus' disciples* who were fishing on the Galilee (John 21:1–14).

8. *More than five hundred brethren.* Jesus appeared unto "above five hundred brethren at once" (1 Corinthians 15:6). Little more is known about this event.

9. *James.* James, an apostle, saw the resurrected Lord (1 Corinthians 15:7).

10. *Eleven apostles.* Jesus appeared to eleven apostles on a mountain in Galilee. "And when they saw him, they worshipped him" (Matthew 28:16–17).

11. *The apostles.* Luke testified that Jesus "shewed himself alive after his passion by many infallible proofs" to his apostles and was "seen of them forty days" (Acts 1:3). (See commentary on "The Apostles Receive Infallible Proofs of Jesus' Resurrection," in this chapter.)

12. *Thousands in Bountiful.* Jesus commanded the Nephites in Bountiful, "Arise and come forth unto me, that ye may thrust your hands into my side, and also that ye may feel the prints of the nails in my hands and in my feet, that ye may know that I am the God of Israel, and the God of the whole earth, and have been slain for the sins of the world" (3 Nephi 11:14). And they felt his wounds and "did see with their eyes and did feel with their hands, and did know of a surety" (3 Nephi 11:15) that he was the resurrected Jesus Christ.

In addition to these eyewitness accounts of the resurrected Jesus in ancient times, a number have seen him in our day:

1. *Joseph Smith and Sidney Rigdon.* "And now, after the many testimonies which have been given of him, this is the testimony, last of all, which we give of him: That he lives! For we saw him, even on the right hand of God, and we heard the voice bearing record that he is the Only Begotten of the Father" (D&C 76:22–23).

2. *Melvin J. Ballard.* This apostle testified, "I know that Jesus lives; for I have seen him!"[1] "I know, as well as I know that I live and look into your faces, that Jesus Christ lives. . . . For in the visions of the Lord to my soul, I have seen Christ's face, I have heard his voice. I know that he lives."[2] He more fully recorded, "I found myself one evening in the dreams of the night in that sacred building, the temple. After a season of prayer and rejoicing I was informed that I should have the privilege of entering into one of those rooms, to meet a glorious Personage, and, as I entered the door, I saw, seated on a raised platform, the most glorious Being my eyes have ever beheld or that I ever conceived existed in all the eternal worlds. As I approached to be introduced, he arose and stepped towards me with extended arms, and he smiled as he softly spoke my name. If I shall live to be a million years old, I shall never forget that smile. He took me into his arms and kissed me, pressed me to his bosom, and blessed me, until the marrow of my bones seemed to melt! When he had finished, I fell at his feet, and, as I bathed them with my tears and kisses, I saw the prints of the nails in the feet of the Redeemer of the world. The feeling that I had in the presence of Him who hath all things in His hands, to have His love, His affections, and His blessing was such that if I ever can receive that which I had but a foretaste, I would give all that I am, and that I ever hope to be, to feel what I then felt."[3]

3. *George Q. Cannon.* President Cannon said, "I know that God lives. I know that Jesus lives; for I have seen Him."[4]

4. *L. John Nuttal.* Brother Nuttal recorded in his diary, "President George Q. Cannon and I have seen the Savior Jesus Christ and conversed with Him face to face and He has talked with me."[5]

5. *Alexander Neibaur.* Brother Neibaur, a Jewish convert from England, testified shortly before his death, "I have seen my Savior! I have seen the prints in His hands. I know that Jesus is the Son of God. I know that this work is true, and that Joseph Smith was a prophet of

God. I would suffer it all and more, far more than I have suffered for that knowledge, even to the laying down of my body on the plains for the wolves to devour!"[6]

6. *Zebedee Coltrin and others.* "Elder Coltrin declared that while the men in the school [of the Prophets] were praying, he saw a personage pass through the room. Joseph Smith asked if the men knew who had appeared to him. Before anyone could answer, the Prophet replied that it was 'Jesus, our elder brother, the Son of God.' The men resumed praying, and once again, Elder Coltrin said he beheld a person in the room 'whose glory and brightness was so great' that he likened it to the burning bush Moses saw. 'Its power was so great,' he said, 'that had it continued much longer I believe it would have consumed us.' After this second personage disappeared, Zebedee Coltrin recalled, Joseph Smith announced that they had just seen 'the Father of Jesus Christ.'"[7]

7. *A number of high priests in Kirtland.* "The High Priests assembled in the school room of the Prophets. . . . Many present had the eyes of their understanding opened by the Spirit of God, so as to behold many things. . . . Many of the brethren saw a heavenly vision of the Savior, and concourses of angels, and many other things."[8]

8. *Orson F. Whitney.* "I thought I was in the garden of Gethsemane, a witness of the Savior's agony, I seemed to be standing behind a tree in the foreground of the picture, from which point I could see without being seen. The Savior, with the Apostles Peter, James and John, entered the garden through a little wicket gate at my right, where he stationed them in a group, telling them to pray. He then passed over to my left, but still in front of me, where he knelt and prayed also. His face, which was towards me, streamed with tears, as he besought the Father to let the cup pass . . . He was much taller than ordinary men, and though meek, far more dignified than any being I had ever beheld; and he wore a look of ineffable tenderness and compassion, even while reproving His disciples. My heart went out to him as never before to anybody or anything; I loved him with all my soul. I wept at seeing him weep, and felt for him the deepest sympathy.

"Then all of a sudden the circumstances changed, though the scene remained the same. Instead of before the crucifixion, it was after. The Savior and the three Apostles, whom he had beckoned to him, now stood in a group at the left, and were about to take their departure, ascending into heaven. I could endure it no longer, but rushed out from behind the tree, fell at his feet, clasped him around the knees and begged him to take me also. With a look of infinite tenderness, as of a father or an elder brother, he stooped, lifted me up and embraced me, saying as he did so in the kindest and gentlest manner possible, while slowly shaking his head and sweetly smiling, 'No, my son, these can go with me: for they have finished their work; but you must stay and finish yours!' Still I clung to him and the contact was so real that I felt the warmth of his bosom as I rested upon it. Gazing up into his face, I once more besought him, 'Well promise me that I will come to you at the last.' Again he smiled sweetly, and there was a look as if he would have gladly granted my request had it been wise to do so. He then said, 'That will depend entirely upon yourself.' I awoke with a sob, and it was morning."⁹

9. *David O. McKay.* I "beheld in vision something infinitely sublime. In the distance I beheld a beautiful white city. . . . I then saw a great concourse of people approaching the city. Each one wore a white flowing robe, and a white headdress. Instantly my attention seemed centered upon their Leader, and though I could see only the profile of his features and body, I recognized him at once as my Savior! The tint and radiance of his countenance were glorious to behold! There was a peace about him which seemed sublime—it was divine! The city, I understood, was his. It was the City Eternal; and the people following him were to abide there in peace and eternal happiness. But who were they? As if the Savior read my thoughts, he answered by pointing to a semicircle that then appeared above them, and on which were written in gold these words: These are They who have overcome the World— who have truly been born again!"¹⁰

JESUS HOLDS THE KEYS OF DEATH AND HELL

Revelation 1:17–18

> *17 And when I saw him, I fell at his feet as dead. And he laid his right hand upon me, saying unto me, Fear not; I am the first and the last:*

*18 I am he that liveth, and was dead; and, behold, I am
alive for evermore, Amen; and have the keys of hell and of
death.*

In Revelation 1:10–16, the apostle John beheld and described the
glorious, resurrected Jesus Christ. Upon seeing the Lord, John fell at
his feet with fear (Revelation 1:17). Jesus laid his right hand on him
to comfort him and commanded him to "fear not." Jesus then uttered
words that identified himself as the resurrected Lord: "I am he that
liveth, and was dead; . . . behold, I am alive for evermore . . . ; [I] have
the keys of hell and of death" (Revelation 1:18). "It is evident," testified George Q. Cannon, "that the Savior had the power of the resurrection within Himself and held the keys. This power He has
received from His Father; for as He says: 'As the Father hath life in
himself, so hath he given to the Son to have life in himself.' (John
5:26.) Jesus was, as He says, 'the resurrection, and the life.' (John
11:25.)"[11]

NOTES AND COMMENTARY

Revelation 1:17 *I saw him.* John's vision of Christ appears to
take place in the celestial kingdom, or, more specifically, "the temple
which is in heaven" (Revelation 14:17). John bore witness that he saw
the Lord in the heavenly temple. Similarly, Joseph Smith and Sidney
Rigdon testified, "For we saw him" (D&C 76:23). Many other
prophets have so testified—and the righteous may see him in his
earthly temple (D&C 97:16; 110:8).

I fell at his feet. Perhaps John fell because he felt great reverence
for the Lord, or maybe he fell because he felt great awe and fear at
being in the presence of such a great and glorious heavenly being.
Other prophets have felt compelled to fall on their faces before the
Lord, including Abraham (Genesis 17:3); Joshua (Joshua 5:14); Peter,
James, and John (Matthew 17:6); and the brother of Jared (Ether 3:6).
So also did the Nephite multitude (3 Nephi 11:12).

he laid his right hand upon me. Like the comforting hand of a loving parent upon a troubled child, the divine hand, accompanied with
the words "Fear not," stilled John's fear. A similar event is recorded
in Matthew's account of the three apostles on the Mount of Trans-

figuration, in which it is recorded that Peter, James, and John "fell on their face, and were sore afraid"; but Jesus touched them and said, "Arise, and be not afraid" (Matthew 17:6–7). It doubtless is significant that John specifies the right hand. The right hand is the hand of authority; it is also the hand used in making covenants; and it is the hand of friendship.

I am the first and the last. In Revelation 1:8, Jesus declares that he is "Alpha and Omega." Alpha and omega are the first and last letters of the Greek alphabet, here signifying Christ as the First and the Last, the Beginning and the End (Revelation 1:17; 21:6; 22:13; Isaiah 41:4; 48:12).

Revelation 1:18 *I am he that liveth, and was dead; . . . I am alive for evermore.* With these statements Jesus bears witness that he is the resurrected Lord. "I am he that liveth, and was dead" is a declaration that Jesus Christ, though once dead, is now alive, appearing to John clothed with all power and glory. So glorious was Jesus' appearance that his "countenance was as the sun shining in his strength" (JST Revelation 1:16). "I am alive for evermore" is an affirmation that Jesus' body has been reunited with his spirit, never to be divided again, forming an eternal, resurrected soul.

keys of hell and of death. To possess keys is to have power, authority, and the right of presidency (Revelation 3:7; 9:1; Matthew 16:19). Jesus has presiding authority over death and hell; he has complete power over all who inhabit the spirit world, including the hosts of evil beings. He has power to bring forth the resurrection and to redeem us from the grave (2 Nephi 9:10–13).[12]

THE ORDINANCE AND KEYS OF THE RESURRECTION

Brigham Young

It is supposed by this people that we have all the ordinances in our possession for life and salvation, and exaltation, and that we are administering in those ordinances. This is not the case. We are in possession of all the ordinances that can be administered in the flesh; but there are other ordinances and administrations that must be administered beyond this world. I know you would like to ask what they are. I will

mention one. We have not, neither can we receive here, the
ordinance and the keys of resurrection. They will be given to
those who have passed off this stage of action and have
received their bodies again. . . . They will be ordained, by
those who hold the keys of the resurrection, to go forth and
resurrect the Saints, just as we receive the ordinance of bap-
tism then receive the keys of authority to baptize others for the
remission of their sins. This is one of the ordinances we can
not receive here [on the earth], and there are many more.[13]

Members of the First Presidency and Quorum of the Twelve
Apostles hold all the keys that are necessary to administer the affairs
of the kingdom of God on earth. These keys, restored by heavenly
messengers to Joseph Smith and Oliver Cowdery, include the keys of
the ministering of angels, the keys of the sealing power, the keys of
the gathering of Israel, the keys to administer the work of the priesthood, and others. Additional Church authorities, such as stake presidents, bishops, and elders quorum presidents, hold keys that pertain
to their respective areas of stewardship. Keys bring order to God's
kingdom and bless individuals as they strive to comply with his commandments and ordinances. Despite the fact that many of God's
earthly ministrants hold keys, there are no mortals who possess the
keys of resurrection; neither does the ordinance of resurrection reside
with members of the human family.

The keys of resurrection are held by Jesus Christ. He obtained the
power of resurrection from his Father. Elder George Q. Cannon bore
witness that "the Savior had the power of the resurrection within
Himself and held the keys. This power He has received from His
Father." Subsequent to his resurrection, Jesus Christ appeared to one
of his mortal ministers and declared, "I am he that liveth, and was
dead; and, behold, I am alive for evermore, Amen; and have the keys
of hell and of death" (Revelation 1:17–18).

THE TEMPLE OF JESUS' BODY

John 2:18–22

18 Then answered the Jews and said unto him, What sign
shewest thou unto us, seeing that thou doest these things?

19 Jesus answered and said unto them, Destroy this temple, and in three days I will raise it up.

20 Then said the Jews, Forty and six years was this temple building, and wilt thou rear it up in three days?

21 But he spake of the temple of his body.

22 When therefore he was risen from the dead, his disciples remembered that he had said this unto them; and they believed the scripture, and the word which Jesus had said.

In the second chapter of his Gospel, the apostle John told of Jesus' cleansing the temple of Herod (John 2:13–22). Shortly before Passover, one area of the temple precinct was filled with Jews selling cattle, sheep, and doves to be used for sacrificial offerings. There were also men exchanging money from foreign currencies to the currency used in Judea at the time. It was in this setting that Jesus made a whip out of cords and drove these traders from his Father's house. The Jews who witnessed this event were likely astonished that one man equipped with a whip would enter the temple, overturn tables, and drive out full-grown men. We presume that never before or since had they witnessed such an event. So they demanded that Jesus give them a sign showing that he had the right to cleanse the temple: "What sign shewest thou unto us, seeing that thou doest these things?" (v. 18).

Jesus answered with a brief response: "Destroy this temple, and in three days I will raise it up" (v. 19). The Messiah gave them a great sign, the sign of his own resurrection. The Jews, however, did not grasp his meaning, supposing that he was referring to Herod's temple, which towered over them even as they spoke. Jesus' words must have puzzled his listeners. It had taken forty-six years to build the temple in the first place—how could this man Jesus rebuild it in three days?

John's Gospel presents four points about the temple of Jesus' body: (1) Jesus would raise up his body three days after it would be destroyed; (2) the Jews had misunderstood Jesus' words about the temple, believing that he was referring to a building of mortar and stone; (3) John supplied the readers of his Gospel with the phrase's correct meaning: "He spake of the temple of his body" (v. 21); and (4) John provided the impact that this prophecy had on the believing community after Jesus' resurrection. He relates that believers *remembered*

Jesus' prophecy about the temple of his body and *believed* his words (John 2:22).

NOTES AND COMMENTARY

John 2:18 *What sign shewest thou unto us.* On many occasions, those who heard Jesus' teachings demanded a sign from him. Generally, however, Jesus refused to give them one (Mark 8:11–12). Once, when a group of scribes and Pharisees asked for a sign, Jesus responded by saying, "An evil and adulterous generation seeketh after a sign; and there shall no sign be given to it, but the sign of the prophet Jonas [Jonah]" (Matthew 12:39). The sign of Jonah is a sign of Jesus' resurrection (see "The Sign of the Prophet Jonah" in chapter 5).

Here, in John 2:19, Jesus gave the Jews another sign of his resurrection: "Destroy this temple," Jesus told them, "and in three days I will raise it up." *This temple* refers to the temple of his body, and *I will raise it up* refers to the resurrection.

Jesus, then, gave two signs to his listeners during his mortal ministry that directly pertain to his resurrection—"the sign of the prophet Jonas" and the sign of the raising of his temple.

John 2:19 *Destroy this temple, and in three days I will raise it up.* The "temple" referred to in this verse is Jesus' own body. Jesus was prophesying of its destruction (by crucifixion) and its subsequent resurrection, three days later. Note that the resurrection would take place by Jesus' own power. He states, "I will raise it up." On another occasion Jesus specifically mentioned three days (Matthew 12:40), having reference to the period immediately before the resurrection.

Jesus uttered the words "Destroy this temple, and in three days I will raise it up" before a crowd in the temple precinct. It is not known just how many personally witnessed this interchange, but his words became widely known among many. For example, some time later, false witnesses stood before the Sanhedrin at Jesus' trial and recalled, "This fellow said, I am able to destroy the temple of God, and to build it in three days" (Matthew 26:61; Mark 14:58). Also, while Jesus was on the cross, he was mocked and jeered: "Thou that destroyest the temple, and buildest it in three days, save thyself. If thou be the Son of God, come down from the cross" (Matthew 27:40).

John 2:20 *Forty and six years was this temple in building.* Jesus' words were confusing to his listeners. They had just witnessed the cleansing of the temple, and now he was talking about destroying it. Even more confusing was his statement that he would raise up the destroyed temple in a mere three days. It had taken forty-six years and hundreds of workmen to rebuild the temple, so how could a single man rebuild it in three days?

John 2:21 *But he spake of the temple of his body.* Jesus' audience misunderstood his words about the temple. John explained to his readers that Jesus referred not to a temple made of stone but to his own body. On several other occasions Jesus' audience misunderstood him, and John added an explanation for his own audience (see, for example, John 11:11–13).

The scriptures contain explicit statements as well as allusions to the Lord as a temple. The Lord revealed to Ezekiel, for instance, that he (the Lord) would be as a "little sanctuary" to the scattered tribes of Israel: "Thus saith the Lord God; Although I have cast [members of the house of Israel] far off among the heathen, and although I have scattered them among the countries, yet will I be to them as a little sanctuary in the countries where they shall come" (Ezekiel 11:16). In another passage, the Psalmist declared, "Lord, thou hast been our dwelling place in all generations" (Psalm 90:1; compare Psalm 91:2). Isaiah prophesied that the Lord "shall be for a sanctuary" unto the righteous but a "stone of stumbling" and a "rock of offense" unto the wicked (Isaiah 8:14). And after describing the celestial city in the book of Revelation, John declared: "I saw no temple therein: for the Lord God Almighty and the Lamb are the temple of it" (Revelation 21:22).

John 2:22 *his disciples remembered that he had said this unto them.* Jesus, at the beginning of his ministry, clearly understood his mission. He foresaw the cross (John 3:14; 12:32–33), his betrayal and death (John 13:19, 21), his burial (John 12:7), and his resurrection.

THE LORD DESTROYS DEATH AND REDEEMS MANKIND

Hosea 13:14

14 I will ransom them from the power of the grave; I will redeem them from death: O death, I will be thy plagues; O grave, I will be thy destruction.

The prophet Hosea reveals that the inhabitants of the kingdoms of Israel (the northern kingdom) and Judah (the southern kingdom) had provoked the Lord by committing numerous sins. "There is no truth," writes Hosea, "nor mercy, nor knowledge of God in the land. By swearing, and lying, and killing, and stealing, and committing adultery, they break out, and blood toucheth blood" (Hosea 4:1–2). Also, "they sin more and more, and have made them molten images of their silver, and idols according to their own understanding" (Hosea 13:2). Because of their sins, the Lord rebuked the people and prophesied that they would experience sorrow, pain, captivity, and destruction.

Notwithstanding their sorrow and destruction, the Lord comforted his people by promising that he would "plague" death, destroy the grave, and redeem his people from the power of death. In other words, though ancient Israel and Judah at the time of Hosea would experience all types of horrors because of their sins against the Lord, eventually they would obtain redemption from death because of the Lord's power to redeem.

Verse 14 presents the Lord's promise of redemption from death and from the grave. It is a poetic expression that features words that correspond with each other. Four phrases begin with "I will," referring to the Lord, who has the role of redeeming humanity from the grave. *Ransom* parallels *redeem; plagues* corresponds with *destruction*. Additionally, *grave* twice parallels *death* in a construction that is arranged chiastically—grave/death/death/grave.

NOTES AND COMMENTARY

Hosea 13:14 *I will.* The pronoun *I* refers to the Lord; the expression *I will* appears four times, summarized as follows: *I will* ransom from the grave, *I will* redeem from death, *I will* plague death, and *I will* destroy the grave. The fourfold repetition emphasizes the essential role of the Lord in humanity's resurrection. He has absolute power over death and the grave.

I will ransom them. "Ransom is an image drawn from ancient economic life. The picture is a slave market or prison. People are in bondage and cannot free themselves. Someone comes and pays the price (provides the ransom) to redeem those in captivity."[14] Those who are dead are like slaves or captives who are in bondage and cannot free themselves. Only Jesus Christ has the power to ransom them. "Ye are bought with a price," wrote Paul (1 Corinthians 6:20), and it was Jesus who paid the price. He did not pay with "corruptible things" such "as silver and gold," but he paid the ransom with his "precious blood" (1 Peter 1:18–19).

power of the grave/redeem them from death. The first phrase literally reads "from the hand of Sheol," *sheol* being a reference to the world of spirits.[15] The grave holds power over the dead in that the dead are captives or in bondage (see D&C 138:18, 31, 42, 50). They will remain in bondage until the Redeemer raises them in the resurrection. As the Psalmist prophesied, "God will redeem my soul from the power of the grave" (Psalms 49:15).

O death, I will be thy plagues. During the Old Testament period, the Lord sent plagues to various individuals or groups who were wicked. For example, "The Lord plagued Pharaoh and his house with great plagues because of Sarai Abram's wife" (Genesis 12:17). The Lord sent various plagues—frogs, lice, swarms of flies, boils, hail, and locusts—upon the Egyptians when they would not release the Israelites from bondage (Exodus 8–10). He also plagued Israel on a number of occasions for their wicked acts—for making the golden calf (Exodus 32:35), for complaining about manna and lusting for flesh (Numbers 11:33), and for murmuring against Moses and Aaron (Numbers 16:41–50). In the last-mentioned plague, 14,700 people died. In light of plagues that kill the body, it is significant that God uses the image of plagues to speak of destroying death itself. That is to say, the resurrection, "the redemption of the soul" (D&C 88:16), will cause death itself to vanish.

O grave, I will be thy destruction. After the Lord resurrects all mankind, graves will no longer exist. They will be destroyed by the Lord, because there will be no need for them. Sepulchres, crypts, and cemeteries will then become only a memory for mortals who were laid to rest in them.

JESUS CHRIST BRINGS TO PASS THE RESURRECTION

Mormon 9:12–13

12 Behold, he created Adam, and by Adam came the fall of man. And because of the fall of man came Jesus Christ, even

the Father and the Son; and because of Jesus Christ came the
redemption of man.

13 And because of the redemption of man, which came by
Jesus Christ, they are brought back into the presence of the
Lord; yea, this is wherein all men are redeemed, because the
death of Christ bringeth to pass the resurrection, which
bringeth to pass a redemption from an endless sleep, from
which sleep all men shall be awakened by the power of God
when the trump shall sound; and they shall come forth, both
small and great, and all shall stand before his bar, being
redeemed and loosed from this eternal band of death, which
death is a temporal death.

Verses 12–13 contain an uncommon structure in which key terms
are presented once and then repeated for emphasis. These key terms—
Adam, fall of man, Jesus Christ, redemption of man—are set forth in a
manner that shows a progression of thought that begins with the
creation of Adam, continues with the Fall, moves on to Jesus Christ
and the redemption of man, and then culminates with humankind
being brought back into the Lord's presence. In other words, the key
terms emphasize that Adam caused the Fall but Jesus Christ brought
the redemption of man. Below, the pertinent lines from verses 12–13
have been arranged with the key words beginning each line so the
reader can more easily identify them:

"Behold, he created
Adam, and by
Adam came the
fall of man. And because of the
fall of man came
Jesus Christ, even the Father and the Son; and because of
Jesus Christ came the
"redemption of man, which came by
Jesus Christ, they are brought back into the presence of
the Lord."

Many truths about death and resurrection are set forth in verse 13.
Christ's death brings about the resurrection; the resurrection may be

defined as "a redemption from an endless sleep"; "sleep" is used as a metaphor for death; God's power will awaken all from the sleep of death; all will awaken at the sound of a trump; "both small and great" will be resurrected; resurrection is also described as being "loosed from [an] eternal band of death."

NOTES AND COMMENTARY

Mormon 9:12 *because of the fall of man came Jesus Christ.* With these words Moroni established the need for Jesus Christ and the redemption that comes through him. Adam and Eve transgressed and fell, bringing death into the world. Jesus Christ had power over death and power to bring immortality and eternal life to humankind. "In order for Adam to regain his original state (to be in the presence of God), an atonement for this disobedience was necessary," explained President Spencer W. Kimball during a conference address in 1978. "In God's divine plan, provision was made for a redeemer to break the bonds of death and, through the resurrection, make possible the reunion of the spirits and bodies of all who had dwelt on earth.

"Jesus of Nazareth was the one who, before the world was created, was chosen to come to earth to perform this service, to conquer mortal death. This voluntary action would atone for the fall of Adam and Eve and permit the spirit of man to recover his body, thereby reuniting body and spirit. Jesus Christ has influenced humanity more than anyone else who ever lived."[16]

because of Jesus Christ came the redemption of man. With these words, plus the first statement of the following verse, Moroni created a brief but powerful chiasmus:

a because of Jesus Christ
b came the redemption of man.
b And because of the redemption of man,
a which came by Jesus Christ

Mormon 9:13 *they are brought back into the presence of the Lord.* The great Redeemer brings all humankind back into God's presence to "stand before his bar" of judgment. "And then cometh the time that he that is filthy shall be filthy still" (Mormon 9:14), but the righteous will be privileged to remain in God's presence forever.

because the death of Christ bringeth to pass the resurrection.
Joseph Fielding Smith clarifies how Jesus' "keys of the resurrection"
empowered Jesus to bring to pass the resurrection. "Christ is the
'resurrection and the life' and the first fruits of them that slept.
Therefore, none could pass from mortality to immortality until our
Savior completed his work for the redemption of man and had
gained the keys of the resurrection, being the first to rise, having
'life in himself' and the power to lay down his life and take it up
again, thus freeing all men from the bondage which the fall had
placed upon them."[17]

bringeth to pass a redemption from an endless sleep. Sleep is a
metaphor for death in many passages of scripture (see, for example, Acts
13:36; 1 Corinthians 15:18; 1 Thessalonians 4:13–14; D&C 43:18;
138:17. See also commentary on 1 Corinthians 15:51 in "The Resurrection Constitutes Victory over Death," in chapter 9). An "endless sleep"
speaks of eternal death, which humankind would have experienced had it
not been for the Redeemer's sacrificial death and subsequent resurrection. All of those who sleep at the time of their resurrection will be
"awakened by the power of God" at the sounding of a trumpet.

when the trump shall sound. Michael, the great archangel, will be
the one privileged to blow the trumpet that wakes the dead (see commentary on 1 Thessalonians 4:16 in "The Doctrine of the Resurrection
Brings Comfort to the Saints," in chapter 9; and the commentary on
D&C 43:18 in "Changed in the Twinkling of an Eye," in chapter 8).

they shall come forth, both small and great. "Small and great," an
expression used also by John (see commentary on Revelation 20:12 in
"The Sea and the Grave Give Up the Dead," in chapter 9) and Joseph F.
Smith (D&C 138:11), expresses the universality of the resurrection.

loosed from this eternal band of death. See commentary on Mosiah
15:20, in "Those Belonging to the First Resurrection," in chapter 8.

RESURRECTION IS POSSIBLE BECAUSE OF CHRIST AND ADAM

1 Corinthians 15:21–22, 45–49

*21 For since by man came death, by man came also the
resurrection of the dead.*

22 For as in Adam all die, even so in Christ shall all be made alive. . . .

45 And so it is written, The first man Adam was made a living soul; the last Adam was made a quickening spirit.

46 Howbeit that was not first which is spiritual, but that which is natural; and afterward that which is spiritual.

47 The first man is of the earth, earthy: the second man is the Lord from heaven.

48 As is the earthy, such are they also that are earthy: and as is the heavenly, such are they also that are heavenly.

49 And as we have borne the image of the earthy, we shall also bear the image of the heavenly.

With reference to Adam and Jesus, Elder Bruce R. McConkie wrote that "no two persons ever born on earth had ministries more intimately and essentially connected."[18] Paul, too, recognized the close connection between Adam and Christ when he wrote that Adam was "the figure of him [Jesus] that was to come" (Romans 5:14). The parallels between their lives are many. For example, Jesus is the Firstborn of the Father; Adam is firstborn of all flesh. "Adam fell that men might be"; Jesus Christ came to "redeem the children of men from the fall" (2 Nephi 2:25–26; see also Mormon 9:12). Adam offered sacrifices unto the Lord, each sacrifice "a similitude of the sacrifice of the Only Begotten of the Father" (Moses 5:7). Christ is the Resurrection (John 11:25); Adam with his trumpet will announce the resurrection (D&C 29:26). Both hold great authority—Jesus stands first in authority, Adam second.[19]

Further parallels are presented in 1 Corinthians 15:21–22 and 15:45–49. Both Adam and Jesus are called *Adam.* Adam is "the first man Adam"; Jesus Christ is "the last Adam." The first Adam is "a living soul" and the last Adam is "a quickening spirit." Adam had a "natural" body and was "of the earth, earthy"; Jesus has a "spiritual" body and is "from heaven." Adam's descendants are first in "the image of the earthy," but later they will be in "the image of the heavenly," as is Christ. Perhaps most significantly, Adam brought temporal death into the world; Christ brought forth power over death, or the resurrection. President Joseph F. Smith sums up: "Just as sure as we go down into the grave, through the transgression of our first parents, by whom death came into the world, so sure will we be resurrected from the dead by the power of Jesus Christ."[20]

NOTES AND COMMENTARY

1 Corinthians 15:21 *by man came death.* Paul refers to Adam, who brought death into the world. Paul explained to the Romans that death came to Adam because of sin: "By one man sin entered into the world, and death by sin; and so death passed upon all men, for that all have sinned" (Romans 5:12).

by man came also the resurrection of the dead. Paul refers to Jesus Christ, who brought forth the resurrection to himself and to all humankind.

Perhaps with 1 Corinthians 15:21 in mind, Joseph F. Smith taught, "Death came upon us without the exercise of our agency; we had no hand in bringing it originally upon ourselves; it came because of the transgression of our first parents. Therefore, man, who had no hand in bringing death upon himself, shall have no hand in bringing again life unto himself; for as he dies in consequence of the sin of Adam, so shall he live again, whether he will or not, by the righteousness of Jesus Christ, and the power of His resurrection."[21]

1 Corinthians 15:22 *For as in Adam all die.* This phrase parallels the opening phrase of verse 21, "For since by man came death." Both phrases begin with *for; man* and *Adam* correspond because *Adam* means "man" or "mankind" in the Hebrew language; and *death* and *die* correspond, one being a noun and the other a verb. Adam, through his transgression, brought physical death into the world.

even so in Christ shall all be made alive. This phrase parallels the second phrase of verse 21, "by man came also the resurrection of the dead." *Man* and *Christ* are corresponding terms, as are *alive* and *resurrection.* Christ overcame the effects of the Fall through his atoning sacrifice and made it possible for all to be resurrected.

1 Corinthians 15:45 *The first man Adam.* The revelations of the Restoration also refer to Adam as "the first man" (D&C 84:16).

a living soul. A mortal, consisting of a body of flesh, blood, and a spirit.

the last Adam was made a quickening spirit. Jesus Christ, the last

Adam, was able to quicken others, or make others immortal souls. *Quicken* is used here and elsewhere to mean *resurrect:* "As the Father raiseth up the dead, and quickeneth them; even so the Son quickeneth whom he will" (John 5:21); "The redemption of the soul is through him that quickeneth all things" (D&C 88:17).

1 Corinthians 15:46 *Howbeit that was not first which is spiritual, but that which is natural; and afterward that which is spiritual.* In an epistle to the Church dated September 6, 1842, Joseph Smith revealed several items regarding baptism for the dead. In the epistle he cited 1 Corinthians 15:46–48 as support for two separate but associated teachings: (1) that "all things may have their likeness." The baptismal font, for example is made in the likeness of the grave—both are usually rectangular cavities found below the surface of the earth. And (2) Joseph Smith wrote, ". . . that which is earthly conforming to that which is heavenly, as Paul hath declared, 1 Corinthians 15:46, 47, and 48." Eventually humankind, who are both natural and earthy, will become immortal, resurrected beings.

1 Corinthians 15:47 *first man is of the earth, earthy.* Adam, the first man, was a mortal being who was formed from "the dust of the ground" (Genesis 2:7). In that sense he was of the earth, earthy. Paul may have had a word play in mind when he stated that Adam was of the earth. The Hebrew word for *earth* is *'adamah,* a feminine form that shares the same root as the Hebrew *'adam,* or Adam. Hence, Adam (and all humankind) is from 'adamah, or mother earth.

1 Corinthians 15:48 *As is the earthy, such are they also that are earthy: and as is the heavenly, such are they also that are heavenly.* During mortality each of Adam's descendants has an earthly body, just as Adam himself did. These earthly bodies are made of clay, or the dust of the earth. Eventually these earthly bodies will be resurrected and will then become heavenly bodies in the likeness of Jesus' heavenly body. Earthly bodies are subject to corruption and death; heavenly bodies are not subject to temporal death and are incorruptible.

1 Corinthians 15:49 *we have borne the image of the earthy, we shall also bear the image of the heavenly.* During mortality, we are in the image of humans, and as such, we are frail, subject to sickness, disease, and death. After the resurrection, however, we will be in the image of Christ and of immortal beings, and death will no longer prevail.

THE APOSTLES RECEIVE INFALLIBLE PROOF OF JESUS' RESURRECTION

Acts 1:2–3, 8, 21–23

> *2 Until the day in which [Jesus Christ] was taken up, after that he through the Holy Ghost had given commandments unto the apostles whom he had chosen:*
>
> *3 To whom also he shewed himself alive after his passion by many infallible proofs, being seen of them forty days, and speaking of the things pertaining to the kingdom of God: . . .*
>
> *8 But ye shall receive power, after that the Holy Ghost is come upon you: and ye shall be witnesses unto me both in Jerusalem, and in all Judea, and in Samaria, and unto the uttermost part of the earth. . . .*
>
> *21 Wherefore of these men which have companied with us all the time that the Lord Jesus went in and out among us,*
>
> *22 Beginning from the baptism of John, unto that same day that he was taken up from us, must one be ordained to be a witness with us of his resurrection.*
>
> *23 And they appointed two, Joseph called Barsabas, who was surnamed Justus, and Matthias.*

In the opening verses of the book of Acts, Luke accounts for many of Jesus' post-resurrection activities among his disciples. During a forty-day period Jesus gave commandments to the apostles and taught them doctrines pertaining to the kingdom of God. Luke emphasized that the apostles were witnesses to Jesus Christ's resurrection, who appeared to them in resurrected form and gave them "many infallible proofs" that he was alive. Having received such proofs, the apostles were then empowered to testify of Jesus Christ's resurrection through-out the known world, namely, in Jerusalem, Judea, Samaria, and "unto the uttermost part of the earth." Luke continued his testimony about the resurrected Lord by citing a portion of Peter's sermon to a large group of Church members. Peter also taught that any man who would be ordained an apostle (such as Matthias) must also become a witness of Jesus Christ's resurrection, together with the other apostles (see Acts 1:15–22).

NOTES AND COMMENTARY

Acts 1:2 *Until the day in which [Jesus Christ] was taken up.* Jesus ministered to his followers for forty days after his resurrection, and then he ascended into heaven. Luke recorded that "he was taken up; and a cloud received him out of their sight" (Acts 1:9).

he through the Holy Ghost. After Jesus Christ's ascension into heaven, the Holy Ghost revealed Jesus' words unto the apostles as they administered the affairs of the kingdom of God upon the earth.

given commandments unto the apostles. During his mortal ministry, Jesus gave his apostles many instructions and commandments to enable them to manage the affairs of the kingdom of God. He sent "them forth to preach" and gave them "power to heal sicknesses, and to cast out devils" (Mark 3:14–15). The apostles, along with other Church officers, served to edify, unify, and perfect the Saints and to preserve the doctrines of the gospel in purity (Ephesians 4:11–14). After his post-resurrection ministry, Jesus gave commandments to the apostles through the Holy Ghost.

whom he had chosen. The phrase recalls Luke 6:13: "When it was day, [Jesus] called unto him his disciples: and of them he chose twelve, whom also he named apostles."

Acts 1:3 *To whom also he shewed himself alive.* Jesus appeared to the apostles after his resurrection and probably also to their companions or friends (see Luke 24:33–36).

after his passion. The Joseph Smith Translation reads here, "after his sufferings." By *passion* (Latin, *passus,* to suffer) Peter refers to Jesus' suffering during the final hours of his mortal life—the beatings, the crown of thorns, Gethsemane, and the cross.

by many infallible proofs. "The Greek word here means, literally, 'sure signs or tokens.' Jesus bore the sure signs or tokens of his atonement, death, and resurrection in his hands, wrists, feet, and side. We learn about similar things in Latter-day Saint temples."[22] The phrase "many infallible proofs" is fundamental to understanding the opening chapter of the book of Acts. Jesus gave his followers *many* (not just one or two) infallible proofs of his resurrection. The proofs that he gave them appealed to many of the human senses. Jesus disciples' saw him. They witnessed him eating tangible food, and later they ate and drank with him. They heard him speak and they conversed with him. During his forty-day ministry, Jesus charged his apostles and disciples to feel his hands and feet, giving them direct physical evidence that he indeed had a resurrected body. Their mortal hands of flesh and blood touched his immortal hands and feet of flesh and bones. To his eleven apostles and others gathered together, Jesus said, "Behold my hands and my feet, that it is I myself: handle me, and see; for a spirit hath not flesh and bones, as ye see me have" (Luke 24:39; compare D&C 129). To Thomas, Jesus said, "Reach hither thy finger, and behold my hands; and reach hither thy hand, and thrust it into my side: and be not faithless, but believing" (John 20:27).

forty days. The resurrected Jesus spent forty days with his disciples before his ascension into heaven. During this period, the "Immortal Lord appeared, conversed, ate with, and touched the Twelve and hundreds (perhaps thousands) of his mortal disciples."[23] During this forty-day ministry, Jesus appeared unto Peter, the Twelve Apostles, five hundred-plus brethren, and James. He also subsequently appeared to Paul (1 Corinthians 15:5–8).

Acts 1:8 *ye shall receive power.* The Lord promised his apostles the power of the Holy Ghost, and having this power they could then "be witnesses unto [him] both in Jerusalem" and in other parts of the known world. Later in the book of Acts, Luke observed that the Lord's witnesses had indeed received power through the Spirit: "They were filled with the Holy Ghost, and they spake the word of God with boldness. . . . And with great power gave the apostles witness of the resurrection of the Lord Jesus" (Acts 4:31, 33).

ye shall be witnesses unto me. The apostles were commanded to be witnesses of the resurrected Savior, a theme that is repeated again and again in Acts (see, for example, Acts 1:22; 2:32; 3:15; 4:20; 5:32; 8:25; 10:39; 13:31; 18:5; 20:21, 24; 22:15, 18, 20; 23:11; 26:16; 28:23). Acts 4:33 records that "with great power gave the apostles witness of the resurrection of the Lord Jesus: and great grace was upon them all." Apostles in our own dispensation as well are special witnesses of the Savior (D&C 27:12; 107:23).

in Jerusalem, and in all Judea, and in Samaria, and unto the uttermost part of the earth. Jesus sets forth the geographical areas in which the apostles are to bear witness of him—Jerusalem, Judah (the southern region of the Holy Land), Samaria (the northern region of the Holy Land), and the rest of the world. The book of Acts recounts the ministry and testimonies of the apostles in these places: Acts 1–7 reports their ministry in Jerusalem, Acts 8:1–11:18 pertains especially to their ministry in Judah and Samaria, and the remaining chapters detail their testimonies and ministry in lands belonging to Gentiles.

Acts 1:21–23 The context of these verses pertains to the vacancy in the quorum of the twelve apostles caused by the departure of Judas. Peter, the chief of the apostles, provides three qualifications for Judas' successor: (1) That person must be a male. Peter said, "Wherefore of these men . . . " (v. 21); (2) that person must have been part of the group who experienced Jesus' ministry ("which have companied with us all the time that the Lord Jesus went in and out among us" (v. 21); and (3) that person must be "a witness with us of [Jesus'] resurrection" (v. 22). Presumably criterion number 2 did not apply to apostles who were called in subsequent decades, such as Paul, although the first and third criteria likely continued to have application.

PAUL IS A WITNESS OF THE RESURRECTION

Acts 13:29–37

> *29 And when they had fulfilled all that was written of [Jesus Christ], they took him down from the tree, and laid him in a sepulchre.*
>
> *30 But God raised him from the dead:*
>
> *31 And he was seen many days of them which came up with him from Galilee to Jerusalem, who are his witnesses unto the people.*
>
> *32 And we declare unto you glad tidings, how that the promise which was made unto the fathers,*
>
> *33 God hath fulfilled the same unto us their children, in*

that he hath raised up Jesus again; as it is also written in the second psalm, Thou art my Son, this day have I begotten thee.

34 And as concerning that he raised him up from the dead, now no more to return to corruption, he said on this wise, I will give you the sure mercies of David.

35 Wherefore he saith also in another psalm, Thou shalt not suffer thine Holy One to see corruption.

36 For David, after he had served his own generation by the will of God, fell on sleep, and was laid unto his fathers, and saw corruption:

37 But he, whom God raised again, saw no corruption.

While preaching the gospel in Asia Minor (modern-day Turkey), Paul and Barnabas stopped in Pisidian Antioch to visit a colony of Jews. On the sabbath day they entered the synagogue and sat down with the congregation. After the customary reading of the law and the prophets, the synagogue leaders invited any in the congregation to teach and exhort others who were present. Paul stood up, made a gesture with his hand, and then taught and testified of Jesus Christ (Acts 13:13–37).

The passage discussed here (Acts 13:29–37) represents a portion of Paul's speech that deals directly with the death and resurrection of Jesus Christ. During his sermon, Paul cited or paraphrased a number of passages from the Old Testament, including Psalm 89:20 (see Acts 13:22), Psalm 2:7 (see Acts 13:33), Isaiah 55:3 (see Acts 13:34), and Psalm 16:10 (see Acts 13:37). By citing scripture, Paul supported his witness that Jesus was indeed Israel's Savior, the Holy One who saw no corruption, the risen Lord.

NOTES AND COMMENTARY

Acts 13:29 *fulfilled all that was written.* Jesus fulfilled all that was written by the prophets of old, who had prophesied of Jesus' life, ministry, death, and resurrection. All such prophecies were fulfilled (see verse 27).

they took him down from the tree. **They** refers to Joseph of Arimathea and Nicodemus, who removed Jesus from the tree or the cross (John 19:38–42). Peter, too, called the cross a tree: "The God of our fathers raised up Jesus, whom ye slew and hanged on a tree" (Acts 5:30). Biblical commentator Joseph A. Fitzmyer explains that the reference to a cross as a tree is found in the Dead Sea Scrolls, which refer back to Deuteronomy 21:22–23. Fitzmyer summarizes: "'Hanging on the tree' was already understood in pre-Christian Palestine as crucifixion, a mode of execution used among Jews even prior to the coming of the Romans (63 B.C.)."[24]

laid him in a sepulchre. The Law of Moses states of a person who is "hanged on a tree," "His body shall not remain all night upon the tree, but thou shalt in any wise bury him that day" (Deuteronomy 21:23). Joseph and Nicodemus, perhaps with this law in mind, buried Jesus in the tomb after removing him from the cross. His body, therefore, did not remain on the tree all night. All four Gospel writers describe Jesus' burial in the tomb followed by the resurrection. Compare also Paul's testimony: "He was buried, and . . . he rose again the third day" (1 Corinthians 15:4).

Acts 13:30 *God raised him from the dead.* In verse 27, Paul summarized that those who had condemned Jesus were "they that dwell at Jerusalem, and their rulers." Now in verse 30, Paul testifies that God raised Jesus from the dead. In the death and resurrection of Jesus, there is a clear contrast between the deeds of mortals and those of God. Those mortals involved in mocking Christ or passing unrighteous judgments upon him directly before his death were "chief priests," "the elders of the people," "Pontius Pilate, the governor," "the multitude," "band of soldiers," "scribes," and "thieves" (Matthew 27:1, 2, 11–12, 20, 24, 27–31, 41, 44). Mortals condemned Christ, conspired to put him to death, and then crucified him. But the final victory belongs to God, who raised Christ from the dead to become an immortal soul. God reversed the destruction of mortals by resurrecting his Son, and this reversal will continue with the resurrection of all humans. Thus Paul's apostolic testimony—"God raised him from the dead"—brings comfort and joy to those who follow Christ.

Acts 13:31 *he was seen.* Paul, in a letter to the Corinthians, provided a partial list of those who saw the resurrected Lord—Peter, James, the other apostles, five hundred brethren, and Paul himself (1 Corinthians 15:5–8). In this synagogue speech he simply summarizes that Jesus Christ "was seen many days of them which came up with him from Galilee to Jerusalem."

many days. Jesus, as a resurrected person, ministered among his disciples for forty days (see Acts 1:3).

from Galilee to Jerusalem. Before his death and resurrection, Jesus "went *throughout every city and village,* preaching and shewing the glad tidings of the kingdom of God" (Luke 8:1; emphasis added). Likewise, after his resurrection, the Lord traveled widely, from "Galilee to Jerusalem," appearing to his disciples and making them witnesses of the resurrection.

who are his witnesses unto the people. This expresses one of the primary goals of Jesus' post-resurrection appearances to his disciples—so that those who witness his resurrection will then bear testimony of him. *People* refers to all who have not yet received the good news of Christ and his resurrection.

Acts 13:32–33 *we declare unto you glad tidings.* This is the good news, or glad tidings, that God has fulfilled the promise made to the fathers that he would raise up a Savior out of the lineage of David, the son of Jesse (see verses 22–23). That Savior was Jesus Christ, and God's promise was fulfilled at the resurrection of Jesus. "God," Paul wrote, "hath fulfilled the [promise] unto us their children, in that he hath raised up Jesus again" (verse 33).

Acts 13:33 *Thou art my Son, this day have I begotten thee.* This phrase, cited by Paul in his sermon, is a direct quotation from Psalm 2:7. (Note that Paul cites Psalm 2:7 again in Hebrews 1:5 and 5:5.) Paul applied the phrase to the resurrected Jesus Christ. Both *Son* and *begotten* are theologically significant expressions that describe Jesus' special relationship with God the Father. In many other passages *Son* is part of a longer title of Jesus Christ. For example, Jesus is called "Son of God" (2 Nephi 25:19), "Son of the Highest" (Luke 1:32), "Son of the Eternal Father" (1 Nephi 11:21), and "Son of the living God" (D&C 14:9). *Begotten,* too, belongs to longer designations of Jesus, such as "Only Begotten" (Moses 6:57), "the Only Begotten of the Father" (D&C 93:11), and the "Only Begotten Son of the Father" (D&C 76:35).

Even as Jesus shared a special relationship with his Father, so too, through spiritual rebirth, righteous individuals may become Jesus' sons and daughters (Mosiah 5:7; 27:25; Ether 3:14; D&C 11:30; 35:2).

Acts 13:34–35 *I will give you the sure mercies of David. . . . Thou shalt not suffer thine Holy One to see corruption.* As part of his discourse on the resurrection, Paul cited two Old Testament passages. He first cited Isaiah 55:3: "I will make an everlasting covenant with you, even the sure mercies of David." The "sure mercies of David" pertains to the promise of the resurrection to King David. Though the king had committed great sins in connection with his affair with Bathsheba, the Lord promised him that his soul would not be left in hell; instead, through the Lord's great mercy, David would receive the resurrection. And if David had the promise of the resurrection, then all may have that same hope.

Next Paul cited the second half of Psalm 16:10: "Neither wilt thou suffer thine Holy One to see corruption." This is a Messianic passage promising that the body of Jesus Christ, the "Holy One," though laid in the tomb for a short period after the crucifixion, would not decay and decompose in the tomb.

Acts 13:36 *For David . . . fell on sleep, and was laid unto his fathers.* According to 1 Kings 2:10, "David slept with his fathers, and was buried in the city of David." As late as the New Testament period, the whereabouts of David's tomb was known (see Acts 2:29).

Acts 13:37 *he, whom God raised again, saw no corruption.* In verses 36–37 Paul contrasts King David and Jesus Christ when he states that David *fell* (asleep in death) but Jesus was *raised* (in the resurrection); also, David "saw corruption" but Jesus Christ "saw no corruption."

MANY SAINTS SEE THE RESURRECTED JESUS

1 Corinthians 15:3–9

3 For I delivered unto you first of all that which I also received, how that Christ died for our sins according to the scriptures;

4 And that he was buried, and that he rose again the third day according to the scriptures:

5 And that he was seen of Cephas, then of the twelve:

6 After that, he was seen of above five hundred brethren at once; of whom the greater part remain unto this present, but some are fallen asleep.

7 After that, he was seen of James; then of all the apostles.

8 And last of all he was seen of me also, as of one born out of due time.

9 For I am the least of the apostles, that am not meet to be called an apostle, because I persecuted the church of God.

The law of witnesses, as revealed to Moses, states, "At the mouth of two witnesses, or at the mouth of three witnesses, shall the matter be established" (Deuteronomy 19:15). The same law was cited during the early Christian period (2 Corinthians 13:1) and then again at the beginning of the dispensation of the fullness of times (D&C 6:28). Paul, perhaps with the law of witnesses in mind, listed a number of the faithful who were privileged to see Jesus Christ's resurrected body. Cephas, approximately five hundred brethren, James, all of the apostles, and Paul were witnesses to the risen Lord. By listing so many who had witnessed the Lord's eternal body, Paul established the matter of the resurrection. Each of these witnesses, and all others who have seen the resurrected Jesus but who were not named by Paul, have no doubt concerning the reality of the resurrection. As President David O. McKay testified, "Let us ask ourselves, and ask sincerely, is it a fact that the crucified Jesus did appear after his death a resurrected being? . . . That the literal resurrection from the grave was a reality to the disciples, who knew Christ intimately, is a certainty. In their minds there was absolutely no doubt. They were witnesses of the fact. They knew because their eyes beheld, their ears heard, their hands felt the corporeal presence of the risen Redeemer."[25]

NOTES AND COMMENTARY

1 Corinthians 15:3–4 *Christ died . . . he was buried . . . he rose again.* Paul, as an apostolic witness of Jesus Christ, bears witness of the Savior's death, burial, and resurrection. Paul's words represent the summation of the Christian message. Joseph Smith plainly asserted, "The fundamental principles of our religion are the testimony of the Apostles and Prophets, concerning Jesus Christ, that He died, was buried, and rose again the third day, and ascended into heaven; and all other things which pertain to our religion are only appendages to it."[26]

according to the scriptures. It is difficult to know to which scriptures Paul was referring when he twice used this phrase (see verses 3–4). He may have had in mind specific passages from the Old Testament, or perhaps he was referring in a general sense to all of the prophets, whose chief message was Jesus Christ, his atoning sacrifice, and his resurrection.

1 Corinthians 15:5 *he was seen of Cephas.* Cephas (Aramaic for *stone;* the name *Peter* in Greek also means *stone*) was Simon Peter. Jesus, upon meeting Simon, named him Cephas. "When Jesus beheld him, he said, Thou art Simon the son of Jona: thou shalt be called Cephas, which is by interpretation, A stone" (John 1:42). Paul mentioned Cephas previously in this epistle (1 Corinthians 1:12; 3:22; 9:5), but here Paul listed Cephas as one who had seen the risen Lord (see also Luke 24:34). It is significant that Cephas was one of the witnesses because he was the chief apostle of his day and the presiding authority of the Church.

then of the twelve. The number refers to the Quorum of the Twelve Apostles, counting Matthias as one of that number, but not Judas.

1 Corinthians 15:6 *he was seen of above five hundred brethren at once.* Paul did not indicate who these brethren were. Perhaps they were attendees of a large priesthood meeting or conference; or possibly they represented a group who were worshiping at a special meeting.

of whom the greater part remain. The majority of the five hundred witnesses were yet alive at the time Paul wrote his epistle to the Corinthians. Others of them, however, had passed away, or "fallen asleep."

1 Corinthians 15:7 *he was seen of James.* This likely refers either to Jesus' brother or to the son of Zebedee, John's brother.

then of all the apostles. Compare verse 5.

1 Corinthians 15:8 *last of all he was seen of me.* Paul, too, saw the resurrected Jesus Christ and served as one of his special witnesses.

1 Corinthians 15:9 *I am the least of the apostles.* Paul wrote to the Ephesians that he was "less than the least of all saints" (Ephesians 3:8). Here he calls himself the "least of the apostles" because of his earlier activity in persecuting God's church.

because I persecuted the church of God. Paul stated straightforwardly that he persecuted Church members; Luke, the author of the book of Acts, gives details: "Saul was consenting unto [Stephen's] death. And at that time there was a great persecution against the church which was at Jerusalem. . . . As for Saul, he made havock of the church, entering into every house, and haling men and women committed them to prison" (Acts 8:1, 3).

CHAPTER 7

THE FORM AND NATURE OF RESURRECTED BEINGS

Resurrected beings have perfect, "superhuman" bodies of flesh and bones. They cannot be injured, harmed, or destroyed. They cannot become sick, diseased, or contaminated with the viruses that plague mortals. These immortal bodies will never expire and will never see corruption of any kind, throughout all the eternities.

Resurrected beings have the power to perform all the noble and elevated functions of mortals (though the powers of procreation are reserved to the exalted). They can speak, converse, reason with and enjoy the company of others, walk, and partake of mortal food. Similar to those of mortals, their bodies are tangible and corporeal, having hands that can touch and feel and perform various functions. They have arms, legs, eyes, a mouth, hair, and other features that they possessed in mortality. Unlike mortals, however, resurrected personages have spirit matter in their bodies in the place of blood. As John Taylor made clear, "When the resurrection and exaltation of man shall be consummated, although more pure, refined and glorious, yet will he still be in the same image, and have the same likeness, without variation or change in any of his parts or faculties, except the substitution of spirit for blood."[1]

In addition, exalted resurrected souls possess powers of various sorts that make them formidable. They have the ability to mingle undetected with mortals. They can hide their glory and resurrected nature while administering to those in mortality. These immortal beings can appear out of nowhere and vanish in an instant. They have the ability to stand in the air and to pass through walls, closed doors, and ceilings (see Joseph Smith—History 1:30, 43).[2]

The appearance of those with exalted resurrected bodies is heavenly because they have been clothed upon with glory from God himself—theirs is a tabernacle made to last forever. They have beautiful skin and a countenance that is lovely, brighter than the noonday sun, and "glorious beyond description" (Joseph Smith–History 1:32). As Brigham Young said, "We bear the image of our earthly parents in their fallen state, but by obedience to the Gospel of salvation and the renovating influences of the Holy Ghost, and the holy resurrection, we shall put on the image of the heavenly, in beauty, glory, power and goodness."[3]

ALL THINGS RESTORED TO THEIR PERFECT FRAME

Alma 40:23–26

23 The soul shall be restored to the body, and the body to the soul; yea, and every limb and joint shall be restored to its body; yea, even a hair of the head shall not be lost; but all things shall be restored to their proper and perfect frame.

24 And now, my son, this is the restoration of which has been spoken by the mouths of the prophets—

25 And then shall the righteous shine forth in the kingdom of God.

26 But behold, an awful death cometh upon the wicked; for they die as to things pertaining to things of righteousness; for they are unclean, and no unclean thing can inherit the kingdom of God; but they are cast out, and consigned to partake of the fruits of their labors or their works, which have been evil; and they drink the dregs of a bitter cup.

Alma used *restored* and *restoration* to describe the resurrection to his son Corianton, whose mind was "worried concerning the resurrection of the dead" (Alma 40:1). The first of three instances of the word *restored* provides a general definition of the resurrection: "The soul shall be *restored* to the body, and the body to the soul" (v. 23; emphasis added). The second instance adds clarity to the first: "Yea, and every limb and joint shall be *restored* to its body; yea, even a hair of the head shall not be lost" (v. 23; emphasis added). The third instance summarizes what will be restored at the resurrection: "All things shall be *restored* to their proper and perfect frame" (v. 23; emphasis added). In verse 24 Alma used the word *restoration*: "This is the restoration of which has been spoken by the mouths of the prophets."

How will such a complete restoration—of every limb and joint, of the head's hair, and of "all things"—be possible? Elder Russell M. Nelson has provided an answer that combines his knowledge as a physician with his testimony as an apostle: "The Lord who created us in the first place surely has power to do it again. The same necessary elements now in our bodies will still be available—at His command. The same unique genetic code now embedded in each of our living cells will still be available to format new ones then. The miracle of the Resurrection, wondrous as it will be, is marvelously matched by the miracle of our creation in the first place."[4]

Notes and Commentary

Alma 40:23 *The soul shall be restored to the body, and the body to the soul.* Alma presented a definition of the resurrection, which is the restoration of the spirit (or "soul") to the body. Some years earlier, Alma's father provided a similar definition when he taught that the resurrection constitutes "spirits uniting with . . . bodies, never to be divided" (Alma 11:45). Centuries before that, Nephi defined the resurrection as when "the spirit and the body is restored to itself again, and all men become incorruptible, and immortal, and they are living souls" (2 Nephi 9:13).

every limb and joint shall be restored to its body. Alma paraphrased Amulek, who affirmed that "both limb and joint shall be restored to its proper frame." See commentary on Alma 11:43 in "The 'Perfect Form' of Resurrected Beings," in this chapter.

yea, even a hair of the head shall not be lost. The resurrection comprehends "every part of the body" (Alma 41:2), even the hair of the head. *Hair* is used elsewhere in scripture to represent physical totality: "there shall not an hair of your head perish" (Luke 21:18); "even the very hairs of your head are all numbered" (Luke 12:7); "for there shall not an hair fall from the head of any of you" (Acts 27:34). Doctrine and Covenants 29:25 explains why even the hair of the head is important to God: "And not one hair, neither mote, shall be lost, for it is the workmanship of mine hand."

Just as Alma said that not a hair of the head would be lost in the resurrection, Brigham Young spoke of the body's "fundamental particles" in a similar context: "When the angel who holds the keys of the resurrection shall sound his trumpet, the peculiar fundamental particles that organized our bodies here . . . —though they be deposited in the depths of the sea, and though one particle is in the north, another in the south, another in the east, and another in the west,—will be brought together again in the twinkling of an eye, and our spirits will take possession of them."[5] (See also commentary on Alma 11:44 in "The 'Perfect Form' of Resurrected Beings," in this chapter.)

all things shall be restored to their proper and perfect frame. "All things" is not an overstatement. Brigham Young taught, "Every material part and portion pertaining to [one's] body, to the temporal organization that constitutes the man, will clothe his spirit again, before he is prepared to receive the place and habitation that is prepared for him."[6]

How perfect will our resurrected bodies be? In general conference, October 1900, President Lorenzo Snow had the resurrection in mind as he addressed the Saints on two occasions. During his first sermon he remarked that after we rise from the dead, "we will have our bodies glorified, made free from every sickness and distress, and rendered most beautiful. There is nothing more beautiful to look upon than a resurrected man or woman. There is nothing grander that I can imagine that a man can possess than a resurrected body."[7] In his second sermon, he remarked that our resurrected bodies will be "glorified" and "free from sickness and death." In fact, "nothing is so beautiful as a person in a resurrected and glorified condition. There is nothing more lovely."[8]

For a discussion of the body's being "perfect" after the resurrection, see commentary on Alma 11:43 in "The 'Perfect Form' of Resurrected Beings," in this chapter.

 Alma 40:24 *this is the restoration of which has been spoken by the mouths of the prophets.* Job, Isaiah, Ezekiel, Daniel, Hosea, Nephi, Jacob, Abinadi, and many other prophets have spoken and written of the resurrection—the restoration of the body to the spirit (see Job

14:13–15; Isaiah 26:19; Ezekiel 37:1–14; Daniel 12:2–3; Hosea 13:14; 2 Nephi 9:3–13; Jacob 4:11–12; Mosiah 15:6–8, 19–20).

Alma 40:25 *then shall the righteous shine forth in the kingdom of God.* After the resurrection, the righteous in God's kingdom will shine with brilliant glory just as the sun shines at noonday (compare also Daniel 12:3 and Matthew 13:43). The resurrected Moroni serves as an example of one who shines with such glory. Joseph Smith described the personage of Moroni with such words as *light, lighter than at noonday, exquisite whiteness, exceedingly white and brilliant, glorious beyond description, countenance truly like lightning, exceedingly light,* and *very bright:* "I discovered a light appearing in my room, which continued to increase until the room was lighter than at noonday, when immediately a personage appeared. . . . He had on a loose robe of most exquisite whiteness. It was a whiteness beyond anything earthly I had ever seen; nor do I believe that any earthly thing could be made to appear so exceedingly white and brilliant. . . . Not only was his robe exceedingly white, but his whole person was glorious beyond description, and his countenance truly like lightning. The room was exceedingly light, but not so very bright as immediately around his person" (Joseph Smith–History 1:31–32).

Alma 40:26 There will be no such light and glory for the wicked, particularly the sons of perdition. Instead, even though they will indeed be resurrected, they will die an "awful death" and they will "die as to things pertaining to things of righteousness" (Alma 40:26). This is called the "second death" and "spiritual death" (Alma 12:16).

THE "PERFECT FORM" OF RESURRECTED BEINGS

Alma 11:41–45

41 Therefore the wicked remain as though there had been no redemption made, except it be the loosing of the bands of death; for behold, the day cometh that all shall rise from the dead and stand before God, and be judged according to their works.

42 Now, there is a death which is called a temporal death; and the death of Christ shall loose the bands of this temporal death, that all shall be raised from this temporal death.

43 The spirit and the body shall be reunited again in its perfect form; both limb and joint shall be restored to its proper frame, even as we now are at this time; and we shall be brought to stand before God, knowing even as we know now, and have a bright recollection of all our guilt.

44 Now, this restoration shall come to all, both old and young, both bond and free, both male and female, both the wicked and the righteous; and even there shall not so much as a hair of their heads be lost; but every thing shall be restored to its perfect frame, as it is now, or in the body, and shall be brought and be arraigned before the bar of Christ the Son, and God the Father, and the Holy Spirit, which is one Eternal God, to be judged according to their works, whether they be good or whether they be evil.

45 Now, behold, I have spoken unto you concerning the death of the mortal body, and also concerning the resurrection of the mortal body. I say unto you that this mortal body is raised to an immortal body, that is from death, even from the first death unto life, that they can die no more; their spirits uniting with their bodies, never to be divided; thus the whole becoming spiritual and immortal, that they can no more see corruption.

Amulek, in the presence of Alma, Zeezrom, and others, formulated one of the most magnificent and masterful statements found in scripture regarding the resurrection. The setting has Amulek responding to Zeezrom, a "man who was expert in the devices of the devil, that he might destroy that which was good" (Alma 11:21). Zeezrom was a master at lying and deception and was full of "craftiness" (Alma 12:1, 3). He "was the foremost to accuse Amulek and Alma, he being one of the most expert among" the lawyers (Alma 10:31).

Zeezrom's question "Is the Son of God the very Eternal Father?" (Alma 11:38) prompted Amulek to testify that Jesus Christ "shall come into the world to redeem his people; and he shall take upon him the transgressions of those who believe on his name; and these are they that shall have eternal life, and salvation cometh to none else" (Alma 11:40). So great were Amulek's words that in due course they silenced Zeezrom and caused him to "tremble under a consciousness of his guilt" (Alma 12:1).

Amulek's words are magnificent because, first of all, he provided very specific details about who will be resurrected: "*all* shall rise from the dead" (v. 41; emphasis added); "*all* shall be raised from this temporal death" (v. 42; emphasis added); and "this restoration shall come to *all,* both old and young, both bond and free, both male and female, both the wicked and the righteous" (v. 44; emphasis added).

Second, Amulek gave a clear definition of what it means to be resurrected: "The spirit and the body shall be reunited again in its perfect form" (v. 43). He then gave additional details: "Both limb and joint shall be restored to its proper frame . . . and even there shall not so much as a hair of their heads be lost; but every thing shall be restored to its perfect frame" (vv. 43–44).

Both the spirit and the body are essential to make a "perfect form." One without the other will never bring perfection. According to President John Taylor, "it requires both body and spirit to make a perfect man, whether in time or eternity."[9]

Third, Amulek presented three unambiguous statements that the resurrection lasts forever. Resurrected beings "can die no more"; "their spirits [unite] with their bodies, never to be divided"; and "thus the whole [become] spiritual and immortal, that they can no more see corruption" (v. 45).

NOTES AND COMMENTARY

Alma 11:41 *the wicked remain as though there had been no redemption made.* The only redemption that comes to the wicked is the resurrection. They cannot gain eternal life (see Alma 11:40), which is reserved for those who believe on the name of Jesus Christ and remain faithful. Thus there is no redemption for the wicked, said Amulek, "except it be the loosing of the bands of death," or the resurrection.

A short time after Amulek completed his response to Zeezrom, Alma "began to speak to [Zeezrom], and to establish the words of Amulek, and to explain things beyond, or to unfold the scriptures beyond that which Amulek had done" (Alma 12:1). In doing so, Alma at one point cited the words of Amulek, that the wicked remain "as though there had been no redemption made" (Alma 12:18), followed by an explanation, "for they cannot be redeemed according to God's justice; and they cannot die, seeing there is no more corruption" (Alma 12:18).

the day cometh that all shall rise from the dead. Amulek emphasized the truth that the resurrection is for everyone who has lived in mortality with his three-time use of the word *all,* in verses 41, 42, and 44. Joseph Smith, too, emphasized the universality of the resurrection when he taught, "All men are born to die, and all men must rise; all must enter eternity."[10]

and stand before God, and be judged according to their works. Several other prophets have linked the resurrection directly to the great judgment, as did Amulek in his speech to Zeezrom. John the Revelator, in fact, linked the two subjects and used key words and phrases identical to those found in Amulek's speech—*dead, stand before God, judged,* and *according to their works.* John wrote, "And I saw the dead, small and great, stand before God; and the books were opened: and another book was opened, which is the book of life: and the dead were judged out of those things which were written in the books, according to their works. And the sea gave up the dead which were in it; and death and hell delivered up the dead which were in them: and they were judged every man according to their works" (Revelation 20:12–13).

Alma, too, linked the resurrection with the judgment. In one passage he repeated, for emphasis, these key words—*God, mercy, atonement, resurrection of the dead,* and *presence.* The passage reads, "But *God* ceaseth not to be *God,* and *mercy* claimeth the penitent, and *mercy* cometh because of the *atonement;* and the *atonement* bringeth to pass the *resurrection of the dead;* and the *resurrection of the dead* bringeth back men into the *presence* of God; and thus they are restored into his *presence,* to be judged according to their works, according to the law and justice" (Alma 42:23; emphasis added).

Alma 11:42 *there is a death which is called a temporal death.* Temporal death occurs when the spirit leaves the mortal body; James wrote, "the body without the spirit is dead" (James 2:26). This is "that death [which] comes upon mankind," Alma explained after Amulek completed his testimony, "yea, the death which has been spoken of by Amulek, which is the temporal death" (Alma 12:24). Temporal death is not the same as "spiritual death" or a "second death," which Alma defines as dying "as to things pertaining unto righteousness": "Then cometh a death, even a second death, which is a spiritual death; then is a time that whosoever dieth in his sins, as to a temporal death, shall also die a spiritual death; yea, he shall die as to things pertaining unto righteousness" (Alma 12:16).

the death of Christ shall loose the bands of this temporal death, that all shall be raised from this temporal death. Amulek touched on the very core of the gospel message—that Jesus Christ's death brings immortality to all humanity.

Alma 11:43 *The spirit and the body shall be reunited again in its perfect form.* Amulek defined resurrection in the simplest of terms. Resurrection is the reunion of one's spirit and body, after death, to a perfect form. Nephi, too, presented a simple definition of resurrection when he wrote, "The spirit and the body is restored to itself again, and all men become incorruptible, and immortal" (2 Nephi 9:13).

Amulek's expression of a "perfect form" is also expressed as a "perfect frame" (Alma 40:23; D&C 138:17) or perfect body. In the April 1949 general conference of the Church, Elder Joseph Fielding Smith instructed, "Those who attain to the blessings of the first or celestial resurrection will be pure and holy, and perfect in body."[11] Almost fifty years later Elder Russell M. Nelson described resurrected bodies as being "perfected": "The Atonement of Jesus Christ became the *immortal creation.* He volunteered to answer the ends of a law previously transgressed. And by the shedding of His blood, His and our physical bodies could become perfected. They could again function without blood, just as Adam and Eve's did in their *paradisiacal* form. Paul taught that 'flesh and blood cannot inherit the kingdom of God; . . . this mortal must put on immortality.' (1 Corinthians 15:50–53.)"[12]

both limb and joint shall be restored to its proper frame. Resurrected bodies will be complete, having every limb, joint, and appendage. "When the body is resurrected," declared President Spencer W. Kimball at the Manila Philippines Area Conference, "we will have our limbs and all our faculties."[13] If a person loses a limb during war, a work-related accident, or in any other circumstance, he or she will have that limb restored in the resurrection. Many of our prophets have so testified. Alma explained to his son that in the resurrection "every limb and joint shall be restored to its body; yea, even a hair of the head shall not be lost" (Alma 40:23).

Joseph Fielding Smith also addressed this topic: "The question is frequently discussed in our classes in Sunday School, Mutual and Priesthood quorums, whether or not a body will come forth deformed, if deformed in this mortal life; or with some part missing, such as if a limb, or other part was lost while in mortal life. The answer has been given in the most emphatic and positive manner in the scriptures. . . . Deformities will be erased and in the resurrection will be made whole."[14]

Another Church authority, Joseph F. Smith, discussed other deformities in light of the resurrection, such as tumors and diseases. "If a man has gone through life with a club foot, or other deformity, will he be raised in the resurrection and have the club foot or deformity, and have to wait until the 'restoration of all things,' before this imperfection is corrected?

"The answer to this is, No! Let us carry this a little farther. If a person through disease passes through the greater part of his life with some deformity—such as diabetes, tumors, consumption—will he have to be subject to such disease until the day of 'restitution of all things'? Certainly not, and it is just as inconsistent to claim that the club foot would have to remain as to say that any of these other deformities or diseases would have to remain."[15]

we shall be brought to stand before God, knowing even as we know now. Things that belong to the world will not remain after the resurrection. "Everything that is in the world," the Lord revealed to Joseph Smith, "whether it be ordained of men, by thrones, or principalities, or powers, or things of name, whatsoever they may be, that are not by me or by my word . . . shall be thrown down, and shall not remain after men are dead, neither in nor after the resurrection" (D&C 132:13). One thing that will remain after the resurrection, however, is the knowledge that we possess in mortality. This will remain with us when we stand before God as resurrected beings; we will be "knowing even as we know now." This accords with Doctrine and Covenants 130:18: "Whatever principle of intelligence we attain unto in this life, it will rise with us in the resurrection."

have a bright recollection of all our guilt. Although both the righteous and the wicked will one day stand before God to be judged, their reactions will be completely different. The righteous will stand before God and will "have a perfect knowledge of their enjoyment, and their righteousness, being clothed with purity, yea, even with the robe of righteousness." The wicked will "have a perfect knowledge of all [their] guilt, and [their] uncleanness, and [their] nakedness" (2 Nephi 9:14; see also Mosiah 3:25). Additionally, the wicked, according to Alma, will stand before "the tribunal of God," and their souls will be "filled with guilt and remorse, having a remembrance of all [their] guilt, yea, a perfect remembrance of all [their] wickedness, yea, a remembrance that [they] have set at defiance the commandments of God" (Alma 5:18).

Alma 11:44 *Now, this restoration shall come to all.* This is the third time that Amulek used the word "all" to describe the scope of those who will receive the resurrection. Earlier in his speech he stated that "all shall rise from the dead" (v. 41) and "all shall be raised from this temporal death" (v. 42); as he concluded his words he testified that "this restoration shall come to all." Then, lest his audience misunderstand his words, Amulek designated those who are included in "all": "both old and young, both bond and free, both male and female, both the wicked and the righteous." In other words, every single soul who has ever lived will rise from the dead, with the spirit restored to the body.

even there shall not so much as a hair of their heads be lost. Alma the Younger testified that "even a hair of the head shall not be lost" at the resurrection (Alma 40:23). Resurrected beings will have a full head of hair because "not so much as a hair" will be lost. The resurrected Jesus is described in two brief statements as having hair on his head: "The hair of his head was white like the pure snow" (D&C 110:3); and "His head and his hairs were white like wool" (Revelation 1:14). The expressions "white like the pure snow" and "white like wool" describe the glory and light that Jesus possesses. Once, when speaking about the resurrection, Joseph Smith said, "The old man with his silvery hairs will glory in bloom and beauty." Then, in order to relate how glorious the resurrection will be, the Prophet added these words: "No man can describe it to you—no man can write it."[16]

God truly is a God of detail, because he promises to resurrect people even down to the hair on their heads; and he is a God of power, because he can complete the promise that "there shall not so much as a hair of their heads be lost." And not just our hair will be restored, but "the very particles that compose our bodies will be brought forth in the morning of the resurrection."[17] (See also commentary on Alma 40:23 in "All Things Restored to Their Perfect Frame," in this chapter.)

but every thing shall be restored to its perfect frame, as it is now, or in the body. Amulek here seems to be speaking of the "perfect frame" as the mortal frame, only without the aging, disease, and deformity that can afflict mortal beings. When we are resurrected to any glory, we will have a body that is much "as it is now," although the glory and power of the body will be different depending on our eternal destiny. Thus, all resurrected bodies are, in this sense, considered "perfect." This "perfect form" is in the image of God, though only those who receive exalted bodies will be glorified as God is, having all the powers and capabilities of the body of a god. On the "perfect form" of resurrected beings, see commentary on verse 43.

shall be brought and be arraigned before the bar of Christ the Son, and God the Father, and the Holy Spirit. Amulek did not reveal *who* will bring all of these resurrected individuals (who were described in the previous verses) before the bar. He stated only that they will "be brought and be arraigned before the bar." Note that God's bar of judgment belongs to all three members of the Godhead— the Father, the Son, and the Holy Ghost.

Alma 11:45 *this mortal body is raised to an immortal body, that is from death.* Earlier in his discourse Amulek defined the resurrection in very simple terms when he taught that "the spirit and the body shall be reunited again in its perfect form" (v. 43). At the conclusion of his words he once again defined resurrection but used different words: "This mortal body is raised to an immortal body, that is from death."

even from the first death unto life. The first death is "the death of the mortal body"; the second death is spiritual death, which is defined as being separated from God.

that they can die no more; their spirits uniting with their bodies, never to be divided. After the resurrection, people will never again need to fear death because their spirits will unite with their bodies for all eternity. "They can die no more," testified Amulek, and their body and spirit will "never . . . be divided." Other prophets have similarly testified: "They cannot die, seeing there is no more corruption" (Alma 12:18); "there shall be no more death" (Revelation 21:4); "they shall rise from the dead and shall not die after" (D&C 63:49); "they shall not any more see death" (D&C 88:116); and "the spirit and the body [are] to be united never again to be divided" (D&C 138:17).

the whole becoming spiritual and immortal. On spiritual bodies, see commentary on 1 Corinthians 15:44 in "Celestial, Terrestrial, and Telestial Bodies at the Resurrection," in this chapter.

THE RESURRECTION IS "THE REDEMPTION OF THE SOUL"

D&C 88:14–17

14 Now, verily I say unto you, that through the redemption which is made for you is brought to pass the resurrection from the dead.

15 And the spirit and the body are the soul of man.

16 And the resurrection from the dead is the redemption of the soul.

17 And the redemption of the soul is through him that quickeneth all things, in whose bosom it is decreed that the poor and the meek of all the earth shall inherit it.

This passage, from a revelation identified as the "olive leaf . . . plucked from the Tree of Paradise, the Lord's message of peace to us,"[18] provides six primary truths that pertain to the soul and its redemption:

- The redemption is "made for" us, earth's inhabitants (v. 14);
- The redemption results in the resurrection (v. 14);

- The spirit and the body constitute man's soul (v. 15);

- The redemption of the soul is the resurrection from the dead (v. 16). ("The redemption of the soul" mentioned in verse 16 is not to be strictly equated with "the redemption" mentioned in verse 14. "The redemption of the soul" speaks specifically of the resurrection, where the body and spirit are redeemed from death. In verse 14, "the redemption" speaks of the redeeming gift of Jesus Christ);

- Jesus Christ made it possible for the soul to be redeemed, or to be resurrected. It is he that "quickeneth all things" (v. 17);

- Jesus Christ made it possible for the meek and the poor to inherit the earth (v. 17).

Those who truly understand the redemption will express great joy, just as Wilford Woodruff did: "There is hardly any principle the Lord has revealed that I have rejoiced more in than in the redemption of our dead; that we will have our fathers, our mothers, our wives and our children with us in the family organization, in the morning of the first resurrection and in the celestial kingdom. These are grand principles. They are worth every sacrifice. When we get home with God and with the prophets and apostles we will rejoice exceedingly. 'Eye hath not seen, nor ear heard, neither have entered into the heart of man, the things which God hath prepared for them that love Him.'"[19]

NOTES AND COMMENTARY

D&C 88:14 *redemption which is made for you.* There is a "great and eternal plan of redemption" (Alma 34:16). It is part of a divine plan that hearkens back to premortal life, long before Adam and Eve were introduced into the Garden of Eden. The plan was "laid from the foundation of the world" so that resurrection from the dead would come to pass (Alma 12:25). It was "made" for all of God's children by a loving father.

The plan calls for a redeemer who would redeem his people, which Redeemer is Jesus Christ. Paul taught that "we have redemption through his [Jesus'] blood" (Ephesians 1:7). The doctrine of redemption through Christ is clearly presented in the Book of Mormon: "redemption cometh in and through the Holy Messiah"

(2 Nephi 2:6); "the resurrection of the dead, and the redemption of the people . . . was to be brought to pass through the power, and sufferings, and death of Christ, and his resurrection and ascension into heaven" (Mosiah 18:2); and "if Christ had not come into the world" then "there could have been no redemption. And if Christ had not risen from the dead . . . there could have been no resurrection" (Mosiah 16:6–7). A modern revelation teaches that "the great atoning sacrifice . . . was made by the Son of God, for the redemption of the world" (D&C 138:2).

D&C 88:15 *the spirit and the body are the soul of man.* Elder James E. Talmage referred to these words in a general conference address: "It has been declared in the solemn word of revelation, that the spirit and the body constitute the soul of man; and therefore, we should look upon this body as something that shall endure in the resurrected state, beyond the grave, something to be kept pure and holy."[20]

The body is formed of "the dust of the ground" (Genesis 2:7), or earth's elements. The spirit also is composed of matter: "All spirit is matter, but it is more fine or pure, and can only be discerned by purer eyes" (D&C 131:7). Genesis 2:7 describes how Adam became a "living soul." "And the Lord God formed man of the dust of the ground, and breathed into his nostrils the breath of life; and man became a living soul" (compare Ezekiel 37:14). All living souls during mortality possess both a spirit and a body; but death comes to mortals when the spirit leaves the body ("the body without the spirit is dead"—James 2:26).

D&C 88:16 *resurrection from the dead is the redemption of the soul.* The plan of redemption will come to pass when the spirit and body are reunited to make an immortal, resurrected soul (see Alma 40:18, 20; 40:23). Hence, the resurrection is the same as the soul's redemption. A latter-day revelation explains that resurrection is "redemption from the bands of death" (D&C 138:16).

D&C 88:17 *redemption of the soul is through him that quickeneth all things.* It is God who quickens all things (1 Timothy 6:13) and brings forth the soul's redemption.

poor and the meek of all the earth shall inherit it. See "The Earth, Too, Will Be Resurrected," in chapter 9.

OUR "EARTHLY HOUSE" VERSUS THE "HOUSE NOT MADE WITH HANDS"

2 Corinthians 5:1–5

1 For we know that if our earthly house of this tabernacle were dissolved, we have a building of God, an house not made with hands, eternal in the heavens.

2 For in this we groan, earnestly desiring to be clothed upon with our house which is from heaven:

3 If so be that being clothed we shall not be found naked.

4 For we that are in this tabernacle do groan, being burdened: not for that we would be unclothed, but clothed upon, that mortality might be swallowed up of life.

5 Now he that hath wrought us for the selfsame thing is God, who also hath given unto us the earnest of the Spirit.

The apostle Paul contrasted mortal bodies with immortal, resurrected bodies, a contrast he also made in his earlier epistle to the Corinthians (see 1 Corinthians 15:53–54). As part of his approach to the subject, Paul employed a number of images in the 2 Corinthians passage. He used the architectural terms *house, tabernacle,* and *building* to describe the nature of mortal and immortal bodies. The mortal body, Paul wrote, is an "earthly house," a "tabernacle" that will eventually be "dissolved." By contrast, a resurrected body is a "building of God," a "house not made with hands" that is "eternal in the heavens," a "house which is from heaven."

Paul also used imagery pertaining to clothing and nakedness; he contrasted *clothed* personages with those who are *naked* and *unclothed.* Similar imagery exists elsewhere. Adam and Eve, for example, "were both naked" (Genesis 2:25; 3:7, 10–11) so the Lord God made "coats of skin, and clothed them" (Genesis 3:21). "Coats of skin" here seems to have a dual meaning, referring to (1) actual garments of skins made out of sheep or other animal skins; and (2) mortal coverings of flesh and skin. Job, too, referred to the clothing of the mortal covering when he declared to God, "Thou hast clothed me with skin and flesh" (Job 10:11).

In Paul's imagery in 2 Corinthians, we are clothed with a body during mortality, "unclothed" of that body at death, and then clothed upon with a glorious body at the resurrection. Nephi also used the words *clothed* and *robe* in the context of the resurrection of the righteous: "The grave [will] deliver up the body of the righteous; and the spirit and the body is restored to itself again, and all men become incorruptible, and immortal, and they are living souls . . . and the righteous shall have a perfect knowledge of their enjoyment, and their righteousness, being clothed with purity, yea, even with the robe of righteousness" (2 Nephi 9:13–14).

Elder Jeffrey R. Holland extended Nephi's imagery in his teachings about the resurrection when he included the words "clothe" and "robe of righteousness": "As a universal gift flowing from the atonement of Christ, the Resurrection will clothe with a permanent, perfected, restored body every spirit ever born into mortality. Furthermore, for every person who accepts the principles and ordinances of the gospel, that person's body will be something of a robe of righteousness. Therein is the redemption of the soul, and therein is a fulness of joy throughout all eternity, including, in its highest order, 'a fulness and a continuation of the seeds forever and ever.' (D&C 132:19)."[21]

Clothe and *clothed* are used by others in reference to the resurrection.[22] Thomas S. Monson spoke of the resurrected Christ being "clothed with an immortal body of flesh and bones."[23] Joseph Smith declared that "we have a knowledge that those we bury here God will bring up again, clothed upon and quickened by the Spirit of the great God."[24] And Brigham Young taught, "In the resurrection everything that is necessary will be brought from the elements to clothe and to beautify the resurrected Saints who will receive their reward. I do not trouble myself about my dead. If they are stripped of their clothing, I do not want to know it."[25]

NOTES AND COMMENTARY

2 Corinthians 5:1 *For we know.* Paul offered his testimony of the resurrection with the words "we know"; for example, "We know . . . we have a building of God, an house not made with hands, eternal in the heavens." In the same context he added further assurance by writing, "Therefore we are always confident" (v. 6) and "We are confident" (v. 8).

our earthly house of this tabernacle were dissolved. "Our earthly house" refers to our mortal body, a tabernacle that will eventually die and be dissolved, meaning it will eventually return to the earth and waste away. "Tabernacle" may be translated as "tent." Our mortal, earthly body is a temporary structure; if it were "dissolved" or quickly "taken down" as a tent is, we still have God's promise of the resurrection.

we have a building of God, an house not made with hands, eternal in the heavens. Our resurrected body will be called a "building of God" because it will be formed by God, unlike our "earthly house," which was created by mortal parents. In the same way, our resurrected body will be called a "house not made with hands," meaning a house not made with *mortal* hands. Our mortal body is temporary in nature. In time it will waste away and return to Mother Earth, unlike our immortal body, which will be "eternal in the heavens."

2 Corinthians 5:2 *we groan.* As humans, we groan because mortality consists of pain, suffering, sickness, disease, and eventual death. In verse 4 Paul expanded his thought: "For we that are in this tabernacle do groan, being burdened." Paul, however, seems to have been referring to groaning that comes from more than mortal pain and sickness. Perhaps he referred to the groaning of mortals who anticipate the freedom that the resurrection will bring to their bodies; "even we ourselves groan within ourselves, waiting for the adoption, to wit, the redemption of our body" (Romans 8:23).

clothed upon with our house which is from heaven. To be clothed with a heavenly house is to be resurrected with a heavenly and glorious body. Paul again used *clothed* in verses 3 and 4 with the same meaning.

2 Corinthians 5:3–4 *If so be that being clothed we shall not be found naked.* To be naked in this context is to be without a body.

not for that we would be unclothed, but clothed upon. Biblical scholar Paul Barnett explains that to be "unclothed" in the context of Paul's address is to be "in the nakedness of death" or "the 'nakedness' of disembodiment following death."²⁶ We are all, like Job, "clothed . . . with skin and flesh" (Job 10:11) during mortality. At death, however, we will become naked or unclothed of our mortal bodies.

that mortality might be swallowed up of life. Two of the many gifts that come to humans through the Savior's atoning sacrifice are those of immortality and eternal life. In fact, God's divine work and glory is "to bring to pass the immortality and eternal life of man" (Moses 1:39).

2 Corinthians 5:5 *he that hath wrought us for the selfsame thing is God.* It is God who clothes us with immortal life. In another epistle, Paul wrote that it is "the Lord Jesus Christ: who shall change this vile body, that it may be fashioned like unto his glorious body" (Philippians 3:20–21).

given unto us the earnest of the Spirit. The New International Version provides a helpful translation for these words: God has "given us the Spirit as a deposit, guaranteeing what is to come." The Spirit is God's pledge or promise (or "earnest money") to us that we will be clothed with immortal life. The Spirit's role in our resurrection is set forth in Romans 8:11: "But if the Spirit of him that raised up Jesus from the dead dwell in you, he that raised up Christ from the dead shall also quicken your mortal bodies by his Spirit that dwelleth in you."

PAUL'S ANALOGY OF SOWN SEEDS

1 Corinthians 15:35–38

> *35 But some man will say, How are the dead raised up? and with what body do they come?*
>
> *36 Thou fool, that which thou sowest is not quickened, except it die:*
>
> *37 And that which thou sowest, thou sowest not that body that shall be, but bare grain, it may chance of wheat, or of some other grain:*
>
> *38 But God giveth it a body as it hath pleased him, and to every seed his own body.*

Paul compared the sowing of seeds in the earth to death and burial, and the maturing and ripening of grain to the resurrection. In his analogy, the sown seed will "die" when it is buried in the ground.

It is then "quickened" when it breaks forth from the ground and produces grain or fruit. The quickening of the seed is comparable to the resurrection of the human soul, according to Paul's analogy. Additionally, Paul called the seed a "body" (vv. 37–38) when he compared it to a person. He credited God for the harvested grain (vv. 37–38), an important point in his analogy, because God is also the power by which people are resurrected.

NOTES AND COMMENTARY

1 Corinthians 15:35 *But some man will say.* Paul was either responding to an actual communication or he was posing rhetorical questions: "How are the dead raised up? and with what body do they come?"

How are the dead raised up? The dead are raised up by God's power. Jesus Christ is the resurrection and the life (John 11:25), and it is through his atoning sacrifice that the resurrection becomes a reality. Paul illustrated this in the following verses about grain.

with what body do they come? A person will be resurrected with a body of celestial, terrestrial, or telestial glory (see "Celestial, Terrestrial, and Telestial Bodies at the Resurrection," in this chapter) or a body without glory.

1 Corinthians 15:36 *that which thou sowest is not quickened, except it die.* When a seed is planted in soil, it decays or "dies," so to speak, and a new plant grows from the decaying seed. Similarly, when our dead bodies are buried or planted in the ground, in due time our bodies will be resurrected and become new, immortal souls. Elder Bruce R. McConkie expressed it this way: "Even as the seed, sown in the ground, decays that a new plant may live, so our mortal bodies return to the dust that they may rise again in a more glorious state."[27]

Paul's comparison of the seed to death and resurrection may have been inspired by a similar analogy provided by Jesus, speaking of his own death. "And Jesus answered them, saying, The hour is come, that the Son of man should be glorified. . . . Except a corn of wheat fall into the ground and die, it abideth alone: but if it die, it bringeth forth much fruit" (John 12:23–24).

1 Corinthians 15:37 *thou sowest not that body that shall be.* Paul continued his analogy of sowing and harvesting seeds, likening them to the resurrection. He called the seed a "body" to make clear the point of comparison with the resurrection. Sowing the seed is comparable to death, and bearing grain is comparable to the resurrection. The seed that is sown is not that which is harvested—it is not "that body that shall be." Rather, that single, decaying seed will produce much grain that will arise from the soil. Similarly, the human body decomposes in the earth, and that decaying body is not the one that will arise, but a beautiful and perfectly restored body will.

it may chance of wheat, or of some other grain. When one sows seed in the ground, it will produce grain according to the kind of seed that was planted. If wheat seeds were planted, then wheat will be harvested; if barley seeds were planted, then barley will be harvested. The same is true in the animal kingdom. If a human is buried in the earth, then at the resurrection a human will arise.

God will judge us according to our deeds and desires, including what we would have received if the entirety of the gospel plan were offered (see D&C 137). Thus, the state of our heart on this earth will have a great influence on our eternal judgment. If a person with a celestial heart is buried in the earth (even if that person did not know of the gospel), at the resurrection a person of celestial glory will arise (by definition, a person with a celestial heart will embrace the whole of the gospel when the opportunity is given). Likewise, those with terrestrial and telestial spirits in mortality will rise with glorified terrestrial and telestial bodies. We must remember, however, that God's eternal plan allows for repentance in the spirit world for those who did not have a full opportunity to receive the gospel in mortality (and only God can judge when that full opportunity has been given).

1 Corinthians 15:38 *But God giveth it a body as it hath pleased him.* Or, "God giveth it [the seed] a body as it hath pleased him." Paul credited God for the successful harvest of sown seeds and likewise, to make the analogy complete, he credited God as the source of the resurrection. God resurrects in an orderly fashion—"and to every seed his own body." That is to say, he does not cause the wheat seeds to produce barley, neither does he cause the human body to rise as a zebra. Wheat seed produces wheat, and human bodies will be resurrected as immortal humans. Those with celestial hearts and desires

...nslate into celestial deeds when truth and light are made available) will be resurrected as glorified celestial beings.

CELESTIAL, TERRESTRIAL, AND TELESTIAL BODIES AT THE RESURRECTION

1 Corinthians 15:39–44

39 All flesh is not the same flesh: but there is one kind of flesh of men, another flesh of beasts, another of fishes, and another of birds.

40 There are also celestial bodies, and bodies terrestrial, and bodies telestial; but the glory of the celestial, one; and the terrestrial, another; and the telestial, another.

41 There is one glory of the sun, and another glory of the moon, and another glory of the stars: for one star differeth from another star in glory.

42 So also is the resurrection of the dead. It is sown in corruption; it is raised in incorruption:

43 It is sown in dishonour; it is raised in glory: it is sown in weakness; it is raised in power:

44 It is sown a natural body; it is raised a spiritual body. There is a natural body, and there is a spiritual body.

Paul compared the light of great heavenly spheres—the sun, moon, and stars—to resurrected bodies. When a person is resurrected, his or her immortal body will have the glory and light that corresponds to the brightness of one of these spheres. Those who have been "sanctified" and have been obedient to celestial law, the law of Christ (see D&C 88:20–21), will receive celestial bodies with the glory of the sun. They will inherit the celestial kingdom, which will also be "sanctified from all unrighteousness, that it may be prepared for the celestial glory." Furthermore, the celestialized earth "shall be crowned with glory, even with the presence of God the Father" (D&C 88:18–19). Those who have not been sanctified or obedient to Christ's law may receive immortal bodies with glory that corresponds to the light of the moon or stars (see also D&C 76:96–98). They will have terrestrial or telestial bodies and will be assigned to the corresponding kingdom,

THE FORM AND NATURE OF RESURRECTED BEINGS

terrestrial or telestial. Elder McConkie taught, "By one degree of obedience or another, all men, in this life, develop either celestial, terrestrial, or telestial bodies (or in the case of those destined to be sons of perdition, bodies of a baser sort). In the resurrection all men receive back again 'the same body which was a natural body,' whether it be celestial, terrestrial, or what have you. That body is then quickened by the glory attending its particular type, and the person receiving the body then goes automatically, as it were, to the kingdom of glory where that degree of glory is found. (D&C 76; 88:16–33; 1 Corinthians 15:35–38)."[28]

Paul comprehended a great deal concerning the three kingdoms of glory to which resurrected beings would be assigned. Joseph Smith informed us that "Paul ascended into the third heavens, and he could understand the three principal rounds of Jacob's ladder—the telestial, the terrestrial, and the celestial glories or kingdoms."[29] Joseph Smith and Sidney Rigdon saw the glory of these kingdoms: "And thus we saw, in the heavenly vision, the glory of the telestial, which surpasses all understanding; and no man knows it except him to whom God has revealed it. And thus we saw the glory of the terrestrial which excels in all things the glory of the telestial, even in glory, and in power, and in might, and in dominion. And thus we saw the glory of the celestial, which excels in all things—where God, even the Father reigns upon his throne forever and ever" (D&C 76:89–92).

NOTES AND COMMENTARY

1 Corinthians 15:39 *All flesh is not the same flesh.* Within the animal kingdom are many different types of flesh, such as beasts, fishes, and birds. At the resurrection, animals will be resurrected according to their kind while upon the earth. Therefore, "in the resurrection a bear has no hope of becoming a bird or a bird a bear. Fish will be resurrected as fish and skunks as skunks."[30] Paul's statement that "all flesh is not the same flesh" is also true of humans. (Note that Paul connected verses 39 and 40 with "also," meaning "in addition"). Some will be resurrected with celestial bodies, others with terrestrial or telestial bodies (see commentary on verse 40).

1 Corinthians 15:40 *celestial bodies, and bodies terrestrial, and bodies telestial.* All people except sons of perdition will be resurrected to one of three different glories, identified by Paul as *celestial, terrestrial,* and *telestial* bodies. A revelation given to Joseph Smith added much understanding to Paul's statement: "They who are of a celestial spirit shall receive the same body which was a natural body; even ye shall receive your bodies, and your glory shall be that glory by which your bodies are quickened. Ye who are quickened by a portion of the celestial glory shall then receive of the same, even a fulness. And they who are quickened by a portion of the terrestrial glory shall receive of the same, even a fulness. And also they who are quickened by a portion of the telestial glory shall receive of the same, even a fulness" (D&C 88:28–31).

Joseph Fielding Smith explained further, "Some will gain celestial bodies with all the powers of exaltation and eternal increase. These bodies will shine like the sun as our Savior's does. . . . Those who enter the terrestrial kingdom will have terrestrial bodies, and they will not shine like the sun, but they will be more glorious than the bodies of those who receive the telestial glory.

"In both of these kingdoms there will be changes in the bodies and limitations. They will not have the power of increase, neither the power or nature to live as husbands and wives, for this will be denied them and they cannot increase.

"Those who receive the exaltation in the celestial kingdom will have the 'continuation of the seeds forever.' They will live in the family relationship. In the terrestrial and in the telestial kingdoms there will be no marriage. Those who enter there will remain 'separately and singly' forever. Some of the functions in the celestial body will not appear in the terrestrial body, neither in the telestial body, and the power of procreation will be removed."[31]

the glory of the celestial, one; and the terrestrial, another; and the telestial, another. People will be assigned kingdoms according to the laws that they obeyed during their time of probation. Those who lived the law of Christ will be assigned to the celestial kingdom. However, "he who is not able to abide the law of the celestial kingdom cannot abide a celestial glory. And he who cannot abide the law of the terrestrial kingdom cannot abide a terrestrial glory. And he who cannot abide the law of the telestial kingdom cannot abide a telestial glory; therefore he is not meet for a kingdom of glory" (D&C 88:22–24).

1 Corinthians 15:41 *glory of the sun.* Those who inherit the celestial kingdom will receive a glory that is as bright as the noon-day sun. These are "they who are just men made perfect through Jesus; . . . these are they whose bodies are celestial, whose glory is that of the sun, even the glory of God, the highest of all, whose glory the sun of the firmament is written of as being typical" (D&C 76:69–70).

glory of the moon. Those who enter the terrestrial kingdom will have glory comparable to the light of the moon. This kingdom includes those "who died without law; . . . who received not the testimony of Jesus in the flesh, but afterwards received it. These are they who are honorable men of the earth, who were blinded by the craftiness of men. . . . These are they who are not valiant in the testimony of Jesus" (D&C 76:72, 74, 75, 79). The glory of the terrestrial differs from the celestial "even as that of the moon differs from the sun in the firmament" (D&C 76:71). Those who receive the terrestrial kingdom will have "bodies terrestrial, and not bodies celestial, and differ in glory as the moon differs from the sun" (D&C 76:78).

glory of the stars. The stars, as viewed from the earth, are comparable to the telestial kingdom and its glory. Those who receive this kingdom include those "who received not the gospel of Christ, neither the testimony of Jesus. . . . These are they who are liars, and sorcerers, and adulterers, and whoremongers, and whosoever loves and makes a lie" (D&C 76:82, 103). The glory of this kingdom "is that of the lesser, even as the glory of the stars differs from that of the glory of the moon in the firmament" (D&C 76:81). Also, "the glory of the telestial is one, even as the glory of the stars is one; for as one star differs from another star in glory, even so differs one from another in glory in the telestial world" (D&C 76:98).

1 Corinthians 15:42 *It is sown in corruption.* The verbs *sown* and *raised* in this verse refer back to the analogy of seeds in verses 35 through 38. See "Paul's Analogy of Sown Seeds," in this chapter.

Corruption refers to mortality. Our mortal bodies are subject to pain, disease, deformity, and death; as a result, they are in bondage. At the resurrection, we will "be delivered from the bondage of corruption into the glorious liberty of the children of God" (Romans 8:21). Paul's language regarding corruption and incorruption is similar to what was taught concerning the resurrection to the Nephites: "Even this mortal shall put on immortality, and this corruption shall put on incorruption, and shall be brought to stand before the bar of God, to be judged of him according to their works whether they be good or whether they be evil" (Mosiah 16:10).

raised in incorruption. Incorruption refers to immortality. After the resurrection, the immortal body will never again suffer corruption. This doctrine was taught beautifully in the Book of Mormon: "I have spoken unto you concerning the death of the mortal body, and also concerning the resurrection of the mortal body. I say unto you that this mortal body is raised to an immortal body, that is from death, even from the first death unto life, that they can die no more; their spirits uniting with their bodies, never to be divided; thus the whole becoming spiritual and immortal, that they can no more see corruption" (Alma 11:45).

1 Corinthians 15:43 *It is sown in dishonour; it is raised in glory.* Our deteriorating, sickly mortal bodies are a direct result of the Fall, which is connected to disobedience, weakness, and dishonor. The resurrected body, however, is the direct result of Jesus Christ's atonement and is therefore associated with glory. Hence, "When Christ, who is our life, shall appear" at his second coming, those who receive resurrected bodies at that time will "also appear with him in glory" (Colossians 3:4).

it is raised in power. God's power causes the resurrection of all individuals.

1 Corinthians 15:44 *It is sown a natural body; it is raised a spiritual body.* The natural body is a mortal body, subject to corruption and a "natural death" (D&C 29:43). The spiritual body is a resurrected body of flesh and bones. Joseph Fielding Smith explained, "When Paul spoke of the spiritual body, he had no reference at all to the spirit body. . . . After the resurrection from the dead our bodies will be spiritual bodies, but they will be bodies that are tangible, bodies that have been purified, but they will nevertheless be bodies of flesh and bones. They will not be blood bodies. They will no longer be quickened by blood but quickened by the spirit which is eternal, and they shall become immortal and shall never die."[32] Therefore, at the resurrection, people will be raised with spiritual bodies, not spirit bodies (see also D&C 88:27).

RESURRECTED PERSONAGES HAVE BODIES OF FLESH AND BONES

D&C 129:1–3

1 There are two kinds of beings in heaven, namely: Angels, who are resurrected personages, having bodies of flesh and bones—

2 For instance, Jesus said: Handle me and see, for a spirit hath not flesh and bones, as ye see me have.

3 Secondly: the spirits of just men made perfect, they who are not resurrected, but inherit the same glory.

On February 9, 1843, the Lord revealed through Joseph Smith the "three grand keys whereby [we] may know whether any administration is from God" (D&C 129:9). In doing so, the Lord revealed a number of truths about "the spirits of just men made perfect" (D&C 129:3) who await the resurrection and "angels, who are resurrected personages, having bodies of flesh and bones" (D&C 129:1). As resurrected personages, Jesus, Peter, James, Moroni, and John the Baptist have bodies of flesh and bones. These and others appeared to Joseph Smith with their tangible, resurrected bodies. Moroni "was a physical being of literal, corporeal, material reality," wrote Elder Mark E. Petersen. In fact, "he held those heavy gold plates in his hands. A block of metal measuring seven-by-seven-by-eight inches could weigh anywhere from thirty to fifty pounds. But Moroni held them in his hands and turned over the pages with his fingers. His were flesh-and-bone hands, resurrected hands."[33] John the Baptist, too, had a tangible, immortal body. He appeared to Joseph Smith and Oliver Cowdery and spoke to them "while he held his hands upon their heads. His was a resurrected body. Theirs were mortal bodies. They felt his hands, the materiality of them, and understood the words which he spoke. This tells us that resurrected beings are tangible, that they can move and act, that they can speak and be understood."[34]

Other resurrected beings, of course, are able to do the same with their flesh-and-bone, resurrected hands. God the Father and Jesus Christ also have bodies of flesh and bones. "The Father has a body of flesh and bones as tangible as man's; the Son also" (D&C 130:22).

Eventually all of the dead will be resurrected and receive bodies of flesh and bones. After envisioning many who were waiting for the resurrection, Joseph F. Smith wrote, "Their sleeping dust was to be restored unto its perfect frame, bone to his bone, and the sinews and the flesh upon them" (D&C 138:17).

NOTES AND COMMENTARY

D&C 129:1 *two kinds of beings in heaven.* The two kinds of beings are angels and "spirits of just men made perfect" (see v. 3). The word *heaven* as used in verse 1 refers to "the abiding places of the righteous dead, be it a degree of glory or paradise."[35]

Angels, who are resurrected personages, having bodies of flesh and bones. Resurrected personages have tangible bodies of flesh and bones. They do not, however, have blood in their veins. This truth Joseph Smith taught on more than one occasion. "All men will be raised from the grave by the power of God, having spirit in their bodies and not blood."[36] Also, "Concerning resurrection, flesh and blood cannot inherit the kingdom of God, or the kingdom that God inherits or inhabits, but the flesh without the blood and the Spirit of God flowing in the veins instead of the blood, for blood is the part of the body that causes corruption. Therefore we must be changed in the twinkle of an eye or have to lay down these tabernacles and leave the blood vanish away. Blood is the corruptible part of the tabernacles."[37] And again, "God Almighty Himself dwells in eternal fire; flesh and blood cannot go there for all corruption is devoured by the fire. 'Our God is a consuming fire.' When our flesh is quickened by the Spirit, there will be no blood in this tabernacle."[38]

In light of these teachings of Joseph Smith, President Spencer W. Kimball taught that a substance that is "finer" than blood would make our bodies immortal: "The spirit, which is supreme in the dual man, transcends the body. It does not decompose but proceeds to the spirit world for further experience, with the assurance that after sufficient preparation there a reunion will take place where the spirit will be housed eternally in a remodeled body of flesh and bones. This time the union will never be dissolved, since there will be no blood to disintegrate and cause trouble. A finer substance will give life to the body and will render it immortal."³⁹

D&C 129:2 *For instance, Jesus said: Handle me and see, for a spirit hath not flesh and bones, as ye see me have.* See also the commentary on Luke 24:39. Joseph Smith referred to Jesus as an example of an angel having a body of flesh and bones. In doing so, the Prophet cited Jesus' saying to his apostles on the occasion when they thought that he was a spirit, "Handle me and see, for a spirit hath not flesh and bones, as ye see me have" (Luke 24:39). On another occasion the Prophet referred to Jesus as an angel: "After [Jesus'] resurrection he appeared as an angel to his disciples."⁴⁰

Jesus' words to his apostles reveal that a resurrected being can be touched ("handled") and seen ("see . . . as ye see") by mortals. A great multitude of people on the American continent felt the "prints of the nails" in the resurrected Lord's hands and feet, and they saw him with their eyes. "The multitude went forth, and thrust their hands into his side, and did feel the prints of the nails in his hands and in his feet; and this they did do, going forth one by one until they had all gone forth, and did see with their eyes and did feel with their hands, and did know of a surety and did bear record, that it was he, of whom it was written by the prophets, that should come" (3 Nephi 11:15). See also the commentary on Luke 24:39 in "The Resurrected Savior Has Flesh and Bones and Partakes of Mortal Food," in this chapter.

D&C 129:3 *the spirits of just men made perfect.* "Just men" are righteous men. In the book of Ezekiel, the Lord teaches that a just man is one who "hath withdrawn his hand from iniquity, hath executed true judgment between man and man, hath walked in my statutes, and hath kept my judgments, to deal truly; *he is just*" (Ezekiel 18:8–9; emphasis added). "Just men made perfect" are they who are *justified,* or "made perfect through Jesus the mediator of the new covenant, who wrought out this perfect atonement through the shedding of his own blood" (D&C 76:69; see also D&C 20:30; Moses 6:60).

Joseph Smith taught his contemporaries much about "the spirits of just men":⁴¹

- "The spirits of the just are exalted to a greater and more glorious work" than they had here on earth.

- When the spirits of the just depart from this earth, they go "to the world of spirits."

- They are "enveloped in flaming fire." When they are revealed to mortals, they "can only be revealed in flaming fire or glory."

- "They are not far from us, and know and understand our thoughts, feelings, and motions, and are often pained therewith."

- "Flesh and blood cannot go" to the place where the spirits of the just are found, "but flesh and bones, quickened by the Spirit of God, can."

- "The spirits of just men are made ministering servants to those who are sealed unto life eternal, and it is through them that the sealing power comes down."

- "Angels have advanced further" than the spirits of the just because "their light and glory" are "tabernacled; and hence they appear in bodily shape."

they . . . are not resurrected, but inherit the same glory. The "spirits of just men" are righteous men and women who have passed from this world but have not yet received their resurrection. In his vision of the spirits in the spirit world on October 3, 1918, President Joseph F. Smith saw "an innumerable company of the spirits of the just," all of whom "had departed the mortal life, firm in the hope of a glorious resurrection" (D&C 138:12, 14).

THE RESURRECTED SAVIOR HAS FLESH AND BONES AND PARTAKES OF MORTAL FOOD

Luke 24:36–43

36 And as they thus spake, Jesus himself stood in the midst of them, and saith unto them, Peace be unto you.

37 But they were terrified and affrighted, and supposed that they had seen a spirit.

38 And he said unto them, Why are ye troubled? and why do thoughts arise in your hearts?

39 Behold my hands and my feet, that it is I myself: handle me, and see; for a spirit hath not flesh and bones, as ye see me have.

40 And when he had thus spoken, he shewed them his hands and his feet.

41 And while they yet believed not for joy, and wondered, he said unto them, Have ye here any meat?

42 And they gave him a piece of a broiled fish, and of an honeycomb.

43 And he took it, and did eat before them.

Luke detailed many of the events that occurred on that particular Sunday on which Jesus rose from the dead. He described the women—the two Marys, Joanna, and others—who approached the tomb with prepared spices but found the tomb empty (Luke 24:1–12). He recounted the two walking on the road to Emmaus who were joined by Jesus Christ (see "The Capabilities of Resurrected Beings," in this chapter). And he presented the account of Jesus' appearance to the group of Saints in the upper room when he showed them the wounds in his feet and hands and ate food in their presence (Luke 24:36–43). Luke's record of these events focuses on Jesus Christ, a resurrected being who is able to vanish and reappear, walk, reason, stand, speak, ask questions and respond, read the minds of others, command, and instruct from the scriptures. Luke's record also shows that Jesus has a tangible body of flesh and bones that can be seen and felt by others and that can eat the food of mortals. In short, Jesus can function as mortals do—and do much more.

Elder Bruce R. McConkie reviewed many of the events recorded in Luke 24, teaching that we will become like Jesus after our resurrection if we remain faithful: "After his resurrection, Jesus walks along the Emmaus road and converses with two of his disciples. He is made known to them in the breaking of bread. Soon thereafter he appears in the upper room to ten of the twelve (Thomas was absent)—and please note, it was to a congregation of saints, which, without question, included the faithful sisters of that day—and to this entire group, not to ten men only, but to the entire group, he says, 'Have ye here any meat?' They bring him a piece of a broiled fish and of honeycomb and he takes it and eats before them. Then they feel the nail marks in his hands and in his feet and thrust their hands into his side. You talk about a teaching situation. That little episode that occurred on the Emmaus road and which was climaxed in the upper room is the paramount illustration in all the revelations that have ever been given as to what kind of a being a resurrected person is and how we, patterned after him, will yet become if we are true and faithful in all things (Luke 24)."[42]

NOTES AND COMMENTARY

Luke 24:36–37 *as they thus spake, Jesus himself stood in the midst of them.* Earlier in the evening, the resurrected Jesus had "vanished" (Luke 24:31) out of the sight of two of his disciples (see "The Capabilities of Resurrected Beings," in this chapter); later, however, he reappeared to the same two and others as they were reporting the events of the day to a gathering of the apostles and a congregation of saints.

Perhaps Jesus' greeting of "Peace be unto you" was given to calm the hearts of his terrified disciples. They recognized him to be Jesus Christ but thought that he was a disembodied spirit who had passed through the walls or the ceiling to stand in their midst (see John 20:19, which states that "the doors were shut where the disciples were assembled"). With the exception of the two disciples from Emmaus, the disciples had never before seen a resurrected personage. In any case, his sudden appearance, apparently out of nowhere, frightened them, and they were terrified because they "supposed that they had seen a spirit" (v. 37).

Luke 24:38 *Why are ye troubled? and why do thoughts arise in your hearts?* Jesus read the thoughts of his disciples, who perhaps thought they were seeing Jesus' spirit and not a tangible body of flesh and bones. In order to allay their fears, Jesus invited them to handle his feet and hands and see that he was solid flesh.

Luke 24:39 *Behold my hands and my feet, that it is I myself: handle me, and see.* Jesus commanded his disciples to "behold . . . handle . . . and see" the marks of the nails in his hands and feet. The marks served as evidence that he had died a terrible death by crucifixion but also that he had risen from the dead. A great number of people examined Jesus' wounds for themselves and became witnesses that the crucified Lord was indeed a resurrected personage. A large Nephite multitude "did feel the prints of the nails in his hands and in his feet . . . and did see with their eyes and did feel with their hands, and did know of a surety and did bear record, that it was he, of whom it was written by the prophets, that should come" (3 Nephi 11:15). On the individual level, the Lord told Thomas, "Reach hither thy finger, and behold my hands; and reach hither thy hand, and thrust it into my side: and be not faithless, but believing." Thomas responded, "My Lord and my God" (John 20:27–28).

Joseph F. Smith wrote that Christ's disciples "examined [Jesus'] wounds with their own hands, to see and feel that he was indeed the same individual, the same person, the same body that was crucified, bearing the same marks that were inflicted upon the body while it was extended upon the cross—all this must go to show to you that the resurrection of Christ was the resurrection of himself, and not his spirit."[43]

for a spirit hath not flesh and bones, as ye see me have. Three truths may be gleaned from this statement: (1) resurrected beings have flesh and bones; (2) spirits do not have flesh and bones; and (3) mortals can see or detect with their eyes—and their sense of touch—that a resurrected personage has flesh and bones. Note that the text specifies "flesh and bones" and not "flesh and blood." Jesus' resurrected body had no blood in it. "The blood [Christ] spilled upon Mount Calvary He did not receive again into His veins," instructed Brigham Young. "That was poured out, and when He was resurrected another element took the place of the blood. It will be so with every person who receives a resurrection; the blood will not be resurrected with the body, being designed only to sustain the life of the present organization. When this is dissolved, and we again obtain our bodies by the power of the resurrection, that which we now call the life of the body, and which is formed from the food we eat and the water we drink, will be supplanted by another element; for flesh and blood cannot inherit the kingdom of God."[44]

Joseph Fielding Smith, too, has explained, "In the resurrection from the dead, the bodies which were laid down natural bodies shall come forth spiritual bodies. That is to say, in mortality the life of the body is in the blood, but the body when raised to immortality shall be quickened by the spirit and not the blood. Hence, it becomes spiritual, but it will be composed of flesh and bones, just as the body of Jesus was, who is the prototype."[45]

Luke 24:40 *when he had thus spoken, he shewed them his hands and his feet.* After he commanded his disciples to "behold . . . handle . . . and see," the Lord then showed them his hands and feet. Perhaps he extended his hands and his feet so that all could see his wounds.

Luke 24:41 *while they yet believed not for joy, and wondered, he said unto them, Have ye here any meat?* Jesus clearly had a plan and a purpose during this appearance to his disciples. He appeared among them without a formal invitation and stood in their midst; he read their thoughts and saw that they were troubled; he commanded them to "behold . . . handle . . . and see"; he showed them his hands and feet; he asked them if they had any meat; and then he ate in their presence.

Luke 24:43 *And he took it, and did eat before them.* Jesus, a glorified, resurrected being, ate fish that had been caught and broiled by mortals, and honeycomb that had been prepared by insects and collected by mortals. "Can a resurrected being eat food of earth? A resurrected being can function upon any lower plane. [An exalted] resurrected personage can do anything that a mortal personage can do, and much besides."[46]

Either on this occasion or during a subsequent visit, Jesus' disciples joined him and partook of food and drank with him. Sometime later, Peter would testify to Cornelius and others, "We are witnesses of all things which [Jesus] did both in the land of the Jews, and in Jerusalem; whom they slew and hanged on a tree: him God raised up the third day, and shewed him openly; not to all the people but unto witnesses chosen before of God, even to us, *who did eat and drink with him* after he rose from the dead" (Acts 10:39–41; emphasis added).

THE CAPABILITIES OF RESURRECTED BEINGS

Luke 24:13–32

13 And, behold, two of them went that same day to a village called Emmaus, which was from Jerusalem about threescore furlongs.

14 And they talked together of all these things which had happened.

15 And it came to pass, that, while they communed together and reasoned, Jesus himself drew near, and went with them.

16 But their eyes were holden that they should not know him.

17 And he said unto them, What manner of communications are these that ye have one to another, as ye walk, and are sad?

18 And the one of them, whose name was Cleopas, answering said unto him, Art thou only a stranger in Jerusalem, and hast not known the things which are come to pass therein these days?

19 And he said unto them, What things? And they said unto him, Concerning Jesus of Nazareth, which was a prophet mighty in deed and word before God and all the people:

20 And how the chief priests and our rulers delivered him to be condemned to death, and have crucified him.

21 But we trusted that it had been he which should have redeemed Israel: and beside all this, to day is the third day since these things were done.

22 Yea, and certain women also of our company made us astonished, which were early at the sepulchre;

23 And when they found not his body, they came, saying, that they had also seen a vision of angels, which said that he was alive.

24 And certain of them which were with us went to the sepulchre, and found it even so as the women had said: but him they saw not.

25 Then he said unto them, O fools, and slow of heart to believe all that the prophets have spoken:

26 Ought not Christ to have suffered these things, and to enter into his glory?

27 And beginning at Moses and all the prophets, he expounded unto them in all the scriptures the things concerning himself.

28 And they drew nigh unto the village, whither they went: and he made as though he would have gone further.

29 But they constrained him, saying, Abide with us: for it

*is toward evening, and the day is far spent. And he went in to
tarry with them.*

*30 And it came to pass, as he sat at meat with them, he took
bread, and blessed it, and brake, and gave to them.*

*31 And their eyes were opened, and they knew him; and he
vanished out of their sight.*

*32 And they said one to another, Did not our heart burn
within us, while he talked with us by the way, and while he
opened to us the scriptures?*

Luke's amazing account of the resurrected Christ's visit with two
mortals provides much information about the capabilities of resurrected beings. Although this account pertains directly to the immortal
Lord, it seems probable that all resurrected beings of a celestial nature
will have the same capabilities. The capabilities are:

Mingling undetected (vv. 16, 31)—Jesus mingled with two mortals
as if he were one of them, but they did not detect that he was
immortal. One of the truths restored through the Prophet Joseph
Smith is that celestial, resurrected beings are able to hide their
glory when among mortals: "A spirit cannot come but in glory; an
angel has flesh and bones; [if they so choose] we see not their
glory."[47] Also, "Spirits can only be revealed in flaming fire or
glory. Angels have advanced further, their light and glory being
tabernacled; and hence they appear in bodily shape."[48]

Speaking and conversing (vv. 17–27)—Perhaps resurrected beings
have some way of communicating among themselves that is
unknown to mortals, but they are yet able to speak and converse
as mortals do. Jesus conversed with his two disciples in a very
natural manner for some time as they walked; he explained passages from the Old Testament to them, and even then they did not
detect that he was the resurrected Lord.

Walking—Jesus walked with the two on the road to Emmaus, a village west of Jerusalem. Unlike Moroni, who stood in the air as he
delivered his message to Joseph Smith and then ascended into
heaven (Joseph Smith–History 1:30, 43), Jesus delivered his message to mortals as he walked on a path to a small village.

Tarrying (v. 29)—At least in some cases, resurrected beings are not in such a hurry that they cannot *tarry* and *abide* with mortals, even when the day is far spent for the mortals.

Sitting down at meat (v. 30)—Jesus sat down at meat with mortals. It is not clear whether or not he ate with them, although as a resurrected being he partook of food on another occasion in the presence of mortals (see Luke 24:42–43).

Vanishing (v. 31)—After conversing, walking, tarrying, and sitting down with his two disciples and expounding the scriptures to them, Jesus vanished from their sight.

In summary, "we know that resurrected beings, containing their glory within themselves, can walk as mortals do on earth; that they can converse and reason and teach as they once did in mortality; that they can both withhold and manifest their true identities; that they can pass with corporeal bodies through solid walls; that they have bodies of flesh and bones which can be felt and handled; that if need be (and at special times) they can retain the scars and wounds of the flesh; that they can eat and digest food; that they can vanish from mortal eyes and transport themselves by means unknown to us."[49]

Or in the words of Brigham Young, "In the resurrection there will be a reunion of the spirits and bodies, and they will walk, talk, eat, drink, and enjoy."[50]

NOTES AND COMMENTARY

Luke 24:13 *two of them went.* The two disciples of Christ were perhaps visiting Jerusalem for Passover. One is identified as Cleopas; the other is not named. Apparently neither was a member of the quorum of the Twelve (see verse 33). Perhaps Jesus chose to appear to two so the truth about the resurrection would be confirmed by "the mouth of two or three witnesses" (2 Corinthians 13:1). Others would accept the testimonies of the two regarding a vanishing personage more readily than the testimony of one.

that same day. The story of the disciples took place the very day of the resurrection. "That same day" continues the sequence of the narrative—the crucifixion took place on Friday (Luke 23:54), the

Lord's body lay in the tomb on Saturday or the Sabbath (Luke 23:56), and now it was "the first day of the week" (Luke 24:1), or Sunday, the day of the resurrection. The fact that the two disciples beheld the resurrected Lord during the day and not after dark adds authority to their account. Nonbelievers and doubters could not make the claim that the two were seeing shadows in the dark rather than a resurrected being.

a village called Emmaus. Luke explained that Emmaus is a village situated about threescore furlongs, or seven miles, west of Jerusalem.

Luke 24:14 *they talked together of all these things which had happened.* The two men conversed about the great events that had occurred during the past three days regarding Jesus' trial, crucifixion, and disappearance from the tomb (see verses 19–24).

Luke 24:15 *Jesus himself drew near, and went with them.* Jesus approached his disciples in a natural manner and then continued with them on their journey. They did not detect that they were walking and conversing with a resurrected being.

Luke 24:16 *their eyes were holden that they should not know him.* The power of God prevented the two men from discerning that it was he who joined them in their walk; that power also prevented them from knowing that he was a resurrected being. At the same time, however, the Lord maintained his identity as Jesus Christ, the son of Mary, the man from Nazareth. President Joseph F. Smith enlightened us on this matter: the resurrected Jesus Christ "preserved His identity, even to the scars of the wounds in His hands and feet and side, . . . so it will be with you and with every son and daughter of Adam, born into the world. You will not lose your identity [at the resurrection] any more than Christ did."[51]

Translated souls, similar to those who are resurrected, can also appear to mortals without being detected (see 3 Nephi 28:18–30).

Luke 24:18 *Art thou only a stranger in Jerusalem.* In verse 17, Jesus asked his disciples, "What manner of communications are these that ye have one to another, as ye walk, and are sad?" Cleopas reacted to this inquiry by asking, "Art thou only a stranger in Jerusalem?" The fact that Cleopas asked if Jesus was a "stranger" gives emphasis to Luke's previous statement that the two disciples' "eyes were holden that they should not know him."

Gods humor?

hast not known the things which are come to pass therein these days? Cleopas' question directed to Jesus is ironic. Cleopas and his traveling companion did not recognize Jesus. They viewed him as a stranger and asked him if he was aware of the great events that had taken place in recent days. The irony was that Jesus was the only one on earth who fully comprehended the events of the past days.

Luke 24:19 *And he said unto them, What things?* Three times Luke wrote of "things" ("all these things which had happened," v. 14; "the things which are come to pass," v. 18; and "What things?" v. 19). It is not until verses 19 through 24 that the *things* are revealed. They pertain to "Jesus of Nazareth" the "prophet mighty in deed and word," his deliverance to the chief priests and rulers, his condemnation to death, his crucifixion, and his vacant tomb, discovered by several women and men.

Luke 24:21 *to day is the third day since these things were done.* "To day" was Sunday, the day of the resurrection. That very morning Jesus' body had reunited with his spirit, creating a glorious immortal soul. Shortly thereafter he appeared as a stranger to two travelers on the road to Emmaus. It was the third day since his death by crucifixion. On more than one occasion Jesus had prophesied that he would "be raised the third day" (Luke 9:22; 13:32; 18:33; cf. 24:7); the two disciples perhaps unwittingly recalled those prophecies by using the expression "the third day."

Luke 24:25 *O fools, and slow of heart to believe all that the prophets have spoken.* The disciples' summary of the things that had happened during the past three days shows a lack of understanding on their part regarding the resurrection. They did know that "Jesus of Nazareth . . . was a prophet mighty in deed and word before God and all the people" (v. 19). But they did not fully comprehend the resurrection, as can be determined by their words in verses 22 through 24. They were "astonished" at the words of the women "which were early at the sepulchre" (v. 22). The women claimed ("they came, saying") that the tomb was empty and that they had "also seen a vision of angels" (v. 23), but others who came to the tomb "saw not" (v. 24).

Jesus responded to the disciples' lack of understanding by saying, "fools" (or foolish, meaning obtuse or imperceptive) and "slow of heart." Jesus' intent was not to say the disciples were idiotic or stupid, but rather to describe them as spiritually imperceptive. His disciples did not fully comprehend the scale and magnitude of the Lord's death and resurrection. They "trusted that it had been [Jesus Christ] which should have redeemed Israel" (v. 21), expecting a political Messiah who would conquer the Roman empire and restore peace and the kingdom to the Jews. Perhaps the two disciples did not realize that Jesus was required "to have suffered these things" so he could "enter into his glory" (v. 26).

Luke 24:27 *beginning at Moses and all the prophets.* During his ministry Jesus regularly cited scripture from the Old Testament while teaching. He cited scripture to his apostles, to his disciples, to Satan, and to the Pharisees and Sadducees; he cited scripture while on the mountain, in the synagogues, in the temple, and on the cross. He repeatedly cited passages that pertained to him and his suffering, death, and resurrection. In this passage, after his resurrection, the Lord once again cited Old Testament passages while walking on the road to Emmaus. Beginning with the writings of Moses (Genesis through Deuteronomy) and continuing with the writings of "all the prophets" (Isaiah, Hosea, Malachi, Joel, Ezekiel, and others), the Lord expounded how the scriptures pertained, unbeknownst to the disciples, to "himself."

Verse 27 emphasizes that "all the prophets" of the Old Testament taught and prophesied of Jesus Christ. Peter testified of such when he said, "To [Jesus Christ] give all the prophets witness" (Acts 10:43). Verse 27 also informs the reader that Jesus knew the writings of the prophets well and that he understood the passages that applied to him, his ministry, his suffering, and his atoning sacrifice.

Luke 24:28–29 Luke did not record the amount of time that the three walked and conversed together before they "drew nigh unto the village." Presumably the two disciples walked the entire six miles from Jerusalem; Jesus, of course, joined them in the course of their walk. As they approached the village, Jesus "made as though he would have gone further," but the two urged him to stay with them because it was almost evening. The two disciples, still not knowing who the stranger was, followed the customs of hospitality and invited him to join them for the evening meal.

Luke 24:30 *he took bread, and blessed it, and brake, and gave to them.* Although Jesus was urged to stay the evening as a guest of his two disciples, he changed the roles and became the host. He took the bread (which was not customarily the role of the guest), blessed and broke it, and gave it to the two. The four verbs—*took, blessed, brake,* and *gave*—recall Jesus' actions when he fed the five thousand. On that occasion "he *took* five loaves and the two fishes, and looking up to heaven, he *blessed* them, and *brake,* and *gave* to the disciples to set before the multitude" (Luke 9:16; emphasis added).

Luke 24:31 *their eyes were opened, and they knew him.* The power of God had prevented the two men from recognizing Jesus; verse 16 explains that the eyes of the two men "were holden that they should not know" him. As Jesus blessed, broke, and gave the bread to them, the eyes of the two were opened and they recognized the Lord. Perhaps the men's eyes were opened at the breaking of the bread because in close quarters with their guest they saw the nail scars in his hands and wrists. Or perhaps the Spirit came upon them.

he vanished out of their sight. After breaking bread with his disciples, Jesus disappeared from their sight. Another resurrected being, Moroni, had the capability to appear and disappear from Joseph Smith's sight (Joseph Smith–History 1:30, 43–44).

Luke 24:32 *Did not our heart burn within us.* The hearts of the two disciples burned with the power of the Holy Ghost because (a) the resurrected, glorified Lord had walked and talked with them, and (b) he had opened the scriptures to them.

A DESCRIPTION OF THE RESURRECTED LORD

Revelation 1:10–16

10 I . . . *heard behind me a great voice, as of a trumpet,*
11 *Saying, I am Alpha and Omega, the first and the last. . . .*
12 *And I turned to see the voice that spake with me. And being turned, I saw seven golden candlesticks;*
13 *And in the midst of the seven candlesticks one like unto*

the Son of man, clothed with a garment down to the foot, and girt about the paps with a golden girdle.

14 His head and his hairs were white like wool, as white as snow; and his eyes were as a flame of fire;

15 And his feet like unto fine brass, as if they burned in a furnace; and his voice as the sound of many waters.

16 And he had in his right hand seven stars: and out of his mouth went a sharp two-edged sword: and his countenance was as the sun shineth in his strength.

While exiled on an island in the Mediterranean Sea, John beheld and described the glorious, resurrected Jesus Christ. Perhaps to capture the magnificence of the vision, John used images and symbols in his attempt to describe the Lord. Jesus' eyes were "as a flame of fire" and his feet were "like unto fine brass, as if they burned in a furnace." The Lord's "head and his hairs were white like wool, as white as snow" and "his voice as the sound of many waters." Perhaps to sum up the glorious appearance, John stated that Jesus' "countenance was as the sun shineth in his strength." The prophets Daniel (Daniel 10:5–6) and Joseph Smith (D&C 110:2–4) also received visions of the Savior and used language similar to that of John in Revelation to describe those visions.

Latter-day descriptions of the resurrected Lord similarly depict the glory that he embodies. Lorenzo Snow noted "what a glorious personage the Savior is and described his hands, feet, countenance, and beautiful white robes, all of which were of such a glory of whiteness and brightness that he could hardly gaze upon Him."[52] David O. McKay "beheld in vision" the Savior and exclaimed that "the tint and radiance of his countenance were glorious to behold! There was a peace about him which seemed sublime—it was divine!"[53] Zebedee Coltrin, a contemporary of Joseph Smith, beheld God "surrounded as with a flame of fire." During the vision, Coltrin "experienced a sensation that it might destroy the tabernacle as it was of consuming fire of great brightness."[54]

John Murdock, another early Church member, gave the following description: "The visions of my mind were opened, and the eyes of my understanding were enlightened, and I saw the form of a man, most lovely, the visage of his face was sound and fair as the sun. His hair a bright silver gray, curled in most majestic form. His eyes a keen penetrating blue, and the skin of his neck a most beautiful white and he was covered from the neck to the feet with a loose garment, pure white, whiter than any garment I have ever before seen. His countenance was most penetrating, and yet most lovely."[55]

NOTES AND COMMENTARY

Revelation 1:10 *great voice.* The great or distinctive voice belongs to Jesus.

as of a trumpet. Here "a trumpet" is used as a symbol, referring to the Lord's voice. His voice is as distinctive as the sound of a trumpet, an instrument used to awaken, herald, proclaim, and call to arms. In a corresponding manner, Alma the Younger wished that he could "speak with the trump of God, with a voice to shake the earth" (Alma 29:1).

Revelation 1:13 *one like unto the Son of man.* John saw Jesus, the "Son of man." Similar phraseology is found elsewhere: Daniel saw "one like the Son of man" (Daniel 7:13; see also Daniel 3:25); John beheld a "white cloud, and upon the cloud one sat like unto the Son of man" (Revelation 14:14); and Abraham recorded that in the pre-mortal council "the Lord said: Whom shall I send? And one answered like unto the Son of Man: Here am I, send me" (Abraham 3:27). The book of Moses enlightens us about Jesus' sacred title, "Son of Man." Moses 6:57 states that in the "language of Adam," God the Father is named "Man of Holiness" and "the name of his Only Begotten is the Son of Man, even Jesus Christ." Thus "Son of Man" is a shortened form of "Son of Man of Holiness."

clothed with a garment down to the foot, and girt about the paps with a golden girdle. In this vision the resurrected Lord appeared in the vestments that symbolically suggest both a priest and a king, wearing a robe and a golden girdle (Exodus 28:4; 39:29).[56] The word *paps* is an archaic word meaning "breasts." The word *girdle* could be translated "sash." The New International Version of the Bible renders this passage as "dressed in a robe reaching down to his feet and with a golden sash around his chest."

Revelation 1:14 *His head and his hairs were white like wool, as* *white as snow.* White is a symbol of light, purity, and triumph; therefore, John saw the Lord in brilliant glory. The word *wool* recalls Jesus as the Lamb of God, who was sacrificed for our sins.

eyes . . . as a flame of fire. (See also Revelation 2:18; 19:12.) Eyes often represent knowledge (D&C 77:4) and here may specifically refer to God's omniscience and ability to penetrate all things. "Flame of fire" describes his brilliant glory. Joseph Smith described Jesus similarly: "His eyes were as a flame of fire" (D&C 110:3).

Revelation 1:15 *feet like unto fine brass.* "Fine brass" suggests beauty and permanence (see also Ezekiel 1:7; Daniel 10:6). John beheld the Lord's glory and beauty, from the head to the feet.

voice as the sound of many waters. The voice of the Lord is as "many waters" (see also Ezekiel 43:2), "as the sound of the rushing of great waters" (D&C 110:3), "like the noise of great waters" (Ezekiel 1:24), "as the voice of many waters, and as the voice of a great thunder" (D&C 133:22), and "like the voice of a multitude" (Daniel 10:6). These expressions seem to describe the power, authority, uniqueness, and intensity that exist in the Lord's voice.

Sometimes the Lord's voice comes more quietly, though still with great power. To the Nephite Saints gathered at the temple of Bountiful, the voice of God "was not a harsh voice, neither was it a loud voice; nevertheless, and notwithstanding it being a small voice it did pierce them that did hear to the center, insomuch that there was no part of their frame that it did not cause to quake; yea, it did pierce them to the very soul, and did cause their hearts to burn" (3 Nephi 11:3).

Revelation 1:16 *his countenance was as the sun shineth in his strength.* Christ's glory is greater than the noonday sun (Malachi 4:2; Matthew 17:2). His servants are compared to the stars (Revelation 1:20), which pale in comparison.

A DETAILED DESCRIPTION OF A RESURRECTED BEING

Joseph Smith–History 1:30–32, 43–44

> 30 *While I was thus in the act of calling upon God, I discovered a light appearing in my room, which continued to increase until the room was lighter than at noonday, when*

immediately a personage appeared at my bedside, standing in
the air, for his feet did not touch the floor.

31 He had on a loose robe of most exquisite whiteness. It
was a whiteness beyond anything earthly I had ever seen; nor
do I believe that any earthly thing could be made to appear
so exceedingly white and brilliant. His hands were naked, and
his arms also, a little above the wrist; so, also, were his feet
naked, as were his legs, a little above the ankles. His head
and neck were also bare. I could discover that he had no other
clothing on but this robe, as it was open, so that I could see
into his bosom.

32 Not only was his robe exceedingly white, but his whole
person was glorious beyond description, and his countenance
truly like lightning. The room was exceedingly light, but not
so very bright as immediately around his person. . . .

43 After this communication, I saw the light in the room
begin to gather immediately around the person of him who
had been speaking to me, and it continued to do so until the
room was again left dark, except just around him; when,
instantly I saw, as it were, a conduit open right up into
heaven, and he ascended till he entirely disappeared, and the
room was left as it had been before this heavenly light had
made its appearance.

44 I lay musing on the singularity of the scene, and mar-
veling greatly at what had been told to me by this extraordi-
nary messenger; when, in the midst of my meditation, I sud-
denly discovered that my room was again beginning to get
lighted, and in an instant, as it were, the same heavenly mes-
senger was again by my bedside.

The most complete and detailed description of a resurrected being
in all scripture is that of Moroni, the great Book of Mormon prophet
who made latter-day appearances to Joseph Smith. Moroni made three
appearances to the Prophet during the night of September 21, 1823,
and another the following day. Subsequent to these visits, Joseph
made a record and detailed the glory and brightness that belonged to
Moroni. Although Joseph admitted that Moroni was "glorious beyond

description" (v. 32), he attempted to describe his glory. Joseph used such words as *light, whiteness, noonday, lightning, white, brilliant,* and *bright.* Some of the expressions are superlatives: "exquisite whiteness" (v. 31), "exceedingly white and brilliant" (v. 31), "exceedingly white" (v. 32), "exceedingly light" (v. 32), and "very bright" (v. 32).

He used comparisons to describe the brightness: "lighter than at noonday" (v. 30) and "countenance truly like lightning" (v. 32). He also compared the "heavenly light" (v. 43) with the "earthly" (v. 31).

In addition to his description of Moroni's glory, Joseph also described the powers of this resurrected personage. Moroni had the power to stand in the air (v. 30), to appear in an instant (vv. 30, 44), and to pass through the ceiling (v. 43).

NOTES AND COMMENTARY

Joseph Smith–History 1:30 *While I was thus in the act of calling upon God.* God responded to Joseph's prayer by sending an angel, who delivered a lengthy message to him, as recorded in Joseph Smith–History 1:33–42.

I discovered a light appearing in my room, which continued to increase until the room was lighter than at noonday. A great light accompanied Moroni during his visitation to Joseph Smith. Correspondingly, when God the Father and his Son appeared to Joseph Smith during the First Vision very bright light accompanied them. Joseph recorded, "I saw a pillar of light exactly over my head, above the brightness of the sun . . . When the light rested upon me I saw two Personages, whose brightness and glory defy all description" (Joseph Smith–History 1:16–17).

when immediately a personage appeared at my bedside. Heavenly messengers have the ability to appear suddenly to mortals, as if out of nowhere. The same phenomenon occurred during Moroni's second visit to the Prophet. Joseph recorded that "in an instant, as it were, the same heavenly messenger was again by my bedside" (v. 44).

standing in the air, for his feet did not touch the floor. Heavenly beings have no need to stand on the floor of homes made by telestial beings. Perhaps they stand above the floor in order to remain elevated above telestial creatures. In several instances the Lord, while visiting his prophets, actually stood on a paved work of precious materials, such as gold (D&C 110:2) or sapphire stone (Exodus 24:10). In any case, Moroni's feet did not touch the floor.

Another example: When the Father and the Son appeared to Joseph Smith during his first vision of them, they, too, stood above him in the air as they delivered their message (Joseph Smith–History 1:17).

When the Lord appeared to Joseph Smith and Oliver Cowdery in the Kirtland temple on April 3, 1836, he stood "upon the breastwork of the pulpit" (D&C 110:2).

Lorenzo Snow saw the resurrected Lord in the Salt Lake Temple standing "about three feet above the floor" and remarked that "it looked as though he stood on a plate of solid gold."[57]

Elder George F. Richards had an inspired dream about Jesus Christ. He wrote, "It is not out of place for us to have important dreams. . . . More than 40 years ago I had a dream which I am sure was from the Lord. In this dream I was in the presence of my Savior as He stood in mid-air."[58]

Joseph Smith–History 1:31 *He had on a loose robe of most exquisite whiteness.* This robe was not made of earthly materials nor by earthly hands. Joseph described it as having "a whiteness beyond anything earthly" and said that he did not "believe that any earthly thing could be made to appear so exceedingly white and brilliant."

His hands were naked, and his arms also . . . so, also, were his feet naked. . . . His head and neck were also bare. Moroni, a resurrected being, wore no wristwatch, bracelet, ring, hat, scarf, socks, or shoes. Nor did he wear a coat, jacket, or sweater, though he appeared from outside of Joseph's home during the night in the month of September in upstate New York. Apparently, resurrected beings have no need for clothing that protects the body or keeps it warm, such as headgear or footgear. Such items are for mortals, to protect them from the elements. Neither do resurrected beings need a mortal's timepiece to tell time.

Joseph Smith–History 1:32 *his whole person was glorious beyond description.* Mortals do not have the capacity or the proper language to adequately describe the glory of a resurrected personage. Similarly, when the Prophet attempted to describe the glory of the

Father and the Son, he acknowledged that their "brightness and glory defy all description" (Joseph Smith–History 1:17). "No man can describe it to you—no man can write it,"[59] he said while teaching the Saints about the appearance of resurrected beings.

his countenance truly like lightning. Lightning, one of the brightest lights known to humankind, is used in an attempt to describe the glory and light that accompanied Moroni.

but not so very bright as immediately around his person. Moroni was the very source of the light that Joseph Smith saw; although it brightened the entire room, it emanated from the angel, his countenance, and his person. It was a "heavenly light" (v. 43). Moroni did not carry a lantern or kerosene lamp. In fact, at the conclusion of this revelation to the Prophet, the light gathered around the angel and left the room dark (see v. 43).

Joseph Smith–History 1:43 *instantly I saw, as it were, a conduit open right up into heaven.* When all things are revealed to us, we will learn about the travel of heavenly beings, the physics of conduits that open into heaven, and the other laws that have not been revealed to mortal beings.

he ascended till he entirely disappeared. Moroni ascended into heaven in a way similar to Jesus Christ's ascension from the Mount of Olives in the presence of witnesses. "And when [Jesus] had spoken these things, while they beheld, he was taken up; and a cloud received him out of their sight" (Acts 1:9).

Joseph Smith–History 1:44 *in an instant, as it were, the same heavenly messenger was again by my bedside.* Resurrected beings are not required to approach mortals as are other mortals—walking, entering through doors, making sounds with each step. Rather, such beings are able to make their approach in an instant, as Moroni did in both his first and second appearances (see also v. 30).

CHAPTER 8

TIMES AND ORDER OF THE RESURRECTION

A s to the resurrection of mankind taking place in an orderly manner," wrote Harold B. Lee, "there can be no doubt, because of the revelations that have been given in this day."[1] In a most perfect manner, God himself has organized, ordered, and appointed the times for the resurrection. He knows the times and seasons of the resurrection of all souls, whether they be Saints or sinners. "Behold, there is a time appointed that all shall come forth from the dead," Alma taught his son. "Now when this time cometh no one knows; but God knoweth the time which is appointed" (Alma 40:4). At appointed times, God will open up graves and through the power of the Atonement reunite the bodies and spirits of humankind.

The first resurrection began with Jesus Christ. It was his right and privilege to be the first of all creatures to rise because he is our Savior and the Firstborn of the Father, and so "that in all things he might have the preeminence" (Colossians 1:18). Christ's resurrection was anticipated in a Mosaic ritual that pertained to the first ripened and choicest produce that was dedicated to the Lord. This produce was called the firstfruits, just as Jesus would later be known as the *firstfruits* of the dead.

The first resurrection also included the Saints who lived and died before Christ's resurrection. Noah, Moses, Elijah, and John the Baptist, for example, were resurrected with Jesus Christ, as were Enoch and his followers (see D&C 133:54–56). Abinadi summarized that "the prophets, and all those that have believed in their words, or all those that have kept the commandments of God" (Mosiah 15:22) would be resurrected with Jesus Christ.

The first resurrection that occurred at Christ's first coming will continue at his second coming. Once again, it will be reserved for the righteous. Brigham Young taught that Joseph Smith "will get his resurrection the first of any one in this Kingdom."[2] He also explained that Joseph Smith "is the man who will be resurrected and receive the keys of the resurrection, and he will seal this authority upon others."[3]

Resurrections subsequent to the first are designed for the ungodly, whose bodies will be required to sleep longer in the graves while their spirits remain in spirit prison.

God has prepared four angels to sound their trumpets, each in his own turn. The sounding of the first trumpet awakens those who lived a celestial law. The sounding of the next three trumpets awaken those who lived terrestrial or telestial laws, or those who will become sons of perdition.

THERE IS A TIME APPOINTED FOR THE RESURRECTION

Alma 40:1–10

1 Now my son, here is somewhat more I would say unto thee; for I perceive that thy mind is worried concerning the resurrection of the dead.

2 Behold, I say unto you, that there is no resurrection—or, I would say, in other words, that this mortal does not put on immortality, this corruption does not put on incorruption— until after the coming of Christ.

3 Behold, he bringeth to pass the resurrection of the dead. But behold, my son, the resurrection is not yet. Now, I unfold unto you a mystery; nevertheless, there are many mysteries which are kept, that no one knoweth them save God himself. But I show unto you one thing which I have inquired diligently of God that I might know—that is concerning the resurrection.

4 Behold, there is a time appointed that all shall come forth from the dead. Now when this time cometh no one knows; but God knoweth the time which is appointed.

5 Now, whether there shall be one time, or a second time, or a third time, that men shall come forth from the dead, it mattereth not; for God knoweth all these things; and it suf-

ficeth me to know that this is the case—that there is a time appointed that all shall rise from the dead.

6 Now there must needs be a space betwixt the time of death and the time of the resurrection.

7 And now I would inquire what becometh of the souls of men from this time of death to the time appointed for the resurrection?

8 Now whether there is more than one time appointed for men to rise it mattereth not; for all do not die at once, and this mattereth not; all is as one day with God, and time only is measured unto men.

9 Therefore, there is a time appointed unto men that they shall rise from the dead; and there is a space between the time of death and the resurrection. And now, concerning this space of time, what becometh of the souls of men is the thing which I have inquired diligently of the Lord to know; and this is the thing of which I do know.

10 And when the time cometh when all shall rise, then shall they know that God knoweth all the times which are appointed unto man.

Alma instructed his son concerning the resurrection, emphasizing that there is a time appointed for the resurrection. In fact, Alma used the word *time* on eighteen occasions in verses 4–10, always with reference to death and the resurrection. Near the beginning of his discourse, Alma taught his son, "There is a time appointed that all shall come forth from the dead" (v. 4); then Alma repeated these words, but with a little variation: "There is a time appointed that all shall rise from the dead" (v. 5); and then to drive home his point he stated again, "There is a time appointed unto men that they shall rise from the dead" (v. 9).

In just a few short verses (vv. 2–10), Alma taught much about the resurrection: (1) "there is no resurrection" until after Christ's coming in mortality; (2) Christ will bring about the resurrection; (3) mortals do not know the appointed time for the resurrection; (4) God does know the appointed time; (5) there may be a first, second, or third time of the resurrection; (6) a period of time exists between death and the resurrection (except for those who are changed "in the twinkling of an eye"); (7) time is measured unto men but not unto God; (8) when people rise in the resurrection, they will know at that time that God knows "all the times which are appointed unto man."

NOTES AND COMMENTARY

Alma 40:2 *resurrection.* In this verse Alma taught two principal doctrines pertaining to the resurrection. First, he defined resurrection with the words *immortality* and *incorruption.* Note the way that he frames his words: "I say unto you, that there is no resurrection—or, I would say, in other words, that this mortal does not put on immortality, this corruption does not put on incorruption. . . ." *Immortality* and *incorruption* are used synonymously in this verse, together with *resurrection.* The bodies of mortals decay and perish because they consist of corruptible material. Resurrected bodies are not subject to decay and will never perish. Second, Alma taught his son that no mortal would be resurrected until after Christ's mortal ministry and his subsequent resurrection.

mortal . . . immortality, corruption . . . incorruption. The Apostle Paul, a world apart from Alma and his son Corianton, and decades later, would also use the terms *mortal, immortality, corruption* (corruptible), and *incorruption* to help his readers understand the resurrection (see 1 Corinthians 15:42, 52–54).

until after the coming of Christ. Christ, the firstfruits of the resurrection (see 1 Corinthians 15:20–23), was privileged to become the first resurrected being. No one was resurrected prior to his resurrection. Brigham Young so testified: "Jesus is the first begotten from the dead, as you will understand. Neither Enoch, Elijah, Moses, nor any other man that ever lived on earth, no matter how strictly he lived, ever obtained a resurrection until after Jesus Christ's body was called from the tomb by the angel. He was the first begotten from the dead."[4] It is only after Christ's resurrection that "this mortal shall put on immortality, and this corruption shall put on incorruption" (Mosiah 16:10).

Alma 40:3 *Behold, [Jesus Christ] bringeth to pass the resurrection of the dead.* This statement is one of the most significant doctrines taught by Alma. Without Jesus and his atoning sacrifice, no one would receive the resurrection. Jesus Christ "is the Master of the resurrection," taught Brigham Young,[5] the power by which all are resurrected.

Now, I unfold unto you a mystery. Alma unfolded the mystery of the resurrection to Corianton, meaning he taught several principles, line upon line, to his son. He taught him that there is a set time for the resurrection (vv. 4–5), that there will be a first resurrection (v. 16), that the resurrection constitutes the reuniting of the spirit and body (v. 18), that all will be resurrected (v. 19), that the resurrection will restore mortals to "their proper and perfect frame" (v. 23), and many other important truths.

Alma 40:4 *Now when this time cometh no one knows; but God knoweth the time which is appointed.* "God knoweth all the times which are appointed unto man" (Alma 40:10), including the time of each man and each woman's death and the time of their resurrection. Mortals, of course, do not have such knowledge. Of these things Joseph F. Smith testified when he wrote that "there will be a glorious reunion of body and spirit. . . . When this time shall come, none but God knoweth, but we do know that all men shall come forth from the dead."[6]

Alma 40:5 *one time, or a second time, or a third time, that men shall come forth from the dead, it mattereth not.* The scriptures make it clear that there is a first resurrection and a last resurrection (Mosiah 15; D&C 76:85). Modern revelation provides many particulars about the different times for the resurrection, which times are signaled by the sounding of trumpets by God's angels (see, for example, D&C 88:94, 96–102). Moreover, Brigham Young spoke specifically about possible third and fourth resurrections: "You read about a first resurrection. If there is a first, there is a second. And if a second, may there not be a third, and a fourth, and so on? Yes; and happy are they who have a part in the first resurrection. Yes, more blessed are they than any others. But blessed also are they that will have part in the second resurrection, for they will be brought forth to enjoy a kingdom that is more glorious than the sectarian world ever dreamed of."[7]

Alma's emphasis to his son, however, is not on whether or not there are different times for the resurrection, but that there is a time appointed for all to rise from the dead.

Alma 40:6 *space betwixt the time of death and the time of the resurrection.* When mortals pass from mortality into the world of spirits they are required to wait for the resurrection. "All men," explained

Alma, "as soon as they are departed from this mortal body, yea, the spirits of all men, whether they be good or evil" will await the resurrection from the world of spirits (Alma 40:11).

Alma 40:7 *what becometh of the souls of men from this time of death to the time appointed for the resurrection?* Alma set forth this question at this point in his address but does not provide the answer until five verses later. In verses 12–14, he explains that righteous spirits "are received into a state of happiness, which is called paradise, a state of rest, a state of peace, where they shall rest from all their troubles and from all care, and sorrow" (Alma 40:12); wicked spirits will experience "weeping, and wailing, and gnashing of teeth . . . yea, in darkness, and a state of awful, fearful looking for the fiery indignation of the wrath of God upon them; thus they remain in this state, as well as the righteous in paradise, until the time of the resurrection" (Alma 40:13–14). (For further discussion on the spirit world, see chapter 3, Conditions and Circumstances of the Dead.)

Alma 40:8 *for all do not die at once.* The plan of salvation requires mortals to live and die upon the earth at various times. It may be possible, since some die during earlier periods and others during later periods, that God in his mercy established different periods for the resurrection. With such a plan, righteous ones who lived and died in earlier dispensations would not be required to wait for their resurrection for long ages. In other words, there may be different times for the resurrection because "all do not die at once." Elder James E. Talmage may have had something similar in mind when he wrote, "No spirit shall remain disembodied longer than he deserves, or than is requisite to accomplish the just and merciful purposes of God. The resurrection of the just began with Christ; it has been in process and shall continue till the Lord comes in glory, and thence onward through the millennium. The final resurrection, or that of the wicked, the resurrection to condemnation, is to be yet later."[8]

JESUS CHRIST, THE FIRSTFRUITS OF THE RESURRECTION

1 Corinthians 15:20, 23–24

> *20 But now is Christ risen from the dead, and become the firstfruits of them that slept. . . .*

23 But every man in his own order: Christ the firstfruits; afterward they that are Christ's at his coming.

24 Then cometh the end, when he shall have delivered up the kingdom to God, even the Father; when he shall have put down all rule and all authority and power.

The Mosaic Law required individual Israelites to bring "the first of the firstfruits of [their] land" (Exodus 23:19) as an offering to the Lord. The firstfruits, including grains and fruits, had to be the first ripened as well as the choicest foods (Numbers 18:12–13). Firstfruits also included selected processed foods, such as olive oil, wine, flour, or dough.

Firstfruits were dedicated to the Lord as an acknowledgment that the land and its produce belonged to him and that all blessings to Israel originated from the Lord. Portions of the firstfruits were provided to the priests for their support and maintenance (Numbers 18:12–13; Deuteronomy 18:4).

In connection with one of the temple rituals, the Israelites selected the firstfruits, brought them in a basket to the temple, and delivered them to the priests. "And the priest shall take the basket out of thine hand, and set it down before the altar of the Lord thy God. . . . And thou shalt set it before the Lord thy God, and worship before the Lord thy God: and thou shalt rejoice in every good thing which the Lord thy God hath given thee, and unto thine house" (Deuteronomy 26:4, 10–11). In another ritual dealing with the firstfruits, individuals brought a sheaf of newly harvested barley and delivered it to a priest in the temple, who then waved it before the Lord (Leviticus 23:9–14).

In symbolic ways the firstfruits offerings pertained to and anticipated Jesus Christ's resurrection. This is in accordance with the Lord's revelation to Moses that "all things bear record of me [Jesus Christ]" (Moses 6:63), as well as Nephi's testimony that "all things which have been given of God from the beginning of the world, unto man, are the typifying of him [Jesus Christ]" (2 Nephi 11:4). In three ways the firstfruits bore record of Christ's resurrection: (1) The planting of seeds in the earth may be likened unto Christ's body being "planted" in the sepulchre at his death (see "Paul's Analogy of Sown Seeds," in chapter 7). Following this analogy, the blossoming of the plants and subsequent ripening of the fruit correspond with the resurrection of Christ, who is called "the firstfruits." (2) The first ripened fruits signify Jesus as the first to rise from the dead, the "firstfruits of them that slept" (1 Corinthians 15:20). (3) The firstfruits also had to be the choicest of the crop. In a very real sense Jesus was and is the choicest of all God's children.

NOTES AND COMMENTARY

1 Corinthians 15:20 *now is Christ risen from the dead.* Paul bore straightforward testimony that Jesus Christ was risen from the dead.

the firstfruits of them that slept. The term *firstfruits* was part of the law of Moses (Deuteronomy 26:1–11; see also Exodus 22:29; 23:19; 34:26; Leviticus 2:12, 14; 23:10–11). The righteous who will be resurrected at Christ's second coming are also called "the first fruits": "They who have slept in their graves shall come forth, for their graves shall be opened; and they also shall be caught up to meet him in the midst of the pillar of heaven—They are Christ's, the first fruits, they who shall descend with him first, and they who are on the earth and in their graves, who are first caught up to meet him; and all this by the voice of the sounding of the trump of God" (D&C 88:97–98).

1 Corinthians 15:23 *every man in his own order.* There is an order of the resurrection that is based on obedience to the gospel. Christ, the most righteous of all, was first to be resurrected. He was the firstfruits. He was followed by the righteous who dwelled in the spirit world at the time of his resurrection (Matthew 27:52–53). Other righteous people will be resurrected at Christ's second coming (see "The Doctrine of the Resurrection Brings Comfort to the Saints," in chapter 9). The wicked will be resurrected last of all.

at his coming. This refers to Christ's second coming. Two groups will be resurrected at Christ's coming, one after the other. The first is those who are caught up to meet Christ "in the midst of the pillar of heaven" (D&C 88:97), both living and dead, who will then descend with him to the earth. These are the faithful who will be resurrected to a celestial glory. The second group is comprised of those who will be resurrected after Christ descends to the earth (see D&C 88:97–99). This second group will be resurrected to a terrestrial glory (see D&C 76:71–79).

1 Corinthians 15:24 *Then cometh the end.* Two prominent events mark the end of the earth as we know it—Christ's deliverance of the kingdom to the Father and Christ's putting down all of humanity's power and authority. The third and fourth trumps will announce the final groups who will be resurrected: telestial beings and sons of perdition, both of whom are wicked (see D&C 88:100–102).

OUR LORD WAS THE FIRST TO RISE

2 Nephi 2:8–9

> *8 Wherefore, how great the importance to make these things known unto the inhabitants of the earth, that they may know that there is no flesh that can dwell in the presence of God, save it be through the merits, and mercy, and grace of the Holy Messiah, who layeth down his life according to the flesh, and taketh it again by the power of the Spirit, that he may bring to pass the resurrection of the dead, being the first that should rise.*
>
> *9 Wherefore, he is the firstfruits unto God, inasmuch as he shall make intercession for all the children of men; and they that believe in him shall be saved.*

Inasmuch as Jesus Christ was "without sin (which no other mortal was), He took the position of Savior and Redeemer, which by right belonged to Him as the first born."[9] It was also "His peculiar right and privilege as the firstborn, the legitimate heir of God, the Eternal Father, to step forth, accomplish and carry out the designs of His Heavenly Father pertaining to the redemption, salvation, and exaltation of man";[10] additionally, it was Jesus Christ's privilege and right to be "the first begotten of the dead" (Revelation 1:5), "the first that should rise . . . the firstfruits unto God" (2 Nephi 2:8–9). The reason that he was "the firstborn from the dead" was so "that in all things he might have the preeminence" (Colossians 1:18).

NOTES AND COMMENTARY

2 Nephi 2:8 *how great the importance to make these things known.* The *things* that are of such great import to all of earth's inhabitants are that the Holy Messiah sacrificed his life and then rose from the dead so that all humankind will rise from the dead and have the privilege, based on their obedience to the Lord's commandments, to return to God's presence. These things are of utmost significance because "redemption cometh in and through the Holy Messiah" (see 2 Nephi 2:6–8).

dwell in the presence of God. Alma arranged his words in a remarkable way, repeating key words in order to emphasize that the atonement made it possible for the dead to be restored to immortal life and then to stand in God's presence. This verse is arranged in the following way so that the reader can easily view the repeated key words:

> "But
> God ceaseth not to be
> God, and
> mercy claimeth the penitent, and
> mercy cometh because of the
> atonement; and the
> atonement bringeth to pass the
> resurrection of the dead; and the
> resurrection of the dead bringeth back men into the
> presence of God; and thus they are restored into his
> presence, to be judged
> according to their works,
> according to the law and justice" (Alma 42:23).

Note the relationship between the repeated key words. The verse begins with an affirmation that God exists (he "ceaseth not be God") followed by the statement that the repentant gain mercy, which mercy comes to them because of the Atonement. The Atonement also produces the resurrection, and it is because of the resurrection that humankind is brought into God's presence. People are restored to God's presence so they can be judged according to their works and according to God's law.

save it be through the merits, and mercy, and grace of the Holy Messiah. It is only through the Holy Messiah, or Jesus Christ, that humankind can gain salvation and return to God's presence. This doctrine is taught repeatedly in the Book of Mormon: "There is none other name given under heaven save it be this Jesus Christ . . . whereby man can be saved" (2 Nephi 25:20); "there is none other salvation save this which hath been spoken of; neither are there any conditions whereby man can be saved except the conditions which I have told you" (Mosiah 4:8); "there is no other head whereby ye can be made free. There is no other name given whereby salvation cometh" (Mosiah 5:8); "there could be no redemption for mankind save it were through the death and sufferings of Christ, and the atonement of his blood" (Alma 21:9); "there is no other way or means whereby man can be saved, only in and through Christ" (Alma 38:9).

who layeth down his life according to the flesh. At his birth and during his mortal ministry, Jesus Christ condescended to come down from his exalted station and live among mortals (1 Nephi 11:16, 26). He was born of a mortal woman (Alma 19:13); he took upon himself flesh and blood (Ether 3:9); he "yieldeth himself . . . into the hands of wicked men" (1 Nephi 19:10); "he suffereth himself to become subject unto man in the flesh, and die" (2 Nephi 9:5), and he "layeth down his life according to the flesh," meaning, he permitted himself to suffer and die.

taketh it again by the power of the Spirit. As the Son of God, Jesus received power from his Father to lay down his life and then take it up again (John 10:17–18; Mosiah 15:7–8), which power was ministered to him by the Holy Spirit. All who receive the resurrection, including Jesus, are "quickened by the Spirit of the great God."[11]

that he may bring to pass the resurrection of the dead. The central message of all God's prophets in every age of the world pertains to Jesus Christ, his atoning sacrifice, and his redeeming acts for all of humankind. To a wicked king and a group of false priests, Abinadi asked, "All the prophets who have prophesied ever since the world began—have they not spoken more or less concerning these things? . . . Yea, and have they not said also that he should *bring to pass the resurrection of the dead . . . ?* (Mosiah 13:33, 35; emphasis added).

2 Nephi 2:8–9 *being the first that should rise. . . . he is the firstfruits unto God.* In agricultural terms, firstfruits are the first of the crop to ripen. Paul wrote, "Now is Christ risen from the dead, and become the firstfruits of them that slept" (1 Corinthians 15:20).

he shall make intercession for all the children of men. Webster's

New World Dictionary defines intercession as "the act of interceding; mediation, pleading, or prayer in behalf of another or others."[12] Jesus, of course, is the Mediator and Advocate who pleads to the Father on behalf of the children of men. In one of his intercessory prayers, he supplicated, "Father, the hour is come; glorify thy Son, that thy Son also may glorify thee: as thou hast given him power over all flesh that he should give eternal life to as many as thou hast given him. . . . I pray for them: I pray not for the world, but for them which thou has given me; for they are thine. . . . Holy Father, keep through thine own name those whom thou hast given me, that they may be one, as we are" (John 17:1–2, 9, 11).

Jesus is the Mediator for "all the children of men." Isaiah so prophesied when he wrote that the Messiah "made intercession for the transgressors" (Isaiah 53:12). Mormon, too, wrote that Jesus "advocateth the cause of the children of men" (Moroni 7:28; see also Mosiah 15:8).

PROPHETS AND OTHERS JOIN CHRIST IN HIS RESURRECTION

D&C 133:54–57

54 Yea, and Enoch also, and they who were with him; the prophets who were before him; and Noah also, and they who were before him; and Moses also, and they who were before him;

55 And from Moses to Elijah, and from Elijah to John, who were with Christ in his resurrection, and the holy apostles, with Abraham, Isaac, and Jacob, shall be in the presence of the Lamb.

56 And the graves of the Saints shall be opened; and they shall come forth and stand on the right hand of the Lamb, when he shall stand upon Mount Zion, and upon the holy city, the New Jerusalem; and they shall sing the song of the Lamb, day and night forever and ever.

57 And for this cause, that men might be made partakers of the glories which were to be revealed, the Lord sent forth the fulness of his gospel, his everlasting covenant, reasoning in plainness and simplicity.

Enoch, Noah, Moses, Elijah, and John the Baptist were resurrected with Jesus Christ. In addition, other prophets, together with a large host of additional people, were resurrected at the same time. Those who lived in Enoch's city appear to be included in this group, as are other Old Testament people who accepted the words of Moses and Noah. During a general conference held in April 1904, Anthon H. Lund provided the following details: "Not only did Christ rise from the dead at that time, but others were seen who had risen from their graves—righteous men and women who died before Christ, and who had the privilege of rising with him. I do not believe that the resurrection then was a general one; I believe it extended to those only who, while upon earth, had proved themselves willing to do all for the kingdom of God, and to whom neither property, honor, nor life itself had been too dear to keep them from carrying out the purposes of God."[13]

At Christ's second coming, Saints who have lived subsequent to his resurrection will arise and join those righteous ones who lived during the Old Testament period. Together, they will stand at Jesus Christ's right hand, clothed in immortal glory, singing praises unto the Lord forever. The resurrection, of course, is one of the greatest "glories" ever revealed to humanity. In fact, the gospel was restored upon the earth to prepare humankind to stand in the Lord's presence and to be "partakers of the glories which were to be revealed" (D&C 133:57).

NOTES AND COMMENTARY

D&C 133:54–55 These two verses list those "who were with Christ in his resurrection." Those listed by name are Enoch, Noah, Moses, Elijah, and John (the Baptist). The verses also refer to unnamed individuals who were resurrected with Jesus—the inhabitants of Enoch's city, the prophets who lived before Enoch, "they who were before" Noah, and "they who were before" Moses. The phrase "and they who were before him," appearing twice in verse 54, may refer to all of the early Saints who believed the prophets and kept God's commandments. Abinadi taught, "The prophets, and all those that have believed in their words, or all those that have kept the commandments of God, shall come forth in the first resurrection; therefore, they are the first resurrection" (Mosiah 15:22).

D&C 133:56 *he shall stand upon Mount Zion, and upon the holy city, the New Jerusalem.* Jesus, together with his resurrected Saints, will visit the two Jerusalems that will exist in the last days, Jerusalem of old and the New Jerusalem. Both cities are called *Mount Zion, holy,* and *Jerusalem* (see, for example, Psalms 48:1–2; 125:1–2; Isaiah 24:23). Each of the old and new Jerusalems will accommodate a temple built unto the Lord, and both will serve as gathering places for the Lord's people. Eventually, perhaps not before the Millennium, God's law will go forth from the two Jerusalems, according to Isaiah's prophecy: "Out of Zion shall go forth the law, and the word of the Lord from Jerusalem" (Isaiah 2:3).[14]

they shall sing the song of the Lamb. The words of the Lamb's song may be those in Revelation 5:9–13. This is a "new song" that will be sung by the twenty-four elders, who represent all exalted Saints. The song addresses Jesus Christ and emphasizes his atoning sacrifice and the resultant benefits for humankind. Or, the Lamb's song may be that which is set forth in Doctrine and Covenants 84:98–102. This song emphasizes the Lord's redemption of his people: "The Lord hath redeemed his people, Israel, according to the election of grace, which was brought to pass by the faith and the covenant of their fathers. The Lord hath redeemed his people . . ." (D&C 84:99–100).

D&C 133:57 *the Lord sent forth the fulness of his gospel.* In the last dispensation the Lord sent his gospel, or "his everlasting covenant," to earth's inhabitants. He did so "for this cause": so that those who would accept his gospel could partake "of the glories which were to be revealed." And with the aim that many would accept his covenant, the Lord presented his gospel in "plainness and simplicity."

THOSE BELONGING TO THE FIRST RESURRECTION

Mosiah 15:20–26

20 *But behold, the bands of death shall be broken, and the Son reigneth, and hath power over the dead; therefore, he bringeth to pass the resurrection of the dead.*

21 And there cometh a resurrection, even a first resurrection; yea, even a resurrection of those that have been, and who are, and who shall be, even until the resurrection of Christ—for so shall he be called.

22 And now, the resurrection of all the prophets, and all those that have believed in their words, or all those that have kept the commandments of God, shall come forth in the first resurrection; therefore, they are the first resurrection.

23 They are raised to dwell with God who has redeemed them; thus they have eternal life through Christ, who has broken the bands of death.

24 And these are those who have part in the first resurrection; and these are they that have died before Christ came, in their ignorance, not having salvation declared unto them. And thus the Lord bringeth about the restoration of these; and they have a part in the first resurrection, or have eternal life, being redeemed by the Lord.

25 And little children also have eternal life.

26 But behold, and fear, and tremble before God, for ye ought to tremble; for the Lord redeemeth none such that rebel against him and die in their sins; yea, even all those that have perished in their sins ever since the world began, that have wilfully rebelled against God, that have known the commandments of God, and would not keep them; these are they that have no part in the first resurrection.

Shortly before his martyrdom, the prophet Abinadi made a number of powerful statements about death and resurrection. Abinadi paid special regard to the fact that Jesus Christ is the power by which all humankind receives the resurrection. Jesus Christ "hath power over the dead" (v. 20); "he bringeth to pass the resurrection of the dead" (v. 20); the righteous "are raised to dwell with God who has redeemed them" (v. 23); "Christ . . . has broken the bands of death" (v. 23); "the Lord bringeth about the restoration of these" (v. 24); "they have a part in the first resurrection . . . , being redeemed by the Lord" (v. 24).

Abinadi also presented truths on the subject of the first resurrection. This resurrection comprises:

- all of the Saints who lived and died before Christ's resurrection. Abinadi specifies who was included in this special group—"the prophets, and all those that have believed in their words, or all those that have kept the commandments of God" (v. 22).

- those who, before Christ's coming, "died . . . in their ignorance, not having salvation declared unto them" (v. 24).

- little children (that is, children who died before the age of accountability).

The resurrection of little children is implied by Abinadi's statement in which he connects "the first resurrection" with "eternal life" (v. 24) and then asserts, "And little children also have eternal life" (v. 25). Two statements revealed to Joseph Smith regarding little children affirm Abinadi's assertion: "Little children are redeemed from the foundation of the world through mine Only Begotten" (D&C 29:46); also, "All children who die before they arrive at the years of accountability are saved in the celestial kingdom of heaven" (D&C 137:10).

Elder Talmage summarized: "The resurrection from the dead was inaugurated by Christ, who had power over death, and who laid down his body and took it up again as and when he willed. (John 10:17–18.) Other resurrections of the righteous dead followed (Matthew 27:52–53; and Book of Mormon 3 Nephi 23:9–10.) This, the first resurrection, or that of the just, has been in operation since John the Baptist, and both Peter and James, each of whom met a martyr's death, have severally appeared upon the earth and ministered in their resurrected bodies in these latter times. (D&C 13; and 27:8–13.) In this circumstance the continuance of service in the Holy Priesthood, through both mortal and resurrected beings, is profoundly exemplified."[15]

NOTES AND COMMENTARY

Mosiah 15:20 *But behold, the bands of death shall be broken.* Abinadi, who had spoken of the "bands of death" earlier in his discourse (see Mosiah 15:8), now repeats the phrase. "Bands of death" is a figurative expression describing the dead who are in "bondage" because of the "absence of their spirits from their bodies" (D&C 138:50). These are bound by the "chains of death" (D&C 138:18); they are "captives" (D&C 138:18, 31, 42), and they are in "prison" (D&C 138:42). Death's bands were broken by the Son of God when he rose from the dead on resurrection morn.

he bringeth to pass the resurrection of the dead. This statement plainly sets forth that Jesus Christ brings about the resurrection. Modern prophets have also so testified: "The atonement made by Jesus Christ brought about the resurrection from the dead and restored life," wrote John Taylor.[16] There are no exceptions to the statement "the Son . . . bringeth to pass the resurrection," for all will rise, whether one wishes it so or not. Joseph F. Smith noted, "You are entities; you have living souls within you; and you will be raised from the dead just as sure as Jesus Christ was raised from the dead. As sure as by Adam you die, so sure by Christ will you be raised from the dead. This is inevitable. It is according to God's plan. He has decreed it, and you cannot help yourselves. Do what you may, you cannot dodge that. It will come just as surely as birth and death come. The resurrection will come to all the children of men."[17]

Mosiah 15:21 *there cometh a resurrection, even a first resurrection.* Abinadi provides two important truths about the first resurrection—its time period and who will be part of it. As for the time period, he says that the first resurrection will take place at the "resurrection of Christ." As for who will take part, the Prophet explains that this resurrection will include "those that have been, and who are, and who shall be, even until the resurrection of Christ." Later Alma used similar language in his instruction to his son: "There is a first resurrection, a resurrection of all those who have been, or who are, or who shall be, down to the resurrection of Christ from the dead" (Alma 40:16). In other words, those who would rise with Christ would be those who lived and died before his resurrection. But Abinadi then offers a qualifier: the first resurrection includes only righteous souls. "The resurrection of all the prophets, and all those that have believed in their words, or all those that have kept the commandments of God, shall come forth in the first resurrection; therefore, they are the first resurrection" (Mosiah 15:22).

This is the "first resurrection" for the righteous who lived and died before Jesus became the first to become an immortal soul. There will be a continuation of the "first resurrection" that will take place at the Second Coming (see D&C 45:44–48, 54; 88:96–98), also designed expressly for the righteous. This first resurrection is connected with Christ's first and second comings to the earth—his coming as a mortal and his coming as an immortal. The first resurrection is also termed "the resurrection of the just" (see D&C 76:50, 65). Elder Talmage has explained regarding the first resurrection, "Two general resurrections are mentioned in the scriptures, and these may be specified as first and final, or as the resurrection of the just and the resurrection of the unjust. The first was inaugurated by the resurrection of Jesus Christ, immediately following which many of the Saints came forth from their graves. A continuation of this, the resurrection of the just, has been in operation since, and will be greatly extended, or brought to pass in a general way, in connection with the coming of Christ in His glory. The final resurrection will be deferred until the end of the thousand years of peace, and will be in connection with the last judgment."[18]

for so shall he be called. The Son of God will be called *Christ,* a Greek word which means "anointed." The Hebrew word that means "anointed" is *Messiah.* Why was the Son of God called Messiah or Christ? Because "Christ . . . was anointed [in the premortal world] with holy oil in heaven, and crowned in the midst of brothers and sisters, while his mother stood with approving virtue, and smiled upon a Son that kept the faith as the heir of all things!"[19]

Mosiah 15:22 *they are the first resurrection.* The first resurrection comprises all the prophets and those who accepted the words of those prophets. All of these, the prophets and their followers, are those who "have kept the commandments of God." Joseph F. Smith, while recording his vision of the redemption of the dead, identified some of these prophets who were part of the first resurrection—Adam, Abel, Seth, Noah, Shem, Abraham, Isaac, Jacob, Moses, Isaiah, Ezekiel, Daniel, Elias, and Malachi (see D&C 138, especially verses 38–46). These and other prophets and Saints from the Old and New Worlds were part of the first resurrection spoken of by Abinadi.

Mosiah 15:23 *They are raised to dwell with God . . . thus they have eternal life.* Those who are part of the first resurrection are privileged to enter the celestial kingdom to dwell with God. They have the promise of eternal life. More specifically, "concerning them who shall come forth in the resurrection of the just . . . they are they who are the church of the Firstborn. They are they into whose hands the Father has given all things—they are they who are priests and kings, who have received of his fulness, and of his glory. . . . Wherefore, as it is written, they are gods, even the sons of God—Wherefore, all things are theirs, whether life or death, or things present, or things to come, all are theirs and they are Christ's, and Christ is God's. . . . These shall dwell in the presence of God and his Christ forever and ever. These are they whom he shall bring with him, when he shall come in the clouds of heaven to reign on the earth over his people. These are they who shall have part in the first resurrection. These are they who shall come forth in the resurrection of the just" (D&C 76:50, 54–56, 58–59, 62–65).

Mosiah 15:24 *these are they that have died before Christ came, in their ignorance, not having salvation declared unto them.* These words likely refer to "all who have died without a knowledge of the gospel, who would have received it if they had been permitted to tarry"; such will rise in the first resurrection, and they "shall be heirs of the celestial kingdom of God" (D&C 137:7). In the words of Abinadi, they will "have eternal life, being redeemed by the Lord" (Mosiah 15:24).

Mosiah 15:25 *And little children also have eternal life.* Abinadi uses the expression "eternal life" three times in this part of his discourse: the prophets and those who believe the words of the prophets will have "eternal life through Christ" (v. 23); those who have "died before Christ came, in their ignorance" will have eternal life (v. 24); and "little children also have eternal life." Although Abinadi did not state explicitly that little children will be part of the first resurrection, certainly that is implied.

Mosiah 15:26 *these are they that have no part in the first resurrection.* To stress his claim about those who will *not* rise up during the first resurrection, Abinadi repeats a number of words and ideas in this verse. The word *tremble* is found twice; the words *sins* and *rebel,* each used twice, are arranged in chiastic order: rebel/sins/sins/rebel. The chiasmus reads: "The Lord redeemeth none such that *rebel* against him and die in their *sins*; yea, even all those who have perished in their *sins* since the world began, that have wilfully *rebelled* against God."

Abinadi repeats the same idea using two expressions: "for the Lord redeemeth none such" corresponds with "these are they that have no part in the first resurrection." Abinadi summarizes his discourse on the first resurrection by stating that the wicked "have no part in the first resurrection." Doctrine and Covenants 76:85 adds to our knowledge of Abinadi's doctrine by connecting sinners with the "last resurrection": "These are they who shall not be redeemed from the devil until the last resurrection, until the Lord, even Christ the Lamb, shall have finished his work."

THE ORDER OF THE RESURRECTION AT THE SOUNDING OF TRUMPS

D&C 88:94, 96–102

> 94 And another angel shall sound his trump. . . .
>
> 96 And the Saints who are upon the earth, who are alive, shall be quickened and be caught up to meet him.
>
> 97 And they who have slept in their graves shall come forth, for their graves shall be opened; and they also shall be caught up to meet him in the midst of the pillar of heaven—
>
> 98 They are Christ's, the first fruits, they who shall descend with him first, and they who are on the earth and in their graves, who are first caught up to meet him; and all this by the voice of the sounding of the trump of the angel of God.
>
> 99 And after this another angel shall sound, which is the second trump; and then cometh the redemption of those who are Christ's at his coming; who have received their part in that prison which is prepared for them, that they might receive the gospel, and be judged according to men in the flesh.
>
> 100 And again, another trump shall sound, which is the third trump; and then come the spirits of men who are to be judged, and are found under condemnation;

101 And these are the rest of the dead; and they live not again until the thousand years are ended, neither again, until the end of the earth.

102 And another trump shall sound, which is the fourth trump, saying: There are found among those who are to remain until that great and last day, even the end, who shall remain filthy still.

The resurrection is well organized and ordered by God. He knows the times and seasons of the resurrection of all souls, whether they be Saints or sinners. At appointed times, he will open the graves and through the power of the Atonement reunite the bodies and spirits of humankind. He has prepared four angels to sound their trumpets, each in his own turn. The sounding of the first trumpet awakens those who lived a celestial law. The sounding of the next three trumpets awakens those who lived terrestrial or telestial laws, or those who will become sons of perdition.

Trumpets make loud, distinct sounds that call to attention and cannot be misunderstood. During Old Testament times, the trumpet was used to awaken, herald, proclaim, and call to arms. "Trumpets played a prominent role in the Israelite temple and may have served as types of the trumpets that sound from the temple in heaven. Nehemiah 12:41 and 1 Chronicles 15:24, for example, 'infer that there were seven trumpets in the temple orchestra.'[20] Trumpets were blown during times of peace and burnt offerings (Numbers 10:10; 2 Chronicles 29:27–28), at certain feasts and at a new moon (Leviticus 23:24; Numbers 29:1), during solemn assemblies and fasting (Joel 2:15), on the Day of Atonement (Leviticus 25:8–9), and at the dedication of the temple (2 Chronicles 5:12–14). The scriptures inform us that the day of the Lord will be announced by the sounding of a trumpet (Joel 2:1; Zephaniah 1:16; see Isaiah 27:13; Zechariah 9:14)."[21]

Revelation 8:1–5 identifies seven angels who will blow their trumpets at the beginning of the seventh thousand-year period of the earth's history to prepare earth's inhabitants for the Second Coming (see also D&C 77:12). The trumpets' blasts bring calamities upon the earth, encouraging people to repent (see Revelation 9:20–21; 16:9, 11, 21). The seven angels who will blow their trumpets, as identified in

Revelation 8:1–5, may be the same angels mentioned in Doctrine and Covenants 88:94–110 who will blast their trumpets.[22]

NOTES AND COMMENTARY

D&C 88:94 *another angel shall sound his trump.* Seven angels, each with a trumpet, signal major events that will occur in connection with the resurrection of humanity. Each angel sounds his trumpet in sequence, one after the other, until the seventh blows his trumpet, signaling, "It is finished; it is finished" (D&C 88:106). The names of the angels are unknown, except for the seventh, who is Michael, the archangel (D&C 88:112).

At the sounding of the first trumpet, two groups will "be caught up to meet" Jesus Christ in the clouds of glory: the Saints who are living as mortals upon the earth will be "quickened and caught up to meet" him, and the righteous dead will also arise and "be caught up to meet" him. Both of these groups constitute "the first fruits, they who shall descend with him first" (see verses 96–98).

D&C 88:96 *the Saints who are upon the earth, who are alive.* Paul's epistle to Church members of Thessalonica indicates that the righteous who are on the earth when Jesus comes again will actually ascend into the clouds to meet him in the air as he descends. The apostle wrote, "We which are alive and remain unto the coming of the Lord shall not prevent [precede][23] them which are asleep. For the Lord himself shall descend from heaven with a shout, with the voice of the archangel, and with the trump of God: and the dead in Christ shall rise first: Then we which are alive and remain shall be caught up together with them in the clouds, to meet the Lord in the air: and so shall we ever be with the Lord" (1 Thessalonians 4:15–17).

D&C 88:97 *they who have slept in their graves shall come forth.* The first trumpet signals the resurrection of those who lived a celestial law—those who will join Christ in the clouds as he descends at his second coming. Three groups of righteous souls will join Christ in the clouds of glory: those who were resurrected in the meridian of time immediately after Christ's own resurrection; those in the spirit world who have awaited the resurrection that occurs at Christ's coming; and mortals who live upon the earth at the time of his coming. Concerning the Saints who are dead, the Lord himself taught, "Then they shall look for me, and, behold, I will come; and they shall see me in the clouds of heaven, clothed with power and great glory; with all the holy angels; and he that watches not for me shall be cut off. But before the arm of the Lord shall fall, an angel shall sound his trump, and the Saints that have slept shall come forth to meet me in the cloud" (D&C 45:44–45).

caught up to meet him. This expression is used three times in this passage (see verses 96, 97, and 98). Paul also wrote, "caught up . . . to meet the Lord" (1 Thessalonians 4:17), as did Joseph Smith: "It is true that in the resurrection the bodies will be caught up to meet the Lord."[24]

D&C 88:98 *They are Christ's, the first fruits, they who shall descend with him first.* The righteous who will be resurrected at Christ's second coming are called "the first fruits." They are like fruits of the tree that are the first to ripen. (See "Jesus Christ, the Firstfruits of the Resurrection," in this chapter.)

D&C 88:99 *the second trump.* This trumpet signals the resurrection of those belonging to the terrestrial order. These will be resurrected at Jesus Christ's coming, subsequent to the resurrection of celestial beings. "After the Lord and the righteous who are caught up to meet him have descended upon the earth, there will come to pass another resurrection. This may be considered as a part of the first, although it comes later. In this resurrection will come forth those of the terrestrial order, who were not worthy to be caught up to meet him, but who are worthy to come forth to enjoy the millennial reign."[25]

who have received their part in that prison. In one meaning, *prison* refers to the entire spirit world. It is called such, in part, because those who have passed from mortality look "upon the long absence of their spirits from their bodies as a bondage" (D&C 138:50; see also D&C 45:17). Peter taught that Jesus "went and preached unto the spirits in prison" (1 Peter 3:19) so that these spirits could be judged, even as those who live in the flesh are judged according to their acceptance or rejection of the gospel (1 Peter 4:6). These spirits are referred to in Doctrine and Covenants 76:73 as "they who are the spirits of men kept in prison, whom the Son visited, and preached the gospel unto them, that they might be judged according to men in the flesh." (For further

discussion of the spirit prison, see chapter 3, Conditions and Circumstances of the Dead.)

D&C 88:100–101 *the third trump.* The third trump signals the
resurrection of those who lived a telestial law during mortality. This
resurrection, designed for the wicked, will occur after the thousand
years of peace upon the earth. During this thousand-year period, these
"shall be thrust down into hell where they shall suffer the wrath of
God until they pay the price of their sinning, if it is possible, by the
things which they shall suffer. . . . This suffering will be a means of
cleansing, or purifying, and through it the wicked shall be brought to
a condition whereby they may, through the redemption of Jesus Christ,
obtain immortality. Their spirits and bodies shall be again united, and
they shall dwell in the telestial kingdom."[26]

D&C 88:102 *the fourth trump.* Those who "remain filthy still"
will be resurrected last of all, at the blowing of the fourth trump. These
are the sons of perdition, who denied the Holy Ghost after receiving
a firm testimony of Christ and who thereafter fought against the
Saints. "They shall die the second death," taught Joseph Smith.
"Those who commit the unpardonable sin are doomed to *Gnolom*—
to dwell in hell, worlds without end. As they concoct scenes of blood-
shed in this world, so they shall rise to that resurrection which is as
the lake of fire and brimstone."[27] These will not inherit a kingdom of
glory after the resurrection but will be assigned to darkness.

The Saints Shall Arise before the Lord's Arm Falls

D&C 45:44–48, 54

> 44 And then they shall look for me, and, behold, I will
> come; and they shall see me in the clouds of heaven, clothed
> with power and great glory; with all the holy angels; and he
> that watches not for me shall be cut off.
>
> 45 But before the arm of the Lord shall fall, an angel shall
> sound his trump, and the Saints that have slept shall come
> forth to meet me in the cloud.
>
> 46 Wherefore, if ye have slept in peace blessed are you; for
> as you now behold me and know that I am, even so shall ye

come unto me and your souls shall live, and your redemption shall be perfected; and the Saints shall come forth from the four quarters of the earth.

47 Then shall the arm of the Lord fall upon the nations.

48 And then shall the Lord set his foot upon this mount, and it shall cleave in twain, and the earth shall tremble, and reel to and fro, and the heavens also shall shake. . . .

54 And then shall the heathen nations be redeemed, and they that knew no law shall have part in the first resurrection; and it shall be tolerable for them.

Doctrine and Covenants 45 provides a number of words and phrases that indicate the timing of certain events associated with Jesus Christ's second coming. Examples include the following: "and *before* the day of the Lord" (D&C 45:42), "and *then*" (D&C 45:44, 48, 51, 53, 54), "but *before*" (D&C 45:45), "*then*" (D&C 45:47, 52, 53), and "at that day" (45:38). Such time-oriented indicators help us understand the sequence of some of the events associated with the resurrection. The righteous will be resurrected "*before* the arm of the Lord shall fall" (D&C 45:45), meaning before the Lord punishes the wicked with righteous judgments. In fact, the Saints will rise to meet Jesus Christ as he comes in "the clouds of heaven" (D&C 45:44). After the Saints have come forth, "*then* shall the arm of the Lord fall upon the nations" (D&C 45:47). It is only after these events—the resurrection of the Saints, the Lord's arm falling upon the nations, and the Lord's standing on the Mount of Olives and appearing to the Jews—that the heathen nations will be resurrected (D&C 45:48–54).

NOTES AND COMMENTARY

D&C 45:44 *they shall see me in the clouds of heaven.* Clouds, located high in the skies and brilliantly white, represent the Lord's glory. After the New Jerusalem temple is built, "a cloud shall rest upon it, which cloud shall be even the glory of the Lord" (D&C 84:5; Ezekiel 10:3–4).

clothed with power and great glory. At his second coming Jesus will be clothed in red garments. A revelation to Joseph Smith portrays Christ coming "down from God in heaven with dyed garments, . . .

clothed in glorious apparel, . . . red in his apparel, and his garments like him that treadeth in the wine-vat" (D&C 133:46, 48; see also Revelation 19:13). Jesus' red garments recall his atoning sacrifice when he bled from every pore (D&C 19:18), thus staining his clothing with his own blood. His red garments also symbolize his treading down the wicked "in the winepress." In his anger he will tread them down, as if they are mere grapes, and the juice will spatter his garments, making them red (see Isaiah 63:1–4).

with all the holy angels. "When Jesus Christ appears in the clouds of glory he will be accompanied by a great number of righteous individuals. Who will these blessed individuals be? Matthew and Luke identified them as 'angels' when they wrote, 'For the Son of man shall come in the glory of his Father with his angels' (Matthew 16:27; Luke 9:26). Mark calls them 'holy angels' (Mark 8:38) and Paul identified those who will accompany Christ as 'Saints' (1 Thessalonians 3:13), as does the Old Testament prophet Zechariah (Zechariah 14:5). Paul wrote an epistle 'to the Saints and faithful brethren in Christ which are at Colosse' (Colossians 1:2) and prophesied 'when Christ, who is our life, shall appear, then shall ye also appear with him in glory' (Colossians 3:4; cf. also 1 Thessalonians 2:19).

"Doctrine and Covenants 76 is the most explicit in its identification of who shall appear with Christ in the sky at his coming. It speaks of individuals who 'received the testimony of Christ,' who kept 'the commandments' and were 'washed and cleansed from all their sins,' who received 'the Holy Spirit by the laying on of the hands,' 'who overcome by faith and are sealed by the Holy Spirit of promise,' 'who are the church of the Firstborn,' and 'who are priests and kings. . . . And are priests of the Most High, after the order of Melchizedek'— these are they who will accompany Christ at his coming, 'These are they whom he shall bring with him, when he shall come in the clouds of heaven to reign on the earth over his people' (D&C 76:51–63)."[28]

D&C 45:45 *before the arm of the Lord shall fall.* The Lord reveals certain events that will occur *before* the Lord's arm comes down, smiting the wicked.

an angel shall sound his trump. It is Michael, the archangel, who will blow the trumpet that calls forth the dead from their graves (D&C 29:26).

come forth to meet me in the cloud. The Saints in the spirit world will receive their resurrection and rise to meet Jesus in the air. Those who are alive on the earth at that time will also be lifted up (see 1 Thessalonians 4:15–17).

D&C 45:46 *if ye have slept in peace blessed are you.* Righteous men and women who reside in the spirit world while awaiting the resurrection are those who sleep in peace. Meanwhile, the wicked reside in hell and are filled with anguish.

D&C 45:47 *Then shall the arm of the Lord fall.* After the righteous have been lifted off the earth and meet Jesus Christ in the clouds, the Lord's righteous judgments will fall upon those who remain on the earth.

D&C 45:48 *then shall the Lord set his foot upon this mount.* This prophecy is very specific about when, where, and how Jesus Christ will appear and rescue the remaining Jews from destruction during a great war (see also Zechariah 14:4). The prophecy also fulfills the words uttered by two heavenly messengers, when Christ ascended from the same Mount of Olives soon after his resurrection. They said, "Ye men of Galilee, why stand ye gazing up into heaven? this same Jesus, which is taken up from you into heaven, shall so come in like manner as ye have seen him go into heaven" (Acts 1:11).

The garden of Gethsemane was located at the mount of Olives, where Christ was "sorrowful and very heavy," prayed to the Father to let the cup pass from him, bled from every pore, and was betrayed by a kiss from Judas (Matthew 26:30–48). On Jesus' former visit to this mount he submitted himself to wicked men; on his future visit he will destroy the wicked.

An Old Testament prophet prophesied of the Lord's standing on the Mount of Olives. Zechariah wrote, "His feet shall stand in that day upon the mount of Olives, which is before Jerusalem on the east" (Zechariah 14:4). A latter-day revelation also sets forth many of the Lord's divine activities during this time: "He shall stand upon the mount of Olivet [another name for the mount of Olives], and upon the mighty ocean, even the great deep, and upon the islands of the sea, and upon the land of Zion" (D&C 133:20).

it shall cleave in twain. Zechariah 14:4 similarly reads, "The mount of Olives shall cleave in the midst thereof toward the east and toward the west, and there shall be a very great valley." Because Christ has complete power over the elements, he will cause the mount to be split in half. And because both the mount and the valley Kidron run north and south, then "half of the mountain shall remove toward the north, and half of it toward the south." As a result, "a very great valley" will be created, through which the Jews will flee to safety.

and the earth shall tremble, and reel to and fro, and the heavens also shall shake. Do these words speak of an earthquake that will occur when the mount splits in two? Once again, Zechariah 14:5 corresponds with Doctrine and Covenants 45 with its reference to an earthquake, one that took place during the reign of Uzziah, king of Judah.

D&C 45:54 *And then shall the heathen nations be redeemed.* The heathen nations are those that have no knowledge of Jesus Christ and his gospel. These are the same as described in Doctrine and Covenants 76:72 as "they who died without law" (see also Romans 2:12). The heathen nations are those that will receive their resurrection after the Saints receive theirs, after the wicked are punished by the falling arm of the Lord (v. 47), and after Jesus stands on the Mount of Olives (v. 48).

THOSE OF THE FIRST RESURRECTION WILL REIGN WITH CHRIST A THOUSAND YEARS

Revelation 20:4–6

4 And I saw thrones, and they sat upon them, and judgment was given unto them: and I saw the souls of them that were beheaded for the witness of Jesus, and for the word of God, and which had not worshipped the beast, neither his image, neither had received his mark upon their foreheads, or in their hands; and they lived and reigned with Christ a thousand years.

*5 But the rest of the dead lived not again until the thousand
years were finished. This is the first resurrection.*

*6 Blessed and holy is he that hath part in the first resur-
rection: on such the second death hath no power, but they
shall be priests of God and of Christ, and shall reign with him
a thousand years.*

Earlier in his vision, John saw the defeat and destruction of the
beast, the false prophet, and the armies of the wicked (see Revelation
18–19). In this section John saw the defeat and imprisonment of their
master, Satan. An angel comes from heaven, captures the devil, and
throws him into a bottomless pit, where he must remain for a thousand
years. The martyrs for Christ, who stood firm in the face of all the persecution and trouble brought by the beast and his followers, will be
called forth in the first resurrection and given power to reign with
Christ on earth. But those who joined the beast will have to wait the
thousand years for the blessing of resurrection.[29]

NOTES AND COMMENTARY

Revelation 20:4 *thrones, and they sat upon them, and judgment
was given unto them.* The kings of the earth, who once occupied the
world's thrones, joined with the beast to fight against the kingdom of
Christ. By the power of Christ they will be defeated and slain
(Revelation 19:21). Then those who stood firm in righteousness will
be blessed to become kings themselves, granted thrones to reign with
Christ throughout the Millennium.

There apparently is a hierarchy of judgment in the time of the
Millennium. First is Christ himself, who rules over all and judges all
(John 5:22; Acts 10:42; Mormon 3:20). Serving under him, the Twelve
Apostles from the meridian dispensation will judge the house of Israel
(Matthew 19:28). The house of Israel in this context apparently means
those who are true Israel, those who are true to their covenants, as
Joseph Smith learned by revelation: "Mine apostles, the Twelve which
were with me in my ministry at Jerusalem, shall stand at my right
hand at the day of my coming in a pillar of fire, being clothed with
robes of righteousness, with crowns upon their heads, in glory even
as I am, to judge the whole house of Israel, even as many as have

loved me and kept my commandments, and none else" (D&C 29:12). John the Revelator, of course, is one of the Twelve who will so judge.

In addition, the Nephite twelve were given the charge to judge the seed of Lehi (1 Nephi 12:9–10; 3 Nephi 27:27; Mormon 3:19). The principle would suggest that there are other divinely appointed leaders of other peoples who also will judge those they serve. Missionaries will be given the responsibility to stand in judgment on those who reject them (D&C 75:20–22). And finally, all Saints shall "judge the world" (1 Corinthians 6:2).

Daniel had a similar vision of the judgment: "I beheld till the thrones were cast down, and the Ancient of days [Adam] did sit, whose garment was white as snow, and the hair of his head like the pure wool: his throne was like the fiery flame, and his wheels as burning fire. A fiery stream issued and came forth from before him: thousand thousands ministered unto him, and ten thousand times ten thousand stood before him: the judgment was set, and the books were opened. . . . I beheld, and the same horn [symbolizing a great world power] made war with the Saints, and prevailed against them; until the Ancient of days came, and judgment was given to the Saints of the most High; and the time came that the Saints possessed the kingdom" (Daniel 7:9–10, 21–22).

they lived. As we see in Revelation 13:15, the righteous are slain for refusing to worship the beast or to receive his mark, giving the beast a temporary victory. But here they rise in the resurrection to live forevermore and to reign victorious with their King.

and reigned with Christ a thousand years. During the thousand years of the Millennium, Christ "will reign personally upon the earth" (Article of Faith 10). With him will reign the martyrs and other righteous people who resisted the pressure to worship the beast and who were raised up in the first resurrection. As the Lord has said, "In mine own due time will I come upon the earth in judgment, and my people shall be redeemed and shall reign with me on earth. For the great Millennium, of which I have spoken by the mouth of my servants, shall come" (D&C 43:29–30).

Revelation 20:5 *the rest of the dead lived not again until the thousand years were finished.* The righteous are resurrected at the coming of the Lord—they were dead but now live again, like their Master (Revelation 2:8). But the wicked must wait until after the Millennium. Their resurrection, with their judgment, is described in Revelation 20:12–13.

This is the first resurrection. For a discussion on the first resurrection, see "The Order of the Resurrection at the Sounding of Trumps," in this chapter.

Revelation 20:6 *Blessed and holy is he that hath part in the first resurrection.* This passage is one of several beatitudes found in Revelation. Those who are blessed to rise first are blessed indeed, for spirits look upon "the long absence of their spirits from their bodies as a bondage" (D&C 138:50). They are further blessed because they are victors over the second death; they are made "priests of God and of Christ," and they are chosen to "reign with him a thousand years." They are holy because they are righteous and because they are made holy by the glorified bodies they are given in the resurrection (D&C 88:28–29).

on such the second death hath no power. The second death, meaning separation from God, has no power over those of the first resurrection. (See also Revelation 2:11.)

"CHANGED IN THE TWINKLING OF AN EYE"

D&C 43:18, 32

> 18 For the day cometh that the Lord shall utter his voice out of heaven; the heavens shall shake and the earth shall tremble, and the trump of God shall sound both long and loud, and shall say to the sleeping nations: Ye Saints arise and live; ye sinners stay and sleep until I shall call again. . . .
> 32 And he that liveth in righteousness shall be changed in the twinkling of an eye, and the earth shall pass away so as by fire.

Many great and glorious events are associated with the resurrection of the righteous. The Lord will speak from heaven, the heavens will shake, the earth will tremble, and God's trumpet will blow, saying, "Ye Saints arise and live." As a blessing to the righteous, the resurrection of the Saints (speaking both individually and collectively) will take place instantaneously, in "the twinkling of an eye." During all of these events the bodies of sinners will remain in their graves until the Lord commands them to arise.

NOTES AND COMMENTARY

D&C 43:18 *the Lord shall utter his voice out of heaven.* During his earthly ministry Jesus prophesied that the dead would hear his voice at the time of the resurrection: "The hour is coming, and now is, when the dead shall hear the voice of the Son of God: and they that hear shall live" (John 5:25; see also 5:28). The very words that Jesus shall utter are perhaps revealed in this passage: "Ye Saints arise and live; ye sinners stay and sleep until I shall call again."

trump of God shall sound both long and loud. A trumpet's sound is very distinct; when it is played "long and loud" it is instantly recognizable. When God's trumpet sounds to beckon the Saints to arise at the resurrection, there will be no uncertainty—they will know that the time has come.

say to the sleeping nations. The dead from all nations shall hear the unmistakable sound of God's trump, but only the Saints will be empowered to arise at the first resurrection. They will "arise and live" while the sinners will remain "asleep" until God calls again. This call for the sinners to arise will take place at the end of the Millennium.

stay and sleep. For commentary on the metaphor of sleep as death, see "Those Who Sleep in the Dust Shall No Longer Slumber," in chapter 5.

D&C 43:32 *changed in the twinkling of an eye.* This expression occurs in many scriptural passages (3 Nephi 28:8; D&C 63:51; 101:31). Mortals who die during the Millennium will be resurrected instantly, as quickly as an eye blinks. These people will certainly be blessed because they will "not sleep in the dust" (D&C 63:51), meaning their bodies will not be buried in the ground.

the earth shall pass away so as by fire. The earth must die and "the elements melt with fervent heat" (2 Peter 3:10) so that the earth will be purified and become a celestial sphere. President Joseph Fielding Smith taught, "This earth is living and must die, but since it keeps the law it shall become celestialized and the abode of celestial beings."[30]

Parley P. Pratt also commented on the earth's death: "This death, or dissolution of the Earth, is a penalty of the original sin . . . so the Earth dies, or undergoes a similar change, not because of the transgression of the children of Adam, but because of the original transgression. But all mankind are made alive from the first death through the resurrection, so the Earth will again be renewed, its elements will again be collected, they will be recombined and reorganized, as when it first issued from the womb of chaos."[31]

MICHAEL'S TRUMP ANNOUNCES THE LAST RESURRECTION

D&C 29:23–29

23 And the end shall come, and the heaven and the earth shall be consumed and pass away, and there shall be a new heaven and a new earth.

24 For all old things shall pass away, and all things shall become new, even the heaven and the earth, and all the fulness thereof, both men and beasts, the fowls of the air, and the fishes of the sea;

25 And not one hair, neither mote, shall be lost, for it is the workmanship of mine hand.

26 But, behold, verily I say unto you, before the earth shall pass away, Michael, mine archangel, shall sound his trump, and then shall all the dead awake, for their graves shall be opened, and they shall come forth—yea, even all.

27 And the righteous shall be gathered on my right hand unto eternal life; and the wicked on my left hand will I be ashamed to own before the Father;

28 Wherefore I will say unto them—Depart from me, ye cursed, into everlasting fire, prepared for the devil and his angels.

29 And now, behold, I say unto you, never at any time have I declared from mine own mouth that they should return, for where I am they cannot come, for they have no power.

Adam, or Michael, has had and will yet have a vital role in the religious history of the earth. God appointed him to be a "prince" and "established his feet, and set him upon high, and [gave] him the keys of salvation under the counsel and direction of the Holy One" (D&C 78:16; see also Daniel 12:1). Michael is the archangel (D&C 88:112). Joseph Fielding Smith explained, "In the eternities before this earth was formed he was the arch-angel. He became Adam when he came to this earth to be the father of the human family."[32] This means that all of God's angels "are under the direction of Michael or Adam, who acts under the direction of the Lord."[33] In addition, it is Adam who will admit people into the Celestial City. Joseph Smith had a vision wherein "he saw Adam open the gate of the Celestial City and admit the people one by one. He then saw Father Adam conduct them to the throne one by one, when they were crowned Kings and Priests of God."[34]

Michael also will have a prominent role at the resurrection. He will be privileged, as the chief angel, to blow the trumpet that awakens the dead from their sleep. At the blast of his trumpet the graves will open and the dead will arise.

NOTES AND COMMENTARY

D&C 29:23 *the heaven and the earth shall be consumed and pass away.* Old, corruptible things will not be able to stand in God's presence after all things become new. After the Millennium, all of the "old things" that remain will be consumed, pass away, and become new (see D&C 29:24). The old heaven and earth must give way so that the new may come. Just as Satan and his followers were cast out of the presence of God—"neither was their place found any more in heaven" (Revelation 12:8)—so will the old heaven and old earth themselves have no place before God. As John recorded in Revelation, "I saw a great white throne, and him that sat on it, from whose face the earth and the heaven fled away; and there was found no place for them" (Revelation 20:11). The earth will be changed to a celestial order after the Millennium.

a new earth. Our earth will "die," but "it shall be quickened again" (D&C 88:26) and become a new earth. In addition, the earth "must needs be sanctified from all unrighteousness, that it may be prepared for the celestial glory; for after it hath filled the measure of its creation, it shall be crowned with glory, even with the presence of God the Father; that bodies who are of the celestial kingdom may possess it forever and ever" (D&C 88:18–20). In general conference, Elder Joseph Fielding Smith taught, "The earth and its heaven shall, after passing away through death, be renewed again in immortality. . . . It shall become celestialized and the abode of celestial beings."[35]

D&C 29:24 *all things shall become new . . . both men and beasts, the fowls of the air, and the fishes of the sea.* It is widely known that men will become renewed at the resurrection; it is perhaps less known that beasts, fowls, and fishes will also "become new." Elder Joseph Fielding Smith taught, "The Lord intends to save, not only the earth and the heavens, not only man who dwells upon the earth, but all things which he has created. The animals, the fishes of the sea, the fowls of the air, as well as man, are to be recreated, or renewed, through the resurrection, for they too are living souls."[36]

Joseph Smith further clarified concerning the salvation of beasts, "John saw the actual beast in heaven, showing to John that beasts did actually exist there. . . .

"John saw curious looking beasts in heaven; he saw every creature that was in heaven,—all the beasts, fowls and fish in heaven,—actually there, giving glory to God. . . .

"I suppose John saw beings there of a thousand forms, that had been saved from ten thousand times ten thousand earths like this,—strange beasts of which we have no conception: all might be seen in heaven. The grand secret was to show John what there was in heaven. John learned that God glorified Himself by saving all that His hands had made, whether beasts, fowls, fishes or men; and He will glorify Himself with them.

"Says one, 'I cannot believe in the salvation of beasts.' Any man who would tell you that this could not be, would tell you that the revelations are not true. John heard the words of the beasts giving glory to God, and understood them. God who made the beasts could understand every language spoken by them. The four beasts were four of the most noble animals that had filled the measure of their creation, and had been saved from other worlds, because they were perfect; they were like angels in their sphere. We are not told where they came from, and I do not know; but they were seen and heard by John praising and glorifying God."[37]

D&C 29:25 *not one hair, neither mote, shall be lost.* God is the great Creator who organized this earth. It is his workmanship, the work of his hands. None of his work will be lost, even a single hair or speck. "All that he created in the beginning, he will glorify in the end—every atom and molecule in its proper place and role."[38]

D&C 29:26–29 These verses refer to the last judgment spoken of in Revelation 20:11–15 where God sits on his "great white throne" (Revelation 20:11) as the great judge of all. John reported that he "saw the dead, small and great, stand before God; and the books were opened: and another book was opened, which is the book of life: and the dead were judged out of those things which were written in the books, according to their works" (Revelation 20:12).

D&C 29:26 *Michael.* Elder Hyrum M. Smith commented on this verse: "The world generally represents Gabriel as sounding the trump that summons the dead. Here we learn that it is Michael. How appropriate that the Ancestor of the race should perform this function! That the father should call his children in the morning of the resurrection day!"[39]

shall sound his trump, and then shall all the dead awake. Michael's trumpet is referred to on several occasions in scripture, where it is called "the trump of God" (1 Thessalonians 4:16; D&C 43:18; D&C 88:98) and the "last trump" (1 Corinthians 15:52). Joseph Smith taught that God "set Adam to watch over [the ordinances], to reveal them from heaven to man, or to send angels to reveal them."[40] Adam has been given a primary responsibility with regard to the resurrection, one of God's ordinances; that responsibility is the sounding of a trumpet that calls forth the dead from their graves.

they shall come forth—yea, even all. For emphasis, the verse twice repeats the word *all.* "Then shall all the dead awake . . . yea, even all."

D&C 29:27 *the righteous shall be gathered on my right hand . . . the wicked on my left hand.* Christ is the speaker of these words, which hearken back to his teachings uttered during his mortal ministry: "When the Son of man shall come in his glory, and all the holy angels with him, then shall he sit upon the throne of his glory: and before him shall be gathered all nations: and he shall separate them one from another, as a shepherd divideth his sheep from the goats: and he shall set the sheep on his right hand, but the goats on the left. Then shall the King say unto them on his right hand, Come, ye blessed of my Father, inherit the kingdom prepared for you from the foundation of the world. . . . Then shall he say also unto them on the left hand, Depart from me, ye cursed, into everlasting fire, prepared for the devil and his angels" (Matthew 25:31–34, 41).

Just as a shepherd gathers his flocks and then separates the sheep from the goats, so will the King of glory gather the nations and separate the righteous from the wicked. Who are the righteous? They are those who fed the hungry, gave drink to the thirsty, clothed the naked, took in strangers, and visited the prisoners in prison. They followed the Good Shepherd, binding themselves to him by covenant, obedience, faith, love, and sacrifice. Who are the wicked? Those who did not feed the hungry, give drink to the thirsty, clothe the naked, take in strangers, and visit the prisoners (Matthew 25:35–45). Those who willfully went their own way, rejecting the word and gift and blessing of the Good Shepherd.

D&C 29:28–29 *Depart from me, ye cursed, into everlasting fire.* After Michael blows his trump to announce the resurrection, and after Jesus Christ judges the nations while sitting on his glorious throne, the wicked will be commanded to depart from the Lord, and they will go into everlasting fire, from whence they will not return because of their powerlessness.

CHAPTER 9

BLESSINGS ASSOCIATED WITH THE RESURRECTION

Nephi taught the doctrine of resurrection along with other significant doctrines and then said, "I speak unto you these things that
ye may rejoice, and lift up your heads forever, because of the blessings which the Lord God shall bestow upon your children" (2 Nephi
9:3). Undeniably, a great number of blessings are associated with the
resurrection. These blessings are designed to benefit God's children
during mortality as they look forward to the resurrection, and more
especially after they have actually received the resurrection. This
chapter examines several of these blessings:

- The doctrine of the resurrection provides much comfort to all who
  have lost a loved one. To know that we will live again in the flesh
  brings great hope and comfort to the grieving heart.

- After the resurrection, family relationships will continue among
  those in the highest glory.

- A correct understanding of the resurrection provides us with a proper
  perspective about life and death and guides us to righteousness.

- If the resurrection were not part of the plan of salvation, we would
  have no hope for the world to come: Jesus Christ would remain
  dead, we would remain in our sins, our dead bodies would lie in
  the graves forever, our spirits would remain "most miserable" forever, and our faith in Christ would be in vain.

- Righteous spirits who await the resurrection while in the spirit
  world are "filled with joy and gladness" (D&C 138:15).

- For a great period of time, perhaps decades, centuries, or even millennia, the grave was victorious in holding the dead captive. But because of Jesus Christ's victory over death and the grave, this captivity does not last. Hence, with Paul we can say, "O death, where is thy sting? O grave, where is thy victory" (1 Corinthians 15:55).

- One of the greatest blessings associated with Jesus Christ's infinite atonement is that all of us will rise from the dead; we will receive incorruptible bodies; and we will not be subject unto the devil.

- The resurrection is universal—all who have lived and died will eventually rise from the dead. This blessing extends to everyone—rich and poor, old and young, male and female. According to Isaiah, "Thy dead men shall live. . . . Awake and sing, ye that dwell in the dust" (Isaiah 26:19).

- Those who are members of the house of Israel are blessed with the understanding that the Lord himself will resurrect us. He will clothe us with flesh, raise us out of our graves, and put his spirit in us. "And ye shall live," God promised (Ezekiel 37:14).

- Parents will have the blessing of being able to rear their children in the resurrection.[1]

- Although the resurrection is universal and all will receive the blessing of immortality, not everyone will be resurrected to eternal life. This greater blessing of eternal life is reserved for the righteous.

- After the power of the resurrection has caused the dead to arise, and after these have stood before God at the bar of judgment, death and hell will be cast into the lake of fire.

- Joseph Smith, through revelation, presented an awe-inspiring doctrine regarding the existence of knowledge and intelligence after the resurrection: intelligence gained in mortality will exist after the resurrection, and those who gain "more knowledge and intelligence" in mortality will have a greater advantage "in the world to come."

- As a blessing for all of humanity, God created the earth so that mortals would have a place to dwell during their probationary period. After the earth has fulfilled the measure of its creation, it will pass through death and then receive the resurrection; then it will become a place for celestial souls to dwell throughout eternity.

THE DOCTRINE OF THE RESURRECTION BRINGS COMFORT TO THE SAINTS

1 Thessalonians 4:13–18 (JST)

13 But I would not have you to be ignorant, brethren, concerning them which are asleep, that ye sorrow not, even as others which have no hope.

14 For if we believe that Jesus died and rose again, even so them also which sleep in Jesus will God bring with him.

15 For this we say unto you by the word of the Lord, that they who are alive at the coming of the Lord, shall not prevent them who remain unto the coming of the Lord, who are asleep.

16 For the Lord himself shall descend from heaven with a shout, with the voice of the archangel, and with the trump of God: and the dead in Christ shall rise first;

17 Then they who are alive, shall be caught up together into the clouds with them who remain, to meet the Lord in the air; and so shall we be ever with the Lord.

18 Wherefore comfort one another with these words.

During general conference in April 1939, David O. McKay affirmed that "the message of the resurrection is the most comforting, the most glorifying ever given to man; for when death takes a loved one from us, we can look with assurance into the open grave and say, 'He is not here,' and 'He will rise again.'"[2] These words recall a similar statement made centuries earlier by another apostle. After writing of the resurrection, Paul wrote, "wherefore comfort one another with these words" (v. 18).

Paul's main purpose in writing this section of the epistle was to give the Christians at Thessalonica comfort regarding their loved ones who had passed away. Twice Paul brought reassurance to his audience—at the beginning of the section he taught them to "sorrow not" (v. 13) concerning those who had died, and at the end of the section he instructed them to "comfort one another with these words," the words found in these verses. How could Paul promise so much comfort? Because, speaking of the righteous, (1) those who have passed on will appear with Jesus at his second coming (v. 14); (2) those who are alive when Jesus comes again will not have precedence over those who are dead (v. 15); and (3) those who are dead will rise first at his coming, and together with the living, they will "meet the Lord in the air" (v. 17). Paul added assurance to his words with the testimony that "Jesus died and rose again" and because of his death and resurrection, the righteous dead will be privileged to come with Jesus at his second coming (v. 14).

NOTES AND COMMENTARY

1 Thessalonians 4:13 *I would not have you to be ignorant.* Inasmuch as Jesus Christ's resurrection was the first to occur in the history of the world, the early Saints did not fully comprehend the doctrine of the resurrection. The Saints at Thessalonica were "ignorant . . . concerning them which [were] asleep" (v. 13). In this section of 1 Thessalonians, Paul addressed Church members' actual concerns about death and resurrection.

them which are asleep. Paul referred to those who have passed on to the world of spirits. *Sleep* is often a metaphor for death (1 Kings 2:10; 1 Corinthians 15:6, 18, 20), and *awakening* is a metaphor for the resurrection (Daniel 12:2).

sorrow not. Paul instructed the Saints that they need not sorrow for those who have died to the same extent that others sorrow. This is because the others "have no hope"—they do not have the Christian hope based on a knowledge of the atonement and resurrection of Jesus Christ. Paul explained in the following verse, "If we believe that Jesus died and rose again, even so them also which sleep in Jesus will God bring with him" (v. 14).

as others which have no hope. Those "without Christ" or " without God in the world" have no hope (Ephesians 2:12) for the life after death, the resurrection, or the eternal blessings that are promised to true followers of Jesus Christ. A modern revelation echoes Paul's words to the Thessalonians: "Thou shalt weep for the loss of them that die, and more especially for those that have not hope of a glorious resurrection" (D&C 42:45).

1 Thessalonians 4:14 *them also which sleep in Jesus.* Paul spoke of a select portion of the dead, those "which sleep in Jesus." *Sleep in Jesus* corresponds with *die in me [Jesus],* found multiple times in Doctrine and Covenants 42:44–47. Both phrases—*sleep in Jesus* and *die in Jesus*—speak of the faithful Christians who have passed away. Death is *sweet* unto such, as the Lord has revealed: "Those that die in me shall not taste of death, for it shall be sweet unto them; and they that die not in me, wo unto them, for their death is bitter" (D&C 42:46–47).

will God bring with him. The righteous will return with Jesus at his second coming (see Zechariah 14:5). He will bring them with him when he returns in power and glory.

1 Thessalonians 4:15 *by the word of the Lord.* Paul wrote with authority, invoking the name of the Lord. He expressed the word of the Lord as one of his apostles, and as one who had the Holy Ghost (see also 1 Corinthians 2:6–16).

they who are alive at the coming of the Lord. Paul here referred to those who will be alive on the earth when Jesus Christ appears at his second coming. These are the individuals who will remain on the earth, having survived the wars, pestilences, and destruction of the last days.

1 Thessalonians 4:16 *Lord himself shall descend from heaven.* Throughout the history of the world, the Lord has delegated many significant tasks to his heavenly messengers. He sent down from heaven Michael, Gabriel, Raphael, Peter, James, John, John the Baptist, and many others to restore keys, make announcements, and conduct divine work (see D&C 110:11–16; 128:20–21). But the Lord will not delegate his second coming to any of his angels. This fact is emphasized with the word *himself* in the expression "the Lord himself shall descend from heaven." Paul and the early Christians understood well that Jesus went to heaven after his ascension from the Mount of Olives (Acts 1:9–11; Romans 8:34; 10:6).

with a shout. This phrase may be translated as "with a command." Who is going to shout when the Lord descends from heaven? It may be Jesus Christ himself, calling the dead to come forth from their graves. Jesus taught, "Marvel not at this: for the hour is coming, in the which all that are in the graves shall hear [my] voice, and they shall come forth; they that have done good, unto the resurrection of life; and they that have done evil, unto the resurrection of damnation" (John 5:28–29; compare also John 11:43).

with the voice of the archangel. The archangel is Michael or Adam (Jude 1:9). It will be his honor to announce Christ's descent from heaven. Other angels, of course, have a role in these events, for they will accompany Christ at his coming (Matthew 25:31).

with the trump of God. Michael will sound the trumpet that calls forth the dead: "Michael, mine archangel, shall sound his trump, and then shall all the dead awake, for their graves shall be opened, and they shall come forth—yea, even all" (D&C 29:26; see also D&C 109:75). His trumpet will be "the last trump: for the trumpet shall sound, and the dead shall be raised incorruptible, and we shall be changed" (1 Corinthians 15:52; see also Matthew 24:31).

the dead in Christ. The "dead in Christ" are "they . . . which are fallen asleep in Christ" (1 Corinthians 15:18), "the dead which die in the Lord" (Revelation 14:13), or they "which sleep in Jesus" (1 Thessalonians 4:14; see comments above). These are they who accepted Jesus Christ and his gospel during mortality. Death will not sever their association with Jesus and his gospel.

shall rise first. The word *first* followed by *then* (v. 17) shows a sequence of events. Paul taught (in verse 15) that the righteous who are living when Jesus appears at his second coming will have no advantage over the righteous dead who await his coming from the spirit world. Here he explains one of the advantages held by those in the spirit world—those who are "dead in Christ shall rise first," and they will be followed by the Saints who are alive at Christ's coming. In fact, the righteous dead are now making preparations for Christ's coming (D&C 61:38–39; 133:57–59).[3]

1 Thessalonians 4:17 *then they who are alive, shall be caught up.* Note that individuals from three spheres of existence—heaven (see Jude 1:14–16), earth (see 1 Corinthians 15:51; D&C 88:96; 101:31), and the spirit world (see D&C 88:97; 109:75)—will be united in the air in a grand reunion at Christ's coming; and Jesus Christ will be both the power by which they unite as well as the focus of the union. Doctrine and Covenants 88:96–98 explains the circumstances of two of those spheres: "The Saints that are upon the earth, who are alive, shall be quickened and be caught up to meet him. And they who have slept in their graves shall come forth, for their graves shall be opened; and they also shall be caught up to meet him in the midst of the pillar of heaven—they are Christ's, the first fruits, they who shall descend with him first, and they who are on the earth and in their graves, who are first caught up to meet him; and all this by the voice of the sounding of the trump of God."

into the clouds. Matthew, Mark, and Luke also testified that Jesus Christ will come in the clouds (Matthew 24:30; Mark 13:26; Luke 21:27). Mark wrote, "Then shall they see the Son of man coming in the clouds with great power and glory."

to meet the Lord in the air. Paul's epistle to Church members of Thessalonica indicates that righteous individuals who are on the earth when Jesus comes again will actually ascend into the clouds to meet him in the air as he descends. In his last farewell, Moroni predicted meeting others in the air as a resurrected soul: "I bid unto all, farewell. I soon go to rest in the paradise of God, until my spirit and body shall again reunite, and I am brought forth triumphant through the air, to meet you before the pleasing bar of the great Jehovah, the Eternal Judge of both quick and dead" (Moroni 10:34).

so shall we be ever with the Lord. The union between the Saints and the Lord will be eternal. During his mortal ministry Jesus promised his disciples that they would one day reunite in a place prepared for them: "If I go and prepare a place for you, I will come again, and receive you unto myself; that where I am, there ye may be also" (John 14:3).

1 Thessalonians 4:18 *comfort one another with these words.* Paul's teachings about death and resurrection are designed to bring comfort to followers of Christ in all periods of history.

FAMILY RELATIONSHIPS IN THE RESURRECTION

Joseph Smith

> *Would you think it strange if I relate what I have seen in vision in relation to [the resurrection]? Those who have died*

in Jesus Christ may expect to enter into all that fruition of joy when they come forth, which they possessed or anticipated here.

So plain was the vision, that I actually saw men, before they had ascended from the tomb, as though they were getting up slowly. They took each other by the hand and said to each other, "My father, my son, my mother, my daughter, my brother, my sister." And when the voice calls for the dead to arise, suppose I am laid by the side of my father, what would be the first joy of my heart? To meet my father, my mother, my brother, my sister; and when they are by my side, I embrace them and they me.[4]

In this passage Joseph Smith introduced an incredibly glorious doctrine to Church members—that righteous families after the resurrection will be united. God revealed these things to the Prophet in vision. Twice Joseph referred to the vision, "I have seen in vision" and "so plain was the vision," and once he stated, "I actually saw . . ." In the same context, Joseph Smith continued, "More painful to me are the thoughts of annihilation than death. If I have no expectation of seeing my father, mother, brothers, sisters and friends again, my heart would burst in a moment, and I should go down to my grave. The expectation of seeing my friends in the morning of the resurrection cheers my soul and makes me bear up against the evils of life. It is like their taking a long journey, and on their return we meet them with increased joy."[5]

Other latter-day authorities have also taught the doctrine of continuing family relationships for the righteous in the resurrection. John Taylor wrote, "It is the gospel that teaches a woman that she has a claim upon a man, and a man that he has a claim upon a woman in the resurrection; it is the gospel that teaches them that, when they rise from the tombs in the resurrection, they will again clasp hands, be reunited, and again participate in that glory for which God designed them before the world was."[6] Anthon H. Lund declared, "We believe in the resurrection . . . that the marriage relation will continue, that husband and wife will dwell together through all eternity, that the love which binds their hearts together upon the earth will not leave them at death, but that it will endure eternally."[7]

UNDERSTANDING THE RESURRECTION GUIDES US TO RIGHTEOUSNESS

1 Corinthians 15:30–34 (JST)

30 And why stand we in jeopardy every hour?

31 I protest unto you the resurrection of the dead; and this is my rejoicing which I have in Christ Jesus our Lord daily, though I die.

32 If after the manner of men I have fought with beasts at Ephesus, what advantageth it me, if the dead rise not? Let us eat and drink; for tomorrow we die.

33 Be not deceived: evil communications corrupt good manners.

34 Awake to righteousness, and sin not; for some have not the knowledge of God: I speak this to your shame.

1 Corinthians 15:30–34 is part of Paul's longer argument for the reality of the resurrection. Paul reasoned that the Lord's servants would not "stand . . . in jeopardy [of persecution] every hour" (1 Corinthians 15:30) if there were no resurrection. He also argued that if there were no resurrection, people would revel and riot, knowing that they would soon die, and that would be the end of things. Those who lack knowledge of the resurrection do not have an appropriate viewpoint to guide them to eternal life.

Those who have a correct knowledge of the resurrection are inclined to live with eternity in mind. Such people look beyond temporal matters and anticipate the world to come. They are better able to resist the world's temptations, overcome troubles associated with mortality, and order their lives in a way that prepares them for the resurrection and judgment. A correct knowledge of the resurrection gives them proper perspective about both temporal and spiritual matters.

NOTES AND COMMENTARY

1 Corinthians 15:30 *why stand we in jeopardy every hour?* With a rhetorical question, Paul taught why Christ's ministers endure peril, persecution, and difficulty as they travel about preaching God's word. In effect, Paul was asking, "Why do we, the Lord's ministers, risk danger and perils so frequently if there is no resurrection? If life ends with death, why would we stand in jeopardy every hour?"

1 Corinthians 15:31 *this is my rejoicing which I have in Christ Jesus.* Although Paul knew that he would eventually die, he rejoiced in the knowledge that his body would one day be joined with his spirit to form an immortal soul. The doctrine of the resurrection of the dead, said Paul, "is my rejoicing." Similarly, Paul wrote in his letter to the Thessalonians that the doctrine of the resurrection brings comfort. "Sorrow not," he wrote, because those who "sleep in Jesus will God bring with him" (1 Thessalonians 4:13–14) at his second coming. Both those whose bodies lie in the graves and those who are alive when Christ returns in glory will be resurrected, explained Paul, "wherefore comfort one another with these words" (1 Thessalonians 4:18).

1 Corinthians 15:32 *what advantageth it me, if the dead rise not?* If there were no resurrection, then Paul and other ministers of Christ would not benefit by preaching the gospel, fighting beasts, or enduring the trials of life.

Let us eat and drink; for tomorrow we die. Prophets often use this expression when portraying those who foolishly seek worldly pleasures with the attitude that there is either no eventual accountability or no postmortal existence. The expression originated with Isaiah as he addressed his fellow Jerusalemites: "Joy and gladness, slaying oxen, and killing sheep, eating flesh, and drinking wine: let us eat and drink; for to morrow we shall die" (Isaiah 22:13). Nephi similarly wrote of those who would live in the last days, "There shall be many which shall say: Eat, drink, and be merry, for tomorrow we die; and it shall be well with us" (2 Nephi 28:7). A character in one of Jesus' parables made a similar statement: "I will say to my soul, Soul, thou hast much goods laid up for many years; take thine ease, eat, drink, and be merry" (Luke 12:19).

1 Corinthians 15:34 *Awake to righteousness.* Paul used a phrase with a double meaning. He first instructed his audience to stir themselves to become righteous. He also used the word *awake* in the context of the resurrection—when the righteous "wake up" from their sleep of death, they will have the same qualities of righteousness as they had in mortality.

WITHOUT CHRIST'S RESURRECTION, OUR FAITH IN HIM IS VAIN

1 Corinthians 15:12–19

> 12 Now if Christ be preached that he rose from the dead, how say some among you that there is no resurrection of the dead?
>
> 13 But if there be no resurrection of the dead, then is Christ not risen:
>
> 14 And if Christ be not risen, then is our preaching vain, and your faith is also vain.
>
> 15 Yea, and we are found false witnesses of God; because we have testified of God that he raised up Christ: whom he raised not up, if so be that the dead rise not.
>
> 16 For if the dead rise not, then is not Christ raised:
>
> 17 And if Christ be not raised, your faith is vain; ye are yet in your sins.
>
> 18 Then they also which are fallen asleep in Christ are perished.
>
> 19 If in this life only we have hope in Christ, we are of all men most miserable.

Paul used rhetorical devices in this section to demonstrate the eternal significance of Jesus Christ's resurrection. One device is Paul's repeated use of *if,* a word that is usually followed by *then,* forming a conditional clause. *If* is used seven times in this passage: "*if* Christ be preached that he rose from the dead " (v. 12); "*if* there be no resurrection of the dead" (v. 13); "*if* Christ be not risen" (v. 14); "*if* so be that the dead rise not" (v. 15); "*if* the dead rise not" (v. 16); "*if* Christ be not raised" (v. 17); "*If* in this life only we have hope in Christ" (v. 19). In another device, Paul repeated five different phrases that pertain to and emphasize the central theme of the resurrection. The five repeated phrases are "no resurrection of the dead" (v. 12, 13); "not risen" (v. 13, 14); "raised up" (twice in v. 15); "dead rise not" (v. 15 and 16); and "raised" (v. 16 and 17).

These devices are tools to teach important doctrines about Christ and his resurrection. Significantly, Paul placed Jesus at the forefront of his discussion by explicitly using the name *Christ* eight times, once per verse. He wished to emphasize that Jesus Christ and his resurrection are essential elements in the Christian faith and understanding.

Paul listed the negative consequences that would attend humanity if there had been no resurrection and if Christ had not risen from the dead. The negative consequences may be summarized as follows: without Christ's resurrection, all men would be miserable; Christ would not be risen and would remain dead (v. 13); the preaching of Christian ministers would be for nothing (v. 14); faith in Christ would be in vain (v. 14); those who testify of Christ would be "false witnesses of God" (v. 15); people would remain in their sins (v. 17); the dead would be in a "perished" state of being (v. 18); and all men would be "most miserable" (v. 19).

NOTES AND COMMENTARY

1 Corinthians 15:12 *if Christ.* Paul began a series of *if/then* statements. *If* often introduces a conditional clause that puts forward the idea "on condition that" or "supposing that." The *if* clause is usually followed by the term *then* (see vv. 13, 14, 16, 18), although this term is sometimes implied rather than expressed (see vv. 12, 15, 17, 19). In the first verse of the section and in subsequent verses, Paul used conditional clauses to make a case for Christ's resurrection.

1 Corinthians 15:13 *if there be no resurrection of the dead, then is Christ not risen.* This passage sets forth a classic conditional clause, having the elements "if . . . then": supposing that there were no resurrection, then Christ of course has not risen from the dead.

1 Corinthians 15:14 *if Christ be not risen, then is our preaching vain, and your faith is also vain.* Without Jesus' resurrection, the preaching and faith of his disciples is for naught.

1 Corinthians 15:15 *we are found false witnesses of God.* The central message of all of the Lord's ministers—prophets, apostles, elders, bishops, and missionaries—is that Jesus died for all humanity, was buried in the tomb, and rose again on the third day. Without his resurrection, all of his servants would be false witnesses.

1 Corinthians 15:16 *if the dead rise not, then is not Christ* *raised.* This phrase restates, for emphasis, the words in verse 13, "if there be no resurrection of the dead, then is Christ not risen."

1 Corinthians 15:17 *if Christ be not raised, your faith is vain; ye are yet in your sins.* Without Christ's resurrection, our faith to be forgiven is for nothing, we could not repent, and we would all remain in our sins.

1 Corinthians 15:18 *Then they also which are fallen asleep in Christ are perished.* If there were no resurrection, then the dead (notwithstanding their faith in Christ and the resurrection) would remain spirits forever. Under such conditions, Paul wrote, the dead would literally have *perished.*

1 Corinthians 15:19 *If in this life only we have hope in Christ, we are of all men most miserable.* How miserable we would be if our hope in Christ were for the duration of mortality only, and there were nothing for us after death—no life, no happiness, and no family relationships. The gospel of Jesus Christ, however, was not designed to bless us for mortality only but also for eternity.

THE RIGHTEOUS IN THE SPIRIT WORLD AWAIT THE RESURRECTION WITH JOY AND GLADNESS

D&C 138:14–19

14 All these had departed the mortal life, firm in the hope of a glorious resurrection, through the grace of God the Father and his Only Begotten Son, Jesus Christ.

15 I beheld that they were filled with joy and gladness, and were rejoicing together because the day of their deliverance was at hand.

16 They were assembled awaiting the advent of the Son of God into the spirit world, to declare their redemption from the bands of death.

17 Their sleeping dust was to be restored unto its perfect frame, bone to his bone, and the sinews and the flesh upon them, the spirit and the body to be united never again to be divided, that they might receive a fulness of joy.

18 While this vast multitude waited and conversed, rejoicing in the hour of their deliverance from the chains of death,

*the Son of God appeared, declaring liberty to the captives
who had been faithful;*

*19 And there he preached to them the everlasting gospel,
the doctrine of the resurrection and the redemption of
mankind from the fall, and from individual sins on conditions
of repentance.*

The words above (verse 14–19) are a selection from President
Joseph F. Smith's recorded vision of the redemption of the dead
received on October 3, 1918. President Smith introduced his vision by
writing, "I sat in my room pondering over the scriptures; and reflect-
ing upon the great atoning sacrifice that was made by the Son of God,
for the redemption of the world; and the great and wonderful love
made manifest by the Father and the Son in the coming of the
Redeemer into the world" (D&C 138:1–3). After presenting additional
introductory words (see verses 4–10), President Smith wrote: "The
eyes of my understanding were opened, and the Spirit of the Lord
rested upon me, and I saw" (verse 11).

With his spiritual eyes opened, President Smith saw a great host
of righteous spirits assembled in the spirit world awaiting the visitation of Jesus Christ. Through the power of his atonement, Christ
would break the bands of death and restore the spirit to the body, giving the resurrected souls liberty and redemption. Before they would
receive the resurrection, however, this host of spirits were "filled with
joy and gladness" (v. 15) as they anticipated receiving perfect bodies
of flesh and bones.

NOTES AND COMMENTARY

D&C 138:14 *All these had departed the mortal life.* "All these"
refers to "an innumerable company of spirits of the just," a "vast multitude," a "vast congregation" (D&C 138:12, 18, 38) of righteous spirits in the spirit world awaiting the appearance of Jesus Christ. These
Saints lived on the earth before Jesus' death. They were named by
President Smith as Adam, Eve, Abel, Noah, Shem, Abraham, Moses,
Isaiah, Ezekiel, Daniel, and Malachi. The group also included the
Nephite prophets and many others (see D&C 138:38–49). The large
company of godly spirits, gathered in "one place," represented a

portion of "the hosts of the dead" (D&C 138:11–12). The remaining spirits—the ungodly—were not part of this select group whom the Lord visited. The ungodly were located in a place where "darkness reigned" (D&C 138:22).

firm in the hope of a glorious resurrection. They were looking forward to not just any resurrection but a *glorious* resurrection. Those faithful to the gospel have hope that extends far beyond mortality and the grave. The faithful have a hope in Christ in this life and "with surety hope for a better world" (Ether 12:4). "If in this life only we have hope in Christ," Paul taught, "we are of all men most miserable" (1 Corinthians 15:19). Mormon, while teaching in the synagogue, asked, "What is it that ye shall hope for?" He responded, "Ye shall have hope through the atonement of Christ and the power of his resurrection, to be raised unto life eternal" (Moroni 7:41).

through the grace of God the Father and his Only Begotten Son, Jesus Christ. The resurrection comes through God's grace, the "divine means of help or strength, given through the bounteous mercy and love of Jesus Christ."[8] Because of the Father's great love for his children, and because of our Savior's devotion to the Father, the great plan of salvation was enacted for all the inhabitants of the earth. Without their great mercy and benevolence—without their grace—there would be no glorious resurrection.

D&C 138:15 *they were filled with joy and gladness, and were rejoicing together.* Joy, gladness, and rejoicing describe the emotions of those who were waiting for "the day of their deliverance." Compare also "fullness of joy," verse 17.

the day of their deliverance at hand. Here the scripture reads "*day* of their deliverance," but verse 18 reads "*hour* of their deliverance." The three expressions, *day, hour,* and *at hand,* specify the temporal nearness of their deliverance. Deliverance was in fact "at hand" for the righteous, for Jesus Christ appeared to them even as they were waiting, conversing, and rejoicing (see verse 18).

How close at hand was their deliverance and resurrection? Matthew recorded that after Jesus' resurrection "the graves were opened; and many bodies of the saints which slept arose, and came out of the graves after his resurrection, and went into the holy city, and appeared unto many" (Matthew 27:52–53). It is likely that many of these righteous spirits seen in vision by President Smith are the same as the Saints mentioned in this passage of Matthew. If so, many of this group were resurrected soon after Jesus' resurrection, which occurred just three days later. "These the Lord taught, and gave them power to come forth, after his resurrection from the dead" (D&C 138:51).

D&C 138:16 *They were assembled.* The words of the vision suggest that this group had congregated ("gathered together," v. 12; "assembled," vv. 16 and 38; "assembly," v. 49) for a prearranged meeting. They were not together by chance or happenstance, for they were "awaiting the advent of the Son of God into the spirit world." Perhaps they had convened in a number of meetings analogous to our general conferences, or maybe they held some kind of orientation meetings to prepare for the visitation of the Son of God. In any case, they were waiting for what would become the most significant *advent* in the history of the spirit world—the visitation of God's Son, who would declare their redemption from death's chains.

to declare their redemption from the bands of death. "Bands of death" is a symbolic expression that defines the state of those who have departed from mortality. *Bands* denotes a captive, like a prisoner or slave. Those who are dead are in bondage, as it were, similar to the way that prisoners are bound or put in chains. The dead described in this vision were like captives because they "looked upon the long absence of their spirits from their bodies as a bondage" (v. 50). Other expressions used throughout the recorded vision are similarly descriptive of one who is held captive—"chains of death" (v. 18); "captives" (vv. 18, 31, 42); "prison" (v. 42); and "them that were bound" (v. 42). Opposite these are words that describe resurrected souls—"deliverance" (vv. 15, 18); "redemption" (vv. 16, 19, 23); and "liberty" (vv. 18, 31, 42). To all disembodied spirits, Jesus is the "Redeemer and Deliverer from death and the chains of hell" (v. 23).

D&C 138:17 *Their sleeping dust was to be restored unto its perfect frame.* See "All Things Restored to Their Perfect Frame," in chapter 7.

bone to his bone, and the sinews and the flesh upon them. In the words of the Lord to Ezekiel, "I will lay sinews upon you, and will bring up flesh upon you, and cover you with skin, and put breath in you, and ye shall live; and ye shall know that I am the Lord" (Ezekiel 37:6). When we become resurrected personages, we will have bones, sinews, and flesh. Unlike mortals, however, "we will not have blood in our veins, but we will have the Spirit of the Lord in our veins so that we can move forward into an everlasting life."⁹

the spirit and the body to be united never again to be divided. President Smith provided this succinct definition of resurrection. See also commentary on Alma 11:45 in "The 'Perfect Form' of Resurrected Beings," in chapter 7.

that they might receive a fulness of joy. Before their resurrection, the righteous spirits "were *filled with joy*" (D&C 138:15; emphasis added) as they anticipated their forthcoming redemption. After their resurrection, however, they received "a *fullness of joy.*" "When eternal spirit and eternal elements are joined again," Elder Hugh B. Brown explained, "man, then an immortal soul, may receive a fulness of joy."¹⁰

D&C 138:18 *While this vast multitude waited and conversed, rejoicing.* Spirits in the spirit world, like mortals, have the capacity to converse with one another, to rejoice, and to sing (see v. 24). Also, like mortals, they are required at times to wait for important events, as this vast multitude waited for the appearance of the Son of God.

the hour of their deliverance from the chains of death. See commentary on verse 16.

the Son of God appeared, declaring liberty to the captives who had been faithful. The wicked did not behold the "Deliverer from death" or hear his voice (vv. 20–21, 23). He "could not go personally" to them "because of their rebellion and transgression" (v. 37). Jesus appeared only to the faithful during his brief visit, which was "limited to the brief time intervening between the crucifixion and resurrection" (v. 27). He preached the gospel to them and prepared and commissioned them to "carry the light of the gospel to them that were in darkness, even to all the spirits of men; and thus was the gospel preached to the dead" (v. 30). The Saints reacted to the appearance of the Savior by rejoicing, bowing before him, acknowledging him as their Redeemer, and singing praises to him (vv. 23–24).

D&C 138:19 *there he preached to them the everlasting gospel.* Jesus Christ taught the great multitude of Saints the gospel, which includes "the doctrine of the resurrection," the doctrine of "the redemption of mankind from the fall," and the doctrine of redemption "from individual sins on conditions of repentance." The doctrine of resurrection was mentioned first, perhaps because this subject was the foremost thing on the minds of the vast group of disembodied spirits. In a short period of time, all or most of the Saints present would receive their resurrection (JST Matthew 27:56). Subsequent to teaching his gospel to the Saints, Christ organized them to go forth and teach the same gospel to the remaining spirits. These taught the gospel to those "who had died in their sins, without a knowledge of the truth" as well as those who had lived and died "in transgression, having rejected the prophets" (v. 32). They taught the first principles and ordinances of the gospel, namely faith, repentance, baptism—in their case, probably vicarious baptism—and the gift of the Holy Ghost (v. 33).

THE RESURRECTION CONSTITUTES VICTORY OVER DEATH

1 Corinthians 15:50–57

> *50 Now this I say, brethren, that flesh and blood cannot inherit the kingdom of God; neither doth corruption inherit incorruption.*
>
> *51 Behold, I shew you a mystery; We shall not all sleep, but we shall all be changed,*
>
> *52 In a moment, in the twinkling of an eye, at the last trump: for the trumpet shall sound, and the dead shall be raised incorruptible, and we shall be changed.*
>
> *53 For this corruptible must put on incorruption, and this mortal must put on immortality.*
>
> *54 So when this corruptible shall have put on incorruption, and this mortal shall have put on immortality, then shall be brought to pass the saying that is written, Death is swallowed up in victory.*
>
> *55 O death, where is thy sting? O grave, where is thy victory?*

*56 The sting of death is sin; and the strength of sin is the law.
57 But thanks be to God, which giveth us the victory
through our Lord Jesus Christ.*

Paul used a number of symbols and images to teach his readers
about the resurrection. He compared death to *sleep,* perhaps because
mortals who pass away seem to "slumber" in the earth. He used the
expression *twinkling of an eye* to indicate the speed at which people will
be resurrected during the millennium. He compared the resurrection to
putting on immortality, as one puts on clothing. He stated that death will
be *swallowed up,* a figure of speech suggesting that death is consumed
just as one consumes food. He addressed death and the grave as if they
were personified. He referred to the *sting* of death, which evokes images
of a scorpion or other creatures that sting their victims. And three times
he termed resurrection as a *victory*—a triumph or conquest—over death.

Jesus is the triumphant one who conquered death. He is completely victorious. As President Joseph Fielding Smith explained,
"Unless every soul is raised, our Savior will not win the victory over
death. His victory must be, and will be, complete, as Paul clearly
declared. In the resurrection the spirit and the body become inseparably connected, that they can never again be divided, and thus they
become immortal."[11]

Howard W. Hunter, during a 1986 general conference, contrasted
Jesus Christ with Alexander the Great. Elder Hunter's purpose was to
demonstrate how Jesus' victory over death was profoundly greater
than Alexander's victory as an earthly conqueror: "Alexander the
Great, king of Macedon, pupil of Aristotle, conqueror of most of the
known world in his time, was one of the world's great young leaders.
After years of exercising military pomp and prowess and after extend-
ing his kingdom from Macedonia to Egypt and from Cyprus to India,
he wept when there seemed to be no more world to conquer. Then, as
evidence of just how ephemeral such power is, Alexander caught a
fever and died at thirty-three years of age. The vast kingdom he had
gained virtually died with him.

"Quite a different young leader also died at what seems such an
untimely age of thirty-three. He likewise was a king, a pupil, and a
conqueror. Yet he received no honors from man, achieved no territorial

conquests, rose to no political station. So far as we know, he never held a sword nor wore even a single piece of armor. But the Kingdom he established still flourishes some two thousand years later. His power was not of this world.

"The differences between Alexander and this equally young Nazarene are many. But the greatest difference is in their ultimate victories. Alexander conquered lands, peoples, principalities, and earthly kingdoms. But he who is called the Perfect Leader, he who was and is the Light and Life of the world—Jesus Christ the Son of God—conquered what neither Alexander nor any other could defeat or overcome: Jesus of Nazareth conquered death."[12]

NOTES AND COMMENTARY

1 Corinthians 15:50 *flesh and blood cannot inherit the kingdom of God.* Mortal tabernacles are composed of flesh, bones, and blood. Blood is the component that brings life to mortals, as the Lord informed Moses: "The life of the flesh is in the blood" (Leviticus 17:11, 14). Immortal beings also have flesh and bones (see D&C 130:22) but do not need the blood flowing through their veins. Therefore, "when our flesh is quickened by the Spirit, there will be no blood in this tabernacle."[13]

1 Corinthians 15:51 *I shew you a mystery.* The mystery that Paul revealed is this—not everyone will be laid to rest at death; the faithful who are alive at Christ's coming will be changed to a resurrected state in the twinkling of an eye.

We shall not all sleep. The righteous during the Millennium will not die and then sleep in the dust (see D&C 63:51) but will die and be resurrected "in the twinkling of an eye." "And he that liveth when the Lord shall come, and hath kept the faith, blessed is he; nevertheless, it is appointed to him to die at the age of man. Wherefore, children shall grow up until they become old; old men shall die; but they shall not sleep in the dust, but they shall be changed in the twinkling of an eye" (D&C 63:50–51; see also D&C 101:31).

but we shall all be changed. At Christ's coming the righteous will be changed, or resurrected. Our "vile body" will be changed and become like the "glorious body" of the resurrected Jesus Christ (Philippians 3:21).

1 Corinthians 15:52 *In a moment, in the twinkling of an eye.* Those who pass away during the Millennium will not sleep in the dust but will die and be resurrected speedily, as quickly as an eye blinks (see also D&C 43:32).

the trumpet shall sound. "Michael, mine archangel, shall sound his trump, and then shall all the dead awake, for their graves shall be opened, and they shall come forth—yea, even all" (D&C 29:26). See also commentary on 1 Thessalonians 4:16.

the dead shall be raised incorruptible. Resurrected beings are immortal and not subject to corruption. Even the most wicked souls— the sons of perdition—will be raised as incorruptible beings. The difference, however, is that the wicked will inherit the devil's kingdom, and the righteous will inherit God's kingdom. Alma 41:4 puts forward the law of restoration: "If their works are evil they shall be restored unto them for evil. Therefore, all things shall be restored to their proper order, every thing to its natural frame—mortality raised to immortality, corruption to incorruption—raised to endless happiness to inherit the kingdom of God, or to endless misery to inherit the kingdom of the devil, the one on one hand, the other on the other."

1 Corinthians 15:53 *For this corruptible must put on incorruption, and this mortal must put on immortality.* Mosiah 16:10 presents the same teaching but changes the order of the words, "This mortal shall put on immortality, and this corruption shall put on incorruption." In both of these passages (1 Corinthians 15:53 and Mosiah 16:10), *corruptible* (or *corruption*) corresponds with *mortal,* and *incorruption* corresponds with *immortality. Put on* in the Corinthians passage suggests that at the resurrection we will be clothed or enrobed in a glorious incorruptible tabernacle.

1 Corinthians 15:54 *put on.* See commentary on verse 53.

the saying that is written, Death is swallowed up in victory. Paul paraphrased Isaiah 25:8, which reads, "He will swallow up death in victory." The full verse from Isaiah reads: "He will swallow up death in victory; and the Lord God will wipe away tears from off all faces; and the rebuke of his people shall he take away from off all the earth: for the Lord hath spoken it." Isaiah listed three things that Jesus Christ will do for his people—he will have victory over death; he who is well "acquainted with grief" (Isaiah 53:3) will wipe away our tears and remove the pains associated with mortality (Revelation 7:17; 21:4; D&C 101:29); and he will remove the disgrace ("rebuke") from his people.

1 Corinthians 15:55 *O death, where is thy sting? O grave, where is thy victory?* In verse 54 Paul paraphrased a passage from Isaiah. Here he rephrased part of Hosea 13:14, using the words *O death* and *O grave.* Paul personified death and the grave when he asked them the whereabouts of their sting and their victory. Death's sting and the grave's victory do not exist, thanks to Jesus Christ's resurrection. According to Mosiah 16:7–8, "If Christ had not risen from the dead, or have broken the bands of death that the grave should have no victory, and that death should have no sting, there could have been no resurrection. But there is a resurrection, therefore the grave hath no victory, and the sting of death is swallowed up in Christ."

1 Corinthians 15:56 *The sting of death is sin.* For those who live unrighteous lives, death will produce a sting. "They that die not in me," saith the Lord, "wo unto them, for their death is bitter" (D&C 42:47). We as Latter-day Saints are commanded to "weep for the loss of them that die, and more especially for those that have not hope of a glorious resurrection" (D&C 42:45).

1 Corinthians 15:57 *thanks be to God, which giveth us the victory through our Lord Jesus Christ.* Because Christ victoriously overcame death, Paul rejoiced as he concluded his teachings on the resurrection—"Thanks be to God." Elder McConkie, too, praised God because Christ gave us victory over death: "To man, nothing is so absolute and final as death; death conquers all; rich and poor, wise and foolish, righteous and wicked, the mighty and the weak—all bow to death, all leave their bodies to rot in the earth. But, praise God!, there is One, even Christ, who, ministering in all the glory of his Father's power, hath gained the victory over the grave, and because of him all men shall live again."[14]

Although Paul's words are ever so brief—"God, which giveth us the victory through our Lord Jesus Christ"—they summarize the greatest victory achieved during earth's history. As Elder Howard W. Hunter taught, "Against the medals and monuments of centuries of men's fleeting victories stands the only monument necessary to mark the eternal triumph—an empty garden tomb."[15]

AN INFINITE ATONEMENT BRINGS FORTH THE RESURRECTION

2 Nephi 9:3–8

3 Behold, my beloved brethren, I speak unto you these things that ye may rejoice, and lift up your heads forever, because of the blessings which the Lord God shall bestow upon your children.

4 For I know that ye have searched much, many of you, to know of things to come; wherefore I know that ye know that our flesh must waste away and die; nevertheless, in our bodies we shall see God.

5 Yea, I know that ye know that in the body he shall show himself unto those at Jerusalem, from whence we came; for it is expedient that it should be among them; for it behooveth the great Creator that he suffereth himself to become subject unto man in the flesh, and die for all men, that all men might become subject unto him.

6 For as death hath passed upon all men, to fulfil the merciful plan of the great Creator, there must needs be a power of resurrection, and the resurrection must needs come unto man by reason of the fall; and the fall came by reason of transgression; and because man became fallen they were cut off from the presence of the Lord.

7 Wherefore, it must needs be an infinite atonement—save it should be an infinite atonement this corruption could not put on incorruption. Wherefore, the first judgment which came upon man must needs have remained to an endless duration. And if so, this flesh must have laid down to rot and to crumble to its mother earth, to rise no more.

8 O the wisdom of God, his mercy and grace! For behold, if the flesh should rise no more our spirits must become subject to that angel who fell from before the presence of the Eternal God, and became the devil, to rise no more.

Jacob, the brother of Nephi, wrote of several wonderful blessings that come to humankind because of the infinite atonement of Jesus Christ. "Rejoice," he said to his brethren, "because of the *blessings* which the Lord God shall bestow upon your children" (v. 3; emphasis added). These blessings pertain to death and the resurrection:

- Though we will die and our bodies "waste away," it is a blessing that "in our bodies we will see God" (v. 4). This means that when we return to God's presence, we shall be fully clothed with glorious resurrected bodies. We will not stand before him as naked spirits, with bodies rotting in the grave.

- Our knowledge that death is a part of God's plan is a blessing (v. 6). His merciful plan includes key points of the plan of salvation—the fall of man, death, and the resurrection.

- The resurrection comes with power, or there is "a power of resurrection," Jacob explained. This power centers on Jesus Christ, he who offered his life for us and raised himself up the third day. Joseph Fielding Smith wrote about this power: "Jesus did for us something that we could not do for ourselves, through his infinite atonement. On the third day after the crucifixion he took up his body and gained the keys of the resurrection, and thus has power to open the graves for all men, but this he could not do until he had first passed through death himself and conquered."[16]

- Christ's atonement is "an infinite atonement" (v. 7), also called "an infinite and eternal sacrifice" (Alma 34:10). This infinite atonement blesses us with incorruptible bodies (v. 7) after we receive the resurrection. It also prevents our bodies from rotting in the earth forever (v. 7) without the hope of a resurrection. And further, the infinite atonement prevents us from becoming "subject to that angel" who "became the devil" (v. 8).

NOTES AND COMMENTARY

2 Nephi 9:3 *that ye may rejoice, and lift up your heads forever.* Jacob explains the doctrine of the resurrection to his brethren with the intent that they will "rejoice and lift up [their] heads forever." The doctrine of the resurrection communicates comfort and joy to the faithful (see 1 Thessalonians 4:18).

blessings which the Lord God shall bestow upon your children. The blessings bestowed upon us, God's children, are identified in the following verses: "in our bodies we shall see God" (2 Nephi 9:4); there will be a resurrection (2 Nephi 9:6, 12); we will escape the awful monster, or death and hell (2 Nephi 9:10); and all humanity will "become incorruptible, and immortal" and "living souls" through the power of the resurrection (2 Nephi 9:13).

2 Nephi 9:4 *our flesh must waste away and die.* The wasting away of the flesh followed by death is the normal process of mortality. Humans on their own cannot avoid or reverse this process. Many through the ages have tried to discover a fountain of youth, but without success. "Nevertheless," said Jacob, meaning "in spite of the wasting away and ultimate death of our bodies," "in our [resurrected] bodies we shall see God." Job, too, realized that his body would be destroyed but that he would yet see the Lord in a resurrected body: "Though after my skin worms destroy this body, yet in my flesh shall I see God" (Job 19:26).

2 Nephi 9:6 *death hath passed upon all men.* All men will pass away. There is no way to escape it. Both the righteous and the wicked, the mighty and the small, the rich and the poor will pass beyond the veil into the world of spirits when their spirits leave their bodies. "All men are born to die,"[17] taught Joseph Smith; and the author of Ecclesiastes explained, "There is no man that hath power over the spirit to retain the spirit; neither hath he power in the day of death" (Ecclesiastes 8:8).

the merciful plan of the great Creator. God's plan is *merciful* because he will not allow our bodies to forever rot in the earth, because he will restore the spirit and the body to a glorious immortal soul, and because he will not permit righteous spirits to be like unto or subject to the devil and his angels. For these reasons, those with spiritual understanding join the prophet Jacob in his acclamations: "O the wisdom of God, his mercy and grace! . . . O how great the goodness of our God . . . O how great the plan of our God" (2 Nephi 9:8, 10, 13).

there must needs be a power of resurrection. Death and the grave grip humanity with a great power (Hosea 13:14; Psalms 49:15), but the power of resurrection is greater still. Jesus Christ is the power of the resurrection. He taught during his mortal ministry, immediately before raising Lazarus from the dead, "I am the resurrection, and the life" (John 11:25). Our prophets, too, have taught that Jesus is the power of the resurrection. Jacob testified, "Ye may obtain a resurrection, according to the power of the resurrection which is in Christ" (Jacob 4:11). And Joseph F. Smith bore witness that "we [will] be resurrected from the dead by the power of Jesus Christ."[18]

the resurrection must needs come unto man by reason of the fall. Mormon 9:12–13 sets forth the connection between the fall of man and the resurrection or redemption of man: "[God] created Adam, and by Adam came the fall of man. And because of the fall of man came Jesus Christ, even the Father and the Son; and because of Jesus Christ came the redemption of man. And because of the redemption of man, which came by Jesus Christ, they are brought back into the presence of the Lord." The key words and concepts of this passage—"Adam," "fall of man," "Jesus Christ," and "redemption of man"—are each repeated twice. Adam is seen as a character parallel to Jesus Christ, and the concept of the fall of man stands opposite to the redemption of man. Through Adam (the apostle Paul designated Adam the "first man Adam") came the "fall of man," but through Jesus Christ (the "last Adam"—1 Corinthians 15:45) came the "redemption of man." A similar passage is found in 1 Corinthians 15:22, where the words are "Adam"/"Christ" and "die"/"alive": "As in Adam all die, even so in Christ shall all be made alive." Because of the eternal roles of Adam and Jesus Christ, men "are brought back into the presence of the Lord."

2 Nephi 9:7 *it must needs be an infinite atonement.* How is Jesus Christ's atonement infinite? "First, it is infinite in the sense that it is timeless—embracing past, present, and future. . . . Second, the atonement of Jesus Christ is infinite in the sense that it conquers the most universal reality in mortal existence—death. . . . Third, the atonement is infinite in that it encompasses all the worlds Christ created. . . . Fourth, the atonement of Jesus Christ is infinite because Christ himself is an infinite being. From his mother, Mary—a mortal woman—he inherited mortality, the capacity to die. On the other hand, he inherited from his Father, the Almighty Elohim, immortality, the power to live forever."[19]

In addition, the Atonement is infinite because it can bless every phase of every life. It is infinite in that it blesses all life on earth, not just human life. And it is infinite in that there is no sin and no suffering that it cannot affect.

save it should be an infinite atonement this corruption could not put on incorruption. Were it not for an infinite atonement, our dead bodies would never become incorruptible through the resurrection. Rather, "this flesh must have laid down to rot and to crumble to its mother earth, to rise no more." For "put on incorruption," see commentary on 1 Corinthians 15:53 in "The Resurrection Constitutes Victory over Death," in this chapter.

2 Nephi 9:8 *O the wisdom of God, his mercy and grace!* The resurrection comes to humankind owing to God's *wisdom, mercy,* and *grace.* How is this so? Jacob explains, "If the flesh should rise no more our spirits must become subject to that angel who fell from before the presence of the Eternal God, and became the devil, to rise no more." Without God's perfect wisdom, mercy, and grace, the dead would never, throughout eternity, have the opportunity to rise again. Instead, the flesh would become like the devil, who will never receive the resurrection. Moreover, without the resurrection, the dead would become subject to the devil. Hence, those who have a "hope of a glorious resurrection" do so "through the grace of God the Father and his Only Begotten Son, Jesus Christ" (D&C 138:14).

if the flesh should rise no more . . . subject to that angel who fell. Verse 8 presents a variety of elements that interact in a significant manner: *flesh* complements *spirits*—together the flesh and the spirit make up the soul; *to rise* stands opposite of *fell*—all flesh will arise at the resurrection because of God's wisdom, mercy, and grace, but the devil fell from God's presence because he lacked wisdom, mercy, and grace; the term *Eternal* in the divine name *Eternal God* is used to call attention to the twice repeated *no more;* in other words, *no more* is an antonym of *eternal.* Other interacting elements include *God* contrasted with *devil;* and *rise no more,* twice repeated to emphasize that without

God's wisdom, mercy, and grace, all flesh would forever remain in their graves.

Joseph Fielding Smith paraphrased and expanded upon Jacob's words "if the flesh should rise no more . . . subject to that angel who fell." He wrote, "If the Savior had not died for the world, man would have remained in his sins. There could have been no resurrection from the dead and the physical body would have gone down into the grave without redemption, while the spirit would have become subject to the devil and his angels eternally."[20]

"THY DEAD MEN SHALL LIVE": THE UNIVERSALITY OF THE RESURRECTION

Isaiah 26:19

> *19 Thy dead men shall live, together with my dead body shall they arise. Awake and sing, ye that dwell in dust: for thy dew is as the dew of herbs, and the earth shall cast out the dead.*

In Isaiah 26:7–18, Israel offered a prayer to the Lord, contemplating different aspects of God's judgments upon the wicked; then in verse 19, the Lord responded to that prayer with a promise of the resurrection and of safety from devastation. The Lord's response presents clear prophetic statements about his own resurrection and that of humanity. The words "Thy dead men shall live, together with my dead body shall they arise" are straightforward, so as not to be misunderstood. In fulfillment of Isaiah's words, the Lord did rise from the dead, as did many of the Saints, for many witnessed his resurrection, including the Nephites at the temple in Bountiful (3 Nephi 11). Others have witnessed the resurrection of Saints (Matthew 27:52–53), and other resurrections are yet to come. In fact, the power of the resurrection will extend to all of God's children born into mortality. Our modern prophets and apostles have made this point over and over. For example:

Joseph F. Smith: "[The Lord] opened the way for every son and daughter of Adam, whether living or dead, to come forth from the grave to a newness of life, to become immortal souls, body and spirit united, never to be severed any more."[21] "Every creature that is born in the image of God will be resurrected from the dead, just as sure as he dies."[22]

James E. Talmage: "The universality of a resurrection is . . . unquestionably affirmed; not only the righteous but even those who merit condemnation are to come forth from their graves in their bodies of flesh and bones."[23]

George Q. Cannon: "Jesus our Lord and Savior died for all, and all will be resurrected—good and bad, . . . people of every race, whether sinners or not; and no matter how great their sins may be, the resurrection of their bodies is sure. Jesus has died for them, and they all will be redeemed from the grave through the atonement which he has made."[24]

Ezra Taft Benson: "Nothing is more absolutely universal than the resurrection. Every living being will be resurrected."[25]

Boyd K. Packer: "With each of us, the resurrection is a certainty."[26]

NOTES AND COMMENTARY

Isaiah 26:19 *Thy dead men shall live.* This is a promise of the resurrection. "All must rise," Joseph Smith said simply, and "all must enter eternity."[27]

together with my dead body shall they arise. The dead body referred to is that of Jesus Christ. This prophecy was fulfilled at Jesus' resurrection. Matthew recorded that after Jesus rose from the dead, "the graves were opened; and many bodies of the Saints which slept arose" (Matthew 27:52).

Awake and sing, ye that dwell in dust. The call is made for those who are dead to awake from the sleep of death and sing praises to the Lord, who made the resurrection possible. Joseph Smith also prophesied, "The graves of the Saints shall be opened; and they shall come forth and stand on the right hand of the Lamb, when he shall stand upon Mount Zion, and upon the holy city, the New Jerusalem; and they shall sing the song of the Lamb, day and night forever and ever" (D&C 133:56; see also D&C 128:22).

for thy dew is as the dew of the morning. The literal reading of the phrase *dew of the morning* is "dew of lights." Isaiah compared resurrected bodies to the dew of the morning because of dew's association with life. "*Dew* is a very important element in Palestine's ecosystem. During the long dry months it is the only moisture the vegetation receives. It became a symbol for life. Light is also an important symbol of life and well-being."[28] Interestingly, dew is also associated with the manna given to the Israelites to save their lives during the exodus (Exodus 16:13–15; Numbers 11:9).

earth shall cast out the dead. This is another reference to the resurrection. The dead will arise from the earth where they have lain. The ground shall no longer hold them captive.

EZEKIEL DETAILS THE HOUSE OF ISRAEL'S RESURRECTION

Ezekiel 37:1–14

1 The hand of the Lord was upon me, and carried me out in the spirit of the Lord, and set me down in the midst of the valley which was full of bones,

2 And caused me to pass by them round about: and, behold, there were very many in the open valley; and, lo, they were very dry.

3 And he said unto me, Son of man, can these bones live? And I answered, O Lord God, thou knowest.

4 Again he said unto me, Prophesy upon these bones, and say unto them, O ye dry bones, hear the word of the Lord.

5 Thus saith the Lord God unto these bones; Behold, I will cause breath to enter into you, and ye shall live:

6 And I will lay sinews upon you, and will bring up flesh upon you, and cover you with skin, and put breath in you, and ye shall live; and ye shall know that I am the Lord.

7 So I prophesied as I was commanded: and as I prophesied, there was a noise, and behold a shaking, and the bones came together, bone to his bone.

8 And when I beheld, lo, the sinews and the flesh came up upon them, and the skin covered them above: but there was no breath in them.

9 Then said he unto me, Prophesy unto the wind, prophesy, son of man, and say to the wind, Thus saith the Lord God;

Come from the four winds, O breath, and breathe upon these slain, that they may live.

10 So I prophesied as he commanded me, and the breath came into them, and they lived, and stood up upon their feet, an exceeding great army.

11 Then he said unto me, Son of man, these bones are the whole house of Israel: behold, they say, Our bones are dried, and our hope is lost: we are cut off for our parts.

12 Therefore prophesy and say unto them, Thus saith the Lord God; Behold, O my people, I will open your graves, and cause you to come up out of your graves, and bring you into the land of Israel.

13 And ye shall know that I am the Lord, when I have opened your graves, O my people, and brought you up out of your graves,

14 And shall put my spirit in you, and ye shall live, and I shall place you in your own land: then shall ye know that I the Lord have spoken it, and performed it, saith the Lord.

Ezekiel saw in vision a great number of dry bones of the Lord's people, members of the house of Israel. God caused Ezekiel to move among the bones, perhaps to comprehend the great number of bones or to make the vision more real. The Lord instructed Ezekiel that he, the Lord, would resurrect those to whom the bones belonged. In fact, the Lord's role in the resurrection was emphasized by a number of statements scattered throughout the section—"I will cause breath to enter into you" (verse 5); "I will lay sinews upon you" (verse 6); I "will bring up flesh upon you" (verse 6); I will "cover you with skin" (verse 6); I will "put breath in you" (verse 6); "I will open your graves, and cause you to come up out of your graves" (verse 12); "I have opened your graves, O my people, and brought you up out of your graves" (verse 13); and I "shall put my spirit in you, and ye shall live" (verse 14). These statements define the resurrection. They also provide hope to members of the house of Israel that their spirits will not remain forever without their bones and other body parts (see verse 11).

Ezekiel knew the vision was from the Lord, and internal evidence supports his view—consider the expression "hear the word of the Lord" (verse 4) as well as the repeated formula "Thus saith the Lord God" (see verses 5, 9, 12). Through his prophet, the Lord used the resurrection as a sign or evidence that Jehovah is God and further emphasized the point through repetition (see verses 6, 13, 14).

A parallel vision to Ezekiel's exists in latter-day scripture. On October 3, 1918, Joseph F. Smith received a vision of Jesus Christ's visit to the spirits of the dead who were awaiting the resurrection. The following day he shared his experience with those who attended general conference. Interesting connections exist between President Smith's vision, now in Doctrine and Covenants 138, and Ezekiel's vision of the resurrection. Some of these connections will be discussed in the following notes and comments. In fact, President Smith saw Ezekiel in vision "among the great and mighty ones who were assembled" in the spirit world (D&C 138:38). He wrote, "Moreover, Ezekiel, who was shown in vision the great valley of dry bones, which were to be clothed upon with flesh, to come forth again in the resurrection of the dead, living souls . . . [was] also there" (D&C 138:43, 46).

NOTES AND COMMENTARY

Ezekiel 37:1 *hand of the Lord was upon me.* This expression indicates that the Spirit of the Lord came upon Ezekiel and empowered him to receive a divine vision or to receive the word of the Lord. The expression appears several times in Ezekiel (see also Ezekiel 1:3; 8:1; 33:22; 40:1). In comparison, President Joseph F. Smith wrote, "The Spirit of the Lord rested upon me" (D&C 138:11) when he envisioned the dead who were awaiting the resurrection.

carried me out in the spirit of the Lord. The Holy Ghost, or the Spirit of the Lord, is the vehicle that enables and empowers people to receive visions and heavenly instructions. During earth's history many, including Adam (Moses 6:64), Elijah (1 Kings 18:12), Nephi (1 Nephi 14:30), the twelve Apostles (1 Nephi 11:29), and Mary (1 Nephi 11:19), have been carried away by the Spirit in order to fulfill the divine purposes of the Lord,

valley which was full of bones. The valley is not named nor is its location known, except that it is not in the land of Israel (see verses

12, 14). In point of fact, the valley is likely a symbolic one, the burial ground for all of the children of Israel who have been scattered throughout the world. Evidence of this interpretation appears later in the vision when the Lord informed Ezekiel that "these bones are the whole house of Israel" (Ezekiel 37:11) rather than a small portion of Israel who had been buried in a particular valley. (And even if a valley large enough to contain all of their bones existed, members of the house of Israel throughout the ages certainly would not all have been buried in a single valley.) Furthermore, the phrase "four winds" (Ezekiel 37:9) indicates a worldwide geography (see commentary, verse 11).

Ezekiel 37:2 *caused me to pass by them round about.* Ezekiel's vision was complete. He did not glance at the bones or look at them from a distance. Rather, the Lord caused him to pass through the bones so that he had a complete understanding of their number, their dryness, and their scattered condition.

there were very many. The vision emphasized a large number of bones. The valley was "full of bones" (Ezekiel 37:1); there were "very many" (Ezekiel 37:2), representing "an exceeding great army" (Ezekiel 37:10), even "the whole house of Israel" (Ezekiel 37:11). Joseph F. Smith too saw in his vision of the dead a great number of people awaiting the resurrection. He "saw the hosts of the dead, both small and great" (D&C 138:11); he saw "an innumerable company of the spirits of the just" (D&C 138:12).

Ezekiel 37:3 *Son of man, can these bones live?* The Lord taught his prophet through interrogation by asking, "Can these bones live?" in other words, can these bones be resurrected? Ezekiel responded simply by stating, "O Lord God, thou knowest."

Ezekiel 37:4 *Prophesy upon these bones . . . O ye dry bones, hear the word of the Lord.* In the book that carries his name, Ezekiel was commanded some two dozen times to prophesy. In this section the Lord commanded him to prophesy three times (see verses 4, 9, and 12). Here he prophesied directly to the bones, commanding them to hear the Lord's word, set forth in verses 5 and 6. Four things are promised to the bones: the Lord will put breath in them, he will lay sinews upon them, he will place flesh upon them, and he will cover them with skin. Of course, dry and lifeless bones cannot comprehend Ezekiel's prophecy; rather his words are directed to members of the house of Israel who will hear or read them.

Ezekiel 37:5 *I will cause breath to enter into you, and ye shall live.* When Adam was created, "the Lord God . . . breathed into his nostrils the breath of life; and man became a living soul" (Genesis 2:7). In a similar way, God resurrects humanity by causing breath to enter them.

Ezekiel 37:6 *And I will lay sinews upon you, and will bring up flesh upon you, and cover you with skin.* One's body consists of more than sinews, flesh, skin, and breath; but these parts of the body perhaps represent the whole body. It would not have been feasible in this revelation for God to name the restoration of every single body part—teeth, hair, eyes, fingernails, and so forth.

and put breath in you, and ye shall live. See commentary on verse 5.

ye shall know that I am the Lord. The resurrection is evidence to all that the God of Ezekiel is the true God. None of the false gods that were worshiped during Ezekiel's time, or that have been worshiped during any other period of the earth, have had the ability to resurrect. Only one God can do so, and when he does, all will know that he is the true God of power.

Ezekiel 37:7 *So I prophesied as I was commanded.* Ezekiel, ever obedient to the Lord's commands, obeyed his voice.

there was a noise, and behold a shaking, and the bones came together, bone to his bone. Ezekiel witnessed the resurrection, here described as a noise, a shaking, and bones coming together, "bone to his bone." President Smith also used the expression "bone to his bone" in his Vision of the Redemption of the Dead. President Smith's words, like Ezekiel's, provide a vivid description of the resurrection: "Their sleeping dust was to be restored unto its perfect frame, bone to his bone, and the sinews and the flesh upon them, the spirit and the body to be united never again to be divided, that they might receive a fulness of joy" (D&C 138:17).

In a manner somewhat parallel to the prophet Ezekiel, Joseph Smith witnessed the resurrection in a vision. Joseph Smith shared a glimpse of what he saw: "Would you think it strange if I relate what I have seen in vision in relation to [the resurrection]? . . . So plain was the vision, that I actually saw men, before they had ascended from the tomb, as though they were getting up slowly. They took each other by the hand and said to each other, 'My father, my son, my mother, my daughter, my brother, my sister.'"[29]

Ezekiel 37:8 *but there was no breath in them.* Ezekiel's prophesying to the bones resulted in a noise, a shaking, and the coming together of bones. However, since God's breath (or Spirit) was not in them, the deceased people did not become immortal souls.

Ezekiel 37:9 *Prophesy unto the wind.* The "four winds" means the whole earth. Perhaps the Lord is telling Ezekiel to prophesy to the whole earth when he says, "Prophesy unto the wind." Or there is another possible interpretation. The same Hebrew word (*ruach*) translated here as *wind* is translated as *spirit* in verse 14. This phrase may then be translated as "prophesy unto the spirit" rather than "prophesy unto the wind." We know from verse 14 and elsewhere (Revelation 11:11) that it is God's Spirit that will cause the resurrection—"And ye shall know that I am the Lord, when I have opened your graves, O my people, and brought you up out of your graves, and shall put my spirit in you, and ye shall live" (verses 13–14). Ezekiel's prophecy "unto the wind [spirit]" will be fulfilled at the second coming when God resurrects the house of Israel.

Come from the four winds. The *four winds* expresses the idea of the totality of the planet Earth. This sense is found in John's book of Revelation, where he writes concerning the "four corners of the earth" and "the four winds of the earth" (Revelation 7:1; see also Daniel 11:4). Ezekiel's prophecy that breath will come from the four winds suggests that life or "breath" will come to all of the dead throughout the earth, whether they were buried in the north or south, east or west, at land or at sea.

Ezekiel 37:10 *So I prophesied as he commanded me.* Once again, Ezekiel was obedient to the Lord's commands (compare verse 7).

breath came into them, and they lived. Here *breath* refers to "the Spirit of life from God" (Revelation 11:11), which will enter into the bodies of the dead at the resurrection and give them life.

stood up upon their feet. Similar language is found in Revelation 11, which tells of the two prophets who will prophesy in Jerusalem during the last days. After their three-and-a-half-year ministry, these two will be martyred, "and their dead bodies shall lie in the street" of Jerusalem. Then, "after three days and an half the Spirit of life from God entered into them, and they *stood upon their feet*" (Revelation 11:8, 11; emphasis added). "Standing," with reference to the resurrected Lord and to other heavenly beings, shows predominance and control (see Revelation 5:6; 7:1; 10:2, 5).[30] Or, simply put, saying they "stood upon their feet" may be designed to show the contrast between a dead body and a living, resurrected one.

an exceeding great army. This large army, or the "whole house of Israel" (37:11), received the Spirit of life from God and became resurrected beings. The Hebrew word here translated as *army* may also be translated as *host,* indicating a large number; hence, "an exceedingly great host."

Ezekiel 37:11 *these bones are the whole house of Israel.* Ezekiel envisioned here the resurrection of members of the house of Israel, not that of the entire world.

Our bones are dried, and our hope is lost: we are cut off for our parts. Without the resurrection, the hope of the members of the house of Israel would be lost forever. Their bones would dry up and their body parts be cut off from their spirits forever.

Ezekiel 37:12 *O my people.* This refers to the house of Israel, who are God's people.

I will open your graves, and cause you to come up out of your graves. Once again God defined the resurrection, which consists of God opening the graves and causing the bodies to come forth from the graves.

bring you into the land of Israel. The Lord himself assured Israel of their eventual return to their land of promise. Note that Ezekiel's vision emphasized the Lord's active role in Israel's return, as indicated by two action verbs—*bring* and *place.* In this verse God promised to *bring* Israel into their land; in verse 14 he stated that he would *place* them in their "own land." God would first cause them to come, then he would set them there, in their promised land.

Ezekiel 37:13 *ye shall know that I am the Lord.* See commentary on verse 6.

Ezekiel 37:14 *shall put my spirit in you, and ye shall live.* God will put his Spirit in us, bringing to pass the resurrection. Paul taught this same doctrine when he wrote, "but if the Spirit of him that raised up Jesus from the dead dwell in you, he that raised up Christ from the dead shall also quicken your mortal bodies by his Spirit that dwelleth in you" (Romans 8:11).

In Ezekiel's prophecy it was the Lord who caused the resurrection—"I have opened your graves, O my people, and brought you up out of your graves, and shall put my spirit in you" (Ezekiel 37:13–14). Neither mortals nor the deceased have power to resurrect themselves. Only God can do so. Joseph Smith taught concerning the role of God's Spirit in the resurrection, "We have a knowledge that those we bury here God will bring up again, clothed upon and quickened by the Spirit of the great God."[31]

I shall place you in your own land. See commentary on verse 12.

then shall ye know that I the Lord have spoken it, and performed it. In verse 6, God revealed to Ezekiel that the house of Israel would know that God is the Lord after he restored their bodies to life. At the conclusion of the section, God affirmed that Israel would know that he had spoken and that he was the one who performed the resurrection and Israel's restoration to the land.

The Righteous Escape the Resurrection of Damnation

John 5:21–29

21 For as the Father raiseth up the dead, and quickeneth them; even so the Son quickeneth whom he will.

22 For the Father judgeth no man, but hath committed all judgment unto the Son:

23 That all men should honour the Son, even as they honour the Father. He that honoureth not the Son honoureth not the Father which hath sent him.

24 Verily, verily, I say unto you, He that heareth my word, and believeth on him that sent me, hath everlasting life, and shall not come into condemnation; but is passed from death unto life.

25 Verily, verily, I say unto you, The hour is coming, and now is, when the dead shall hear the voice of the Son of God: and they that hear shall live.

26 For as the Father hath life in himself; so hath he given to the Son to have life in himself;

27 And hath given him authority to execute judgment also, because he is the Son of man.

28 Marvel not at this: for the hour is coming, in the which all that are in the graves shall hear his voice,

29 And shall come forth; they that have done good, unto the resurrection of life; and they that have done evil, unto the resurrection of damnation.

The preceding verses serve two principal purposes:

1. They speak of the relationship between God and his Son (note that the word *Father* is used five times and *Son* seven times). Jesus instructed his listeners regarding a number of doctrinal truths that clarify his position in relation to the Father. The Father delegated divine activities to his Son when he gave him authority to "execute judgment" (vv. 22, 27), sent him to the earth to deliver God's word (v. 24), and gave to him to have life in himself (v. 26). Because of Jesus' participation in divine activities, "all men should honour the Son, even as they honour the Father" (v. 23). In fact, those who fail to honor the Son consequently fail to honor the Father. One cannot honor the Father without giving honor to his Son.

2. The verses also teach the doctrine of the resurrection. Certain words in Jesus' discourse referred to this important theme, speaking of both death and life. On the one hand he used the terms *dead* (twice), *death,* and *graves* in the context of resurrection; on the other hand he spoke of *raiseth up, quickeneth* (twice), *everlasting life, life* (five times), *come forth,* and *resurrection* (twice). *Judgment* is a sub-theme that exists in these verses (see vv. 22, 27) because at the resurrection all humankind will be judged and receive the resurrection of life or of damnation.

Mention should be made here of an especially significant event that occurred in Church history. As Joseph Smith was reading and translating John 5:29 on February 16, 1832, he and Sidney Rigdon received a vision. Joseph recorded the setting: "Upon my return from Amherst conference, I resumed the translation of the Scriptures. From sundry revelations which had been received, it was apparent that many important points touching the salvation of man, had been taken from the Bible, or lost before it was compiled. It appeared self-evident from what truths were left, that if God rewarded every one according to the deeds done in the body the term 'Heaven,' as intended for the Saints' eternal home must include more kingdoms than one. Accordingly, on the 16th of February, 1832, while translating St. John's Gospel, myself and Elder Rigdon saw the following vision."[32]

This vision, recorded as Doctrine and Covenants 76, sets forth many important truths about the resurrection, the degrees of glory, and the celestial, terrestrial, and telestial kingdoms. Verses 16 and 17 especially are important to our understanding of the resurrection: "Speaking of the resurrection of the dead, concerning those who shall hear the voice of the Son of Man: and shall come forth; they who have done good, in the resurrection of the just; and they who have done evil, in the resurrection of the unjust."

NOTES AND COMMENTARY

John 5:21 *For as the Father raiseth up the dead, and quickeneth them; even so the Son quickeneth whom he will.* To *quicken* is to "give life." The Father has power to give life to the dead, restoring them to mortality or resurrecting them to immortality. He empowered Jesus as well to restore life to the dead, as Paul explained in an epistle: "The last Adam was made a quickening spirit" (1 Corinthians 15:45). Jesus himself taught, "The Son quickeneth whom he will." Jesus demonstrated this power a number of times during his mortal ministry. One remarkable example is the raising of Lazarus (John 11:41–44).

Subsequent verses in the passage under discussion (John 5:21–29) reveal more about Jesus and his power to quicken "whom he will." Verses 25 and 28 through 29 report that those who have passed on will in time hear the Son's voice and rise from their graves, some to "the resurrection of life" and others to "the resurrection of damnation."

John 5:22 *For the Father . . . hath committed all judgment unto* *the Son.* Jesus possesses all privileges and rights connected with divine judicial authority—he is at the same time advocate, mediator, and judge. According to the scriptures, he is the "advocate with the Father" (1 John 2:1; D&C 29:5). He is also the "one mediator between God and men, the man Christ Jesus" (1 Timothy 2:5). As the advocate and the mediator, he has power to "make intercession" (Mosiah 15:8). As the judge, he has a "judgment seat" (Romans 14:10) and a judgment bar, called the "bar of Christ" (Alma 11:44). God the Father not only committed all judgment unto Jesus Christ; he also "ordained" him "to be the Judge of the quick and dead" (Acts 10:42).

John 5:23 *That all men should honour the Son, even as they honour the Father.* Jesus is equal with the Father in power to bring life to the dead; he also possesses life in himself, as does the Father, and he has the authority to judge earth's inhabitants. Because of his equality with the Father on these and other divine matters, "all men" are required to give honor to the Son in the same way that they honor the Father. And those who do not honor the Son do not honor the Father.

John 5:24 *He that heareth my word, and believeth on him that sent me, hath everlasting life.* Hearing Jesus' word and *believing* in the Father are vital elements in humanity's efforts to obtain everlasting life. Hearing does not simply connote receiving words in one's ears; it also signifies acting upon or obeying the words of Christ. To other audiences in other settings, Jesus presented additional doctrines regarding everlasting life: "Verily, verily, I say unto you, If a man keep my saying, he shall never see death" (John 8:51), and "these are written, that ye might believe that Jesus is the Christ, the Son of God; and that believing ye might have life through his name" (John 20:31; see also John 11:26).

John 5:25 *The hour is coming, and now is, when the dead shall hear the voice of the Son of God.* To place emphasis on this sentence, the Lord repeats it, though with a little variation, in verse 28: "The hour is coming, in the which all that are in the graves shall hear his voice." The words prophesy that Jesus Christ would soon visit the dead in the spirit world. "The hour is coming" indicates that his visit would be imminent. This visit was spoken of by Isaiah more than seven hundred years earlier: "They shall be gathered together, as prisoners are

gathered in the pit, and shall be shut up in the prison, and after many
days shall they be visited" (Isaiah 24:22); also, "The Spirit of the Lord
God is upon me; because the Lord hath anointed me to preach good
tidings unto the meek; he hath sent me to bind up the brokenhearted,
to proclaim liberty to the captives, and the opening of the prison to
them that are bound" (Isaiah 61:1).

Other scripture provides insight about the phrase "the dead shall
hear the voice of the Son of God." It is possible that the Lord's voice
will be uttered loudly, in the form of a shout, as Paul wrote: "The Lord
himself shall descend with a shout" (1 Thessalonians 4:16). In any
case, the exact words that Jesus will utter may have been revealed to
Joseph Smith: "The day cometh that the Lord shall utter his voice out
of heaven; the heavens shall shake and the earth shall tremble, and the
trump of God shall sound both long and loud, and shall say to the
sleeping nations: Ye Saints arise and live; ye sinners stay and sleep
until I shall call again" (D&C 43:18).

John 5:26 *For as the Father hath life in himself; so hath he given
to the Son to have life in himself.* The manner in which God can have
life in himself remains a mystery. Mortals do not have life in themselves and are dependent on God for food, water, and breath as well
as resurrection and eternal life. In addition to having life in himself,
God has the power to create life in man and beast, to restore the dead
to mortality, and to resurrect the dead to immortality and eternal life.

John 5:27 *And hath given him authority to execute judgment
also, because he is the Son of man.* This verse presents the precise reason why God authorized Jesus to be the judge and to execute judgment on the world—"because he is the Son of man." "Son of man" is
a shortened form of "Son of Man of Holiness"; in other words, he is
the Son of God the Father, whose divine title is Man of Holiness.
Jesus, as God's only begotten Son, was empowered by the Father to
execute judgment upon the inhabitants of the world.

John 5:28 *for the hour is coming.* See commentary on verse 25.

John 5:29 *And shall come forth.* Every man, woman, and child
who is dead will come forth when their graves are opened at the voice
of the Lord and the sounding of Michael's trumpet. As the Lord has
revealed, "Before the earth shall pass away, Michael, mine archangel,

shall sound his trump, and then shall all the dead awake, for their graves shall be opened, and they shall come forth—yea, even all" (D&C 29:26).

the resurrection of life . . . the resurrection of damnation. The "resurrection of life" or "the resurrection of the just" (D&C 76:17) is designed for those who have lived godly lives. According to the times and orders of resurrection, these will be resurrected before the wicked. The "resurrection of damnation" or "the resurrection of the unjust" (D&C 76:17) will consist of those whose deeds have been evil and whose lives have been filled with darkness. All of the dead, of course, will receive a resurrection, but some "shall awake . . . to everlasting life" and others "to shame and everlasting contempt" (Daniel 12:2).

THE SEA AND THE GRAVE GIVE UP THE DEAD

Revelation 20:11–15

11 And I saw a great white throne, and him that sat on it, from whose face the earth and the heaven fled away; and there was found no place for them.

12 And I saw the dead, small and great, stand before God; and the books were opened; and another book was opened, which is the book of life: and the dead were judged out of those things which were written in the books, according to their works.

13 And the sea gave up the dead which were in it; and death and hell delivered up the dead which were in them: and they were judged every man according to their works.

14 And death and hell were cast into the lake of fire. This is the second death.

15 And whosoever was not found written in the book of life was cast into the lake of fire.

John saw in vision the resurrection of the dead and their subsequent judgment. He envisioned the dead coming forth from the sea and that "death and hell delivered up the dead which were in them" (v. 13). All of the resurrected dead will stand before God, the great judge who sits upon his great white throne. They will be judged according to their deeds, which deeds are recorded in both earthly and heavenly books (see also D&C 128:6–8). According to John, three things will be cast into the lake of fire—death, hell, and those whose names are not written in the book of life.

NOTES AND COMMENTARY

Revelation 20:11 *a great white throne.* This throne symbolizes God's kingship and power. It is called "great" to suggest that it is no ordinary throne but one fit for the king of all creation. White may symbolize victory or purity and righteousness—or a combination of these attributes of God. In addition, the word *white* (Greek *leukos*) may mean "bright" or "gleaming."[33] God dwells in "everlasting burnings,"[34] and his throne would therefore be white, bright, and gleaming. For other references to the throne, see Revelation 4:2–3, 9; 5:1, 7, 13; 6:16; 7:10, 15; 19:4; 21:5.

him that sat on it. The being on the throne is God, the Eternal Father.

from whose face the earth and the heaven fled away. "When the thousand years are ended, and men again begin to deny their God, then will I spare the earth but for a little season; and the end shall come, and the heaven and the earth shall be consumed and pass away, and there shall be a new heaven and a new earth. For all old things shall pass away, and all things shall become new, even the heaven and the earth, and all the fulness thereof" (D&C 29:22–24). These things will come by the power of God.

there was found no place for them. The old heaven and earth must give way so that the new may come (Revelation 21:1). Just as Satan and his followers were cast out of the presence of God—"neither was their place found any more in heaven" (Revelation 12:8)—so will the old heaven and the old earth themselves have no place before God. The earth will be changed to a celestial order after the Millennium (see Revelation 21:1).

Revelation 20:12 *the dead, small and great, stand before God.* These are "the rest of the dead" who were not resurrected earlier (Revelation 20:5). The righteous dead have already been raised up unto glory (Revelation 20:4). All who remain—whether strong or weak, rich or poor, famous or insignificant in the eyes of the world—

will be raised from the dead to stand before God the Judge to determine what their eternal reward or punishment will be.

the books were opened. Joseph Smith explained, "You will discover in this quotation [Revelation 20:12] that the books were opened; and another book was opened, which was the book of life; but the dead were judged out of those things which were written in the books, according to their works; consequently, the books spoken of must be the books which contained the record of their works, and refer to the records which are kept on the earth [which probably includes Church records of ordinances and Church histories]. And the book which was the book of life is the record which is kept in heaven; the principle agreeing precisely with the doctrine which is commanded you in the revelation contained in the letter which I wrote to you previous to my leaving my place [D&C 127]—that in all your recordings it may be recorded in heaven" (D&C 128:7; see also Daniel 7:10).

another book was opened, which is the book of life. Those whose names are recorded in the book of life are saved from being cast into the lake of fire, which is the second death. As Jesus said to the apostles, "Rejoice not, that the spirits are subject unto you; but rather rejoice, because your names are written in heaven" (Luke 10:20).

The book of life figures prominently in the book of Revelation (3:5; 13:8; 17:8; 20:12, 15; 21:27; 22:19). This book contains the names of those who will receive eternal life. It is the "record which is kept in heaven" (D&C 128:7), which contains the names of the righteous (Alma 5:58). The book belongs to the Lamb (21:27), who blots out the names of sinners from it (Exodus 32:32–33) but does not remove the names of those who overcome the world and are clothed in white raiment.

the dead were judged out of those things which were written in the books, according to their works. The things we do here on earth are entered into the record books of both heaven and earth, and our works form the basis of our judgment. Jacob wrote, "When all men shall have passed from this first death unto life, insomuch as they have become immortal, they must appear before the judgment-seat of the Holy One of Israel; and then cometh the judgment, and then must they be judged according to the holy judgment of God" (2 Nephi 9:15).

Paul later testified, "Every one of us shall give account of himself to God" (Romans 14:12).

As mentioned earlier, the dead here are those who were not worthy to come forth in the first resurrection but were reserved until after the Millennium. The righteous will also likely stand before the judgment bar at this time but only to have their earlier judgment—and blessing of glory—confirmed.[35] For examples of individuals and groups that received an earlier judgment, see Revelation 20:4; Mosiah 15:21–25; D&C 101:30–31; 132:37.

Joseph Smith gave a valuable and comforting lesson on the judgment: "The Great Parent of the universe looks upon the whole of the human family with a fatherly care and paternal regard; He views them as His offspring, and without any of those contracted feelings that influence the children of men. . . . [He] will judge all men, not according to the narrow, contracted notions of men, but, 'according to the deeds done in the body whether they be good or evil,' or whether these deeds were done in England, America, Spain, Turkey, or India. He will judge them, 'not according to what they have not, but according to what they have,' those who have lived without law, will be judged without law, and those who have a law, will be judged by that law. . . . He will award judgment or mercy to all nations according to their several deserts, their means of obtaining intelligence, the laws by which they are governed, the facilities afforded them of obtaining correct information, and His inscrutable designs in relation to the human family; and when the designs of God shall be made manifest, and the curtain of futurity be withdrawn, we shall all of us eventually have to confess that the Judge of all the earth has done right."[36]

President Joseph Fielding Smith added this insight: "Every man will be judged according to his works, his opportunities for receiving the truth, and the intent of his heart."[37]

Revelation 20:13 *the sea gave up the dead which were in it.* The sea may represent the resting place of those whose bodies are lost to the knowledge of humanity. Though their bodies were carried away, and no one knows their final resting place, even these will be resurrected. In addition, "It was widely believed that those lost at sea had no access to Sheol (Hades); in specifically naming the sea, John emphasized that he was describing the *general* resurrection."[38]

death and hell delivered up the dead which were in them. According to Jacob, the brother of Nephi, death is the state in which body and spirit are separated, and hell is the state of spiritual death. Those in both states will all be brought forth in the great, universal resurrection. Jacob said, "O how great the goodness of our God, who prepareth a way for our escape from the grasp of this awful monster; yea, that monster, death and hell, which I call the death of the body, and also the death of the spirit. And because of the way of deliverance of our God, the Holy One of Israel, this death, of which I have spoken, which is the temporal, shall deliver up its dead; which death is the grave. And this death of which I have spoken, which is the spiritual death, shall deliver up its dead; which spiritual death is hell; wherefore, death and hell must deliver up their dead, and hell must deliver up its captive spirits, and the grave must deliver up its captive bodies, and the bodies and the spirits of men will be restored one to the other; and it is by the power of the resurrection of the Holy One of Israel" (2 Nephi 9:10–12).

Revelation 20:14 *death and hell were cast into the lake of fire.* This is a symbolic way of saying that death and hell will be destroyed. "Jesus Christ . . . hath abolished death," Paul wrote (2 Timothy 1:10), and he likewise abolishes hell for all who attain to a state of glory. The lake of fire is a hell for those who are cast into it (Satan, his angels, and the sons of perdition), and that hell will continue through the eternities (D&C 29:38; 76:44; 2 Peter 2:4). But for those who are "heirs of salvation" (D&C 76:88), meaning all who attain to a kingdom of glory, death and hell will forever cease to exist.

This is the second death. The torture of the second death—which means to suffer eternal *spiritual* death—is typified by the lake of fire.

Revelation 20:15 *whosoever was not found written in the book of life was cast into the lake of fire.* Many will be cast into the lake of fire: the beast and the false prophet, the devil, death and hell, and all those who names are not found in the book of life (Revelation 19:20; 20:10, 14, 15).

INTELLIGENCE GAINED IN MORTALITY
REMAINS IN THE RESURRECTION

D&C 130:18–19

18 Whatever principle of intelligence we attain unto in this life, it will rise with us in the resurrection.

19 And if a person gains more knowledge and intelligence in this life through his diligence and obedience than another, he will have so much the advantage in the world to come.

The forty-nine words presented in Doctrine and Covenants 130:18–19 compose a concise and awe-inspiring statement about the existence of knowledge and intelligence after the resurrection. The statement presents three principal truths:

1. Intelligence gained in mortality will exist after the resurrection.

2. Knowledge and intelligence are gained in mortality through "diligence and obedience."

3. Those who gain "more knowledge and intelligence" in mortality will have a greater advantage in the "world to come."

NOTES AND COMMENTARY

D&C 130:18 *Whatever principle of intelligence we attain unto in this life, it will rise with us in the resurrection.* By intelligence is meant "light and truth." "The glory of God is intelligence," the Lord revealed to Joseph Smith on May 6, 1833, "or, in other words, light and truth" (D&C 93:36).

The knowledge and intelligence that we gain in mortality will remain with us as we pass from mortality to the spirit world. Joseph Smith made three statements that broaden our understanding about the possession of knowledge in the world of spirits: "Knowledge saves a man; and in the world of spirits no man can be exalted but by knowledge."[39] "A man is saved no faster than he gets knowledge."[40] "There are a great many wise men and women too in our midst who are too wise to be taught; therefore they must die in their ignorance, and in the resurrection they will find their mistake."[41]

At the reunion of our spirits and bodies, the level of intelligence that we gain in mortality will "rise with us in the resurrection." Nephi similarly taught that all humankind, whether wicked or righteous, will rise at the resurrection with knowledge. On the one hand, the wicked will have "a perfect knowledge of all [their] guilt, and [their] uncleanness, and [their] nakedness." On the other hand, "the righteous shall have a perfect knowledge of their enjoyment, and their righteousness, being clothed with purity, yea, even with the robe of righteousness" (2 Nephi 9:14).

In a conference address given in October 1937, Elder Albert E. Bowen provided this summary: "It is fair to conclude that spiritual and mental growth can be attained only by obedience to the laws on which they are predicated. If through diligence, observance of correct principles, discipline of the mind and of the spirit, a man attains to a fine development of personality in this life, surely it is not unreasonable to suppose that that will be his imperishable possession and glory in the life he enters upon after death. On the contrary, if through lethargy or sin his self-realization in this life is dwarfed, he shall be handicapped to that extent as he enters upon the new world."[42]

D&C 130:19 *if a person gains more knowledge and intelligence in this life.* Verse 18 introduced the idea of people gaining "intelligence" in this life; verse 19 pairs "knowledge" with "intelligence," hence reading "knowledge and intelligence."

through his diligence and obedience. Intelligence is gained through diligence and obedience (see also D&C 93:28). It is also lost through disobedience: "That wicked one cometh and taketh away light and truth, through disobedience, from the children of men, and because of the tradition of their fathers" (D&C 93:39; see also Alma 12:9–11).

advantage in the world to come. All individuals will have an "advantage in the world to come" if they gain "more knowledge and intelligence in this life." It may be said that God has the greatest advantage of all because he possesses "greater knowledge." Joseph Smith explained, "In knowledge there is power. God has more power than all other beings, because he has greater knowledge; and hence he knows how to subject all other beings to him. He has power over all."[43]

THE RESURRECTION OF ANIMALS

Joseph Fielding Smith

The Lord intends to save not only the earth and the heavens, not only man who dwells upon the earth, but all things which he has created. The animals, the fishes of the sea, the fowls of the air, as well as man, are to be recreated, or renewed, through the resurrection, for they too are living souls.[44]

Our latter-day prophets have made numerous statements about God's eternal plan for animals. Joseph Fielding Smith's statement indicates that animals, fish, and fowl will be renewed through the resurrection. The reason for their resurrection, he explains, is that they "are living souls." Brigham Young taught concerning the resurrection of both the earth and living things that are on it: "And the earth is resurrected? Yes, and every living thing on the earth."[45]

God's eternal plan for living creatures extends beyond their resurrection. Church authorities have taught the following regarding animals:

Each animal and creature has been endowed with a spirit. "God created the beasts as well as man, creeping things, the fowls of the air and placed in each a spirit in the exact likeness of its body, or more properly, created every creature in the likeness of its spirit. Therefore they are living entities entitled to the mercies of Jesus Christ and to receive the resurrection. . . .

"So we learn that all things were created by our Eternal Father, and there is nothing which has life that he did not create; moreover every thing shall live again receiving the benefit of the resurrection. This proves that every thing having life, is endowed with a spirit, and had a fall."[46]

Although members of the animal kingdom have spirits, this does not mean they are God's offspring. Joseph Fielding Smith clarified that "the Lord has said that not only has man a spirit, and is thereby a living soul, but likewise the beasts of the field, the fowl of the air, and the fish of the sea have spirits, and hence are living souls. But this does not make them kinsmen to the sons and daughters of God. They are our Father's creations, not his offspring, and that is the great difference between man and beast."[47]

The perfection of the animal creation. Joseph F. Smith, John R. Winder, and Anthon H. Lund, comprising the Church's First Presidency, composed the following regarding the eventual perfection of animals and the joy they will receive. "[God] made the tadpole and the ape, the lion and the elephant; but He did not make them in His own image, nor endow them with Godlike reason and intelligence. Nevertheless, the whole animal creation will be perfected and perpetuated in the Hereafter, each class in its 'distinct order or sphere,' and will enjoy 'eternal felicity.' That fact has been made plain in this dispensation. (D&C 77:3.)"[48]

Some animals or beasts will exist in heaven. Joseph Smith presented these significant words about John the Revelator's vision of beasts in heaven: "John saw curious looking beasts in heaven; he saw every creature that was in heaven, all the beasts, fowls and fish in heaven, actually there, giving glory to God. . . . John learned that God glorified Himself by saving all that His hands had made, whether beasts, fowls, fishes or men; and He will glorify Himself with them."[49]

Beasts in heaven give glory to and communicate with God. "Says one, 'I cannot believe in the salvation of beasts.' Any man who would tell you that this could not be, would tell you that the revelations are not true. John heard the words of the beasts giving glory to God, and understood them. God who made the beasts could understand every language spoken by them. The four beasts [in Revelation 4:6-9] . . . were seen and heard by John praising and glorifying God."[50]

THE EARTH, TOO, WILL BE RESURRECTED

D&C 88:17–21, 25–26

17 And the redemption of the soul is through him that quickeneth all things, in whose bosom it is decreed that the poor and the meek of the earth shall inherit it.

18 Therefore, it must needs be sanctified from all unrighteousness, that it may be prepared for the celestial glory;

19 For after it hath filled the measure of its creation, it shall be crowned with glory, even with the presence of God the Father;

20 That bodies who are of the celestial kingdom may possess it forever and ever; for, for this intent was it made and created, and for this intent are they sanctified.

21 And they who are not sanctified through the law which I have given unto you, even the law of Christ, must inherit another kingdom, even that of a terrestrial kingdom, or that of a telestial kingdom. . . .

25 And again, verily I say unto you, the earth abideth the law of a celestial kingdom, for it filleth the measure of its creation, and transgresseth not the law—

26 Wherefore, it shall be sanctified; yea, notwithstanding it shall die, it shall be quickened again, and shall abide the power by which it is quickened, and the righteous shall inherit it.

As members of the Church we are required to "teach . . . and be instructed" about "things both in heaven and in the earth, and under the earth" (D&C 88:78–79). Doctrine and Covenants 88 presents a number of teachings about the earth and its role in the salvation of the human family: Christ is the power by which the earth was made (D&C 88:10); the earth moves in its times and seasons through God's law (D&C 88:42–43); the earth will fill "the measure of its creation" (D&C 88:19, 25); and the earth is obedient, in that it "abideth the law of a celestial kingdom" (D&C 88:25).

Perhaps most significantly, the earth was "made and created" so that celestial souls could inherit it (D&C 88:20). Specifically, "the poor and the meek of the earth shall inherit" the earth (D&C 88:17); celestialized bodies will "possess [the earth] forever and ever" (D&C 88:20); and "the righteous shall inherit" the earth (D&C 88:26). In the end, the earth will "be crowned with glory," which is "the presence of God the Father" (D&C 88:19).

Before it obtains celestial glory, the earth must pass through death and resurrection. Doctrine and Covenants 88 affirms that the earth "shall die" and "be quickened again" (D&C 88:26), or receive a resurrection, and it will "be sanctified" (D&C 88:26). Prophets and other authorities of our dispensation have written regarding the earth's resurrection. Brigham Young asked, "And the earth is resurrected?" and then explained, "Yes, and every living thing on the earth that has abided the law by which it was made. Then that which you and I respect, are fond of, and love with an earthly love, will become divine, and we can then love it with that affection which it is not now worthy of."[51] On another occasion, President Young taught, "The earth is organized for a glorious resurrection."[52] A popular commentary on the Doctrine and Covenants states, "The entrance to celestial glory is through death and resurrection (v. 14)." "And the Earth itself must pass through the same process, in order to become the dwelling-place of celestial beings (vv. 18–20)."[53]

NOTES AND COMMENTARY

D&C 88:17 *redemption of the soul.* See "The Resurrection Is 'the Redemption of the Soul,'" in chapter 7.

him that quickeneth all things. To "quicken" is to give life. It is God "who quickeneth all things" (1 Timothy 6:13).

meek inherit the earth. After the earth is changed and becomes a celestial kingdom, then the meek (see also Luke 6:20; D&C 38:20) will inherit it. The Psalmist prophesied, "The meek shall inherit the earth. . . . The righteous shall inherit the land, and dwell therein for ever" (Psalm 37:11, 29). Perhaps Jesus Christ had this psalm in mind when he presented the beatitude "Blessed are the meek: for they shall inherit the earth" (Matthew 5:5). A number of revelations recorded in the Doctrine and Covenants refer to the inheritance of the righteous, which is "the earth from generation to generation, forever and ever" (D&C 56:20; see D&C 38:20; 45:58; 57:5; 59:2; 63:20).

D&C 88:18 *sanctified from all unrighteousness.* The context pertains to the earth, which eventually will be sanctified from the unrighteousness that plagues its inhabitants. Two passages from the Book of Moses describe the filth and corruption that existed on the earth during the time of Enoch and Noah. Enoch "looked upon the earth; and he heard a voice from the bowels thereof, saying: Wo, wo is me, the mother of men; I am pained, I am weary, because of the wickedness of my children. When shall I rest, and be cleansed from the filthiness which is gone forth out of me? When will my Creator sanctify me, that I may rest, and righteousness for a season abide upon my face?"

(Moses 7:48). Moses 8:28–30 describes the earth at the time of Noah: "The earth was corrupt before God, and it was filled with violence. And God looked upon the earth, and, behold, it was corrupt, for all flesh had corrupted its way upon the earth. And God said unto Noah: The end of all flesh is come before me, for the earth is filled with violence, and behold I will destroy all flesh from off the earth."

According to the verses presented in this section, the earth will be sanctified for three purposes: (1) to prepare it for "celestial glory" (v. 18); (2) to prepare it for "the presence of God the Father" (v. 19); and (3) to prepare it to become a celestial kingdom for celestial souls (v. 20). That sanctification will also come because the earth kept the law of its existence and fulfilled the measure of its creation (see D&C 88:19, 25).

prepared for the celestial glory. The earth will be cleansed in two stages. First, at the dawn of the Millennium, "the earth will be renewed and receive its paradisiacal glory" (Article of Faith 10), meaning it will become a terrestrial place. At this stage "every corruptible thing, both of man, or of the beasts of the field, or of the fowls of the heavens, or of the fish of the sea, that dwells upon all the face of the earth, shall be consumed; and also that of element shall melt with fervent heat." Then, after all corruptible things are destroyed, "all things shall become new, that [God's] knowledge and glory may dwell upon the earth" (D&C 101:24–25). Then, at the end of the Millennium, the earth will be sanctified and prepared for celestial glory. In D&C 29:22–24 the Lord said, "When the thousand years are ended, and men again begin to deny their God, then will I spare the earth but for a little season; and the end shall come, and the heaven and the earth shall be consumed and pass away, and there shall be a new heaven and a new earth. For all old things shall pass away, and all things shall become new, even the heaven and the earth, and all the fulness thereof, both men and beasts, the fowls of the air, and the fishes of the sea."[54]

D&C 88:19 *it hath filled the measure of its creation.* After the Millennium, the earth will have completed the purpose for which it was created, to serve as a dwelling place for God's children. It has served as a dwelling place for them during their probationary state, and it will eventually serve as a dwelling place for celestial beings.

it shall be crowned with glory. Glory will be upon the earth because God the Father, an eternal and glorious being, will grace the earth with his presence. According to Brigham Young, "This earth is our home, it was framed expressly for the habitation of those who are faithful to God, and who prove themselves worthy to inherit the earth when the Lord shall have sanctified, purified and glorified it and brought it back into his presence, from which it fell far into space. . . . When the earth was framed and brought into existence and man was placed upon it, it was near the throne of our Father in heaven. And when man fell . . . the earth fell into space, and took up its abode in this planetary system, and the sun became our light. This is the glory the earth came from, and when it is glorified it will return again unto the presence of the Father, and it will dwell there, and these intelligent beings that I am looking at, if they live worthy of it, will dwell upon this earth."[55]

D&C 88:20 *for this intent was it made and created.* Verse 20 describes the purpose that the earth was "made and created"—so that "bodies who are of the celestial kingdom may possess it forever and ever."

D&C 88:21 *must inherit another kingdom, even that of a terrestrial kingdom, or that of a telestial kingdom.* Although our earth is destined to become a celestial kingdom, other earths will eventually become terrestrial or telestial kingdoms. According to Joseph Fielding Smith, "Other earths, no doubt, are being prepared as habitations for terrestrial and telestial beings, for there must be places prepared for those who fail to obtain celestial glory, who receive immortality but not eternal life. . . . Every earth, whether created for celestial glory, or for terrestrial or telestial, will have to pass through the condition of death and the resurrection, just the same as our earth will have to do."[56]

D&C 88:25 *the earth abideth the law of a celestial kingdom.* The earth, when it is resurrected, will become a celestial kingdom, designed for people who have been resurrected with celestial bodies. "This earth, every part of it, will be celestial; not one-third telestial and one-third terrestrial. It will be celestial—and only celestial beings shall dwell upon it."[57]

D&C 88:26 *Wherefore, it shall be sanctified.* Earlier in the revelation, the Lord said that the earth "must needs be sanctified from all unrighteousness" (see v. 18). For emphasis, the Lord here repeats, "Wherefore, it shall be sanctified."

yea, notwithstanding it shall die. "The earth itself will die, and its elements be dissolved through the agency of a fire," taught Orson Pratt. "This death, or dissolution of the earth is a penalty of the original sin. . . . But all mankind are made alive from the first death through the resurrection, so that the earth will again be renewed, its elements will again be collected, they will be recombined and reorganized as when it first issued from the womb of chaos."[58] "The earth has to undergo a change analogous to death and is to be regenerated in a manner comparable to a resurrection. . . . The Lord, in a revelation through Joseph Smith, the prophet, tells plainly of the eventual death and subsequent quickening of the earth. These are his Words: [D&C 88:25–26 quoted]."[59]

it shall be quickened again. Inasmuch as the earth "abideth the law of the celestial kingdom" and "transgresseth not the law" (D&C 88:25), it will be quickened or restored to life subsequent to its death. The earth's quickening is possible because of the atoning sacrifice of Jesus Christ.

shall abide the power by which it is quickened. Jesus Christ is the power by which the earth will be resurrected. The earth, ever obedient to God, will become a quickened or resurrected sphere.

the righteous shall inherit it. See commentary on D&C 88:17.

NOTES

INTRODUCTION

1. Quoted in *Improvement Era,* June 1969, 123.
2. Quoted by Brown in *Improvement Era,* June 1967, 28.
3. *Teachings of the Prophet Joseph Smith,* 324.

PART 1:
UNDERSTANDING DEATH

1. Faust, *Ensign,* May 1979, 54, 59.
2. *Teachings of Gordon B. Hinckley,* 153.
3. Nelson, *Ensign,* May 1992, 72.
4. McConkie, *Ensign,* November 1976, 106.

CHAPTER 1: DEATH IS PART
OF GOD'S PLAN

1. Brown, *Improvement Era,* June 1967, 28.
2. Smith, *Gospel Doctrine,* 428.
3. Kimball, *Faith Precedes the Miracle,* 99, 101, 103, 106.
4. Packer, Conference Report, October 1975, 147.
5. *Discourses of Brigham Young,* 368.
6. Kimball, *Journal of Discourses,* 12:180.
7. Woodruff, *Journal of Discourses,* 22:348.
8. *Teachings of Spencer W. Kimball,* 45.
9. Young, *Journal of Discourses,* 17:14.
10. *Teachings of Spencer W. Kimball,* 37.
11. McConkie, *Ensign,* November 1976, 107.

12. Packer, *Ensign,* November 1988, 21.
13. Smith, *History of the Church,* 4:553–54.
14. McKay, *Gospel Ideals,* 75.
15. Smith, *Gospel Doctrine,* 453–54.
16. Benson, *Come unto Christ,* 78; see also Smith, *History of the Church,* 3:29.
17. McConkie, *Mormon Doctrine,* 685.
18. Smith, *Answers to Gospel Questions,* 5:95.
19. Benson, *Come unto Christ,* 78.
20. See *Discourses of Wilford Woodruff,* 149.
21. Benson, *Come unto Christ,* 78.
22. Woodruff, *Journal of Discourses,* 19:228.
23. Smith, *History of the Church,* 6:365; italics added.
24. Smith, *Utah Genealogical and Historical Magazine,* October 1940, 196.
25. Woodruff, *Journal of Discourses,* 19:229.
26. *Discourses of Wilford Woodruff,* 152.
27. Smith, *History of the Church,* 6:313–14.
28. Smith, Conference Report, April 1942, 26.
29. *Teachings of the Prophet Joseph Smith,* 191–92.
30. Smith, *History of the Church,* 6:183–84.
31. Cannon, *Journal of Discourses,* 22:129–31.
32. Smith, *Church News,* 27 March 1949, 21.
33. Smith, *History of the Church,* 6:184.
34. Widtsoe, *Utah Genealogical and*

Historical Magazine, October 1934, 189–90.

35. See Sperry, *Voice of Israel's Prophets,* 325.
36. *Discourses of Brigham Young,* 402.
37. Smith, *Doctrines of Salvation,* 2:166.
38. Smith, *Gospel Doctrine,* 438.
39. Penrose, Conference Report, April 1906, 86–87.
40. *Discourses of Brigham Young,* 379.

CHAPTER 2: MORTALITY AND DEATH

1. *Webster's New Collegiate Dictionary,* 10th edition, s.v. mortal, mortuary, mortician, murder.
2. Young, *Journal of Discourses,* 5:54.
3. Nelson, *The Gateway We Call Death,* 5, 8.
4. Clark, Conference Report, October 1940, 17.
5. Kimball, *Journal of Discourses,* 3:108.
6. Cited in Andrus and Andrus, *They Knew the Prophet,* 62.
7. *Sermons and Missionary Services of Melvin J. Ballard,* 234.
8. Kimball, *BYU Speeches of the Year,* 6 December 1955, 6, 9, 11–12.
9. Maxwell, *All These Things Shall Give Thee Experience,* 99.
10. Woodruff, *Leaves from My Journal,* 54–55.
11. *Teachings of Spencer W. Kimball,* 38.
12. Smith, *Gospel Doctrine,* 43.
13. McConkie, *Ensign,* November 1976, 107.
14. Cannon, *Gospel Truth,* 61.
15. Smith, *History of the Church,* 5:127.
16. Nelson, *The Gateway We Call Death,* 36–37.
17. Cannon, *Juvenile Instructor,* July 1868, 100.
18. Smith, *History of the Church,* 5:126.
19. Nelson, *The Gateway We Call Death,* 22.
20. Grant, *Gospel Standards,* 361.
21. Madsen, in *Deity and Death,* 71.
22. Smith, *Gospel Doctrine,* 428.
23. Packer, *Ensign,* November 1988, 19, 20, 21.
24. Cowley, *Wilford Woodruff, His Life and Labors,* 622.
25. *Teachings of Spencer W. Kimball,* 42.
26. Smith, *History of the Church,* 5:361.
27. For a helpful discussion on the doctrine of burial, see Spencer J. Palmer, *New Era,* July 1972, 34–36.
28. Dummelow, *A Commentary on the Holy Bible,* 31; see also Genesis 24:2, 9.

CHAPTER 3: CONDITIONS AND CIRCUMSTANCES OF THE DEAD

1. Packer, *Teach Ye Diligently,* 276.
2. Nelson, *Ensign,* November 1998, 86.
3. *Teachings of Spencer W. Kimball,* 44.
4. Cannon, *Journal of Discourses,* 10:370.
5. Smith, *History of the Church,* 3:387.
6. Smith, *History of the Church,* 6:311.
7. Smith, *Gospel Doctrine,* 277.
8. Smith, *Gospel Doctrine,* 455.
9. Smith, *Gospel Doctrine,* 277.
10. Pratt, *Journal of Discourses,* 1:7–9; see also Pratt, *Key to the Science of Theology,* 50–53.
11. Smith, *History of the Church,* 4:575.
12. Kimball, Conference Report, April 1968, 73–74.
13. Quoted by W. Grant Bangerter, in *Ensign,* November 1988, 81.
14. *Teachings of Spencer W. Kimball,* 41.
15. *Discourses of Brigham Young,* 379.
16. *Sermons and Missionary Services of Melvin J. Ballard,* 240, 245.
17. McConkie and Millet, *Doctrinal Commentary on the Book of Mormon,* 3:256.
18. McConkie, *Mormon Doctrine,* 762.
19. Cannon, *Gospel Truth,* 58.
20. Cannon, *Gospel Truth,* 73.
21. Smith, *Answers to Gospel Questions,* 2:85; see also Kimball, *Journal of Discourses,* 3:112–13; McConkie, *Doctrinal New Testament Commentary,* 1:520; 3:297.
22. *Discourses of Brigham Young,* 376–77.
23. *Teachings of Harold B. Lee,* 57.
24. *Sermons and Missionary Services of Melvin J. Ballard,* 184.
25. *Sermons and Missionary Services of Melvin J. Ballard,* 241–42.

26. Walter Bowen, "Spirit World," in *Encyclopedia of Mormonism,* 1408.
27. See *Discourses of Wilford Woodruff,* 245, for a prophetic example of this analogy.
28. Smith, *Gospel Doctrine,* 448; emphasis added.
29. *Teachings of Harold B. Lee,* 58; see also *Discourses of Brigham Young,* 376–77; Pratt, *Key to the Science of Theology,* 126.
30. Pratt, *Key to the Science of Theology,* 126.
31. Cannon, *Gospel Truth,* 60.
32. Ludlow, *Principles and Practices,* 225.
33. Maxwell, *That Ye May Believe,* 94.
34. *Sermons and Missionary Services of Melvin J. Ballard,* 241–42; see also Ludlow, *Principles and Practices,* 219.
35. Ballard, *Three Degrees of Glory,* 31.
36. See Smith, *Gospel Doctrine,* 455.
37. Cannon, *Gospel Truth,* 58.
38. Dyer, *Who Am I?* 490–91; see also Pratt, *Key to the Science of Theology,* 126.
39. *Teachings of the Prophet Joseph Smith,* 310.
40. Widtsoe, *Program of the Church,* 224.
41. Smith, *Teachings of the Prophet Joseph Smith,* 353.
42. McConkie, *Mormon Doctrine,* 762.
43. Young, *Journal of Discourses,* 3:369–70.
44. Quoted in West, *Profiles of the Presidents,* 153.
45. *Discourses of Wilford Woodruff,* 288–89.
46. See Smith, *History of the Church,* 4:598–99; *Discourses of Brigham Young,* 378, 468; McConkie, *New Witness for the Articles of Faith,* 309.
47. Smith, *History of the Church,* 6:316.
48. *Discourses of Brigham Young,* 379.
49. *Discourses of Brigham Young,* 379.
50. Smith, *History of the Church,* 6:52.
51. Smith, *Doctrines of Salvation,* 2:158; see also McConkie, *Doctrinal New Testament Commentary,* 1:521.
52. See M. Catherine Thomas, "Paradise," in *Encyclopedia of Mormonism,* 1062.
53. Smith, *History of the Church,* 6:52.
54. Kimball, *Journal of Discourses,* 4:135–37; this experience is also quoted in Russell M. Nelson, *The Gateway We Call Death,* 96–99.
55. Smith, *Gospel Doctrine,* 439.
56. Smith, *Gospel Doctrine,* 439.
57. *Discourses of Brigham Young,* 380.
58. Smith, *Gospel Doctrine,* 448.
59. For further discussion on the gulf separating the two parts of the spirit world, see "The Gulf between Righteous and Wicked," in chapter 3.
60. *Teachings of the Prophet Joseph Smith,* 367; see also D&C 138:58.
61. McConkie, *Ensign,* August 1976, 11; see also Young, *Journal of Discourses,* 3:95.
62. *Discourses of Brigham Young,* 377; see also *Teachings of Harold B. Lee,* 58.
63. Kimball, *Journal of Discourses,* 2:150.
64. *Teachings of the Prophet Joseph Smith,* 310.
65. See McConkie, *Mortal Messiah,* 4:241.
66. Whitney, *Life of Heber C. Kimball,* 464.
67. Talmage, Conference Report, April 1930, 95–96.
68. *Teachings of the Prophet Joseph Smith,* 357.
69. For a helpful and thorough discussion on the early apostasy and latter-day restoration of the gospel, including the views of the early apostles on the subject, see Kent P. Jackson, *From Apostasy to Restoration.*
70. Nibley, *Mormonism and Early Christianity,* 105–6, 108.
71. Smith, Conference Report, April 1911, 124.
72. Smith, *Utah Genealogical and Historical Magazine,* April 1926, 148–49.
73. Young, *Journal of Discourses,* 4:285.
74. *Discourses of Wilford Woodruff,* 288–89; a more complete account of this experience is found in chapter 3 of this book.
75. *Discourses of Brigham Young,* 378.
76. Smith, *Gospel Doctrine,* 134.
77. *Words of Joseph Smith,* 370.
78. Lee, *Decisions for Successful Living,* 119; see also Kimball, *Faith Precedes*

the Miracle, 101; Lee, Conference
Report, October 1942, 73.

79. Snow, *Millennial Star,* 22 January 1894,
50.

80. Woodruff, *Collected Discourses,* vol. 4;
as cited in Packer, *The Holy Temple,*
203, 206.

81. Young, *Journal of Discourses,* 13:76.

82. Maxwell, *That Ye May Believe,* 94.

83. Young, *Journal of Discourses,* 17:142.

84. Snow, *Millennial Star,* 22 January 1894,
50.

85. See "We Continue in the Same Spiritual
Condition When We Die," in this
chapter.

86. Young, *Journal of Discourses,* 3:731.

87. Quoted in Abraham H. Cannon Journal,
5 April 1894, spelling and punctuation
standardized; cited in *Collected
Discourses,* vol. 4.

88. *Sermons and Missionary Services of
Melvin J. Ballard,* 229–30.

89. Pratt, *Journal of Discourses,* 1:12.

90. Woodruff, *Collected Discourses,* vol. 4;
as cited in Packer, *The Holy Temple,*
203, 206.

91. Kimball, *Miracle of Forgiveness,* 168.

92. See Talmage, *Vitality of Mormonism,*
258–59.

93. Kimball, *Ensign,* May 1978, 4.

94. Maxwell, *Church News,* 1 September
1990, 7.

95. Romney, *Ensign,* March 1971, 16.

96. *Discourses of Brigham Young,* 410.

97. Pratt, *Journal of Discourses,* 1:13.

98. *Wilford Woodruff, History of His Life
and Labors,* 415.

99. Taylor, *Gospel Kingdom,* 31.

100. Oaks, *Ensign,* November 1998, 39.

101. *Teachings of the Prophet Joseph Smith,*
120.

102. *Teachings of the Prophet Joseph Smith,*
325.

103. Smith, *From Prophet to Son,* 37–39.

104. Smith, Conference Report, April 1916,
4.

105. Lee, *Relief Society Magazine,* February
1964, 85.

106. *Teachings of Ezra Taft Benson,* 35.

107. Ballard, *Crusader for Righteousness,*
219.

108. Woodruff, Conference Report, April
1880, 9–10.

109. Woodruff, *Journal of Discourses,*
21:317–18.

110. *Teachings of Spencer W. Kimball,* 42.

111. Grant, *Gospel Standards,* 195.

112. Woodruff, *Journal of Discourses,*
22:333–34.

113. Smith, *Gospel Doctrine,* 435, 437.

114. *Teachings of Harold B. Lee,* 415.

115. *Autobiography of Parley P. Pratt,* 261,
262.

116. Grant, *Gospel Standards,* 364–65.

117. *Discourses of Wilford Woodruff,*
292–93.

118. *Discourses of Brigham Young,* 409.

119. Woodruff, *Journal of Discourses,*
19:229.

120. Ballard, *Church News,* 20 January 1940,
2.

121. *Sermons and Missionary Services of
Melvin J. Ballard,* 230.

122. Haight, *Ensign,* May 1993, 25.

123. *Discourses of Brigham Young,* 379.

124. *Discourses of Brigham Young,* 409.

125. Widtsoe, *Utah Genealogical and
Historical Magazine,* July 1931, 104.

126. Smith, *Gospel Doctrine,* 436.

127. Whitney, *Saturday Night Thoughts,*
307–8.

128. Cannon, *Gospel Truth,* 64.

129. Young, *Journal of Discourses,* 6:73; see
also 5:54–55.

130. Smith, *History of the Church,* 3:392.

CHAPTER 4: CHRIST HAS POWER OVER DEATH

1. Lee, *Decisions for Successful Living,*
179–80.

2. Whitney, *Improvement Era,* May 1916,
608–9.

3. Grant, *Gospel Standards,* 366.

4. LeRoi C. Snow, *Improvement Era,*
September 1929, 881, 883–86.

5. Smith, *Church News,* 5 January 1935, 6.

6. Part of that vision is recounted and
discussed elsewhere in this book; see
"Missionary Work in the Spirit World"
in chapter 3; and "The Righteous in the

Spirit World Await the Resurrection with Joy and Gladness" in chapter 9.

7. President Smith also saw Joseph Smith and others from the last dispensation in the spirit world. Some have supposed from that these brethren were present when Christ visited the spirit world immediately after his death. But, as Joseph Fielding McConkie explains, "A more careful reading of the vision does not sustain that conclusion. President Smith said that those who were present at the time of Christ's visit were those 'who had been faithful in the testimony of Jesus while they lived in mortality; and who had offered sacrifice in the similitude of the great sacrifice of the Son of God, and had suffered tribulation in their Redeemer's name' (D&C 138:12–13). Some in our dispensation have certainly been faithful in the testimony of Jesus and suffered tribulation in their Redeemer's name, but it would not be accurate to say that they had offered animal sacrifice, which was in similitude of the sacrifice of Christ, which had just taken place. A list of those present when Christ appeared in the spirit world is then given (see D&C 138:38–49). It starts with Adam and Eve and mentions such notables as Abel, Seth, Noah, Shem, Abraham, Isaac, Jacob, Moses, Isaiah, Ezekiel, Daniel, Elias, Malachi, and Elijah. In addition, it notes that the Book of Mormon prophets were also present. These 'had looked upon the long absence of their spirits from their bodies as a bondage' (D&C 138:50). Those present were then given the 'power to come forth' from the grave after the resurrection of Christ (D&C 138:51).

"There is no thought in all of this that the unborn are present. It simply doesn't fit to suppose that the unborn would be given the power of resurrection. This marvelous vision was followed by another in which President Smith saw the spirit world as it was at that time (3 October 1918). It is in this vision that he mentions seeing those of our dispensation who had died. Of them he said, 'I beheld that the faithful elders of this dispensation, when they depart from mortal life, continue their labors in the preaching of the gospel' (D&C 138:57).

"The change of scene, including time and place, is common to visions of this sort. Joseph Smith's vision on the degrees of glory (see D&C 76) does this same thing, as does Nephi's account of the dream both he and his father had of the tree of life (see 1 Ne. 11:1)." (McConkie, *Answers: Straightforward Answers to Tough Gospel Questions*, 82–83.)

8. For a commentary on these verses, see Parry, Parry, and Peterson, *Understanding Isaiah*, 541–43.

9. McConkie, *Mortal Messiah*, 4:243.

10. Nibley, *Mormonism and Early Christianity*, 118; see original source for footnotes accompanying quotations in this excerpt.

11. These statements of Job must be counterbalanced by his later expression of faith: "I know that my redeemer liveth, and that he shall stand at the latter day upon the earth: And though after my skin worms destroy this body, yet in my flesh shall I see God: Whom I shall see for myself, and mine eyes shall behold, and not another; though my reins be consumed within me" (Job 19:25–27).

12. Young, *Journal of Discourses*, 7:171.

PART 2: UNDERSTANDING THE RESURRECTION

1. See Talmage, *House of the Lord*, 66; McKay, Conference Report, April 1944, 120.

2. *Teachings of Gordon B. Hinckley*, 28.

3. Holland, *Christ and the New Covenant*, 238.

4. Hinckley, "The Empty Tomb Bore Testimony," *Ensign*, May 1988, 66.

5. Taylor, *Mediation and Atonement*, 178–79.

6. Maxwell, *BYU Speeches,* 8 Nov. 1977, 181.

CHAPTER 5:
THE RESURRECTION:
FORESHADOWED WITH TYPES

1. McConkie, *Mormon Doctrine,* 641.
2. Young, *Journal of Discourses,* 8:28; see also, Smith, *History of the Church,* 5:362, and Lee, *Church News,* 19 April 1941, 7–8.
3. Penrose, *Improvement Era,* July 1919, 752, 754.
4. *Discourses of Brigham Young,* 374.
5. Penrose, *Improvement Era,* July 1919, 752, 754.
6. Taylor, *Journal of Discourses,* 13:230.
7. Smith, *Journal of Discourses,* 2:263.
8. *Teachings of the Prophet Joseph Smith,* 278.
9. Joseph Smith taught, "Hades, the Greek, or Shaole, the Hebrew: these two significations mean a world of spirits. Hades, Shaole, paradise, spirits in prison, are all one; it is a world of spirits" (*History of the Church,* 5:425).
10. Carson, "Matthew," in *The Expositor's Bible Commentary,* ("Matthew, Mark, Luke"), 8:296.
11. *Teachings of the Prophet Joseph Smith,* 170.
12. Richards, *Journal of Discourses,* 25:236–37.
13. *Teachings of the Prophet Joseph Smith,* 170–71.
14. Smith, *Doctrines of Salvation,* 2:300–301.
15. McConkie, Millet, and Top, *Doctrinal Commentary on the Book of Mormon,* 4:191.

CHAPTER 6: JESUS CHRIST
AND THE RESURRECTION

1. Ballard, *Deseret Weekly News,* 31 October 1896, 610.
2. Ballard, Conference Report, April 1920, 40.
3. Recorded in his diary for May 14, 1917; also in Hinckley, *Sermons and*

Missionary Services of Melvin Joseph Ballard, 156.
4. Cannon, *Deseret Weekly News,* 6 October 1896, 610.
5. L. John Nuttal Diary, April 20, 1893.
6. See "Alexander Neibaur" in *Utah Genealogical and Historical Magazine,* April 1914, 62; cf. *Journal of Discourses,* 11:279.
7. Backman, *The Heavens Resound,* 267.
8. Smith, *History of the Church,* 1:334–35; see also *History of the Church,* 2:432.
9. *Jensen's Biographical Encyclopedia,* 1:660–61; Whitney, *Through Memories Halls,* 82.
10 McKay, *Cherished Experiences,* 102.
11. Cannon, *Juvenile Instructor,* April 1891, 220.
12. On Jesus' possession of keys, see *Teachings of the Prophet Joseph Smith,* 323; *Discourses of Brigham Young,* 378; *Discourses of Wilford Woodruff,* 26–27; Smith, *Doctrines of Salvation,* 2:267.
13. *Discourses of Brigham Young,* 397–98.
14. Dominy, "Atonement," *Holman Bible Dictionary,* 131.
15. Smith, *History of the Church,* 5:425.
16. Kimball, Conference Report, April 1978, 7–8.
17. Smith, *Doctrines of Salvation,* 2:301.
18. McConkie, *Doctrinal New Testament Commentary,* 2:392.
19. *Teachings of the Prophet Joseph Smith,* 157.
20. Smith, *Millennial Star,* 12 March 1896, 162.
21. Smith, *Improvement Era,* March 1908, 385.
22. Ogden and Skinner, *New Testament Apostles Testify of Christ,* 30.
23. McConkie, *Doctrinal New Testament Commentary,* 2:22.
24. Fitzmyer, *The Acts of the Apostles,* 337.
25. McKay, Conference Report, April 1939, 112.
26. *Teachings of the Prophet Joseph Smith,* 121.

CHAPTER 7: THE FORM AND NATURE OF RESURRECTED BEINGS

1. Taylor, *Mediation and Atonement,* 166.
2. As we consider the nature and powers of resurrected beings, it should be noted that mortals on earth have had experience only with those who have been resurrected to a celestial (and perhaps) exalted glory. Prophets have recorded some of the powers of such beings, but the specific powers and abilities of those who will be resurrected to other glories have not been revealed.
3. *Discourses of Brigham Young,* 374.
4. Nelson, Conference Report, April 1992, 103–4.
5. *Discourses of Brigham Young,* 372.
6. *Discourses of Brigham Young,* 373.
7. Snow, Conference Report, October 1900, 4.
8. Snow, Conference Report, October 1900, 63.
9. Taylor, *Government of God,* 27.
10. Smith, *History of the Church,* 6:366.
11. Smith, Conference Report, April 1949, 137.
12. Nelson, Conference Report, October 1996, 45.
13. Kimball, Manila Philippines Area Conference, August 1975, 51.
14. Smith, *Church History and Modern Revelation,* 2:301.
15. Smith, *Gospel Doctrine,* 30.
16. Smith, *History of the Church,* 6:366.
17. Young, *Journal of Discourses,* 8:28.
18. Smith, *History of the Church,* 1:302.
19. Woodruff, *Millennial Star,* 22 September 1890, 596.
20. Talmage, Conference Report, October 1913, 117.
21. Holland, *Christ and the New Covenant,* 244.
22. See also Talmage, *Articles of Faith,* 344–45.
23. Monson, Conference Report, April 1988, 63.
24. Smith, *History of the Church,* 5:362.
25. *Discourses of Brigham Young,* 374–75, see also Young, *Journal of Discourses,* 8:28.
26. Barnett, *The Second Epistle to the Corinthians. The New International Commentary on the New Testament,* 263–64.
27. McConkie, *Doctrinal New Testament Commentary,* 2:398.
28. McConkie, *Doctrinal New Testament Commentary,* 1:196.
29. *Teachings of the Prophet Joseph Smith,* 304–5. Joseph Smith also comprehended the three kingdoms, as recorded in D&C 76. Concerning this recorded revelation, Joseph Smith wrote, "That document is a transcript from the records of the eternal world" (*History of the Church,* 1:252).
30. McConkie and Ostler, *Revelations of the Restoration,* 631.
31. Smith, *Doctrines of Salvation,* 2:287–88.
32. Smith, Conference Report, April 1917, 62–63.
33. Petersen, *Ensign,* May 1978, 63.
34. Gordon B. Hinckley, Priesthood Restoration Commemoration Fireside, 15 May 1988.
35. McConkie and Ostler, *Revelations of the Restoration,* 1042.
36. Smith, *History of the Church,* 4:555.
37. Smith, *Words of Joseph Smith,* 370–71.
38. Smith, *History of the Church,* 6:366.
39. Kimball, *BYU Speeches,* 6 September 1977, 140.
40. Smith, *History of the Church,* 4:425.
41. Smith, *History of the Church,* 6:51–52.
42. McConkie, *Ensign,* April 1975, 71.
43. Smith, *Gospel Doctrine,* 463.
44. *Discourses of Brigham Young,* 374.
45. Smith, *Improvement Era,* March 1916, 430.
46. James E. Talmage, Conference Report, April 1928, 93.
47. *Teachings of the Prophet Joseph Smith,* 162.
48. Smith, *History of the Church,* 6:51, see also *History of the Church,* 4:425.
49. McConkie, *Ensign,* December 1980, 14.
50. *Discourses of Brigham Young,* 375.

51. Smith, Conference Report, April 1912, 135.
52. Snow, *Improvement Era,* September 1933, 677.
53. McKay, *Cherished Experiences,* comp. by Clare Middlemiss, 102.
54. Cook, *The Revelations of the Prophet Joseph Smith,* 187.
55. Backman, *The Heavens Resound,* 267.
56. Mounce, *Book of Revelation,* 58.
57. Snow, *Improvement Era,* September 1933, 677.
58. Richards, Conference Report, October 1946, 139.
59. Smith, *History of the Church,* 6:366.

Chapter 8: Times and Order of the Resurrection

1. Lee, *Church News,* 19 April 1941, 7-8.
2. *Discourses of Brigham Young,* 468.
3. *Discourses of Brigham Young,* 116.
4. *Discourses of Brigham Young,* 374.
5. *Discourses of Brigham Young,* 374.
6. Smith, *Gospel Doctrine,* 448.
7. *Discourses of Brigham Young,* 374.
8. Talmage, *Vitality of Mormonism,* 294.
9. Taylor, *Mediation and Atonement,* 136-37.
10. Taylor, *Mediation and Atonement,* 136.
11. Smith, *History of the Church,* 5:362.
12. *Webster's New World Dictionary,* 733.
13. Lund, Conference Report, April 1904, 6.
14. For additional commentary on the two Jerusalems and on Isaiah 2:3, see Parry, Parry, and Peterson, *Understanding Isaiah,* 26-27.
15. Talmage, *Vitality of Mormonism,* 293.
16. Taylor, *Mediation and Atonement,* 178.
17. Smith, *Millennial Star,* 15 March 1906, 164-65.
18. Talmage, *Articles of Faith,* 348.
19. Phelps, *Times and Seasons,* 1 January 1845, 758.
20. Ford, *Revelation: Introduction, Translation and Commentary,* Anchor Bible Commentary, 38:136.
21. Parry and Parry, *Understanding the Book of Revelation,* 105.
22. See Parry and Parry, *Understanding the Book of Revelation,* 104-5.

23. This archaic meaning of *prevent* is found in the footnote of this verse in the LDS edition of Bible.
24. *Words of Joseph Smith,* 197-98.
25. Smith, *Doctrines of Salvation,* 2:296.
26. Smith, *Doctrines of Salvation,* 2:297-98.
27. *Teachings of the Prophet Joseph Smith,* 361.
28. Parry and Parry, *Understanding the Signs of the Times,* 423.
29. For a verse-by-verse commentary on Revelation 20:4-6, see Parry and Parry, *Understanding the Book of Revelation,* 267-73.
29. Smith, Conference Report, October 1928, 99-100.
30. Pratt, *Journal of Discourses,* 1:331.
31. Smith, *Church History and Modern Revelation,* 1:309.
32. Dahl and Cannon, *Teachings of Joseph Smith,* 21.
33. Joseph Smith's vision was reported by Heber C. Kimball; see Dahl and Cannon, *Teachings of Joseph Smith,* 22.
34. Smith, Conference Report, October 1928, 99-100.
35. Smith, Conference Report, October 1928, 99-100.
36. Smith, *History of the Church,* 5:343-44.
37. Robinson and Garrett, *A Commentary on the Doctrine and Covenants,* 1:203.
38. Smith and Sjodahl, *Doctrine and Covenants Commentary,* 154.
39. Dahl and Cannon, *Teachings of Joseph Smith,* 21.

Chapter 9: Blessings Associated with the Resurrection

1. Smith, *History of the Church,* 6:316.
2. McKay, Conference Report, April 1939, 115.
3. See also Smith, *History of the Church,* 3:390.
4. Smith, *History of the Church,* 5:361-62.
5. Smith, *History of the Church,* 5:362.
6. Taylor, *Gospel Kingdom,* 33-34.
7. Lund, Conference Report, April 1907, 56.

8. Bible Dictionary, 697.

9. Kimball, *Manila Philippines Area Conference,* August 1975, 51.

10. Brown, *BYU Speeches,* 25 March 1958, 7–8.

11. Smith, *Improvement Era,* December 1942, 829.

12. Hunter, Conference Report, April 1986, 18.

13. *Teachings of the Prophet Joseph Smith,* 367.

14. McConkie, *Doctrinal New Testament Commentary,* 2:403.

15. Hunter, *Ensign,* May 1986, 15.

16. Smith, *Utah Genealogical and Historical Magazine,* April 1926, 146–48.

17. Smith, *History of the Church,* 6:366.

18. Smith, *Millennial Star,* 12 March 1896, 162.

19. Joseph Fielding McConkie and Robert L. Millet, *Doctrinal Commentary on the Book of Mormon,* 1:238.

20. Smith, *Improvement Era,* January 1916, 199.

21. Smith, *Improvement Era,* May 1903, 505.

22. Smith, *Millennial Star,* 12 March 1896, 162.

23. Talmage, *Jesus the Christ,* 210.

24. Cannon, *Juvenile Instructor,* February 1900, 124.

25. Benson, *Ensign,* April 1992, 2.

26. Packer, *Our Father's Plan,* 50.

27. Smith, *History of the Church,* 6:366.

28. Watts, *Isaiah 1–33,* 342.

29. Smith, *History of the Church,* 5:361–62.

30. See Parry and Parry, *Understanding the Book of Revelation,* 69–70, 92–93.

31. Smith, *History of the Church,* 5:362.

32. Smith, *History of the Church,* 1:252–53.

33. Mounce, *Book of Revelation,* 375.

34. Smith, *History of the Church,* 6:317.

35. McConkie, *Doctrinal New Testament Commentary,* 3:576–77.

36. *Teachings of the Prophet Joseph Smith,* 218.

37. Smith, *Doctrines of Salvation,* 2:21.

38. Harrington, *Revelation,* vol. 16 of Sacra Pagina Series, 203.

39. Smith, *History of the Church,* 6:314.

40. *Teachings of the Prophet Joseph Smith,* 217.

41. Smith, *History of the Church,* 5:424.

42. Bowen, Conference Report, October 1937, 86.

43. Smith, *History of the Church,* 5:340.

44. Smith, Conference Report, October 1928, 100.

45. *Discourses of Brigham Young,* 375.

46. Smith, *Man: His Origin and Destiny,* 194, 204–5.

47. Smith, *Church News,* 15 February 1941, 1.

48. Joseph F. Smith, John R. Winder, Anthon H. Lund, *Improvement Era,* November 1909, 81.

49. Joseph Smith, *History of the Church,* 5:343–44.

50. Joseph Smith, *History of the Church,* 5:343–44.

51. *Discourses of Brigham Young,* 375.

52. *Discourses of Brigham Young,* 101.

53. Smith and Sjodahl, *Doctrine and Covenants Commentary,* 543.

54. See McConkie and Ostler, *Revelations of the Restoration,* 630.

55. Young, *Journal of Discourses,* 17:143.

56. Smith, *Doctrines of Salvation,* 1:72–73.

57. Hinckley, *Sermons and Missionary Services of Melvin J. Ballard,* 257–58.

58. Pratt, *Journal of Discourses,* 1:332. On the death of the earth, see also Smith, *Doctrines of Salvation,* 1:72–73.

59. Talmage, *Sunday Night Talks by Radio,* 1931, 353–55.

BIBLIOGRAPHY

"Alexander Neibaur," *Utah Genealogical and Historical Magazine,* April 1914, 53–63.

Andrus, Hyrum L., and Helen Mae Andrus. *They Knew the Prophet.* Salt Lake City: Deseret Book, 1999.

Backman, Milton V., Jr. *The Heavens Resound.* Salt Lake City: Deseret Book, 1983.

Ballard, Melvin J. *Crusader for Righteousness.* Salt Lake City: Bookcraft, 1977.

———. Conference Report, April 1920, 35–41.

———. *Deseret Weekly,* October 31, 1896, 610.

———. "The Inspiration of Temple Work," *Deseret News, Church News Section,* 20 January 1940, 2, 8.

———. *Three Degrees of Glory.* Salt Lake City: Magazine Printing & Publishing, 1975.

Bangerter, W. Grant. "The Quality of Eternal Life," *Ensign,* November 1988, 80–82.

Barnett, Paul. *The Second Epistle to the Corinthians. The New International Commentary on the New Testament.* Grand Rapids, Mich.: Eerdmans, 1997.

Benson, Ezra Taft. *Come unto Christ.* Salt Lake City: Deseret Book, 1983.

———. "The Meaning of Easter," *Ensign,* April 1992, 2–4.

———. *Teachings of Ezra Taft Benson.* Salt Lake City: Bookcraft, 1988.

Bowen, Albert E. Conference Report, October 1937, 84–89.

Bowen, Walter. "Spirit World," in *Encyclopedia of Mormonism.* Edited by Daniel H. Ludlow. New York: Macmillan, 1992.

Brown, Hugh B. "Immortality," *Improvement Era,* June 1967, 26–28.

———. "What Is Man and What May He Become," in *Brigham Young University Speeches of the Year,* 1–7. Provo, Utah: Brigham Young University, 25 March 1958.

Cannon, George Q. *Deseret Weekly News.* 6 October 1896, 610.

———. "Editorial Thoughts," *Juvenile Instructor,* July 1868, 100.

———. "Editorial Thoughts," *Juvenile Instructor,* April 1891, 218–25.

———. "Editorial Thoughts," *Juvenile Instructor,* February 1900, 123–24.

———. *Gospel Truth: Discourses and Writings of President George Q. Cannon.* Edited by Jerreld L. Newquist. Salt Lake City: Deseret Book, 1987.

Carson, D. A. "Matthew," in *The Expositor's Bible Commentary,* Volume 8 ("Matthew, Mark, Luke"). 12 vols. Edited by Frank E. Gaebelein. Grand Rapids, Mich.: Zondervan, 1984.

Clark, J. Reuben. Conference Report, October 1940, 7–18.

Cook, Lyndon. *The Revelations of the Prophet Joseph Smith. A Historical and Biographical Commentary of the Doctrine and Covenants.* Salt Lake City: Deseret Book, 1985.

Cowley, Matthias F. *Wilford Woodruff, His Life and Labors.* Salt Lake City: Bookcraft 1964.

Dahl, Larry E., and Donald Q. Cannon, eds. *The Teachings of Joseph Smith: First President of The Church of Jesus Christ of Latter-day Saints.* Salt Lake City: Deseret Book, 1997.

Dominy, Bert. "Atonement," *Holman Bible Dictionary*. Edited by Trent C. Butler. Nashville: Holman Bible Publishers, 1991.

Dummelow, J. R. *A Commentary on the Holy Bible*. New York: Macmillan, 1908.

Dyer, Alvin R. *Who Am I?* Salt Lake City: Deseret Book, 1970.

Evans, Richard L. "And What of Death?" *Improvement Era*, June 1969, 123.

Faust, James E. "The Refiner's Fire," *Ensign*, May 1979, 53–59.

Fitzmyer, Joseph A. *Acts of the Apostles*. New York: Doubleday, 1997.

Ford, J. Massyngberde. *Revelation: Introduction, Translation and Commentary*. Vol. 38 of *Anchor Bible Commentary*. New York: Doubleday, 1975.

Grant, Heber J. *Gospel Standards: Selections from the Sermons and Writings of Heber J. Grant*. Edited by G. Homer Durham. Salt Lake City: Bookcraft, 1998.

Haight, David B. "Personal Temple Worship," *Ensign*, May 1993, 23–25.

Harrington, Wilfrid J. *Revelation*. Collegeville, Minn.: Liturgical Press, 1993.

Hinckley, Bryant S. *Sermons and Missionary Services of Melvin Joseph Ballard*. Salt Lake City: Deseret Book, 1949.

Hinckley, Gordon B. Priesthood Restoration Commemoration Fireside, 15 May 1988.

———. *Teachings of Gordon B. Hinckley*. Salt Lake City: Deseret Book, 1998.

Holland, Jeffrey R. *Christ and the New Covenant: The Messianic Message of the Book of Mormon*. Salt Lake City: Deseret Book, 1997.

Holy Bible. Authorized King James Version. Salt Lake City: The Church of Jesus Christ of Latter-day Saints, 1979.

Hunter, Howard W. "An Apostle's Witness of the Resurrection," *Ensign*, May 1986, 15–17.

———. Conference Report, April 1986, 17–20.

———. "He is Risen," *Ensign*, May 1988, 16–17.

Jackson, Kent P. *From Apostasy to Restoration*. Salt Lake City: Deseret Book, 1996.

Jensen's Biographical Encyclopedia, 1:660–661.

Journal of Discourses. 26 vols. London: Latter-day Saints' Book Depot, 1854–86.

Kimball, Spencer W. "Absolute Truth," in *Brigham Young University Speeches of the Year*, 137–43. Provo, Utah: Brigham Young University, 6 September 1977.

———. Conference Report, April 1968, 73–78.

———. Conference Report, April 1978, 4–9.

———. *Faith Precedes the Miracle*. Salt Lake City: Deseret Book, 1972.

———. Manila Philippines Area Conference, August 1975, 51.

———. *Miracle of Forgiveness*. Salt Lake City: Bookcraft, 1971.

———. *Teachings of Spencer W. Kimball*. Edited by Edward L. Kimball. Salt Lake City: Bookcraft, 1982.

———. "Tragedy or Destiny," in *Brigham Young University Speeches of the Year*, 1–14. Provo, Utah: Brigham Young University, 6 December 1955.

———. "The True Way of Life and Salvation," *Ensign*, May 1978, 4–7.

Lee, Harold B. Conference Report, October 1942, 71–73.

———. *Decisions for Successful Living*. Salt Lake City: Deseret Book, 1973.

———. "Easter Morning—A Newness of Life," *Deseret News, Church News Section*, 19 April 1941, 7–8.

———. "The Influence and Responsibility of Women," *Relief Society Magazine*, February 1964, 84–89.

———. *Teachings of Harold B. Lee*. Edited by Clyde J. Williams. Salt Lake City: Bookcraft, 1998.

Ludlow, Victor L. *Principles and Practices of the Restored Gospel*. Salt Lake City: Deseret Book, 1992.

Lund, Anthon H. Conference Report, April 1904, 5–8.

———. Conference Report, April 1907, 53–59.

Lyon, Jack M., Linda Ririe Gundry, and Jay A. Parry, eds. *Best-Loved Stories of the LDS People.* Salt Lake City: Deseret Book, 1997.

Madsen, Truman G. "Distinctions in the Mormon Approach to Death and Dying," in *Deity and Death: Selected Symposium Papers.* Edited by Spencer J. Palmer. Provo, Utah: Religious Studies Center, Brigham Young University, 1978, 61–76.

Maxwell, Neal A. "All Hell Is Moved," in *Brigham Young University Speeches of the Year,* 175–81. Provo, Utah: Brigham Young University, 8 November 1977.

———. *All These Things Shall Give Thee Experience.* Salt Lake City: Deseret Book, 1979.

———. "Apostles Testify of Temples' Importance," *Deseret News, Church News Section,* 1 September 1990, 7.

———. *That Ye May Believe.* Salt Lake City: Bookcraft, 1992.

McConkie, Bruce R. "The Dead Who Die in the Lord," *Ensign,* November 1976, 106–8.

———. *Doctrinal New Testament Commentary.* 3 vols. Salt Lake City: Bookcraft, 1965–73.

———. "Drink from the Fountain," *Ensign,* April 1975, 70–72.

———. "Gaining a Testimony of Jesus Christ," *Ensign,* December 1980, 10–15.

———. *Mormon Doctrine.* 2d ed. Salt Lake City: Bookcraft, 1966.

———. *The Mortal Messiah: From Bethlehem to Calvary.* 4 vols. Salt Lake City: Deseret Book, 1979–1981.

———. "A New Commandment: Save Thyself and Thy Kindred," *Ensign,* August 1976, 6–11.

———. *A New Witness for the Articles of Faith.* Salt Lake City: Deseret Book, 1993.

McConkie, Joseph Fielding. *Answers: Straightforward Answers to Tough Gospel Questions.* Salt Lake City: Deseret Book, 1998.

McConkie, Joseph Fielding, and Robert L. Millet (with Brent L. Top for volume 4). *Doctrinal Commentary on the Book of Mormon.* 4 vols. Salt Lake City: Bookcraft, 1987–92.

McConkie, Joseph Fielding, and Craig J. Ostler. *Revelations of the Restoration.* Salt Lake City: Deseret Book, 2000.

McConkie, Joseph Fielding, and Donald W. Parry. *A Guide to Scriptural Symbols.* Salt Lake City: Bookcraft, 1990.

McKay, David O. *Cherished Experiences.* Compiled by Clare Middlemiss. Salt Lake City: Deseret Book, 1955.

———. Conference Report, April 1939, 111–15.

———. Conference Report, April 1944, 119–25.

———. "For the Perfecting of the Saints," *Improvement Era,* June 1968, 2–3.

———. *Gospel Ideals.* Salt Lake City: Bookcraft, 1998.

Monson, Thomas S. Conference Report, April 1988, 60–64.

Mounce, Robert H. *The Book of Revelation.* Grand Rapids, Mich.: Eerdmans, 1977.

Nelson, Russell M. Conference Report, April 1992, 101–5.

———. Conference Report, October 1996, 44–48.

———. "The Doors of Death," *Ensign,* May 1992, 72–74.

———. *The Gateway We Call Death.* Salt Lake City: Deseret Book, 1995.

———. "We Are Children of God," *Ensign,* November 1998, 85–87.

Nibley, Hugh. *Mormonism and Early Christianity.* Edited by Todd M. Compton and Stephen D. Ricks. Salt Lake City: Deseret Book; Provo, Utah: Foundation for Ancient Research and Mormon Studies, 1987.

Nuttal, John L. Diary, April 20, 1893.

Oaks, Dallin H. "The Aaronic Priesthood and the Sacrament," *Ensign,* November 1998, 37–40.

Ogden, D. Kelly, and Andrew C. Skinner. *New Testament Apostles Testify of Christ.* Salt Lake City: Deseret Book, 1998.

Packer, Boyd K. Conference Report, October 1975, 145–49.

———. "Funerals—A Time for Reverence," *Ensign,* November 1988, 18–21.

———. *The Holy Temple.* Salt Lake City: Bookcraft, 1980.

————. *Our Father's Plan.* Salt Lake City: Deseret Book, 1994.

————. *Teach Ye Diligently.* Salt Lake City: Deseret Book, 1991.

Palmer, Spencer J. "What about Cremation?" *New Era,* July 1972, 34–36.

Parry, Donald W., and Jay A. Parry. *Understanding the Signs of the Times.* Salt Lake City: Deseret Book, 1999.

Parry, Donald W., Jay A. Parry, and Tina M. Peterson. *Understanding Isaiah.* Salt Lake City: Deseret Book, 1998.

Parry, Jay A., and Donald W. Parry. *Understanding the Book of Revelation.* Salt Lake City: Deseret Book, 1998.

Penrose, Charles W. Conference Report, April 1906, 85–91.

————. "The Firstborn, the Resurrection and the Life," *Improvement Era,* July 1919, 747–55.

Petersen, Mark E. "Evidences of Things Not Seen," *Ensign,* May 1978, 61–63.

Phelps, William W. "The Answer," *Times and Seasons,* 1 January 1845, 758.

Pratt, Parley P. *Autobiography of Parley P. Pratt.* Salt Lake City: Deseret Book, 2000.

————. *Key to the Science of Theology; A Voice of Warning.* Salt Lake City: Deseret Book, 1978.

Richards, George F. Conference Report, October 1946, 137–41.

Robinson, Stephen E., and H. Dean Garrett. *A Commentary on the Doctrine and Covenants,* vols. 1 and 2. Salt Lake City: Deseret Book, 2000.

Romney, Marion G. Conference Report, April 1982, 5–10.

————. "Temples—The Gates to Heaven," *Ensign,* March 1971, 12–16.

Smith, Hyrum M., and Janne M. Sjodahl. *The Doctrine and Covenants Commentary: Containing Revelations Given to Joseph Smith, Jr., the Prophet.* Salt Lake City: Deseret Book, 1972.

Smith, Joseph. *History of The Church of Jesus Christ of Latter-day Saints.* Edited by B. H. Roberts. 2d ed. rev. 7 vols. Salt Lake City: The Church of Jesus Christ of Latter-day Saints, 1980.

————. *Teachings of the Prophet Joseph Smith.* Selected by Joseph Fielding Smith. Salt Lake City: Deseret Book, 1976.

————. *The Words of Joseph Smith: The Contemporary Accounts of the Nauvoo Discourses of the Prophet Joseph.* Edited by Andrew F. Ehat and Lyndon W. Cook. Orem, Utah: Grandin Book, 1991.

Smith, Joseph F. Conference Report, April 1912, 134–38.

————. Conference Report, April 1916, 1–8.

————. "Discourse by President J. F. Smith," *Millennial Star,* March 12, 1896, 161–64.

————. *From Prophet to Son: Advice of Joseph F. Smith to His Missionary Sons.* Compiled by Hyrum M. Smith III and Scott G. Kenney. Salt Lake City: Deseret Book, 1981.

————. *Gospel Doctrine.* 5th ed. Salt Lake City: Deseret Book, 1977.

————. "The Gospel in Precept and Example," *Millennial Star,* March 15, 1906, 161–66.

————. "I Know That My Redeemer Lives," *Improvement Era,* March 1908, 379–90.

————. "A Sermon of Purity," *Improvement Era,* May 1903, 501–6.

Smith, Joseph F., John R. Winder, and Anthon H. Lund. "The Origin of Man," *Improvement Era,* November 1909, 5–81.

Smith, Joseph Fielding. *Answers to Gospel Questions.* 5 vols. Salt Lake City: Deseret Book, 1957–1966.

————. *Church History and Modern Revelation.* 2 vols. Salt Lake City: Council of the Twelve Apostles of The Church of Jesus Christ of Latter-day Saints, 1946–49.

————. Conference Report, April 1911, 124–26.

————. Conference Report, April 1917, 58–65.

————. Conference Report, October 1928, 99–102.

————. Conference Report, April 1942, 25–28.

————. Conference Report, April 1949, 134–37.

———. *Doctrines of Salvation.* Compiled by Bruce R. McConkie. 3 vols. Salt Lake City: Bookcraft, 1954–66.

———. "Heirs to Exaltation," *Deseret News, Church News Section,* 5 January 1935, 2, 6.

———. "Is Man Immortal?" Part I. *Improvement Era,* January 1916, 195–99.

———. "Is Man Immortal?" Part III. *Improvement Era,* March 1916, 425–31.

———. "Latter-day Temple Work," *Utah Genealogical and Historical Magazine,* October 1940, 193–200.

———. *Man: His Origin and Destiny.* Salt Lake City: Deseret Book, 1954.

———. "The Resurrection," *Deseret News, Church News Section,* 15 February 1941, 1, 7.

———. "The Resurrection," *Improvement Era,* December 1942, 780–81, 827–31.

———. "Salvation for the Dead," *Utah Genealogical and Historical Magazine,* April 1926, 145–56.

———. "Temple Session Suggested for Melchizedek Priesthood," *Deseret News, Church News Section,* 27 March 1949, 21.

Snow, LeRoi C. "An Experience of my Father's," *Improvement Era,* September 1933, 677, 679.

———. "Raised from the Dead," *Improvement Era,* September 1929, 881–86.

Snow, Lorenzo. Conference Report, October 1900, 1–5, 60–63.

———. "Discourse by President Lorenzo Snow," *Millennial Star,* January 1894, 49–53.

Sperry, Sidney B. *Voice of Israel's Prophets.* Salt Lake City: Deseret Book, 1952.

Stuy, Brian H., ed. *Collected Discourses Delivered by President Wilford Woodruff, His Two Counselors, the Twelve Apostles, and Others.* Vol. 4. Burbank, Calif.: B.H.S. Pub., 1992.

Talmage, James E. *The Articles of Faith.* 12th ed. Salt Lake City: The Church of Jesus Christ of Latter-day Saints, 1924.

———. Conference Report, October 1913, 116–21.

———. Conference Report, April 1928, 91–97.

———. Conference Report, April 1930, 94–98.

———. *Jesus the Christ.* 3d ed. Salt Lake City: The Church of Jesus Christ of Latter-day Saints, 1916.

———. *Sunday Night Talks: A Series of Radio Addresses relating to the Doctrines of the Church of Jesus Christ of Latter-day Saints.* Salt Lake City: The Church of Jesus Chris of Latter-day Saints, 1931.

———. *Vitality of Mormonism.* Salt Lake City: Deseret Book, 1948.

Taylor, John. *Gospel Kingdom: Selections from the Writings and Discourses of John Taylor, Third President of The Church of Jesus Christ of Latter-day Saints.* Selected by G. Homer Durham. Salt Lake City: Bookcraft, 1998.

———. *Government of God.* Salt Lake City: Lloyd Cottrell, 1966. Facsimile reprint of the 1852 edition published by S. W. Richards, Liverpool.

———. *The Mediation and Atonement.* Salt Lake City: Deseret News, 1882.

Thomas, M. Catherine. "Paradise," in *Encyclopedia of Mormonism.* Edited by Daniel H. Ludlow. New York: Macmillan, 1992, 1062.

Watts, John D. W. *Isaiah 1–33.* Waco, Tex.: Word Books, 1985.

Webster's New Collegiate Dictionary. 10th ed. Springfield, Mass.: Merriam-Webster, 1993.

Webster's New World Dictionary. Edited by David B. Guralnik. New York: World Publishing, 1970.

West, Emerson Roy. *Profiles of the Presidents.* Salt Lake City: Deseret Book, 1980.

Whitney, Orson F. *Life of Heber C. Kimball.* Salt Lake City: Deseret Book, 2001.

———. *Saturday Night Thoughts: A Series of Dissertations on Spiritual, Historical and Philosophic Themes.* Salt Lake City: Deseret News, 1927.

———. *Through Memories Halls: The Life Story of Orson F. Whitney as Told by Himself.* Independence, Mo.: Zion's Printing and Publishing Co., 1930.

———. "We Walk by Faith," *Improvement Era,* May 1916, 608–9.

Widtsoe, John A. "Genealogical Activities in Europe," *Utah Genealogical and Historical Magazine,* July 1931, 96–106.

———. *Program of the Church of Jesus Christ of Latter-day Saints.* Salt Lake City: Deseret Book, 1941.

———. "The Worth of Souls," *Utah Genealogical and Historical Magazine,* October 1934, 189–90.

Woodruff, Wilford. Conference Report, April 1880, 6–14.

———. "Discourse by President W. Woodruff," *Millennial Star,* 22 September 1890, 593, 596.

———. *The Discourses of Wilford Woodruff.* Selected by G. Homer Durham. Salt Lake City: Bookcraft, 1990.

———. *Leaves from My Journal.* Salt Lake City: Juvenile Instructor's Office, 1882.

Young, Brigham. *Discourses of Brigham Young.* Selected by John A. Widtsoe. Salt Lake City: Deseret Book, 1941.

Scripture Index

GENESIS

2:7, pp. 13, 201, 227
2:25, p. 228
3:7, 10–11, 21, p. 228
12:17, p. 195
17:3, p. 188
17:5 (JST), p. 170
24:2, 9, p. 354
32:1, p. 122
37:34, p. 55
47:29, p. 57
47:29–30, p. 55
49:29–32, p. 56
50:4–13, 24–25, p. 56

EXODUS

8–10, p. 195
13:19, p. 56
16:13–15, p. 327
22:29, p. 268
23:19, pp. 267, 268
24:10, p. 259
28:4, p. 255
32:32–33, p. 341
32:35, p. 195
34:26, p. 268
34:29–35, p. 181
39:29, p. 255

LEVITICUS

2:12, 14, p. 268
13–14, p. 163
23:9–14, p. 267
23:10–11, p. 268
23:24, p. 281
25:8–9, p. 281

NUMBERS

10:10, p. 281
11:9, p. 327
11:33, p. 195
16:41–50, p. 195
18:12–13, p. 267
19, p. 163
29:1, p. 281

DEUTERONOMY

18:4, p. 267
19:15, p. 210
21:22–23, p. 207
26:1–11, p. 268
26:4, p. 267
32:22, p. 95

JOSHUA

5:14, p. 188

RUTH

1:17, p. 55

1 SAMUEL

2:6, p. 174
3:17, p. 55
14:44, p. 55

2 SAMUEL

3:9, 31, p. 55
3:31–33, p. 53
3:35, pp. 53, 55
22:4–7, p. 145

1 KINGS

2:10, p. 209
18:12, p. 329

2 KINGS

4:32–37, p. 141

1 CHRONICLES

15:24, p. 281

2 CHRONICLES

5:12–14, p. 281
29:27–28, p. 281

NEHEMIAH

12:41, p. 281

JOB

1:21, p. 63
10:11, pp. 229, 231
10:20–22, p. 153
14:1–2, 7–12, p. 153
19:26, p. 322
21:23–26, p. 14
34:15, pp. 13, 14
34:20, pp. 13, 15

PSALMS

2:7, pp. 206, 208
16:9, p. 144
16:10, pp. 144, 206, 209
18:2–6, p. 145
23:1, 3–4, p. 36
33:18–20, p. 140
37:11, 29, p. 349

40:17, p. 145
48:1–2, p. 274
49:12–20, p. 63
49:15, pp. 195, 323
55:3, p. 49
55:4, pp. 47, 49
55:5, p. 47
70:5, p. 145
86:12, p. 145
86:13, pp. 95, 145
88:3–4, 6–8, 14–18, p. 50
89:20, p. 206
90:1, p. 193
91:2, p. 193
110:4, p. 169
116:15, p. 47
125:1–2, p. 274
144:2, p. 145

PROVERBS

5:3–5, p. 96
7:10, 27, p. 96
9:13–18, p. 96

ECCLESIASTES

2:16, p. 14
3:1–8, p. 16
5:15–16, p. 63
8:8, pp. 14, 322
12:7, pp. 12, 13

ISAIAH

2:3, pp. 274, 360
8:14, p. 193
9:1, p. 36
9:2, pp. 35, 107
15:3, p. 55
22:13, p. 307
24:22, p. 338
25:8, p. 318
26:7–18, p. 325
26:19, pp. 217, 299, 325,
    326
27:13, p. 281
38:1–5, p. 140
53:3, p. 319
53:12, p. 272
55:3, pp. 206, 209
61:1, pp. 149, 338
61:2, p. 149

63:1–4, p. 286
65:20, p. 31

EZEKIEL

1:3, p. 329
1:7, p. 256
8:1, p. 329
10:3–4, p. 285
11:16, p. 193
18:8–9, p. 241
32:3–6, 11–12, p. 139
33:22, p. 329
37:1, pp. 329, 330
37:1–14, pp. 217, 327
37:2–3, 10, p. 330
37:4–6, 9, pp. 329, 330
37:5, 7–10, p. 332
37:5–6, 11–14, p. 328
37:5–7, p. 331
37:11–12, pp. 330, 333
37:13, p. 329
37:13–14, pp. 332, 334
37:14, pp. 227, 229, 330
40:1, p. 329
43:2, p. 256

DANIEL

3:25, p. 255
7:9, p. 290
7:10, pp. 290, 341
7:13, p. 255
8:16, p. 122
9:21, p. 122
10:6, p. 256
12:1, p. 294
12:2, pp. 161, 163, 164, 217,
    301, 339
12:3, pp. 163, 165, 217

HOSEA

4:1–2, p. 194
13:2, p. 194
13:14, pp. 143, 193, 194,
    319, 323

JOEL

2:1, 15, p. 281

OBADIAH

1:21, pp. 29, 30

JONAH

1:2, 4, p. 166
1:15–16, p. 161
1:17, pp. 161, 166
2, p. 161
2:2, 3, 6, p. 167
2:10, p. 166
3:4–8, p. 168

ZEPHANIAH

1:16, p. 281

ZECHARIAH

9:11, p. 147
9:14, p. 281
14:4, pp. 287, 288
14:5, pp. 286, 288, 302

MALACHI

4:2, p. 256

MATTHEW

5:4, p. 51
5:5, p. 349
10:8, p. 141
11:4–5, p. 141
12:39, pp. 165, 166, 192
12:40, pp. 165, 167, 192
12:41, pp. 165, 168
13:43, p. 217
16:13–18, p. 101
16:27, p. 286
17:1–9, p. 181
17:2, p. 256
17:6, pp. 188, 189
17:7, p. 189
19:28, p. 289
22:31–32, p. 19
24:30, p. 304
24:31, p. 303
25:31, p. 303
25:31–45, p. 297
26:30–48, p. 287
26:61, p. 192
27:40, p. 192
27:52, pp. 268, 313, 325, 326
27:53, pp. 268, 313, 325
27:56 (JST), p. 315
28:9, p. 183
28:16–17, p. 184

MARK

3:14–15, p. 203
8:11–12, p. 192
8:38, p. 286
12:26, p. 19
13:26, p. 304
14:58, p. 192
16:6, p. 183

LUKE

1:5–19, 26–27, p. 122
1:32, p. 208
1:76–79, p. 35
4:16–19, p. 149
6:13, p. 203
6:20, p. 349
7:12–15, p. 141
8:1, p. 208
9:16, p. 253
9:22, p. 251
10:20, p. 341
12:7, p. 215
12:19, p. 307
13:32, p. 251
16:19–31, p. 83
16:22, 24, p. 84
16:26, 31, p. 85
18:33, p. 251
20:38, p. 19
21:18, p. 215
23:54, p. 249
23:56, p. 250
24, pp. 243, 244
24:1, 14–16, 18–24, p. 250
24:1–12, p. 243
24:13, 29–31, 33, 42–43, p. 249
24:13–32, pp. 181, 246
24:17–27, p. 248
24:19, 21–25, p. 251
24:21, 26–29, p. 252
24:30–32, p. 253
24:31, 36–38, p. 244
24:33–36, p. 203
24:34, pp. 183, 211
24:36–43, pp. 242, 243
24:39, pp. 184, 204, 241, 244
24:40–41, 43, p. 246
24:48, p. 184

JOHN

1:42, p. 211
2:13–22, p. 191
2:18–20, 22, p. 192
2:18–22, p. 190
2:21, 22, p. 193
3:14, p. 193
5:21, pp. 201, 336
5:21–29, pp. 334, 336
5:22, pp. 289, 335, 336
5:23–25, p. 337
5:25, pp. 146, 292
5:26–29, p. 338
5:27, p. 335
5:28, p. 292
5:28–29, p. 165
5:29, p. 336
8:51, p. 337
10:17–18, pp. 271, 276
11:11–13, p. 193
11:11–45, p. 141
11:21–26, pp. 162, 172, 173
11:23–25, p. 174
11:25, pp. 183, 199, 232, 323
11:26, pp. 175, 337
11:41–44, p. 336
11:43, p. 303
12:7, 32–33, p. 193
12:23–24, p. 232
13:19, 21, p. 193
14:3, p. 304
14:27, p. 51
17:1–2, 9, 11, p. 272
19:38–42, p. 206
20:16, p. 183
20:19, p. 244
20:24–25, p. 184
20:27, p. 204
20:27–28, pp. 184, 245
20:31, p. 337

ACTS

1–7, p. 205
1:2–3, 8, 21–23, p. 202
1:2–3, 9, 15–22, p. 203
1:3, pp. 184, 208
1:8, 22, p. 204
1:9, p. 260, 302
1:10, p. 302

1:11, pp. 287, 302
1:21–23, p. 205
2:29, p. 209
2:32, p. 204
3:15, p. 204
3:21, p. 101
4:20, p. 204
4:31, 33, p. 204
5:32, p. 204
8:1, 3, p. 212
8:1–11:18, p. 205
8:25, p. 204
10:39, pp. 204, 246
10:40–41, p. 246
10:42, pp. 19, 289, 337
10:43, p. 252
13:22–23, p. 208
13:29–37, pp. 205, 206
13:30–31, p. 207
13:31, p. 204
13:32, p. 208
13:33, pp. 167, 208
13:34–37, p. 209
18:5, p. 204
20:21, 24, p. 204
22:15, 18, 20, p. 204
23:11, p. 204
26:16, p. 204
27:34, p. 215
28:23, p. 204
28:24, p. 111

ROMANS

2:12, p. 288
5:12, pp. 16, 200
5:14, p. 199
6, p. 170
6:3–4, p. 170
6:3–11, pp. 161, 168
6:4, p. 167
6:5–6, p. 171
6:7, 9–11, p. 172
8:11, pp. 231, 334
8:23, p. 230
8:34, p. 302
10:6, p. 302
10:13–15, p. 115
11:26–27, p. 146
14:10, p. 337
14:11, p. 77
14:12, p. 342

1 CORINTHIANS

1:12, p. 211
2:6–16, p. 302
3:22, p. 211
6:2, p. 290
6:20, p. 195
9:5, p. 211
15:3–4, pp. 209, 210, 211
15:4–8, p. 207
15:5, p. 183, 204
15:5–9, p. 209, 211
15:6, pp. 184, 204, 301
15:7–8, p. 204
15:12–19, pp. 308, 309
15:13, 17–19, p. 310
15:18, pp. 198, 301, 303
15:19, pp. 154, 312
15:20, pp. 154, 266, 268,
    271, 301
15:20–23, p. 264
15:21–22, pp. 198, 199, 200
15:22, pp. 154, 323
15:23, p. 268
15:23–24, p. 266
15:24, p. 269
15:29, p. 21
15:30–34, pp. 306, 307
15:35–37, pp. 231, 232
15:37–38, p. 232
15:38, pp. 231, 233
15:39–40, p. 235
15:39–44, p. 234
15:41–42, p. 237
15:42, 52–54, p. 264
15:43–44, p. 238
15:44, p. 225
15:45, pp. 200, 323, 336
15:45–49, p. 198
15:46–49, p. 201
15:50–51, 54–55, p. 317
15:50–53, p. 221
15:50–57, p. 315
15:51, pp. 198, 303
15:52, pp. 180, 296, 303
15:52–54, p. 318
15:53, p. 324
15:53–54, p. 228
15:55–57, pp. 48, 137, 319

2 CORINTHIANS

5:1, p. 229
5:1–5, p. 228
5:2–6, p. 230
5:5, p. 231
5:7, p. 77
6:9, p. 9
12:2, 4, p. 86
13:1, pp. 210, 249

EPHESIANS

1:7, p. 226
2:12, p. 301
4:11–14, p. 203
4:22–24, p. 171

PHILIPPIANS

2:10, p. 77
3:21, p. 317

COLOSSIANS

1:2, p. 286
1:18, pp. 261, 269
2:12, p. 169
2:20, p. 170
3:3, p. 170
3:4, pp. 238, 286
3:9, p. 171

1 THESSALONIANS

2:19, p. 286
3:13, p. 286
4:13–14, pp. 198, 307
4:13–15, p. 301
4:13–18, p. 300
4:14–16, p. 302
4:14–18, p. 159
4:15, p. 303
4:15–17, pp. 82, 282, 287
4:16, pp. 198, 296, 318, 338
4:17, pp. 283, 301, 303
4:18, pp. 300, 304, 307, 322

1 TIMOTHY

2:5, p. 337
6:7, p. 63
6:13, pp. 227, 349

2 TIMOTHY

1:10, p. 343
2:11, p. 170

HEBREWS

1:5, p. 208
1:14, p. 121
7:17, p. 169
7:27, p. 172
9:28, p. 172
10:10, p. 172
11:35, p. 141
13:2, p. 182

JAMES

2:26, pp. 12, 220

1 PETER

1:18–19, p. 195
3:18, pp. 146, 150
3:18–20, pp. 91, 104
3:19, pp. 146, 151, 283
4:5, p. 19
4:6, pp. 19, 91, 104, 151,
    283

2 PETER

2:4, p. 343
3:10, p. 292

1 JOHN

2:1, p. 337
4:12, p. 107

JUDE

1:9, p. 303

REVELATION

1:5, p. 269
1:8, p. 189
1:10, 13–14, p. 255
1:10–16, pp. 188, 253
1:15, p. 256
1:16, pp. 189, 256
1:17, pp. 187, 188, 189, 190
1:18, pp. 98, 183, 188, 189,
    190
2:7, p. 86
2:8, 11, p. 291

2:18, p. 256
3:7, p. 189
4:2–3, 9, p. 340
4:6–9, p. 347
5:1, 7, 13, p. 340
5:6, p. 333
5:9–13, p. 274
6:16, p. 340
7:1, pp. 332, 333
7:10, 15, p. 340
7:17, p. 319
8:1–5, pp. 281, 282
9:1, p. 189
9:20–21, p. 281
10:2, 5, p. 333
11:11, p. 332
12:8, pp. 294, 340
13:15, p. 290
14:13, pp. 47, 303
14:14, p. 255
14:17, p. 188
16:9, 11, 21, p. 281
19:4, p. 340
19:12, p. 256
19:13, p. 286
19:20, p. 343
19:21, p. 289
20:4, pp. 289, 340, 342
20:4–6, pp. 288, 360
20:5, pp. 290, 340
20:6, p. 291
20:10, 14–15, p. 343
20:11, pp. 294, 296, 340
20:11–15, pp. 296, 339
20:12, pp. 198, 296, 340, 341
20:12–13, pp. 220, 291
20:13, pp. 339, 342
21:1, p. 340
21:4, pp. 137, 225, 319
21:5, p. 340
21:6, p. 189
21:22, p. 193
22:13, p. 189

1 NEPHI

11:1, p. 357
11:14, p. 122
11:16, 26, p. 271
11:19, 29, p. 329
11:21, p. 208

12:9–10, p. 290
14:30, p. 329
19:10, p. 271
31:20, p. 159

2 NEPHI

1:13, p. 94
1:15, p. 144
2:6, p. 227
2:6–8, p. 270
2:8, pp. 151, 269
2:8–9, pp. 269, 271
2:11, 25, p. 16
2:21, 27, p. 76
2:22–23, p. 15
2:25–26, p. 199
2:29, p. 96
4:32, p. 103
9:3–4, 6–8, p. 321
9:3–8, p. 320
9:3–13, p. 217
9:4, p. 322
9:5, p. 271
9:6, pp. 14, 16, 17, 322
9:7, p. 323
9:7–9, pp. 145, 154
9:8, pp. 322, 324
9:10, pp. 94, 144, 154, 322
9:10–13, pp. 142, 189
9:11, p. 145
9:12, pp. 84, 94, 146, 322
9:13, pp. 84, 146, 215, 221, 229, 322
9:14, pp. 229, 345
9:15, pp. 72, 341
9:16, p. 67
9:19, p. 142
9:27–28, 30, p. 97
9:31, 34–35, 37–39, p. 98
11:4, pp. 160, 267
18:19, p. 3
25:17–18, p. 182
25:19, p. 208
25:20, p. 271
26:10, p. 96
28:7, p. 307
28:15, 20, p. 96
28:21, 22, p. 97
33:6, p. 144

JACOB

4:11, p. 323
4:11–12, p. 217

ENOS

1:23, p. 48

MOSIAH

2:38, p. 98
3:2, p. 122
3:5, p. 141
3:15, p. 160
3:25, p. 223
4:8, p. 271
5:7, p. 209
5:8, p. 271
13:33, 35, p. 271
15:6–8, 19–20, p. 217
15:7–8, p. 271
15:8, pp. 272, 276, 337
15:20, 24, pp. 275, 276
15:20–26, p. 274
15:21, p. 277
15:22, pp. 261, 274, 276, 277, 278
15:23, p. 275
15:23–26, p. 279
15:25, pp. 21, 276
15:26, p. 48
16:6–9, p. 144
16:7–8, p. 319
16:10, pp. 238, 264, 318
18:2, p. 227
18:9, p. 51
27:10–11, p. 122
27:25, p. 209
27:31, p. 77

ALMA

5:6–11, 13, p. 118
5:7–10, p. 103
5:18, p. 223
5:58, p. 341
7:12, p. 144
10:7, p. 122
10:31, p. 218
11:21, 38, 40, p. 218
11:40, 41, p. 219
11:41–42, p. 223
11:41–45, p. 217

11:42, p. 220
11:43, pp. 215, 216, 221, 224
11:44, pp. 216, 223, 337
11:45, pp. 215, 224, 238, 314
12:1, 41–45, p. 219
12:11, pp. 96, 98, 103
12:15, p. 77
12:16, pp. 217, 221
12:18, p. 220
12:22, pp. 36, 37, 38
12:24, pp. 36, 38, 221
12:25, p. 226
12:26–27, pp. 36, 40
12:27, pp. 41
13:16, p. 160
13:30, pp. 94, 103
15:3, p. 99
19:13, p. 271
21:9, p. 271
22:14, pp. 48, 145
25:15, p. 160
26:13–16, p. 119
26:14, p. 103
27:28, pp. 152, 154
30:18, p. 153
33:22, p. 72
34:10, p. 321
34:16, p. 226
34:31–33, 35, p. 39
34:34, pp. 66, 68
34:35, pp. 66, 69
36:11, 14, p. 99
37:36–37, p. 45
38:9, p. 271
39:19, p. 121
40:1, p. 214
40:1–10, pp. 262, 263
40:2, pp. 167, 264
40:3, p. 264
40:4, pp. 261, 265
40:5, 10, p. 265
40:6, pp. 73, 75, 265
40:6–16, p. 17
40:7, pp. 73, 75, 266
40:8, p. 266
40:11, pp. 69, 72, 85, 89, 266
40:12, pp. 85, 89, 266
40:13–14, pp. 89, 92, 266
40:16, pp. 265, 277

40:18–19, p. 265
40:21, p. 92
40:23, pp. 215, 221, 222, 223, 224, 265
40:23–26, p. 214
40:24, pp. 215, 216
40:25, pp. 165, 217
40:26, p. 217
41:2, p. 215
41:4, p. 318
42:2, 4–6, 8–9, 11, 15, p. 11
42:4, 6–16, p. 18
42:4, 13, p. 37
42:5, p. 17
42:7, 10, p. 38
42:9, 11, p. 40
42:23, pp. 220, 270

HELAMAN

13:7, p. 122
14:17, p. 144

3 NEPHI

7:17–18, p. 122
7:19, p. 141
11, p. 325
11:3, p. 256
11:12, p. 188
11:14, p. 184
11:15, pp. 184, 241, 245
11:23–26, p. 169
11:38, p. 102
12:27–30, p. 97
18:1–13, p. 103
23:9–10, p. 276
26:15, p. 141
27:27, p. 290
28:7–9, pp. 175, 178, 179, 180
28:8, p. 292
28:15–23, 27–32, 36–40, p. 175
28:15, 17–18, 23, 29, p. 180
28:18–30, p. 250
28:18–29, p. 181
28:27–28, pp. 178, 182
28:30, pp. 178, 181
28:31–32, 38–40, p. 182
28:37, 40, p. 179
28:39, pp. 178, 179

4 NEPHI

1:5, p. 141

MORMON

3:19, p. 290
3:20, p. 289
6:7, p. 49
8:16–17, p. 97
9:4, p. 92
9:12, pp. 197, 199
9:12–13, pp. 195, 323
9:13, pp. 164, 197
9:14, p. 197

ETHER

3:6, pp. 60, 188
3:15, 17, p. 60
3:9, p. 271
3:14, p. 209
3:16, pp. 59, 62
12:4, p. 312

MORONI

7:25, 29, 31–32, p. 121
7:28, p. 272
7:41, p. 312
8:5–22, p. 20
8:12–21, p. 97
10:14, pp. 120, 121
10:26, p. 45
10:32–33, p. 172
10:34, p. 304

DOCTRINE AND COVENANTS

6:28, p. 210
10:24–26, p. 96
11:30, p. 209
13, p. 276
14:9, p. 208
17:8, p. 102
18:5, p. 103
19:15–20, p. 100
19:16–17, p. 150
19:18, pp. 150, 286
20:30, p. 241
20:35, p. 121
20:73, p. 169
21:1, p. 28

27:12, p. 205
29:5, p. 337
29:12, p. 290
29:13, p. 47
29:22–24, p. 340
29:23–24, p. 294
29:23–29, p. 293
29:24, p. 295
29:25, p. 215
29:25–29, p. 296
29:26, pp. 199, 303, 318, 339
29:28–29, p. 297
29:38, p. 343
29:42, p. 38
29:43, pp. 17, 38, 238
29:46, pp. 21, 276
35:2, p. 209
38:5, p. 92
38:20, p. 349
42:43, p. 43
42:43–48, p. 40
42:44–47, pp. 44, 302
42:45, pp. 50, 302, 319
42:46–47, pp. 47, 48
42:48, p. 45
43:18, pp. 164, 198, 291, 292, 338
43:29–30, p. 290
43:32, pp. 14, 75, 100, 291, 292, 318
45, p. 288
45:17, pp. 73, 91
45:42, 44, 51–53, p. 285
45:44–48, pp. 278, 284
45:45, pp. 285, 286
45:46, p. 287
45:47–48, pp. 285, 287, 288
45:48–54, p. 285
45:54, pp. 278, 284, 288
45:58, p. 349
56:20, p. 349
57:5, p. 349
59:2, pp. 86, 349
61:38–39, p. 303
63:2–4, p. 139
63:3–4, p. 140
63:20, p. 349
63:49, pp. 47, 225
63:50–51, pp. 30, 31, 317
63:51, p. 292

68:25–27, p. 21
75:20–22, p. 290
76, pp. 235, 357, 359
76:14, p. 113
76:16–17, p. 336
76:17, p. 339
76:22–23, p. 185
76:23, p. 188
76:35, p. 208
76:44, 88, p. 343
76:50, 54–56, 58–59, 62–65, p. 279
76:50, 65, p. 278
76:50–51, p. 170
76:51–63, p. 286
76:59, p. 139
76:66, p. 30
76:69, p. 241
76:69–72, 74–75, 78–79, 82, p. 237
76:70–74, 84, p. 95
76:73, pp. 113, 283
76:81, 98, pp. 95, 237
76:84, 104, p. 93
76:85, pp. 93, 98, 265, 280
76:86, pp. 94, 107
76:89–92, p. 235
76:96–98, p. 234
76:103, pp. 97, 237
76:106, pp. 93, 98
76:110, p. 77
77:2, p. 62
77:3, p. 347
77:4, p. 256
77:12, p. 281
84:2, 32, p. 30
84:5, p. 285
84:16, p. 200
84:45–46, p. 39
84:99–100, p. 274
88:10, 42–43, 78–79, p. 348
88:14, pp. 225, 226, 349
88:14–17, 116, pp. 225, 226
88:15, pp. 12, 227
88:16, pp. 195, 227
88:16–33, p. 235
88:17, pp. 201, 227, 348, 349, 352
88:17–21, p. 347
88:18, pp. 234, 349, 350, 352

88:18–20, pp. 295, 349
88:19, pp. 234, 348, 350
88:20, 25, pp. 348, 351
88:20–21, p. 234
88:21, p. 351
88:22–24, p. 237
88:25–26, pp. 347, 352
88:26, pp. 294, 348, 352
88:27, p. 239
88:28–31, p. 236
88:73, p. 119
88:94, pp. 280, 282
88:96, pp. 282, 303
88:96–98, pp. 278, 283
88:96–101, p. 82
88:96–102, p. 280
88:97, pp. 268, 282, 303
88:97–99, p. 268
88:98, pp. 282, 283, 296
88:99, p. 283
88:100–102, pp. 269, 284
88:106, p. 282
88:112, pp. 282, 294
93:11, p. 208
93:28, 39, p. 345
93:33, pp. 60, 73
93:33–34, pp. 19, 157
93:36, p. 344
97:16, p. 188
98:14, p. 17
98:22, pp. 101, 102, 103
101:24–25, p. 350
101:29, pp. 31, 319
101:30–31, p. 342
101:31, pp. 292, 303, 317
101:31–32, p. 31
104:18, p. 97
107:23, p. 205
109:75, p. 303
110:2, p. 259
110:2–4, p. 254
110:3, p. 256
110:8, p. 188
110:11–16, p. 302
121:23, p. 97
124:85, p. 47
124:85–86, p. 45
124:86, p. 47
124:100, pp. 140, 142
127, p. 341
128:5, pp. 21, 26

128:6–8, p. 340
128:7, p. 341
128:12–13, p. 169
128:15–17, p. 26
128:15–19, p. 21
128:18–19, p. 28
128:20, p. 122
128:20–21, p. 302
128:22, pp. 21, 29, 326
129, p. 204
129:1, pp. 122, 239, 240
129:2, pp. 239, 241
129:3, pp. 239, 240, 241
129:4–9, p. 139
129:9, p. 239
130:5, p. 122
130:18–19, pp. 344, 345
130:22, p. 240
131:1–4, p. 95
131:7, pp. 60, 62, 65, 227
132:13–14, pp. 64, 66
132:15, p. 65
132:19, p. 229
132:37, p. 342
133:20, p. 288
133:22, p. 256
133:46, 48, p. 286
133:54–55, p. 273
133:54–56, p. 261
133:54–57, p. 272
133:56, pp. 30, 274, 326
133:57, pp. 273, 274
133:57–59, p. 303
137, p. 233
137:7, pp. 24, 279
137:7–9, p. 110
137:10, pp. 20, 21, 276
138, p. 278
138:1, 6–12, p. 106
138:1–3, p. 311
138:2, p. 227
138:4–10, 32–33, p. 311
138:11, pp. 31, 198, 329, 330

138:11–12, 22, p. 312
138:11–16, p. 149
138:12, pp. 242, 311, 314, 330
138:12–17, p. 72
138:14, pp. 242, 311, 324
138:14–19, pp. 31, 310
138:15, pp. 31, 298, 312, 314
138:16, pp. 106, 227, 313, 314
138:17, pp. 198, 221, 225, 240, 312, 313, 331
138:18, pp. 195, 277, 311, 312, 314
138:19, p. 315
138:19–21, 24, 27, 33, 49, 116, p. 314
138:20–22, 29–32, p. 91
138:23, pp. 146, 314
138:29, p. 106
138:29–30, p. 103
138:30, pp. 107, 108, 115, 314
138:31, pp. 117, 277, 314
138:32–35, p. 115
138:33–34, 58–59, p. 117
138:37, pp. 108, 314
138:38, pp. 311, 314, 329
138:38–46, p. 278
138:38–49, pp. 311, 357
138:42, pp. 195, 277, 314
138:43, p. 329
138:50, pp. 72, 91, 195, 283, 291, 314, 357
138:51, pp. 313, 357
138:57, pp. 109, 117, 119
138:58, p. 355
138:59, p. 119

MOSES

1:11, pp. 180, 181
1:39, p. 231

3:5, p. 74
3:9, p. 74
3:7, p. 14
3:16–17, pp. 1, 15
4:8–25, p. 15
5:6, p. 122
5:7, p. 199
6:28, p. 97
6:48, pp. 15, 16
6:57, pp. 208, 255
6:59, p. 16
6:60, p. 241
6:63, pp. 160, 267
6:64, p. 329
7:48, p. 350
7:57, p. 92
8:28–30, p. 350

ABRAHAM

3:25, p. 76
3:27, p. 255

JOSEPH SMITH– HISTORY

1:16–17, p. 258
1:17, p. 260
1:30, pp. 213, 248, 253, 258, 260
1:30–32, pp. 256, 259
1:30–33, 68–72, p. 122
1:31, p. 259
1:31–32, p. 217
1:32, pp. 214, 259
1:43, pp. 213, 248
1:43–44, pp. 253, 256, 259, 260
1:44, p. 258

ARTICLES OF FAITH

10, pp. 290, 350

SUBJECT INDEX

Abel, 148, 278, 311

Abinadi, 274–80

Abraham: in paradise, 148, 311; in first resurrection, 272, 278

Abraham's bosom, 83–84

Accountability, age of, 20–21

Adam (and Eve): probationary period of, 10–11, 36–37; fall of, 15, 195–202; need of savior for, 40; in paradise, 148, 311; connection of, with Christ, 199–202, 323; in paradisiacal form, 221; creation of, 227; in first resurrection, 278; as judge, 290

Age of man, 30–31

Agency, 76, 116

Alexander the Great, 316–17

Alma the Younger: on place of death in plan of salvation, 10–11; experiences torments of hell, 99–100; on times appointed for resurrection, 262–66, 277

Amulek, 217–25

Angels, ministering: communicate with man, 120–22; know thoughts and actions, 123; bring blessings and truth, 128–30, 131–32; accompany loved ones in death, 130–31; assist with family history work, 132–34; work through the priesthood, 134–36; as translated beings, 175–82; as resurrected beings, 239–41; accompany Christ at Second Coming, 286

Animal life: spiritual creation of, 74; resurrection of, 235, 295, 346–47

Apostasy, 101

Apostles (in meridian of time): see resurrected Christ, 183–84, 202–5;

witness of Christ, 208–11, 242–46; to judge house of Israel, 289

Apostles (Nephite), 290

Appointed unto death, 40–45

Atonement: necessity of, 18; removes fear of death, 137–38; men redeemed from hell through, 144–45; Christ suffers for sins through, 150–51; tokens of, 203; brings forth the resurrection, 320–21; as infinite, 323–24

Attitudes, 68–69, 80

Awakening, 161, 163–65, 301

Ballard, Melvin J.: on importance of mortality, 39–40; on knowledge we will have in spirit world, 67–68, 114; on righteous spirits wanting to reunite with the body, 73, 77–78; on children having adult spirits, 78; on communication with spirit world, 124, 132–33; sees resurrected Christ, 185

Baptism: of little children, 20; symbolizes resurrection, 161, 168–72

Baptism for the dead: as welding link for generations, 21–23; as key to gates of hell, 102; symbol of, 201

Barnabas, 206

Barnes, Lorenzo Dow, 56

Barnett, Paul, 230–31

Benson, Ezra Taft: on mothers raising children who have died, 20–21; on equal opportunity to hear gospel, 24; on ordinances for dead, 24, 25; on closeness of spirit world, 124; on universality of resurrection, 326

Bier, 55

Birth, 163

Blessings, priesthood, 41, 43

Blood, 240, 245, 317

Body: when separated from spirit, 12–13, 73, 77–78; is formed from dust, 13–15, 201, 227, 230; is fashioned after the spirit, 60, 62; restoration and perfection of, 214–17, 221–22, 223–24; never again separated from spirit, 225; mortal, as imperfect, 238. *See also* Resurrected beings, Translated beings

Bondage: separation of spirit and body as, 72–73, 77–78, 276–77, 313; mortality as, 237–38

Book of life, 341

Bowen, Albert E., 345

Bowen, Walter, 74

Brass, fine, 256

Brown, Hugh B., 10, 314

Burial, 55–57

Cannon, Abraham H., 131–32

Cannon, George Q.: on dead seeking salvation through mortals, 27; on faithful dying in the Lord, 46; on wicked fearing death, 49; on knowledge of spirit world, 59; on retaining same feelings after death, 69; on being taken home to God, 70–71; on spirit world as probationary, 76–77; on diversity of spirits in spirit world, 78–79; administers to George A. Smith, 127; on evil spirits, 135–36; sees resurrected Christ, 185; on Christ holding keys of resurrection, 188, 190; on universality of resurrection, 326

Carmel, dews of, 29

Carson, D. A., 167

Celestial kingdom: little children inherit, 20–21; as paradise, 86; inheritors of, 113, 117, 234, 236–37; eternal increase within, 236; resurrection of those who inherit, 268, 279; Michael admits righteous into, 290, 294

Cephas, 211. *See also* Peter

Character, 64, 67–69, 112

Chiasmus, 197, 280

Children, little: death of, 20–21; salvation of, 21, 24, 86; adult spirits of, 78; come forth in first resurrection, 276, 279

Christiansen, ElRay, 64

Church of Jesus Christ of Latter-day Saints, The: teachings of, are alone on salvation for the dead, 23; responsibility of, to take gospel to living and dead, 26; members of, as saviors on Mount Zion, 29; faithful members of, dying in the Lord, 46–48; funerals in, 53–55; has knowledge of spirit world, 59, 74; growth of, in mortality and spirit world, 116; as judge, 290

Cicero, 1

Clark, J. Reuben, 34

Clawson, Rudger, 141–42

Clement of Alexandria, 151

Cleopas, 183, 242, 247, 249–51

Clothing, imagery of, 228–29

Clouds, 285

Coats of skin, 228–29

Coltrin, Zebedee, 186, 254

Columbus, Christopher, 132

Comfort, from knowledge of resurrection, 298, 300–304

Communication with spirit world: blessing of, 120–22; from spirits who watch and help, 122–24; from past leaders, 124–28; from loved ones, 128–32; to facilitate temple work, 132–34; comes through priesthood, 134–36

Corpses, 163

Corruption, 237

Covenant promises, 64

Cowdery, Oliver, 190, 239, 259

Creation, spiritual, 74

Cross, 206–7

Crucifixion, 206–7

Curse formula, 55

Damnation, 96

Daniel: in paradise, 148, 311; on death as sleep, 164; on resurrection, 165; describes resurrected Christ, 254; in first resurrection, 278; on judgment, 290

Darkness, spiritual, 35–36

David, sure mercies of, 209

Death, physical or temporal: as part of plan of salvation, 11, 15–19, 321; as a birth, 12–13; quickness of, 15; from transgression of Adam and Eve, 15–16, 36–37, 75; in the Millennium, 30–31;

being appointed unto, 40–45; is feared by wicked, 48–50, 152–54; Christ redeems all men from, 143–46, 315–20; comes to all, 221; drawing comfort at, of loved one, 300–304; will cease to exist, 343

Death, spiritual: as result of the Fall, 15, 18, 36–38; hell as condition of, 93–94; Christ redeems men from, 143–46; no glorification of body in, 217; as lake of fire, 340–41, 343

Deformities, 222

Degrees of glory, 93–96, 234–37, 343. See also Celestial kingdom, Telestial kingdom, Terrestrial kingdom

Dew, 29, 326–27

Disobedience, 345

Dispensation of the fulness of times: unifies all dispensations, unfolds mysteries, 22, 28; work to do be done in, 80–81, 108; receives fulness of gospel, 274

Donne, John, 2

Dust, 13–15, 201

Dyer, Alvin R., 79

Dying in the Lord, 34, 44, 45–47

Earth: spirit world resides on, 76; paradisiacal glory of, 85; celestialization of, 234, 292–95, 340, 347–52

Earthquake, 288

Egypt, 139–40

Elias, 148, 278

Elijah, 27, 260, 272–73

Emmaus, 246, 250

Enoch and followers, 260, 272–73

Equality, of requirements and opportunity, 23–26, 112, 115

Esau, 30

Eternal increase, 236

Eternal life, 279. See also Celestial kingdom

Eulogies, 54–55

Eusebius, 152

Eyes of Christ, 256

Ezekiel: in paradise, 148, 311; in first resurrection, 278; on resurrection of house of Israel, 327–34

Faith: to follow Christ, 33; to be healed, 41, 43; in the spirit world, 77

Fall: as part of plan of salvation, 10–11;

from transgression of Adam and Eve, 15–16; effects of, 36–38; resurrection because of, 195–202, 323; imperfect mortal bodies result of, 238

Family history work, 132–34

Family organization, 26–28, 87, 304–6

Fasting, 55

Faust, James E., 7–8

Fear of death, 47–50, 152–54

First fruits, 82, 260, 266–68

First resurrection: Christ as first fruits of, 261, 263–64, 266–69, 271; others coming forth in, with Christ, 261, 272–73, 276–78; timing of, known to God, 262–63, 265; Second Coming continues, 268, 274; those coming forth in, 279, 303; at sounding of first trump, 282, 287; those in, will live through Millennium, 290–91; will occur instantaneously, 291–92; calling forth of, 326

First Vision, 258

Fitzmyer, Joseph A., 206–7

Founding Fathers, 132

Franklin, Benjamin, 2

Funerals, 53–55

Gates of hell, 101–3

Glory: resurrected body associated with, 217, 238, 259–60; resurrected beings can hide, 248

Godhead, 224

God the Father: being taken home to, 69–72; has power over life and death, 139; raises Christ from dead, 207; quickens all things, 227, 231–33; has resurrected body, 240; has set schedule for resurrections, 260, 265; wisdom, mercy, and grace of, 324–25; gives power to the Son, 334–37; final judgment by, 340–42

Gospel of Jesus Christ: is taught to all in spirit world, 107–9, 115; acceptance of, in spirit world, 110–16; fulness of, in last dispensation, 274

Grace, 312

Grant, B. F., 130–31

Grant, Caroline, 87

Grant, Heber J.: on death of wife, 51–52; has vision of spirit world, 126; on death of son, 130–31; on loved ones who have died, 138–30

Grant, Jedediah M.: on visit to spirit world, 86–88; visits Wilford Woodruff in spirit, 125; faithfulness of, 126

Grant, Margaret, 87

Graves, 195

Grief, 51–52

Guilt, 223

Hades, 79, 359 n. 9

Haight, David B., 133

Hair, restoration of, 223–24

Hannah, 174

Happiness, eternal, 18

Harris, Martin, 100

Harvest, 231–33

Healings, 40–45

Hell: as spirit world, 79, 83–84; meanings of, 93–94; purpose of, 95–96; those who will be in, 96–98; those in, to be resurrected, 98, 146; gates of, 101–3; being redeemed from, 143–46

Herod's Temple, 190–93

Hezekiah, 140

Hinckley, Gordon B., 8, 239

Hippolytus, 151

Holland, Jeffrey R., 229

Holy Ghost: as Comforter at times of death, 54; as Holy Spirit of promise, 66; early apostles receive, 204; as vehicle for visions, 329

Holy Spirit of promise, 65–66

Hope, 301, 308–15

Hugo, Victor, 1–2

Hunter, Howard W.: on significance of resurrection, 157, 158; on Christ's complete victory, 316–17, 319–20

Idolatry, 166–67

Immortality: of spirits, 10, 12, 58, 60–62; as incorruption, 238, 264

Incorruption, 238, 264, 318, 324

Individuality, 60–61

Intelligence, 344–45

Intelligences, 60–62

Intercession, 272

Isaac, 148, 272–73, 278

Isaiah, 148, 278, 311

Israel, house of, 289, 327–34

Israelites, ancient: funerals of, 52, 55; burials of, 55–56

Jacob (Israel): burial request of, 55, 57; in paradise, 148; in first resurrection, 272, 278

James: transfiguration of, 180–81; sees resurrected Christ, 184, 203–4, 211; resurrection of, 239, 276

Jensen, Ella, 141–42

Jensen, Jacob, 141–42

Jerusalem, 30, 274, 287

Jesus Christ: as author of plan of mercy, 18, 270–72; as judge of living and dead, 19, 117, 289, 334–37; as dayspring, 35–36; as guide and support in mortality, 45–47; comforts us in mourning, 51; as example of eternal spirit, 58; shows himself while in the spirit, 59–60; will be acknowledged by all spirits, 77, 113; bridges gulf in spirit world, 84–85, 90–91; organizes missionaries for spirit world, 104–7; teaches in paradise, 105–7, 146–52; has power over life and death, 139–42, 187–89, 315–20, 323; raises Lazarus from the dead, 141, 161–62, 172–75; redeems all men from death, 143–46, 315–20; overcomes fear of death, 152–54; is focus of baptism ordinance, 169–72; holds keys of resurrection, 190; connection of, with Adam, 198–202, 323; as Redeemer, 226–27; as Mediator, 272; as Christ and Messiah, 278. See also Atonement, Second Coming

Jesus Christ, resurrection of: introduces ordinances for dead, 24; Christ is seen by many following, 183–89, Christ prophesies, 190–93; promises to destroy death, 193–95; necessity of, 197; apostles bear witness of, 202–5, 244–45; Paul bears witness of, 205–9; other Saints bear witness of, 209–12, 244–45; body of Christ after, 239–41, 242–46; Christ's appearance on road to Emmaus following, 247–53; description of Christ following, 253–56; as first fruits, 260, 263, 264, 266–69

Joanna, 243

Job, 152–53, 358 n. 11

John: transfiguration of, 180–81; sees resurrected Christ, 185–86, 188–89; describes resurrected Christ, 253–56
John the Baptist: calling of, 35; resurrected body of, 239; is resurrected with Christ, 260, 272–73
Jonah, 161, 165–68
Joseph of Arimathea, 206–7
Joseph of Egypt, 56, 57
Joy, 16, 310–15
Judas, 205
Judgment: of Christ, of living and dead, 19, 296, 335–37; of opportunity to hear gospel in mortality, 23, 117; for appointed resurrection, 40, 82; partial, at death, 75, 90; final, when all shall confess Christ, 77, 113; final, linked to resurrection, 220, 223; hierarchy of, at time of Millennium, 289–90; by God, after Millennium, 340–42
Just men made perfect, 239, 241–42

Keys, to resurrection, 189–90, 198
Kimball, Heber C.: on spirits longing to be free, 34–35; on Heber J. Grant's visit to spirit world, 86–87; on righteous and wicked in spirit world, 91–92; on souls in hell, 95; visits Wilford Woodruff in spirit, 125
Kimball, Spencer W.: on knowledge of death in pre-earth existence, 11–12; on death as a birth, 12; on body being perfected, 13; on death coming to all, 14; on death and healings, 41–42; on dying in the Lord, 44; on funeral eulogies, 54–55; on immortality of spirit, 58; on leaving behind temporal things, 63; on character remaining unchanged after death, 67; on being needed as a missionary in the spirit world, 109–10; on repentance in the spirit world, 117; on temple work for the dead, 119; on prophets attending temple dedications, 125–26; on need for a Savior for Adam, 197; on perfected, resurrected body, 221–22, 240–41
Kindred dead, 25, 26
Kingdom of God on earth, 190
Knowledge: goes beyond death, 64, 222–23;

will be the same after death, 67–68, 114; will rise in resurrection, 344–45
Korihor, 153

Lamanites, 118–19
Law of Moses, 160, 267
Lazarus: is raised from the dead, 141, 336; symbolizes resurrection, 161–62, 172–75
Lee, Harold B.: on spirits going to God, 71; on earth as spirit world, 76; on righteous spirits as missionaries in spirit world, 110; on closeness of spirit world, 124; relates story of John Wells and son, 128; on atonement of Christ tempering death, 137; on order of resurrection, 260
Leprosy, 163
Light, 258, 327
Light of Christ, 39, 76
Lineages, 111
Ludlow, Victor L., 77
Luke: sees resurrected Christ, 183–84, 202–3; records events of resurrected Christ, 243–44, 247–42
Lund, Anthon H., 273, 305–6, 347

Madsen, Truman, 52
Malachi, 148, 311, 278
Mankind, fallen state of, 37–38
Marriages, earthly, 65–66
Martha, 173–74
Martyrs, 289
Mary (mother of James), 183, 243
Mary Magdalene, 183, 243
Matter, 227
Matthias, 202, 211
Maughn, Peter, 127
Maxwell, Neal A.: on spirits being needed in the spirit world, 42; on walking by faith in the spirit world, 77; on success of spirit world missionary work, 111; on hastening the work on both sides of the veil, 119–20; on joy of the resurrection, 158
McAllister, Brother, 132
McConkie, Bruce R.: on choosing how death will be, 9; on necessity of death, 17; on no second chance to gain salvation, 24; on dying in the Lord, 46; on having same attitudes after death, 69;

on life in the spirit world, 79–80; on
Christ teaching in paradise, 150; on
Jonah's experience as symbolic of
resurrection, 161; on interconnection of
Adam and Christ, 199; on death as
sowing seeds, 232; on being resurrected
to a degree of glory, 235; on capability
of resurrected beings, 243–44, 249; on
Christ's victory over death, 319
McConkie, Joseph Fielding, 323–24, 358 n. 7
McKay, David O.: on death of children, 20;
on significance of resurrection, 157;
sees resurrected Christ, 187, 254; on
witnesses of resurrected Christ, 209; on
comforting doctrine of resurrection, 300
Mercy, 37
Michael (Adam): to sound trump for
resurrection, 198, 282, 286–87, 293–94,
296–97, 338–39
Millennium: death and resurrection during,
30–31, 75, 82, 292, 316–17; doing work
for dead in, 31–32; state of wicked
during, 82; celestial and terrestrial
beings reside on earth during, 283, 290,
350; earth celestialized following, 350
Misery, 16
Missionaries, 117, 290
Missionary work: for living and dead, 29;
during Millennium, 82–83; Christ
organizes, for spirit world, 104–7, 152,
314–15; righteous performing, in spirit
world, 108–10; success of, in spirit
world, 110–16
Monson, Thomas S., 229
Moon, 235, 237
Moriah, Mount, 30
Morning, 162–63
Moroni, 217, 239, 256–60
Mortality: as result of Fall, 15–16; as part of
God's plan, 16–19; having opportunity
to hear gospel in, 23; as gift, 33–34; as
probationary state, 39; as corruption,
238
Moses: in paradise, 149, 311; transfiguration
of, 180–81; in first resurrection, 260,
272–73, 278
Mothers, 20–21
Mourning, 50–52
Murdock, John, 254–55
Mysteries of God, 28

Neibaur, Alexander, 185–86
Nelson, Russell M.: on life and death, 8–9,
34; on near-death experience, 48–49; on
grief and mourning, 51; on spirit
providing personality, 58; on restoration
of body at resurrection, 215, 221
Nephites, 184
Nephites, Three, 175–82
New Jerusalem, 30, 274
Nibley, Hugh, 101–2, 151
Nicodemus, 206–7
Nineveh, 168
Noah: in paradise, 148; in first resurrection,
260, 272–73, 278
Nuttal, L. John, 185

Oaks, Dallin H., 121
Obedience: as protection against hell, 103,
337; from knowledge of resurrection,
306; intelligence gained through, 344–
45
Olives, Mount of, 287–88
Opportunity to hear the gospel, 23–26, 112,
117
Opposition, 16, 112
Ordinances for dead: performed after
Atonement, 24; done by proxy, 24–25,
119–20; efficaciousness of, 25; all, must
be completed, 25; seals families
together, 26–29
Outer darkness, 92

Packer, Boyd K.: on death, 12; on death as
mechanism of rescue, 18; on funerals
within the Church, 53–54; on
immortality of spirit, 58; on universality
of resurrection, 326
Paradise: righteous go to, 75, 78–79;
meaning of, 85–86; description of,
86–89; Christ teaches in, 105–7,
146–52; resurrection of those in, 143,
146
Paradisiacal form, 221
Partridge, Edward, 108
Patten, David, 112
Paul: likens baptism to resurrection,
168–72; sees resurrected Christ, 204,
209; bears witness of resurrection,
205–9; contrasts mortal and resurrected

bodies, 228–31; likens sowing seeds to death and resurrection, 231–24
Penrose, Charles W., 32, 163
Perdition, sons of, 269, 284
Perfection: to family organization, 26; of body in resurrected beings, 214–17, 221–22
Personality, 58
Perspective, 306
Peter (Cephas): transfiguration of, 180–81; sees resurrected Christ, 183; resurrection of, 239, 276
Peterson, Mark E., 239
Phelps, William W., 278
Plagues, 195
Plant life, 74
Pond, Stillman, death of family of, 7–8
Pratt, Orson, 352
Pratt, Parley P.: on characteristics of spirit, 61–62; on spirit world as probationary, 76; on grades of spirits in spirit world, 114–15; on communication with spirit world, 120–21; is needed in the spirit world, 128; receives ministering angel, 128–30; on earth's becoming celestialized, 293
Pre-earth existence, 11–12, 74
Priest, 169
Priesthood: goes beyond death, 64; righteous missionaries in spirit world have, 107; will direct spirit communication, 134–36; power of, to raise the dead, 140–42
Probationary state: earth life as, 10–11, 36–38, 76; extends beyond mortality, 39–40, 76–77
Promises, earthly, 65–66
Prophets: hold sealing keys, 65–66; influence Church while in spirit world, 126–27; come forth in first resurrection, 277–78
Proxy, 24–25

Quick, 19
Quicken, 201, 236, 336

Raised from the dead, 140–42, 162
Ransom, 194–95
Red, symbolism of, 286
Redemption: necessity of, 18, 36–40, 226;

vision of, of the dead, 72, 104–6, 107, 115, 119, 146–49, 278, 310–11, 329–31, 358 n. 7; Christ as author of plan of, 143–46, 194–95; is not for the wicked, 219–20
Relationships, 64, 81, 304–6
Religions, in spirit world, 79, 114
Remorse, 223
Repentance: to receive blessings of plan of redemption, 18, 37–38, 144–46; of dead for salvation, 23, 28; of those in spirit world, 39, 84–85, 94, 116–19; as putting off of old self, 171
Responsibility, 26
Restitution, law of, 138
Restoration of body, 214–17
Resurrected beings: as different from translated beings, 162, 178; as different from mortal beings, 213; bodies of, 214–17, 221–22, 223–24, 230; capabilities of, 239–44, 247–49, 256–60
Resurrection: death necessary for, 17; raising children renewed in, 20–21; baptism for dead as evidence of, 26; of those in Millennium, 30; personal, depends on judgment, 40; coming forth in, amid Saints, 56; things of the Lord remain after, 66; being in the same spiritual condition after, 66–69, 344–45; times appointed for, 75, 81–82, 98, 261–66; redeems all men from death, 143–46, 151, 220, 277, 325–26; as most significant event, 157; awakening from sleep as type of, 161, 163–65; Jonah's experience as type of, 161, 165–68; baptism as type of, 161, 168–72; Lazarus raised from dead as type of, 161–62, 172–75; translated beings as type of, 162, 178–85; ordinances and keys of, 189–90; because of Adam and Christ, 195–202; bodies glorified and restored at, 214–17, 221–22, 223–24, 318; is linked to final judgment, 220, 334–39; is redemption of the soul, 227; blessings from, 298–99; comfort from knowledge of, 300–306; obedience, perspective, and righteousness from knowledge of, 306–8; hope from knowledge of, 308–10; joy from knowledge of, 310–15; as victory over death, 315–20; infinite atonement as

part of, 320–25; of house of Israel,
327–34; after Millennium, 339–44; of
animals, 346–47; of earth, 348–52. *See
also* First resurrection; Jesus Christ,
resurrection of
Richards, Franklin D., 177–78
Richards, George F., 259
Rigdon, Sidney, 185, 336
Righteous: die in the Lord, 44–48, 302–3;
mourning and grieving for, 52; funerals
of, 53–55; will be the same after death,
66–69, 80–81; will be in God's realm
after death, 71–72; anxiously await the
resurrection, 71–72, 310–15; go to
paradise, 75, 78–79, 83–84, 86–89, 266;
come forth in the first resurrection, 82,
165, 261, 273–74, 277–80, 282–83,
303–4, 312–13; are teaching in the spirit
world, 109–10, 315; at judgment day,
223; characteristics of, 297; death and
resurrection of, in Millennium, 315–18
Righteousness, 307–8
Romney, Marion G., 120, 157
Roskelley, Bishop, 127

Sacrifice, animal, 172
Salome, 183
Salvation: different grades of, 96; comes
only through Christ, 270–71
Salvation for the dead, 21–29
Salvation, plan of: includes death, 10–11,
15–19; equal opportunities and blessings
in, 26; is enacted for all earth's
inhabitants, 312; is merciful, 322
Sanctification of earth, 349–52
Satan: can be followed after death, 69;
power of, as chains of hell, 103; teaches
fear of death, 153–54; is bound for
thousand years, 289; is cast into hell,
343
Saul, 212. *See also* Paul
Savior, need for, 40
Saviors on Mount Zion, 29–30
School of the Prophets, 186
Sealings, 27–29, 66
Second Coming: spirit world will change at,
81–82; will continue first resurrection,
262, 268, 273, 278, 280–83; sequence of
events of, 284–88; righteous will be
with Christ at, 302–4

Second estate, 77
Seeds, sown, analogy of, 231–34
Seth, 148, 278
Shadow of death, land of, 35–36
Shem, 148, 278, 311
Sibylline Discourses, 151
Signs, seeking, 166–67, 192
Sin, 16, 44–45, 171
Sleep: as death, 161, 163–65, 197, 198, 301
Smith, Alvin, 47, 50
Smith, Carlos, 108
Smith, George A., 125, 127–28
Smith, Hyrum: is preaching gospel in spirit
world, 80–81, 109; visits men while in
spirit world, 125
Smith, Hyrum M. (son of Joseph F.),
122–23, 296
Smith, Joseph: on understanding death, 3,
322; on death of little children, 20, 276;
on salvation for the dead, 20–23, 27; as
translator, 28; on spreading forth of
gospel, 29; on saviors on Mount Zion,
29; on importance of mortality, 39; on
death of brother Alvin, 47, 50; on
burials, 56–57; on nature of spirit, 60,
62; on paradise and spirit prison, 79; on
activities in spirit world, 80–81; is
preaching in spirit world, 80–91, 108–9,
112; on relationships in spirit world, 81;
on missionaries in spirit world, 83, 109;
on closeness of spirit world to us, 86; on
spirits released from spirit prison, 91; on
misery of wicked, 92; on torments of
hell, 100; on telestial kingdom, 113–14;
on ministering angels, 122, 123; visits
and watches over earth, 124–26; on evil
spirits, 135, 136; on sign seekers, 166;
on translated beings, 177, 178; sees
resurrected Christ, 185, 186; keys of
gospel restored to, 190; on baptism for
the dead, 201; on testimony of the early
apostles, 210–11; on Moroni, 217,
256–60; on restoration of resurrected
beings, 223–24, 229; on degrees of
glory, 235, 236, 336; sees resurrected
beings, 239; on bodies of flesh and
bone, 240; on just men made perfect,
241; on resurrected beings disguising
their glory, 248; on resurrected Christ,
254; on capabilities of resurrected
beings, 258–59; on sons of perdition,

284; on Michael, 294; on resurrection of animals, 295, 347; on family relationships at resurrection, 304–5, 332; on universality of resurrection, 326; on role of God's spirit in resurrection, 334; on resurrection of righteous, 338; on judgment of God, 342; on knowledge going with man into spirit world, 344; on knowledge of God, 344–45

Smith, Joseph F.: on hope of eternal life, 11, 44; on dead helping in the Millennium, 32; on not mourning righteous who die, 52–53; on individuality of spirits, 60–61; on vision of redemption of dead, 72, 104–6, 107, 115, 116–17, 119, 146, 147–49, 278, 310–11, 329–31, 358 n. 7; on partial judgment at death, 74–75, 90; on adult spirit appearing as child, 78; on righteous in spirit world, 88–89, 109; on communication with heavenly beings, 122–23, 134; on slumber before the resurrection, 164; on connection of Adam to Christ, 199–200; on perfection of resurrected body, 222, 240; on spirits of the just, 242; on Christ's resurrected body, 245, 250; on timing of the resurrections, 265; on resurrection for all, 277, 325; on power of Christ to resurrect, 323; on resurrection of animals, 347

Smith, Joseph Fielding: on ordinances for the dead, 24; on doing ordinances for kindred dead, 25, 26, 27–28; on work of the Millennium, 32; on being taken home to God, 71; on accepting Christ in the spirit world, 84; on dead being taught the gospel, 108; on Christ holding keys to resurrection, 198; on perfected, resurrected body, 221, 222, 238–39, 245–46; on being resurrected to degree of glory, 236; on earth becoming celestialized, 292, 295, 351–52; on Michael, 294; on resurrection of animals, 295, 346–47; on Christ's complete victory over death, 316; on atonement of Christ, 321, 325; on judgment of God, 342

Smith, Joseph, Sr., 80–81, 108

Snow, Lorenzo: on success of spirit world missionary work, 110, 114; raises Ella

Jensen from the dead, 141–42; on our bodies glorified in the resurrection, 216; describes resurrected Christ, 254, 259

Son of man, 255, 338

Soul of man, 226–27

Spirit(s): transcends mortality, 10, 12, 58, 138; returns to spirit world, at death, 13–14, 74–75; are alive unto God, 19; long to be free of mortality, 34–35; nature of, 59–62, 240; remain the same after death, 66–69, 112; await reuniting with body, 72–73, 77–78; adult, of children who died, 78; diversity of, in spirit world, 78–79, 113–15; as promise of resurrection, 231; as breath of resurrection, 332. See also Angels, ministering

Spirit prison: wicked go to, 75, 78–79; meaning of, 89–93; righteous to be missionaries in, 104–7; Christ does not go into, 106–7, 148–49

Spirit world: missionaries teach gospel in, 23–24, 29, 81–82, 103–10; spirits waiting in, 27–28; veil lifted from, during Millennium, 32; probationary state during, 39–40, 75–77; some spirits needed in, 42; as rest from mortal labors, 47; Latter-day Saint knowledge of, 59; some difficulties removed in, 67–68, 93, 111–12; spirit enters, on death, 74–75, 79; as here on earth, 76; work being done in, 80–81; relationships in, 81; gulf between righteous and wicked in, 83–85, 90–91; description of, by Heber J. Grant, 86–88; as spirit prison, 91; Christ appears in, 105–7, 147–49; success of missionary effort in, 110–16; repentance while in, 116–19, 144; communication of, with those on earth, 120–36

Spirits, evil, 135–36

Spiritual gifts, 64, 120, 135

Stars, 235, 237

Sun, 234–237

Talmage, James E.: on different grades of salvation and damnation, 96; on soul of man, 227; on resurrection at different times, 266; on first resurrection, 276, 278; on universality of resurrection, 326

Taylor, John: on actions of angels, 121; on resurrection of all, 157, 277; on type of resurrection, 164; on resurrected beings, 213; on restoration of body with spirit, 219; on family relationships in resurrection, 305
Taylor, Joseph E., 130
Telestial kingdom: inheritors of, 95, 113, 117, 236–37; will not enjoy presence of Father or Son, 107; resurrection of those who inherit, 269, 284
Temple: as place for ordinances for dead, 25, 27, 29, 119; as Mount Zion, 30; Jesus Christ as, 193
Tennyson, Alfred, Lord, 2–3
Terrestrial kingdom: inheritors of, 95, 113, 117, 236–37; resurrection of those who inherit, 268, 283
Tertullian, 152
Testimony, 64
Thomas, 184
Thomas, M. Catherine, 85
Throne of God, 340
Transfiguration, 180–81
Translated beings: as angels, 121–22; as type of resurrection, 162, 175–82; can appear undetected, 250
Translation, 14, 30–31, 75, 82, 282
Tree of knowledge of good and evil, 15
Tree of life, 17, 40, 86
Trials: death as part of earthly, 16–17; are fewer in spirit world, 67–68, 93, 111–12, 116
Trumpet: symbolizes Christ's voice, 255; sounds order of the resurrection, 280–82, 283, 292
Turning of hearts of fathers, 27–28
Types and shadows, 160

Voice of Lord, 255, 256

Washington, George, 132
Wells, John, 128
Wesley, John, 132
White, symbolism of, 256
Whitney, Horace K. and Helen Mar, 7–8
Whitney, Orson F.: on spirit communication, 134–35; on death as returning home, 137–38; sees resurrected Christ, 186
Wicked: fear death, 44–45, 48–50; weeping

for, 50; may not change after death, 67–69, 80; will be in God's realm after death, 71; go to spirit prison, 75, 78–79, 83–84, 90–93; during Millennium, 82; suffer torments of hell, 93–96, 98–100; sins of, 96–98; resurrection of, 219–20, 279–80; at judgment day, 223; await resurrection, 266; characteristics of, 297
Widtsoe, John A., 29–30, 134
Winder, John R., 347
Witnesses: for ordinances for dead, 26; apostles as, 202–5; Paul as, 206–9; other Saints as, 209–12
Wood, Edward J., 132–33
Woodruff, Wilford: on death as a birth, 12, 74; on ordinances for dead done as proxy, 24–25; on doing our duty for salvation for the dead, 25; on healing of his wife, 42–43; on his funeral plans, 54; on righteous works in spirit world, 80; sees Joseph Smith in vision, 80–81, 108, 124–25; on success of spirit world missionary work, 110–11, 112, 116; on those in spirit world observing mortal life, 121, 124; on righteous men called to spirit world, 127, 131–32; signers of Declaration of Independence appear to, 132; on plan of redemption, 226
Worldly goods, 63–64
Worlds, other, 351

Young, Brigham: on death as a birth, 12, 163; on rejoicing of spirit without body, 13; on work to do in Millennium, 31, 32; on mortality, 33; on character unchanged after death, 67, 80; on spirits going to God after death, 71; on relationships in spirit world, 81; on paradise, 89; on spirit world as place, 91; on teaching gospel in spirit world, 108–9; is missionary in spirit world, 109; on success of spirit world missionary work, 111; describes conditions of spirit world, 111–12; on temple work for the dead, 120; visits Wilford Woodruff in spirit, 125; on ministering angels teaching redemption of the dead, 132; on dead ancestors helping with temple work, 133–34; on evil influences, 136; on death of sister,

154; on morning of resurrection, 162; on ordinance and keys of the resurrection, 189–90; on countenance of resurrected beings, 214; on restoration of body at resurrection, 216, 229, 245; on capability of resurrected beings, 249; on resurrection of Joseph Smith, 262; on Christ as Master of the resurrection, 264; on number of resurrections, 265; on resurrection of animals, 346; on resurrection and celestialization of earth, 349, 350

Young, Fanny, 154

Zarahemla, people of, 118
Zeezrom, 98–99, 218
Zion, Mount, 29–30, 274